Hands-on Guide to the Red Hat® Exams

RHSCA™ and RHCE® Cert Guide and Lab Manual

Damian Tommasino

Pearson
800 East 96th Street
Indianapolis, Indiana 46240 USA

Hands-on Guide to the Red Hat® Exams

ISBN-13: 978-0-321-76795-0
ISBN-10: 0-321-76795-0

Library of Congress Cataloging-in-Publication data is on file.
Printed in the United States of America

First Printing: May 2011

Trademarks

Warning and Disclaimer

Bulk Sales

Que Publishing offers excellent discounts on this book when ordered in quantity for bulk purchases or special sales. For more information, please contact

U.S. Corporate and Government Sales
1-800-382-3419
corpsales@pearsontechgroup.com

For sales outside of the U.S., please contact
International Sales
international@pearson.com

Editor-in-Chief
Mark Taub

Executive Editor
Debra Williams Cauley

Senior Development Editor
Chris Zahn

Managing Editor
Sandra Schroeder

Project Editor
Mandie Frank

Copy Editor
Chuck Hutchinson

Indexer
Tim Wright

Proofreader
Megan Wade

Technical Editor
Robert P.J. Day

Editorial Assistant
Kim Boedigheimer

Book Designer
Gary Adair

Composition
Mark Shirar

Contents at a Glance

Table of Contents

About the Author

Damian Tommasino is currently a Linux system administrator at TradeCard and CEO of Modular Learning, Inc., an online IT training company. His current certifications include RHCE, RHCSA, MCSA, CCNA, CCENT, MCP, Security+, Network+, and A+. He has a popular blog called Security Nut (http://secnut.blogspot.com) that covers Red Hat, Linux, security, and more. Damian also spends time over at techexams.net helping out in the forums and conversing with friends.

Acknowledgments

I'd like to thank both Chris Zahn and Debra Williams Cauley at Pearson for all their help in making this book a reality. This book would not have been possible without them and the rest of the team at Pearson. It has been wonderful to work with both of them.

We Want to Hear from You!

As the reader of this book, *you* are our most important critic and commentator. We value your opinion and want to know what we're doing right, what we could do better, what areas you'd like to see us publish in, and any other words of wisdom you're willing to pass our way.

As an Editor in Chief for Pearson IT Certification, I welcome your comments. You can email or write me directly to let me know what you did or didn't like about this book—as well as what we can do to make our books better.

Please note that I cannot help you with technical problems related to the topic of this book. We do have a User Services group, however, where I will forward specific technical questions related to the book.

When you write, please be sure to include this book's title and author as well as your name, email address, and phone number. I will carefully review your comments and share them with the author and editors who worked on the book.

Email: feedback@quepublishing.com

Mail: Mark Taub
         Editor in Chief
         Pearson IT Certification
         800 East 96th Street
         Indianapolis, IN 46240 USA

Reader Services

Visit our website and register this book at www.informit.com/title/9780321767950 for convenient access to any updates, downloads, or errata that might be available for this book.

Preface

This book was written as a lab guide to help individuals pass the RHCSA (EX200) and RHCE (EX300) exams. It is meant for those with different amounts of experience, from novice to expert, and is structured to make it easy for any reader to find what he is looking for. The book contains 22 chapters and two full-length lab exams.

Book Features

Each chapter includes the following elements to aid your learning:

- **Opening topics list**—This list defines the topics to be covered in the chapter; it also lists the corresponding Red Hat objectives.

- **Review Questions**—Review questions help reinforce what you learned and help you identify what you may need to review.

- **Answers to Review Questions**—Answers are provided for each of the review questions.

- **Labs**—Chapters conclude with several lab-based exercises that provide hands-on training and also help you to see what questions on the actual exam might be like.

The labs also include scripts that can help you with troubleshooting. The scripts use the following syntax:

- v_script_name   Used to verify a service or configuration
- t_script_name   Used to cause trouble on your system

I have also included two full-length labs at the end of the book intended to give you an experience like that of the real exam as well as examples of what the real exam might cover.

I have also produced an additional set of scripts that you can download that will purposely cause trouble on your system. You can download them from

- http://sourceforge.net/projects/rhcelabscripts/

Exam Registration and Costs

To register for the Red Hat exams, you must visit Red Hat's site at http://www.redhat.com/training and enroll online. The price for the new RHCSA exam is $399, and it is 2 hours in length. With the addition of the RHCSA certification, the price of the RHCE exam has been reduced to $399 (down from $799).

The RHCE exam is also 2.5 hours in length. Each exam is performance based, meaning it is given in the form of labs. With the addition of the RHCSA certification, you are now required to obtain the RHCSA before you can become RHCE certified. You can still take the RHCE exam; however, you will not receive the certification until you have completed and passed both exams.

LPIC, RHCE, and Other Things You Should Know

The Red Hat exams are a big undertaking, particularly if you have never taken a performance-based exam before. There is the unknown element of what to expect on the exam plus the amount of material you need to be familiar with. Before sitting for either of the Red Hat exams, you might want to consider completing the LPIC-1 exam series. Why? The Red Hat exams test experience and skill, not just your ability to memorize content within a book. There is also a certain skill set that you need before you take the Red Hat exams. You are expected to know basic Linux commands, to be able to navigate around a system, and to be able to perform basic file operations. Being able to effectively use some form of text editor is a good thing, too.

The LPIC-1 certification is broken down into two exams: LPIC 101 and LPIC 102. The material covered in both of these exams is equivalent to the knowledge a junior system administrator should have, and it gives you a solid foundation for taking on the Red Hat exam material. Although many topics overlap between the LPIC-1 material and the Red Hat exams, this will only help to reinforce your understanding of particular topics. You should look through the exam objectives of the LPIC-1 exams to gain a better understanding of some of the prerequisite skills required. The objectives for the LPIC-1 exams are very detailed, so they will help you identify any weak areas you might have:

- LPIC-101

  http://www.lpi.org/eng/certification/the_lpic_program/lpic_1/
  exam_101_detailed_objectives
- LPIC-102

  http://www.lpi.org/eng/certification/the_lpic_program/lpic_1/
  exam_102_detailed_objectives

If you already have a solid set of Linux skills, you should have no problem starting out here. If you don't, you can still proceed with this book but will need to put in some extra effort in areas you don't fully understand. One question I see frequently is, "Should I take the LPIC exams if I'm an RHCSA/RHCE?" My answer is always yes! The reason behind this is that the Red Hat exams are vendor specific, whereas the LPIC-1 exams are vendor neutral. They focus more on implementing services and working with Linux from an unbiased perspective. Holding both certifications adds diversity to your resume, and the exams shouldn't be hard to pass with the amount of overlap in the material between the Red Hat exams and the LPIC-1 exams.

You should know the following topics (prerequisites) before you start studying for the Red Hat exams. This is by no means a complete list!

- How to use a text editor (vim, emacs, or nano)
- File system hierarchy structure
- Different types of media (/dev/sda versus /dev/hda)
- File operations:

pwd	~	find	w
path	cat	locate	who
ls	more	cp	
echo	less	mv	
cd	tail	ln	
sort	head	wc	

- How to search with grep
- Command piping
- The basics of sed and awk
- Compression:
  - tar
  - gunzip
  - bzip2
- Networking basics:
  - ping
  - netstat
  - ifconfig
- IP addresses, subnets, and gateways
- How to use a command line and a GUI-based email client

If you lack the experience, the introduction to this book covers a majority of these prerequisite commands. Although it shouldn't count as a replacement for learning all these commands individually, the introduction can get you up to speed quickly if you have little to no current Linux experience.

Self-Study and Experience

One of the biggest debates I see among those studying for the Red Hat exams is, "Should I self-study or take a course?" I am a self-study person and have yet to find a halfway decent course for a price that wouldn't give a person a heart attack. The problem that most people seem to encounter with taking a course is the cost. Simply put, they are not cheap! The average price for a Red Hat training course is around $3,000, and such a course typically consists of four to five days of classroom training (which means footing the bill and taking time off work).

NOTE   Red Hat offers an eLearning (or online version) of its training course for about half the price. I highly recommend that you DO NOT take this class because the learning experience is very different from that given in the classroom.

The benefits to taking a course, however, are that it is tailored specifically for the exams and the instructors can help you with questions. With the self-study option, you have to balance what you think important topics are (more likely to be tested on) versus less important topics (not likely to appear on the exam). This is really a strong point of the LPIC-1 exams: They list a "weight" for each topic, so you know how heavily it will count on the exam. If you spend the time researching the experience others have had on the Red Hat exams and read through the Red Hat Exam Prep Guide, you will start to get a feel for what topics are more likely to appear on the exam.

Experience plays another big factor in taking the Red Hat exams. After much research and talking to those who have taken the exams, I believe the amount of experience presented in Table P-1 would be required for each exam.

Table P-1   Experience Recommended for the Red Hat Exams

Exam	Years of Experience
LPIC-101/102	0–1 year
LPIC-201/202	2 years
RHCSA	2 years
RHCE	3 years

Although these are only my recommendations, you will probably find, with a little research on the Web, they are pretty accurate. As you probably know too, everyone is different and learns at different rates. The biggest difference between the two exams is that the Red Hat exams are all hands-on (performance based), whereas the

LPIC-1 exams are multiple choice. Unless you truly know what you are doing and have experience in the technologies listed in the Red Hat Exam Prep Guide, you will not pass the Red Hat exams. Don't worry, though, because a little experience (either at home or on the job) and some lab work will fix that. I hope that you will have both, which makes the learning process slightly easier and more rewarding.

Materials from Red Hat

No exam would be complete without a listing of what you should know. In Red Hat's case, the company has created a prep guide that lists the topics you need to know for the exams. With the release of Red Hat Enterprise Linux 6 and the addition of the RHCSA, the exam prep guide has become more specific about what you are required to know for the Red Hat exams. This book covers every topic you need to know for both exams. Before you begin studying, review the prep guide for each exam. If you don't have one printed out or saved already, you can get it here:

- Red Hat RHCSA Exam Prep Guide

   https://www.redhat.com/certification/rhcsa/objectives/

- Red Hat RHCE Exam Prep Guide

   https://www.redhat.com/certification/rhce/objectives/

I have also included a copy of each in the next two sections of this preface. If you have taken an earlier version of the RHCE, you may notice that the required objectives have become more specific about what you need to know. This is good because they leave you with less guessing to do. One of the great benefits of the Red Hat exams is that they don't list any specific technology that you must know. For example, if the exam requires that you block access to a particular service, you can choose to use TCP Wrappers, iptables, or the security of the service itself. This approach is good because, just as in the real world, there is always more than one way to do something. Another example might be the exams requiring you to set up outgoing mail using SMTP. You could use the Sendmail service or Postfix. As long as the system is allowed to send out mail, the exams don't care how you accomplish it. The only exception, of course, is unless the exams specifically ask you to use a particular service. These requirements will be useful as you study and practice for the exams in case you already have experience with a particular service.

> **EXAM TIP**
> It is worth noting that although you have some freedom on the exam to implement different technologies, Red Hat may ask you do something in a particular way. Going back to the example of blocking something on the system, you may use any method you like, unless Red Hat says that you need to specifically use iptables.

To aid you in setting up, configuring, and securing everything needed for the exams, Red Hat also provides documentation for its operating system. With the release of Red Hat Enterprise Linux 6, the documentation layout has also changed. The documentation guides are broken down into different sections instead of the two guides (installation guide and deployment guide) that were previously given. The following documentation is available from Red Hat:

- Installation Guide

    http://docs.redhat.com/docs/en-US/Red_Hat_Enterprise_Linux/6/
    html/Installation_Guide/index.html

- Managing Confined Services

    http://docs.redhat.com/docs/en-US/Red_Hat_Enterprise_Linux/6/html/
    Managing_Confined_Services/index.html

- Migration Planning Guide

    http://docs.redhat.com/docs/en-US/Red_Hat_Enterprise_Linux/6/html/
    Migration_Planning_Guide/index.html

- Security-Enhanced Linux

    http://docs.redhat.com/docs/en-US/Red_Hat_Enterprise_Linux/6/html/
    Security-Enhanced_Linux/index.html

- Security Guide

    http://docs.redhat.com/docs/en-US/Red_Hat_Enterprise_Linux/6/html/
    Security_Guide/index.html

- Storage Administration Guide

    http://docs.redhat.com/docs/en-US/Red_Hat_Enterprise_Linux/6/html/
    Storage_Administration_Guide/index.html

- Virtual Server Administration

    http://docs.redhat.com/docs/en-US/Red_Hat_Enterprise_Linux/6/html/
    Virtual_Server_Administration/index.html

- Virtualization Guide

    http://docs.redhat.com/docs/en-US/Red_Hat_Enterprise_Linux/6/html/
    Virtualization/index.html

You can find these guides available in HTML, EPUB, and PDF format. These guides are helpful tools when you're studying for the exams because they provide more command options than can be covered in any book. I recommend that you keep them close by as a reference.

RHCSA Exam Prep Guide

Understand and Use Essential Tools

- Access a shell prompt and issue commands with the correct syntax.
- Use input-output redirection (>, >>, |, 2>, etc.).
- Use grep and regular expressions to analyze text.
- Access remote systems using SSH and VNC.
- Login and switch users in multi-user runlevels.
- Archive, compress, unpack, and uncompress files using tar, star, gzip, and bzip2.
- Create and edit text files.
- Create, delete, copy, and move files and directories.
- Create hard and soft links.
- List, set, and change standard ugo/rwx permissions.
- Locate, read, and use system documentation including man, info, and files in /usr/share/doc.

Operate Running Systems

- Boot, reboot, and shut down a system normally.
- Boot systems into different runlevels manually.
- Use single-user mode to gain access to a system.
- Identify CPU and memory-intensive processes, adjust process priority with renice, and kill processes.
- Locate and interpret system log files.
- Access a virtual machine's console.
- Start and stop virtual machines.
- Start, stop, and check the status of network services.

Configure Local Storage

- List, create, delete, and set partition types for primary, extended, and logical partitions.
- Create and remove physical volumes, assign physical volumes to volumes groups, and create and delete logical volumes.
- Create and configure LUKS-encrypted partitions and logical volumes to prompt for password and be available at system boot.

- Configure systems to mount file systems at boot by using Universally Unique ID (UUID) or labels.
- Add new partitions, logical volumes, and swap to a system non-destructively.

Create and Configure File Systems

- Create; mount; unmount; and use ext2, ext3, and ext4 file systems.
- Mount, unmount, and use LUKS-encrypted file systems.
- Mount and unmount CIFS and NFS network file systems.
- Configure systems to mount ext4, LUKS-encrypted, and network file systems automatically.
- Extend existing unencrypted ext4 formatted logical volumes.
- Create and configure set-GID directories for collaboration.
- Create and manage access control lists (ACLs).
- Diagnose and correct file permission problems.

Deploy, Configure, and Maintain Systems

- Configure network and hostname resolution statically or dynamically.
- Schedule tasks using cron.
- Configure systems to boot into a specific runlevel automatically.
- Install Red Hat Enterprise Linux automatically using kickstart.
- Configure a physical machine to host virtual guests.
- Install Red Hat Enterprise Linux systems as virtual guests.
- Configure systems to launch virtual machines at boot.
- Configure network services to start automatically at boot.
- Configure a system to run a default configuration HTTP server.
- Configure a system to run a default configuration FTP server.
- Install and update software packages from the Red Hat Network, a remote repository, or from the local file system.
- Update the kernel package appropriately to ensure a bootable system.
- Modify the system bootloader.

Manage Users and Groups

- Create, delete, and modify local user accounts.
- Change passwords and adjust password aging for local user accounts.
- Create, delete, and modify local groups and group memberships.
- Configure a system to use an existing LDAP directory service for user and group information.

Manage Security

- Configure firewall settings using system-config-firewall or iptables.
- Set enforcing and permissive modes for SELinux.
- List and identify SELinux and file process context.
- Restore default file contexts.
- Use Boolean settings to modify system SELinux settings.
- Diagnose and address routine SELinux policy violations.

RHCE Exam Prep Guide

System Configuration and Management

- Route IP traffic and create static routes.
- Use iptables to implement packet filtering and configure network address translation (NAT).
- Use /proc/sys and sysctl to modify and set kernel run-time parameters.
- Configure a system to authenticate using Kerberos.
- Build a simple RPM that packages a single file.
- Configure a system as an iSCSI initiator that persistently mounts an iSCSI target.
- Produce and deliver reports on system utilization (processor, memory, disk, and network).
- Use shell scripting to automate system maintenance tasks.
- Configure a system to log to a remote system.
- Configure a system to accept logging from a remote system.

HTTP/HTTPS

- Install the packages needed to provide the service.
- Configure SELinux to support the service.

- Configure the service to start when the system is booted.
- Configure the service for basic operation.
- Configure host-based and user-based security for the service.
- Configure a virtual host.
- Configure private directories.
- Deploy a basic CGI application.
- Configure group-managed content.

DNS

- Install the packages needed to provide the service.
- Configure SELinux to support the service.
- Configure the service to start when the system is booted.
- Configure the service for basic operation.
- Configure host-based and user-based security for the service.
- Configure a caching-only name server.
- Configure a caching-only name server to forward DNS queries (forwarding server).

FTP

- Install the packages needed to provide the service.
- Configure SELinux to support the service.
- Configure the service to start when the system is booted.
- Configure the service for basic operation.
- Configure host-based and user-based security for the service.
- Configure anonymous-only downloads.

NFS

- Install the packages needed to provide the service.
- Configure SELinux to support the service.
- Configure the service to start when the system is booted.
- Configure the service for basic operation.
- Configure host-based and user-based security for the service.
- Provide network shares to specific clients.
- Provide shares suitable for group collaboration.

Samba

- Install the packages needed to provide the service.
- Configure SELinux to support the service.
- Configure the service to start when the system is booted.
- Configure the service for basic operation.
- Configure host-based and user-based security for the service.
- Provide network shares to specific clients.
- Provide shares suitable for group collaboration.

SMTP

- Install the packages needed to provide the service.
- Configure SELinux to support the service.
- Configure the service to start when the system is booted.
- Configure the service for basic operation.
- Configure host-based and user-based security for the service.
- Configure a mail transfer agent (MTA) to accept inbound email from other systems.
- Configure an MTA to forward (relay) email through a smart host.

SSH

- Install the packages needed to provide the service.
- Configure SELinux to support the service.
- Configure the service to start when the system is booted.
- Configure the service for basic operation.
- Configure host-based and user-based security for the service.
- Configure key-based authentication.
- Configure additional options described in documentation.

NTP

- Install the packages needed to provide the service.
- Configure SELinux to support the service.
- Configure the service to start when the system is booted.
- Configure the service for basic operation.
- Configure host-based and user-based security for the service.
- Synchronize time using other NTP peers.

Setting Up the Lab

Throughout this book, I show you how to use different systems to set up services, perform configurations, and implement security. In many forums I often see people asking how to set up labs or practice for the Red Hat exams. The lab used throughout this book is built completely on top of VirtualBox. VirtualBox is like VMware in that it allows you to virtualize systems. If you don't have VirtualBox, you should grab a copy because it is free to use and very helpful when practicing labs.

■   VirtualBox

   http://www.virtualbox.org/wiki/Downloads

Because you will be using many different machines in the lab environment, Chapter 1 describes how to set up Red Hat Enterprise Linux (RHEL). You can install RHEL on your own or follow along in Chapter 1 to completely set up the lab.

Table P-2 presents a layout of the lab used here. Each ID is a different virtual machine.

Table P-2   Lab Layout

ID	Hostname	Red Hat Version	IP Address	Network
1	RHEL01	RHEL6	DHCP	Bridged
			172.168.1.1	Internal
2	RHEL02	RHEL6	172.168.1.2	Internal
3	Client01	RHEL5	172.168.1.10	Internal
4	Client02	RHEL6	172.168.1.20	Internal

As you can see, four machines are used. The first is a dual-homed server that also serves as the gateway for all the internal clients. A majority of the configuration work takes place on this server, and you use the second server (RHEL02) as a backup. The two client machines are to simulate users on the network. The reason I set up the network like this for you is that all testing and configuration are done in a controlled environment (which is a good habit to get into). If something ever happens on the internal network, it doesn't affect the rest of the external (home) network. Some other details for the lab setup include those shown in Table P-3.

Table P-3 Lab Layout

Host	Drive	Size	Layout
RHEL01	Disk 1	20GB	Default
	Disk 2	8GB	
	Disk 3	8GB	
	Disk 4	8GB	
RHEL02	Disk 1	10GB	Default
RHEL02	Disk 1	10GB	Default
Client01	Disk 1	10GB	Default

All virtual machines use 384MB of RAM for memory. I also disabled the sound device for each virtual system because I never use it, but that is entirely up to you.

> **NOTE**   All drives in VirtualBox are considered IDE and use the /dev/hdx format.

In the first chapter, you set up each virtual machine for the lab. If you have experience working with VirtualBox, you can set up your lab with the outlined requirements beforehand; otherwise, you can follow along in the first chapter.

No network is complete without documentation and a diagram to finally tie it all together. The network is represented in Figure P-1.

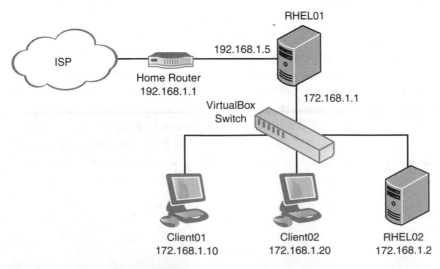

Figure P-1 The network diagram.

NOTE   In case you're thinking you don't have the hardware to host this number of machines or you don't know how you'll virtualize an entire lab, think again. These four virtual machines each use 384MB of RAM (1.5GB total). The host machine that I use is a laptop so that my lab is portable, and it has a dual-core processor with 3GB of RAM. I have also tested this lab setup on a Pentium 4 with 4GB of RAM. Both host machines were able to run the full virtual lab with no problems or delays. If you have some trouble with performance, you can also drop the amount of memory on RHEL02, Client01, or Client02 to 256MB of RAM. The primary host (RHEL01) is the only machine that really needs the extra memory.

CAUTION   Don't create the three 4GB drives for host RHEL01 just yet! One of the limitations in VirtualBox is that you can have only four devices attached to a system at one time. To get the operating system installed, you need to have a CD-ROM device attached, and if you create the four drives listed here, you will have no room left for the CD-ROM. After you complete Chapter 1, you can remove the CD-ROM device and create the three extra 4GB drives that you will need later.

Who Should Read This Book?

The Red Hat exams are some of the most challenging exams in the Linux arena. This book is meant to be used as a hands-on lab guide to readers with all types of backgrounds. Whether you are just starting out or are a seasoned system administrator, this book helps you learn or fine-tune your skills to take the Red Hat exams. Although those just starting out need to put in more effort to learn some of the skills discussed in this book, it is possible to gain the required skills for the exams. While this book teaches you the necessary skills, the key to passing the Red Hat exams is practice, practice, practice.

How This Book Is Organized

This book is laid out in a logical format that flows from cover to cover. Although you could jump around, each chapter builds on where the previous one left off, allowing you to build a system and understand how it works from the ground up. Although each chapter covers a different set of exam objectives, the first half of the book (Chapters 2 through 12) deals primarily with the RHCSA exam. The second half of the book (Chapters 13 through 21) covers the RHCE exam.

Chapter 1, "Installation," is an introductory chapter designed to help you install the Red Hat Enterprise Linux operating system and set up your virtual lab. The virtual lab that you set up will help you with the labs in each chapter, allowing you to build your hands-on skills for the real exams.

The first half of the book, Chapters 2 through 12, covers the following topics:

- **Chapter 2, "System Initialization"**—This chapter focuses on how to manage system services, system runlevels, and everything that occurs during the boot process. It also looks at how services work and are started and stopped.

- **Chapter 3, "Disks and Partitioning"**—This chapter addresses partitioning Red Hat systems. It discusses basic partitions, LVM, and RAID. Also covered are swap partitions and advanced use of LVM for in-depth storage management. This chapter prepares you to work with file systems in Chapter 4.

- **Chapter 4, "File Systems and Such"**—This chapter follows up where Chapter 3 left off. It describes file systems, how they work, and how to manage them. Also discussed are the new LUKS encryption options and file system security.

- **Chapter 5, "Networking"**—This chapter is all about networks. Nothing can happen unless you can communicate with other systems. This chapter describes how to set up and troubleshoot network connections and client-side DNS problems.

- **Chapter 6, "Package Management"**—This chapter examines how to install, search for, and remove software from Red Hat systems. It covers many different ways to work with packages, including building your own packages and package repositories.

- **Chapter 7, "User Administration"**—No system would be complete without users. This chapter covers user administration (creating, managing, and deleting). Also covered are switching between users and client-side authentication.

- **Chapter 8, "Network Installs"**—To make life easier, you can use automated installations. This chapter covers kickstart and how it can aid in the installation of Red Hat Enterprise Linux. Also covered is hands-free installation with DHCP and PXE boot clients.

- **Chapter 9, "System Logging, Monitoring, and Automation"**—This chapter dives into system logging and monitoring and how to interpret that data. It looks at different ways to find problems (or their answers). Also discussed is the automation of system monitoring.

- **Chapter 10, "The Kernel"**—This chapter discusses updating and tuning the kernel properly. Although the kernel is not a huge topic, it is important to address critical security issues with any system.

- **Chapter 11, "SELinux"**—This chapter covers one of the most complex topics in the book. It describes how to set up and work with SELinux without giving you a headache. Also covered is how to work with SELinux Boolean values to allow services to run properly.

- **Chapter 12, "System Security"**—This chapter talks all about system security, including TCP Wrappers, firewall rules, and security policies. Because firewall rules play a heavy role in all services, the second half of the book covers this topic in particular.

The second half of the book, Chapters 13 through 21, covers the following topics:

- **Chapter 13, "Remote Access"**—This chapter demonstrates how to remotely and securely manage your Red Hat systems. It covers SSH, the most popular remote management tool in Linux. Also covered is VNC for remote desktop management.

- **Chapter 14, "Web Services"**—This chapter discusses how to set up and manage Apache web servers. Because it is the most widely deployed web server in the world, this is a big topic in the Linux arena. This chapter also covers the Squid web proxy and how to use it in conjunction with Apache.

- **Chapter 15, "NFS"**—This chapter discusses network file systems. A great choice for centralized storage, NFS has many benefits over its SMB and FTP counterparts. Also covered in this chapter is connecting clients to NFS servers.

- **Chapter 16, "Samba"**—This chapter discusses Samba and how to set it up. As Samba progresses more and more, integration with Windows becomes easier for Linux systems. The chapter describes how to set up basic shares and printer services for Windows and Linux systems.

- **Chapter 17, "FTP"**—This chapter explains how to set up and use an FTP server. FTP is great for sharing files both securely and insecurely. The chapter describes the benefits of both, including how to troubleshoot FTP issues.

- **Chapter 18, "DNS"**—This chapter discusses how DNS works, server setup, and management of DNS servers. Although this is one of the most complex topics in the book, it is one of the easiest to work with after you understand it. This chapter also delves into different types of DNS servers.

- **Chapter 19, "Network Services"**—This chapter discusses setting up the core network services for your network. Topics include DHCP servers, NTP for time management, and more.

- **Chapter 20, "Email Services"**—This chapter explains how to properly set up different types of mail servers. Because email is one of the most critical business components, it is essential to understand how to work with this technology. The chapter also covers how to secure your mail servers so you don't get overrun by spammers.

- **Chapter 21, "Troubleshooting"**—This chapter discusses different troubleshooting steps for a variety of topics. Although this chapter doesn't cover all troubleshooting topics discussed throughout the book, it does cover the big topics that you should know for the exam.

The last chapter deals with Red Hat's newest addition, virtualization:

■ **Chapter 22, "Virtualization with KVM"**—This chapter discusses how to use virtualization with Red Hat Enterprise Linux 6. It talks about installation, setup, and configuration of virtual machines. Also discussed is how to monitor your virtual machines when they are in use.

Also included are two full exams that simulate what the real exams are like. The lab activities will help you prepare by asking you to accomplish various tasks, which is very similar to the real exam. There is one practice exam for each of the Red Hat exams this book covers. If you can comfortably make it through the full exams in the allotted time, then you should be in good shape for the real exam! In addition to the 22 chapters and 2 full labs, this book provides end of chapter questions and tasks to help you prepare for the exam. There are also additional troubleshooting scripts available for download at http://sourceforge.net/projects/rhcelabscripts.

This introduction covers the following subjects:

- **File and Directory Management**—This section explains how to navigate, create, move, and explore files and directories on the system.

- **File Permission Basics**—This section explores file permissions and how the system uses them.

- **Using a Text Editor**—This section covers using a text editor effectively from the command line.

- **Regex**—This section covers regular expressions and how they are used for pattern matching.

- **I/O Redirection**—This section covers how to pipe commands and redirect output.

- **Compression and Archiving**—This section explains how to compress and archive files and directories.

The following RHCSA exam objectives are covered:

- Access a shell prompt and issue commands with the correct syntax

- Use input-output redirection (>, >>, |, 2>, and so on)

- Use grep and regular expressions to analyze text

- Archive, compress, unpack, and uncompress files using tar, star, gzip, and bzip2

- Create and edit text files

- Create, delete, copy, and move files and directories

- Create hard and soft links

- List, set, and change standard ugo/rwx permissions

- Locate, read, and use system documentation including man, info, and files in /usr/share/doc

Introduction

Everyone has to start somewhere, and Linux administrators and engineers are no exception. If you have purchased this book, I imagine that your goal is to pass the Red Hat exams (RHCSA and RHCE) while acquiring or improving your current Linux skills. This introduction covers user-level commands that you will be required to know before you embark on your journey of becoming a system administrator or engineer. These skills and commands are all essential for knowing how to work with Linux, not just Red Hat. Although the current *Red Hat Exam Prep Guide* doesn't list (and can't) all the commands covered in this introduction, everything covered here is required for you to get through the rest of this book. This is in no way a complete list of every user-level command, but it is everything you need to get started. Many of the topics here are also covered later in the book. If you already have a decent set of Linux skills, most of this introduction will probably be a review for you.

File and Directory Management

For you to be able to work with different parts of the system, you need to know how to get around the system! In this section, we look at the following basic commands:

`ls`	Displays the contents of a directory
`cp`	Copies files or directories from one location to another
`mv`	Moves or renames files and directories
`cd`	Changes the current location
`rm`	Deletes files or directories
`touch`	Creates empty files
`mkdir`	Creates a directory
`pwd`	Shows the present working directory
`file`	Displays the type of a file
`head`	Displays the beginning of a file
`tail`	Displays the end of a file

This might seem like a lot of commands to start with; however, they are all quite simple to use, which makes explaining them easy. First, let's start by displaying a directory on the system using the ls command.

Step 1.   List the contents of the current directory:

```
# ls
Desktop  Documents  Downloads  Music  Pictures  Public  Templates
Videos
```

Although you can't tell because this book is black and white, these directories are displayed in blue, alerting the user to the fact that they are indeed directories. Although it's great to have all these directories, how do you know where you are on the system? To view your current location, you can use the pwd command.

Step 2.   Show the current location:

```
# pwd
/home/user01
```

Presently, you are in user01's home directory, so the output of the ls command was all directories that belong to user01. Let's move out of user01's home directory into one of the subdirectories. Using the cd command, you can move between different directories.

Step 3.   Move down one level into the Documents directory:

```
# cd Documents/
```

REAL-WORLD TIP

The trailing slash (/) is optional when you're using the cd command. It indicates that the name being specified is a directory.

Step 4.   Now view the current location again:

```
# pwd
/home/user01/Documents
```

What if you want to move up one level to the directory you just came from? If you use ls, you don't see the user01 directory listed. You can, however, view two special directories.

Step 5.   View all hidden directories with the `ls -a` command:

```
# ls -a
.  ..
```

Notice what seems like just a bunch of dots? They actually stand for two special types of directories. The first—the single .—stands for the current directory. The second—double ..—is the directory above where you currently are located.

Step 6.   To get back to the previous user01 directory, use the following:

```
# cd ..
```

Step 7.   Verify with the `pwd` command:

```
# pwd
/home/user01
```

Now you should be able to navigate around the system.

Let's move on to creating files and directories. First, let's look at directory creation.

Syntax: `mkdir [option] DIRECTORY`

Options:

  `-p`   Creates a parent directory as needed

  `-v`   Provides verbose output

Step 1.   Create a new directory called test:

```
# mkdir test
```

Step 2.   Create a new set of directories within one another:

```
# mkdir -p another/quick/test
```

Because none of the directories you just chose exist, they are all created, including the subdirectories named quick and test.

Step 3.   Verify the directory creation with the `ls` command:

```
# ls another
quick
```

```
# cd another

# ls
Test
```

Step 4.   Return to the home directory:

```
# cd /home/user01
#pwd
/home/user01
```

As you will see throughout this book, there are a lot of quick tricks to navigating the system. Because the directories were all created successfully, let's move on to files. Using the touch command, you can create blank files.

Step 5.   Create a file called test1:

```
# touch test1
```

Step 6.   Verify its existence:

```
# ls
test1
```

Sometimes files need to be created before you can use them, which is why the touch command is useful. You might also want to use a blank file as a placeholder for something later. If you are ever unsure what type of file something is, you can use the file command to find out.

Step 1.   Check the file type of test1:

```
# file test1
test1: empty
```

Step 2.   Check the type of the password file on the system:

```
# file /etc/passwd
passwd: ASCII text
```

Along with being able to create and determine file types, you need to be able to read them as well. There are many times, however, when you don't need to read the whole file (think log files), but instead can just view a few entries from that file. Using the tail and head commands, you can view either the beginning or the end of a file.

Syntax: head [options] FILE

Options:

- n   Specifies the number of files to print

- v   Provides verbose output

Syntax: `tail [options] FILE`

Options:

`-n`   Specifies the number of files to print

`-f`   Continuously displays the end of file (useful for logs)

`-v`   Provides verbose output

Step 1.   View the beginning of the messages log file:

```
# head /var/log/messages
Dec 5 03:13:06 RHEL01 dhclient: DHCPREQUEST on eth0 to
172.27.100.163 port 67
Dec 5 03:13:10 RHEL01 dhclient: DHCPREQUEST on eth0 to
255.255.255.255 port 67
Dec 5 03:13:20 RHEL01 dhclient: DHCPREQUEST on eth0 to
172.27.100.163 port 67
Dec 5 03:13:29 RHEL01 dhclient: DHCPREQUEST on eth0 to
255.255.255.255 port 67
Dec 5 03:13:30 RHEL01 dhclient: DHCPREQUEST on eth0 to
172.27.100.163 port 67
Dec 5 03:13:43 RHEL01 dhclient: DHCPREQUEST on eth0 to
255.255.255.255 port 67
Dec 5 03:13:44 RHEL01 dhclient: DHCPREQUEST on eth0 to
172.27.100.163 port 67
Dec 5 03:13:50 RHEL01 dhclient: DHCPREQUEST on eth0 to
255.255.255.255 port 67
```

Step 2.   View the end of the messages log file:

```
# tail /var/log/messages
Dec 11 08:11:04 RHEL01 dhclient: DHCPDISCOVER on eth0 to
255.255.255.255 port 67 interval 13
Dec 11 08:11:04 RHEL01 dhclient: DHCPOFFER from 172.27.100.163
Dec 11 08:11:04 RHEL01 dhclient: DHCPREQUEST on eth0 to
255.255.255.255 port 67
Dec 11 08:11:04 RHEL01 dhclient: DHCPACK from 172.27.100.163
Dec 11 08:11:04 RHEL01 NET[26281]: /sbin/dhclient-script : updated
/etc/resolv.conf
Dec 11 08:11:04 RHEL01 dhclient: bound to 172.27.100.226 — renew-
al in 40864 seconds.
Dec 11 08:18:00 RHEL01 abrt[26389]: saved core dump of pid 26388
(/usr/libexec/fprintd) to /var/spool/abrt/ccpp-1292073480-
26388.new/coredump (757760 bytes)
Dec 11 08:18:00 RHEL01 abrtd: Directory 'ccpp-1292073480-26388'
creation detected
Dec 11 08:18:00 RHEL01 abrtd: Crash is in database already (dup of
/var/spool/abrt/ccpp-1291114420-26066)
```

You can see that being able to look at different sections of a file without actually opening it is really useful, particularly when it comes to looking at log files. Now that you know where one of the log files is, why don't you copy it to the /home/user01 directory? You can use the `cp` command for this.

Syntax: `cp [options] SOURCE DEST`

Options:

-R   Copies recursively

-v   Provides verbose output

Step 1.   Copy the log file into the user01 home directory:
```
# cp /var/log/messages /home/user01
```

Step 2.   You also could use the following:
```
# cp /var/log/messages .
```

Remember that the dot (.) represents the current location. After the messages log file is copied over, you should probably rename it for safekeeping. You can use the mv command to accomplish this in addition to moving the file to a new location.

Syntax: mv [options] SOURCE DEST

Options:

-v   Provides verbose output

Step 3.   Rename the file by specifying the filename and the new name of the file:
```
# mv messages messages.bak
```

Step 4.   With the file renamed, move it to the test directory for safekeeping:
```
# mv messages.bak test/
```

Because you specified a directory this time, the file was moved instead of renamed. You can also verify that the file was moved correctly.

Step 5.   List the contents of the test directory:
```
# ls test
messages.bak
```

What if you moved this file by mistake? In that case, you would need to delete it to make room for a new one. You can use the rm command to remove files or directories.

Syntax: rm [options] FILE

Options:

-R   Deletes recursively

-f   Forces deletion

-v   Provides verbose output

Step 1.   Delete the messages.bak file:

```
# cd test
# rm messages.bak
rm: remove regular file `messages.bak'? y
```

Notice that you are prompted to delete the file? By using the -f option, you can skip the confirmation. While you're deleting things, also remove the test directory.

Step 2.   Delete the test directory:

```
# cd ..
# rm -Rf test/
```

Because this example uses the -f option, there is no confirmation and the directory is just deleted. Here's one thing you need to make a note of: You must use the -R option to delete directories. If you don't use the -R option, you get a warning message about the directory not being empty.

By now, you should be able to get around the system, create and remote files and directories, and view files and their types. It may seem as though we moved fast through this section, but these are really basic commands and anyone with any Linux experience should know most of them.

File Permission Basics

Just like every operating system, Linux comes with a set of permissions that it uses to protect files, directories, and devices on the system. These permissions can be manipulated to allow (or disallow) access to files and directories on different parts of the system. Here are some of the commands you can use to work with permissions:

chmod   Changes the permissions of files or directories

chown   Changes the owner and group of files or directories

ls -l   Displays file permissions and ownership of files or directories

ll   Same as ls -l

umask   Defines or displays the default permissions for creation of files or directories

Before starting to use commands, let's look at how permissions work first. Linux permissions are implemented through the properties of files and defined by three separate categories. They are broken down into the following:

User   Person who owns the file

Group   Group that owns the file

Other   All other users on the system

Permissions in Linux can be assigned one of two ways. You can use the mnemonic or a single digit to represent the permissions level.

Operation	Digit	Mnemonic	Description
Read	r	4	View file contents
Write	w	2	Write to or change
Execute	x	1	Run the file

Let's start by looking at file permissions before changing them. You can view the home directory from one of the users I have set up. To view a file's or directory's permissions, you can use two different commands.

Step 1.   View file permissions for user01's home directory:

```
# ll /home/user01
total 32
drwxr-xr-x. 2 user01 user01 4096 Dec 11 07:43 Desktop
drwxr-xr-x. 2 user01 user01 4096 Dec 11 07:43 Documents
drwxr-xr-x. 2 user01 user01 4096 Dec 11 07:43 Downloads
-rw-rw-r--. 1 user01 user01    0 Dec 11 07:44 file1
-rw-rw-r--. 1 user01 user01    0 Dec 11 07:44 file2
drwxr-xr-x. 2 user01 user01 4096 Dec 11 07:43 Music
drwxr-xr-x. 2 user01 user01 4096 Dec 11 07:43 Pictures
drwxr-xr-x. 2 user01 user01 4096 Dec 11 07:43 Public
drwxr-xr-x. 2 user01 user01 4096 Dec 11 07:43 Templates
drwxr-xr-x. 2 user01 user01 4096 Dec 11 07:43 Videos
```

Step 2.   You could also use the following:

```
# ll -s /home/user01
total 32
drwxr-xr-x. 2 user01 user01 4096 Dec 11 07:43 Desktop
drwxr-xr-x. 2 user01 user01 4096 Dec 11 07:43 Documents
drwxr-xr-x. 2 user01 user01 4096 Dec 11 07:43 Downloads
-rw-rw-r--. 1 user01 user01    0 Dec 11 07:44 file1
-rw-rw-r--. 1 user01 user01    0 Dec 11 07:44 file2
drwxr-xr-x. 2 user01 user01 4096 Dec 11 07:43 Music
drwxr-xr-x. 2 user01 user01 4096 Dec 11 07:43 Pictures
drwxr-xr-x. 2 user01 user01 4096 Dec 11 07:43 Public
drwxr-xr-x. 2 user01 user01 4096 Dec 11 07:43 Templates
drwxr-xr-x. 2 user01 user01 4096 Dec 11 07:43 Videos
```

Here, you can see 10 different options that can be set on the file. The first field determines whether it is a directory. Desktop is a directory as denoted by the d in the first field. The next three fields each represent the owner, the group, and other. For example, file1 is not a directory, the owner of the file can read and write to this file, the group can read and write, and all others can only read the file. You can also see that file2 has the same permissions. The owner and group are listed after the permissions, and for all files in this directory, the owner is user01 and the group is user01. Users and groups are used to control who has access to files and directories.

Now that you know how to view the permissions of files and directories, let's look at how to modify them. Let's start with changing the owner and group of a file using the `chown` command. There is another user called user02 you can use.

Syntax: `chown [option] [user] [: [group]]`

Options:

`-R`	Acts recursively
`-v`	Provides verbose output

Step 3. Change the owner of file1 from user01 to user02:
```
# chown user02 file1
```

Step 4. Change the group of file2 from user01 to user02:
```
# chown :user02 file2
```

Step 5. Now check the permissions again:
```
# ll
-rw-rw-r--. 1 user02 user01    0 Dec 11 07:44 file1
-rw-rw-r--. 1 user01 user02    0 Dec 11 07:44 file2
```

You can see that the user for file1 and group for file2 were changed appropriately. Currently, both files are set up to allow only other users to read them. What if you want to allow all users on your system to make changes to this file? In that case, you can use the `chmod` command to change permissions.

Syntax: `chmod [options] FILE`

Options:

`-R`	Acts recursively
`-v`	Provides verbose output

Step 6. Change the permissions in the "other" section to allow write access to this file:
```
# chmod 666 file1
```

Step 7.   View the permissions change:

```
# 11
-rw-rw-rw-. 1 user02 user01     0 Dec 11 07:44 file1
```

Now user02, group user01, and everyone else on the system have read and write access to this file. You might be wondering where I got 666 for the permissions? When you assign permissions with numerical values, you add up the values of the permissions for each section. Because I wanted to keep the user and group permissions the same, I needed to make sure that they each had read (4) and write (2) permissions (4 + 2 = 6). Because I want the "other" group to be the same, I just continued with the same numerical value, which is where the 666 permissions come from. Being able to manipulate permissions isn't a difficult task but may take some practice to understand at first.

The last command that we look at is umask. You may be wondering where the permissions came from when we first created file1 and file2? They were given 664 as their default permissions upon creation, but where did that number come from? When users are created, they are assigned a umask value that defines all permissions for files and directories that users create. Let's look at how that works.

When files are created, they are given the default permissions 666 or rw-rw-rw- and directories are given the default permissions 777 or rwxrwxrwx. The umask command takes the default permissions and modifies them according to its mask value (through subtraction). Here is an example of how they are calculated:

File's default permissions	666 = 110 110 110 (in binary)
Subtract the umask	002 = 000 000 010 (in binary)
Value you get afterward	664 = 110 110 100 (in binary)

Now you have the default permissions 664 as shown previously. This calculation is the same with directories:

Directory's default permissions	777 = 111 111 111 (in binary)
Subtract the umask	002 = 000 000 010 (in binary)
Value you get afterward	775 = 111 111 101 (in binary)

Now you have the default permissions 775 as shown previously.

Step 8.   You can display the current value of the umask to find out what it is set to by calling the umask command:

```
# umask
0002
```

All files and directories have a leading 0, which is used for more advanced permissions. For now, just know that it is there but that you can leave it off when calculating directory permissions. You can also supply a value to umask to be able to change it, but this is not recommended.

If you don't understand the information covered here, that's all right because Chapter 7, "User Administration," deals with users, user creation, and advanced file permissions more closely. However, you should know how to set file permissions and understand how they are calculated before moving on.

Using a Text Editor

Being able to use a text editor is probably one of the most critical skills to have as a system administrator. You constantly need to edit config files, write scripts, or make changes to system files...all of which require you to use a text editor. The three most popular editors available today include

vi or vim	Text editor with great flexibility
emacs	Similar to vi, an advanced text editor with many features
nano	A basic text editor for quick editing

For the Red Hat exams, you need to know how to use the vim text editor. It is installed by default with Red Hat Enterprise Linux 6, although it isn't the only editor available. Vim is an enhanced version of vi with syntax highlighting for programming. You can install additional text editors if the packages for them are available during the exam. Personally, I use nano for most of my quick edits and vim for any config file building from scratch or programming.

Let's look at some of the options for vim.

Syntax: vim [arguments] [file]

Arguments:

-R	Opens a file in read-only mode
-b	Specifies binary mode
+	Starts at the end of the file
+<num>	Starts at line <num>

Vim functions in three different modes: command mode, insert mode, and last line mode. When you first start working with a file, you are in command mode. Here, you can issue commands that allow you to move around your file without actually inserting text into the file. When you're ready to insert text into the file, you can use i or a to move into insert mode, enabling you to insert text at the cursor location. To move out of insert mode back into command mode, just press the Esc key. The last mode you can enter is last line mode, which you enter by typing a colon (:). In this mode, you can issue additional commands to save, quit, and do even more.

There are some additional options you should know for command mode.

Commands for command mode:

e	Moves to the end of a word
b	Moves to the beginning of a word
$	Moves to the end of a line
H	Moves to the first line onscreen
L	Moves to the last line onscreen
i	Enters insert mode
a	Appends after the cursor
o	Opens a new line below and inserts
O	Opens a new line above and inserts
R	Enters insert mode but replaces characters instead of inserting
dd	Deletes the current line
x	Deletes text under the cursor
yy	Yanks (copies) the current line
p	Pastes the yanked line
u	Undoes the last action

Commands for last line mode:

:n	Jumps to line n
:w	Writes the file to disk
:q	Quits vim
:q!	Quits without saving changes

Using vim is rather confusing at first if you have not used it before. I suggest you create and work with some sample files before continuing so that you become more familiar with it. You can also practice with nano and emacs to see the difference in how the editors work. Although nano is quicker to pick up and easier to use, it is not as flexible or powerful as vim or emacs. There is a huge war between system administrators over which text editor is better—vim or emacs. I won't choose sides, but I will say you should try both and see which you are more comfortable with.

Regex

From time to time, you need to hunt down something specific on your system, whether it's a file itself, something within a file, or through a script. In Linux, you can use regular expressions (also known as *regex*) that enable you to find specific information. Regex uses special expressions in combination with any of the following:

Literal	Any character used in a search or matching expression
Metacharacter	One or more special characters with special meaning
Escape sequence	Use of metacharacters as a literal

Regex is one of those topics that either you pick up or it causes tons of frustration and headaches. Just like anything else though, the more you practice and look at examples, the more you should begin to pick up on how it works and how to use it more efficiently.

In this section, we look at only a single command called grep, which can be used with regex. To start, let's look at the options that can be used with it.

Syntax: grep [options] PATTERN [file]

Options:

-w	Forces PATTERN to match whole words only
-x	Forces PATTERN to match whole lines only
-E	Makes PATTERN an extended regular expression
-f	Obtains PATTERN from a file
-v	Inverts the match (prints nonmatching lines)
-m [NUM]	Stops after NUM matches
-R	Acts recursively when searching through directories
—color=[WHEN]	Displays output in color; WHEN is always, auto, or never

The hardest thing to understand when you're starting with regex is how to build a pattern to find what you're looking for. You not only need to know which option to use when calling the grep command, but also need to understand pattern options. Let's go through what some of these options include.

Metacharacters:

[ ]	Matches anything inside the brackets, either individually or as a whole, including letters or numbers. Be aware that lower- and uppercase letters are different.
-	Creates a range; for example, one through nine would be 1-9. This dash can also be used to search for a range of letters such as a-z or A-Z. There are no spaces between characters when using a range.
^	Negates a search when used inside brackets. The caret is used outside brackets to find only lines that begin with a given string.
$	Similar to a caret outside brackets, finds lines based on their ending character or string.
.	Finds any character in its position.
*	Matches any character zero or more times.
( )	Combines multiple patterns.
¦	Finds left or right values, which is very useful in combination with ( ).

These characters should be enough to get you started. The following text is used in the file_example file for all regex examples.

Step 1.   Copy the following into a file called file_example:

```
My original text
Another line with the number 3

Search for the word "me"
I contain 5and6
Skip me
and me

0 + 1 = 1
Above this line is a math equation...duh!
```

Step 2.   For the bracket example, look for S[ek] as a pattern:

```
# grep S[ek] file_example
Search for the word "me"
Skip me
```

You can see that two lines were returned from the file. The first line was returned because it contained the word *Search*, which has *Se* in it. The second line contains the word *Skip*, which matches the *Sk*.

Step 3.   Try another match with c[or] as the pattern:

```
# grep c[on] file_example
I contain 5and6
```

Here, both letters are matched in the word *contain*. Now let's check out how range works in a pattern.

Step 4.   Search for any line that contains a number using [0-9] as the pattern:

```
# grep [0-9] file_example
Another line with the number 3
I contain 5and6
0 + 1 = 1
```

You can see all lines with any number between zero and nine were returned. Can you think of another way you could have returned only lines that contained numbers and no words?

Step 5.   Search for all letters (both lower- and uppercase) with [A-Za-z] as your pattern and then invert your selection:

```
# grep -v [A-Za-z] file_example
0 + 1 = 1
```

Let's run through a few more examples to finish this section.

Step 6.   Search for all lines beginning with the letter *S*:

```
# grep ^S file_example
Search for the word "me"
Skip me
```

Step 7.   Find any line that ends in the word *me*:

```
# grep me$ file_example
Skip me
and me
```

Step 8.   Find all lines that begin with uppercase *A* or lowercase *a* and have any number of characters after it:

```
# grep ^[Aa]. file_example
Another line with the number 3
and me
Above this line is a math equation...duh!
```

As you are probably starting to realize, there is an infinite number of combinations you can use to hunt down lines or words in a file. Using regular expressions is a huge topic, and there are many great books dedicated to it. For the purposes of this book, we have covered enough for you to find what you're looking for in files. Make sure that you keep practicing with the sample and even system config files trying to find different combinations. If you're having trouble with the results of matches, I highly recommend using the —color=always options with your grep command. This highlights on your terminal what is actually being matched by your pattern, allowing you to get some better insight into what the pattern is actually looking for.

I/O Redirection

Sometimes you need to use the output from a command more than once. To accomplish this, you can redirect the output of commands using some neat command-line tricks. Let's look at the following commands:

sort	Sorts the output of a command or file
wc	Provides a word or line count
cat	Displays the contents of a file
uniq	Lists all the unique lines in a file or command output
echo	Outputs or displays a string
cut	Divides a string or output

There are also a few characters you can use to direct or redirect output of commands. These characters are

>	Directs output to a file or device (overwrites if the file exists)
<	Directs input from the file or device
>>	Appends output or text to a file (creates if the file doesn't exist)
¦	Pipes the output of one command to another
&&	Combines commands

This might be a lot of commands to take in at once if you've never worked with them before. After we go through a few examples, most of these commands and characters will make more sense.

Step 1.   Use the echo command to output some text to a file:

```
# echo "This is some sample text" > file_example
```

Normally, the echo command just displays the text you have given it back to the screen, but because you are using the output direction character, the output is pushed to the file specified instead.

Step 2.   Verify that the text was output correctly by viewing the contents of the file:

```
# cat file_example
This is some sample text
```

Having this line in a file provides a good chance to look at the cut command.

Syntax: cut OPTION [FILE]

Options:

-d   Specifies a delimiter

-f   Displays a particular field

Because you know what is in the text file you just created, why not pick it apart using the cut command?

Step 3.   Display the third field of the text using the space as a delimiter:

```
# cut -d " " -f3 file_example
some
```

You can see that with this kind of command you can select which piece of a string or text file you'd like. Now that you know how to put some text in a file and pick it apart, see whether you can put these commands together. Using the pipe character (|), you can combine the two previous commands to make one command pipe into another.

Step 4.   Combine the two commands into a single line:

```
# cat file_example | cut -d " " -f3 file_example
some
```

Here, the cat command normally outputs the contents of the file named file_example. However, instead, the output is sent to the cut command for further processing. Instead of piping the commands together, you can also use && to have one command execute after another.

Step 5.   Execute one command and then another:

```
# echo "This is some more text" > file_example && cut -d " " -f3
file_example
some
```

So far, you've seen some creative ways to output text to files and manipulate the text in the file. What if you output text to a file and then run the same command a second time?

Step 1.   View the current contents of the sample file:

```
# cat file_example
This is some more text
```

Step 2.   Output some more text to this file:

```
# echo "Different text" > file_example
```

Step 3.   Verify the contents of the file again:

```
# cat file_example
Different text
```

What happened to the original text? When you use the >, the output is sent to a file or device. However, it always overwrites what is in the current file or device. If you want to append text, you can use the same character twice.

Step 4.   Append text to the file instead of overwriting it:

```
# echo "My original text" >> file_example
```

Step 5.   Verify the contents of the file:

```
# cat file_example
Different text
My original text
```

Step 6.   Run the same exact command again and view the contents of the file:

```
# echo "My original text" >> file_example && cat file_example
Different text
My original text
My original text
```

Notice there are now two lines with the same text. What if this was a config file for a service with duplicate data? In that case, you can use the uniq command to pull only unique lines from a file, making sure that there are no duplicates.

Step 7.   View only unique lines in the sample file, create a new file based on the output, and view the contents of this new file:

```
# uniq file_example > uniq_file && cat uniq_file
Different text
My original text
```

Now that you've been through a few commands and characters, you're ready to start working with the rest of the commands and some real files. Suppose you are looking through the /etc/passwd file for a particular user. When you view the contents of this file, you notice that they are not in order.

Step 1.   Display the contents of /etc/passwd:

```
# cat /etc/passwd
root:x:0:0:root:/root:/bin/bash
bin:x:1:1:bin:/bin:/sbin/nologin
daemon:x:2:2:daemon:/sbin:/sbin/nologin
adm:x:3:4:adm:/var/adm:/sbin/nologin
lp:x:4:7:lp:/var/spool/lpd:/sbin/nologin
sync:x:5:0:sync:/sbin:/bin/sync
shutdown:x:6:0:shutdown:/sbin:/sbin/shutdown
halt:x:7:0:halt:/sbin:/sbin/halt
mail:x:8:12:mail:/var/spool/mail:/sbin/nologin
uucp:x:10:14:uucp:/var/spool/uucp:/sbin/nologin
operator:x:11:0:operator:/root:/sbin/nologin
games:x:12:100:games:/usr/games:/sbin/nologin
gopher:x:13:30:gopher:/var/gopher:/sbin/nologin
nobody:x:99:99:Nobody:/:/sbin/nologin
dbus:x:81:81:System message bus:/:/sbin/nologin
usbmuxd:x:113:113:usbmuxd user:/:/sbin/nologin
avahi-autoipd:x:170:170:Avahi IPv4LL Stack:/var/lib/avahi-
autoipd:/sbin/nologin
vcsa:x:69:69:virtual console memory owner:/dev:/sbin/nologin
rpc:x:32:32:Rpcbind Daemon:/var/cache/rpcbind:/sbin/nologin
rtkit:x:499:499:RealtimeKit:/proc:/sbin/nologin
abrt:x:498:498::/etc/abrt:/sbin/nologin
nscd:x:28:28:NSCD Daemon:/:/sbin/nologin
haldaemon:x:68:68:HAL daemon:/:/sbin/nologin
nslcd:x:65:55:LDAP Client User:/:/sbin/nologin
saslauth:x:497:495:"Saslauthd user":/var/empty/saslauth:/sbin/nolo-
gin
avahi:x:70:70:Avahi mDNS/DNS-SD Stack:/var/run/avahi-
daemon:/sbin/nologin
ntp:x:38:38::/etc/ntp:/sbin/nologin
rpcuser:x:29:29:RPC Service User:/var/lib/nfs:/sbin/nologin
pulse:x:496:494:PulseAudio System Daemon:/var/run/pulse:/sbin/nolo-
gin
sshd:x:74:74:Privilege-separated SSH:/var/empty/sshd:/sbin/nologin
tcpdump:x:72:72::/:/sbin/nologin
```

How are you supposed to find anything in this mess? You could do some searching with regex to find a specific user, but what if you just need a little organization in your life? If that's the case, you can use the sort command to make heads or tails of this mess.

Syntax: sort [options] [FILE]

Options:

-b   Ignores leading blanks

-f   Ignores case

-n   Compares according to numerical string value

-r   Sorts in reverse order

Step 2.   Display the /etc/passwd file again, this time in a sorted format:

```
# sort /etc/passwd
abrt:x:498:498::/etc/abrt:/sbin/nologin
adm:x:3:4:adm:/var/adm:/sbin/nologin
apache:x:48:48:Apache:/var/www:/sbin/nologin
avahi-autoipd:x:170:170:Avahi IPv4LL Stack:/var/lib/avahi-
autoipd:/sbin/nologin
avahi:x:70:70:Avahi mDNS/DNS-SD Stack:/var/run/avahi-
daemon:/sbin/nologin
bin:x:1:1:bin:/bin:/sbin/nologin
daemon:x:2:2:daemon:/sbin:/sbin/nologin
dbus:x:81:81:System message bus:/:/sbin/nologin
games:x:12:100:games:/usr/games:/sbin/nologin
gdm:x:42:42::/var/lib/gdm:/sbin/nologin
gopher:x:13:30:gopher:/var/gopher:/sbin/nologin
haldaemon:x:68:68:HAL daemon:/:/sbin/nologin
halt:x:7:0:halt:/sbin:/sbin/halt
lp:x:4:7:lp:/var/spool/lpd:/sbin/nologin
mail:x:8:12:mail:/var/spool/mail:/sbin/nologin
nfsnobody:x:65534:65534:Anonymous NFS User:/var/lib/nfs:/sbin/nolo-
gin
nobody:x:99:99:Nobody:/:/sbin/nologin
nscd:x:28:28:NSCD Daemon:/:/sbin/nologin
nslcd:x:65:55:LDAP Client User:/:/sbin/nologin
ntp:x:38:38::/etc/ntp:/sbin/nologin
operator:x:11:0:operator:/root:/sbin/nologin
postfix:x:89:89::/var/spool/postfix:/sbin/nologin
pulse:x:496:494:PulseAudio System Daemon:/var/run/pulse:/sbin/nolo-
gin
root:x:0:0:root:/root:/bin/bash
rpcuser:x:29:29:RPC Service User:/var/lib/nfs:/sbin/nologin
rpc:x:32:32:Rpcbind Daemon:/var/cache/rpcbind:/sbin/nologin
rtkit:x:499:499:RealtimeKit:/proc:/sbin/nologin
saslauth:x:497:495:"Saslauthd user":/var/empty/saslauth:/sbin/nolo-
gin
shutdown:x:6:0:shutdown:/sbin:/sbin/shutdown
sshd:x:74:74:Privilege-separated SSH:/var/empty/sshd:/sbin/nologin
sync:x:5:0:sync:/sbin:/bin/sync
tcpdump:x:72:72::/:/sbin/nologin
usbmuxd:x:113:113:usbmuxd user:/:/sbin/nologin
uucp:x:10:14:uucp:/var/spool/uucp:/sbin/nologin
vcsa:x:69:69:virtual console memory owner:/dev:/sbin/nologin
```

This sorted output is much better and makes it easier to read. Why stop here, though? What if you want to know how many users are listed in this file? You could count the lines in this file, or you could use the wc command to do it for you.

Syntax: wc [option] [FILE]

Options:

-c	Prints the byte count
-m	Prints the character count
-l	Prints the number of lines
-w	Prints the word count

Step 3.   Determine how many lines are in the /etc/passwd file:

```
# wc -l /etc/passwd
35 /etc/passwd
```

At this point, we have covered a bunch of commands for piping and redirection. We saw not only some simple examples, but also some practical uses. Make sure you are comfortable piping, redirecting, or combining commands for efficiency. Being able to pass the Red Hat exams requires that you have good time management skills, which you can accomplish by being able to use fewer commands more efficiently.

Compression and Archiving

One of the great things about Linux is that many things don't have a standard. This allows for various implementations and customizations among many different software programs and practices. This also can be a downfall. As you will learn when you become a system administrator, backups are the number one priority. If something should crash or become corrupt and you can't restore it because you aren't keeping up with your backups or you just don't keep any, you may be looking for a new job. Although we don't address backup programs here, this is a good lead into archiving and compression. For that task, we look at a single command in this section:

tar   Used for compressing and archiving files and directories

The tar utility has a monstrous number of options, so it would be impossible to cover them all here. Instead, let's focus on some common options used in this book.

Syntax: tar [options] [FILE]

Options:

-c	Creates a new archive
-d	Finds differences between the archive and file system
-f	Specifies the archive file to use
-p	Preserves files and directory permissions
-t	Lists the files in an archive
-v	Produces verbose output

Right away, you should be able to see that this little utility would be perfect to create an archive of files and directories that you could keep as a backup. Although using this tool solely as a backup strategy isn't recommended, it is useful for transferring a group of files and directories quickly. Let's look at some examples showing how to use the tar command.

Step 1. Create some random blank files:

```
# touch file1 file2 file3 another_file
```

Step 2. With the files in place, create a simple archive containing these files:

```
# tar cvf sample.tar file1 file2 file3 another_file
file1
file2
file3
another_file
```

Step 3. Of course, you know that you can also use some of the other tricks you learned already to make this task easier:

```
# tar cvf sample.tar <file>
another_file
file1
file2
file3
```

When an archive is created, you can also apply compression to reduce the amount of space the archive file takes up. Although multiple types of compression are supported with the use of tar, we look only at gunzip (.gz) and bzip2 (bz2) here.

Step 4. Let's re-create the archive using the gunzip compression:

```
# tar cvf sample.tar.gz <file>
another_file
file1
file2
file3
```

Step 5.   View the current directory to see the two current archive files:

```
# ls
sample.tar
sample.tar.gz
```

If these archives contained actual files instead of the blank ones, you'd notice that the .tar.gz file is smaller than the normal .tar file. Suppose now that you are working for a software company and the developers just sent over a build called Dec2010_MyApp.tar.gz. You need to deploy it to all your application servers, but you first need to uncompress and then extract it from the remaining .tar file. Before you deploy this build file (Dec2010_MyApp.tar.gz) to the application servers, a developer asks you to check for a file called file5.jsp within the build file. How can you tell whether this file is in the build without uncompressing and untarring the build?

Step 6.   Use the -t option to list all the contents within the build file:

```
# tar tf Dec2010_MyApp.tar.gz
MyApp/
MyApp/build.xml
MyApp/app.config
MyApp/config/
MyApp/config/file3.sql
MyApp/config/file1.jcml
MyApp/config/file2.xml
MyApp/source/
MyApp/source/file4.jar
MyApp/source/file3.jar
MyApp/source/file5.jsp
```

As you can see, the file is indeed in the build. If this build were much larger, however (which they usually are), you could also use the grep command to filter out just the file you were looking for.

Step 7.   Query only for the file you want within the build file:

```
# tar tf Dec2010_MyApp.tar.gz ¦ grep file5.jsp
MyApp/source/file5.jsp
```

Step 8.   Query again for the same thing, but with this command, use -v for additional information:

```
# tar tvf Dec2010_MyApp.tar.gz ¦ grep file5.jsp
-rw-r--r-- root/root          0 2010-12-10 11:51
MyApp/source/file5.jsp
```

Step 9.   Now extract this build file verbosely:

```
# tar xvf Dec2010_MyApp.tar.gz
MyApp/
MyApp/build.xml
MyApp/app.config
```

```
MyApp/config/
MyApp/config/file3.sql
MyApp/config/file1.jcml
MyApp/config/file2.xml
MyApp/source/
MyApp/source/file4.jar
MyApp/source/file3.jar
MyApp/source/file5.jsp
```

Again, you know that this build file is small, so there is no harm in allowing the extra output to see what files you're getting. You can leave out the verbose option when extracting large archives, and you get a new command prompt after the extraction is finished. You can see how the tar command is quite useful for many purposes and plays a large role in the real world. Make sure you're comfortable creating, extracting, and looking through archives, both compressed and uncompressed.

Summary

Think we've covered a lot? Unfortunately, this is only the tip of the iceberg when it comes to Linux. As mentioned at the beginning of this introduction, all the tools discussed here are user-level commands that you need to know to continue in this book. If you haven't seen many of the things described here, don't panic! Everyone learns at different speeds, and with some practice and repetition, you will quickly pick up everything. Remember, this book is a lab manual; hands-on is the number-one way to learn how to work with Red Hat and any other Linux operating system. Now let's move on to Chapter 1 on how to install Red Hat Enterprise Linux 6.

This chapter covers the following subjects:

■ **Starting the Installation—**This section covers the installation and setup of the Red Hat Enterprise Linux operating system.

■ **Verifying the Installation—**After you complete the installation, this section shows you how to verify that the installation was successful.

## CHAPTER 1

Installation

The first step when working with any new operating system is learning how to install it. This is an essential first step because the installation and setup affect how the system will be used post-install. This chapter covers the installation of Red Hat, the first steps to take post-install, and some other helpful tips to watch out for during the installation. Although the installation of Red Hat is no longer covered on the exam itself, installing Red Hat is an important subject. The first system you build will define a "template" for what your future installs will look like. It is common to build a kickstart server as well, which will automate the entire process of installation. Before we get ahead of ourselves, though, let's start with the basic installation process.

Starting the Installation

Let's start with a typical installation of Red Hat Enterprise Linux. The first virtual machine is going to be called RHEL01, and we'll walk through the installation here together. You should follow along with the install instructions to get a feel for how RHEL is installed. At the end of this chapter, you will reinstall Red Hat Enterprise Linux on this virtual machine as part of Lab 1 (the first task of Lab 1 to be exact).

Step 1. Create a new virtual machine in VirtualBox, with 384MB of RAM, and name it RHEL01.

Step 2. Make sure that the installation CD is in the drive (or attached as an ISO), and boot from the CD. If you don't press Enter at the first screen, it will begin to boot automatically after the timeout threshold (about 3 seconds). The installation process should begin at this point.

Step 3. The first option should be obvious because choosing a language affects the rest of the installation process. You also need to choose your keyboard layout at this point.

Step 4. Next comes the storage layout of the system. You don't need any crazy configuration here, so choose the basic option and move on (see Figure 1-1).

Step 5.   The next screen allows you to choose a hostname for your system. Notice the option on the bottom left to configure networking as well (see Figure 1-2). You don't need to make any changes to the network adapters for now; by default they are set to receive an IP address via Dynamic Host Configuration Protocol (DHCP). If you want to change an interface to have a static IP address, you could configure that here.

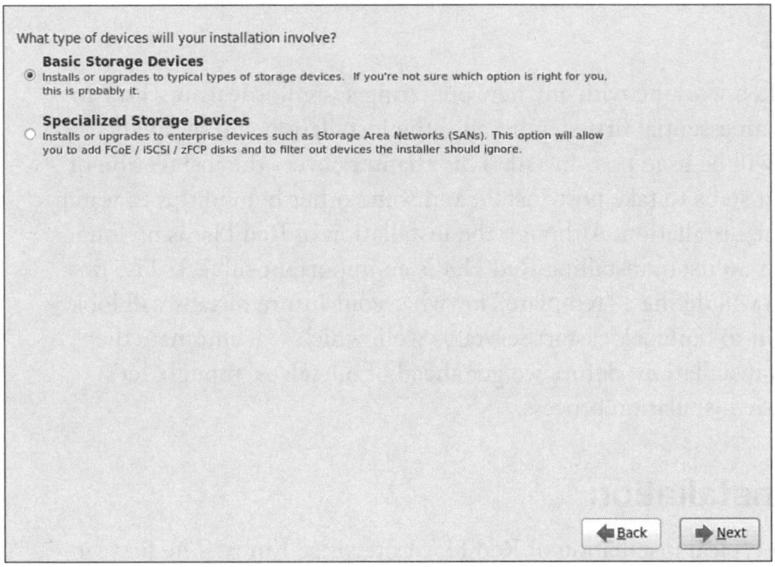

What type of devices will your installation involve?

Basic Storage Devices
◉ Installs or upgrades to typical types of storage devices. If you're not sure which option is right for you, this is probably it.

Specialized Storage Devices
○ Installs or upgrades to enterprise devices such as Storage Area Networks (SANs). This option will allow you to add FCoE / iSCSI / zFCP disks and to filter out devices the installer should ignore.

◀ Back   ➡ Next

Figure 1-1   Storage selection.

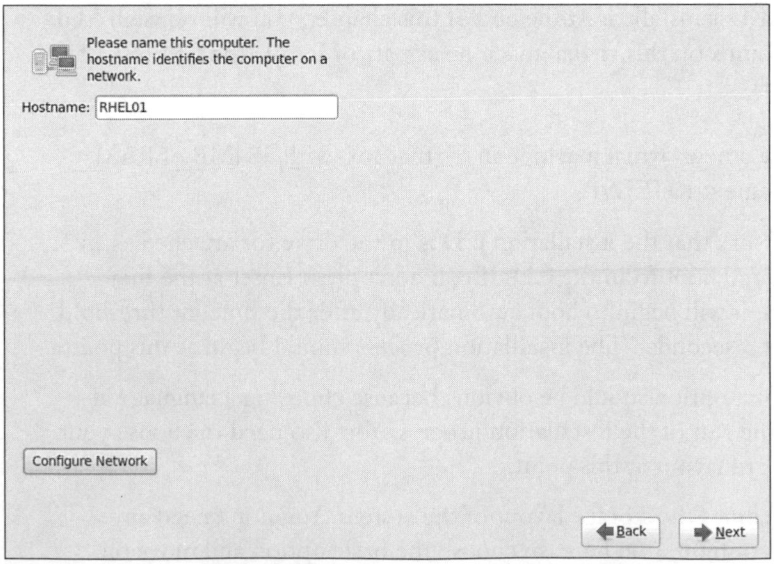

Please name this computer. The hostname identifies the computer on a network.

Hostname: RHEL01

Configure Network

◀ Back   ➡ Next

Figure 1-2   Set the hostname.

Step 6. Select your time zone. For me, it's America/New York.

Step 7. Choose a root password (see Figure 1-3). Make sure that this password is something strong that no one else will be able to guess. The root user basically has full access to anything on the system, so it's not a good idea to use something that can be guessed on the first try.

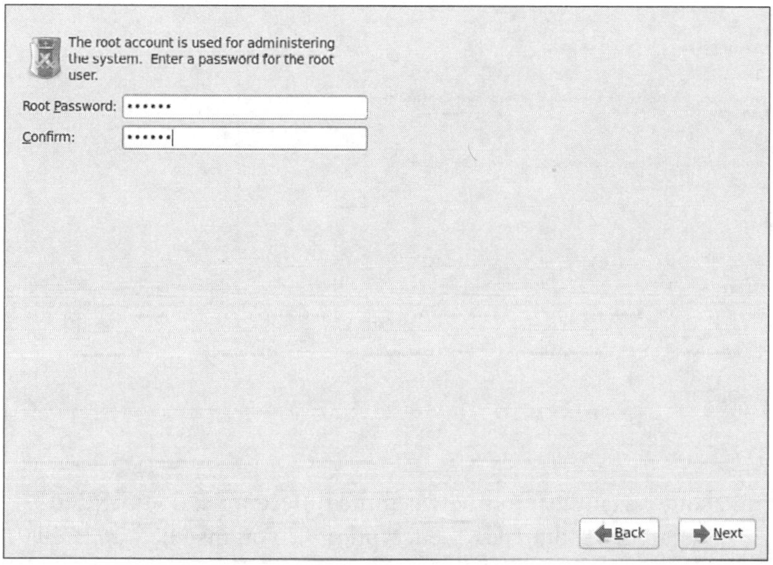

Figure 1-3   Choose a root password.

Step 8. Next, go to the partition layout screen. This screen is the place where you will probably spend the most time (see Figure 1-4). Here, you create the partitions for your new installation. For the purpose of getting through the install, select Use All Space. You could create a custom partition scheme (which will probably always happen with future installs), but it is not necessary here. By default, Red Hat uses logical volume management (covered in depth in Chapter 3, "Disks and Partitioning") when creating a default layout so that all your partitions (with the exception of /boot) are on logical volumes. To create a custom layout, you need to check the box on the bottom allowing you to modify the partitioning layout. New in Red Hat Enterprise Linux 6 (RHEL6), you can also choose to encrypt your system (using LUKS). If you'd like to do this, just check the box on the bottom. After you choose to continue, the partition table is written to the system drives.

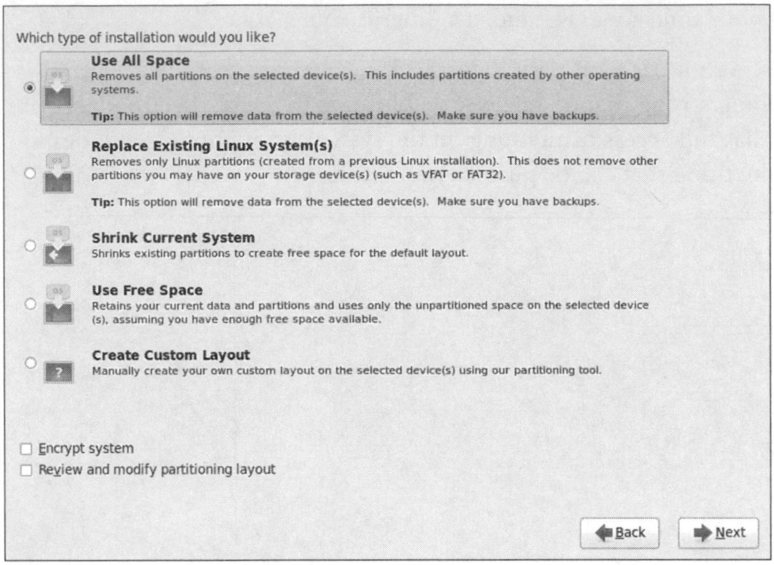

Figure 1-4   Partition creation.

MIGRATION TIP

You need to be careful about certain features between the different versions of Red Hat. Here, I'm specifically talking about LUKS encryption. If you installed updated versions of Red Hat Enterprise Linux 5 (such as version 5.4 or 5.5), you will notice that the LUKS encryption option is available during installation. However, the official Red Hat documentation states that only Red Hat Enterprise Linux 6 supports LUKS encryption. Although I try to point out many of these differences throughout the book, make sure you understand when certain features are available for use (via updates) and when they are officially supported.

REAL-WORLD TIP

Many system administrators have their own way of creating partition layouts, and sometimes that is even dictated through company requirements. Due to individual taste, and the fact that I will start a war discussing the topic of "what should be laid out where," I do not describe how to create a custom partitioning scheme based on any standards. There are, however, two important points to know. One is that the /boot partition can never be part of a Logical Volume Manager (LVM) layout. Second, you should spend time and plan ahead as to how you want your partitions laid out because a little planning now will save you from a big headache later.

Step 9.   Now you can select which packages you want installed. This process can get very detailed because you can choose a package group and then individual packages within the group. For my install, I'm going to leave the defaults, which install the base system with no desktop manager (see Figure 1-5). You need to know how to configure different packages and installations by hand, so allowing the system to install them now isn't going to help in the long run.

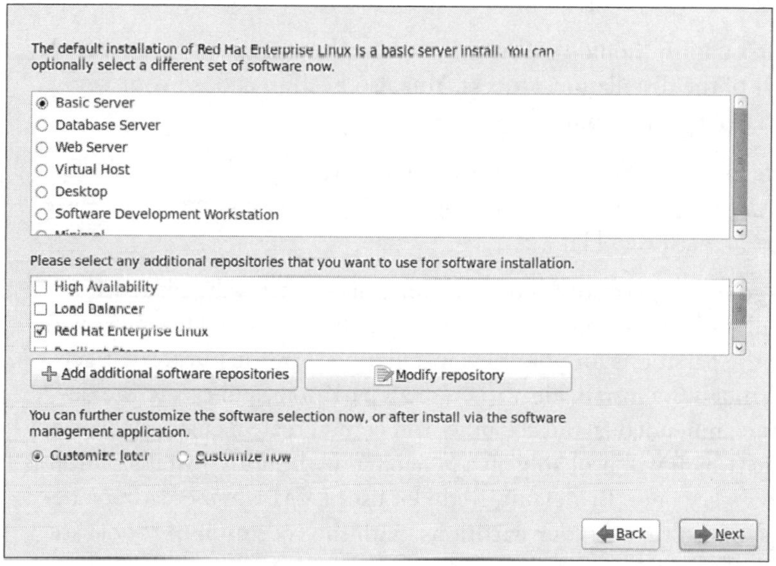

Figure 1-5 Package selection.

After you click Next, the installation of the operating system begins. This process can be fairly quick (10 minutes) or slightly longer (30 minutes) depending on which software packages you chose to install and other configuration options. When the installation is complete, you are prompted to reboot the system. After the system has rebooted, make sure that you either remove the CD from the drive or set the system to boot from the primary disk so as not to start the installation process all over again. This completes the installation of Red Hat Enterprise Linux 6.

An Older Install with RHEL5

I have included this section for those who are still running Red Hat Enterprise Linux 5 (RHEL5). Let's face it, new operating systems offer great new features and stability, but no one upgrades all his systems the moment a new release comes out. This takes careful planning, testing, and coordination.

Let's revisit the installation process using RHEL5 for the operating system. You should notice how the installation process and order have changed with the move to RHEL6. If you'd like to practice along with this section, you can install RHEL5 on your Client01 virtual machine.

Step 1.   Create a new virtual machine in VirtualBox with 384MB of RAM, and name it Client01.

Step 2.   Make sure that the installation CD is in the drive (or attached as an ISO), and boot from the CD. If you don't press Enter at the first screen, it will begin to boot automatically after the timeout threshold (about 3 seconds). The installation process should begin at this point.

Step 3.   The first option should be obvious because choosing a language affects the rest of the installation process. You also need to choose your keyboard layout at this point.

Step 4.   You are prompted to enter an installation number, which you can skip for now. Because you are just setting up a lab, you don't need to register the system with Red Hat.

Step 5.   Next, go to the partition layout screen. This screen is the place where you will probably spend the most time (see Figure 1-6). Here, you will create the partitions for your new installation. For the purpose of getting through the install, elect to erase all partitions and create the default recommended layout for now. You could create a custom partition scheme (which will probably always happen with future installs), but it is not necessary here. By default, Red Hat uses LVM when creating a default layout so that all your partitions (with the exception of /boot) are on logical volumes.

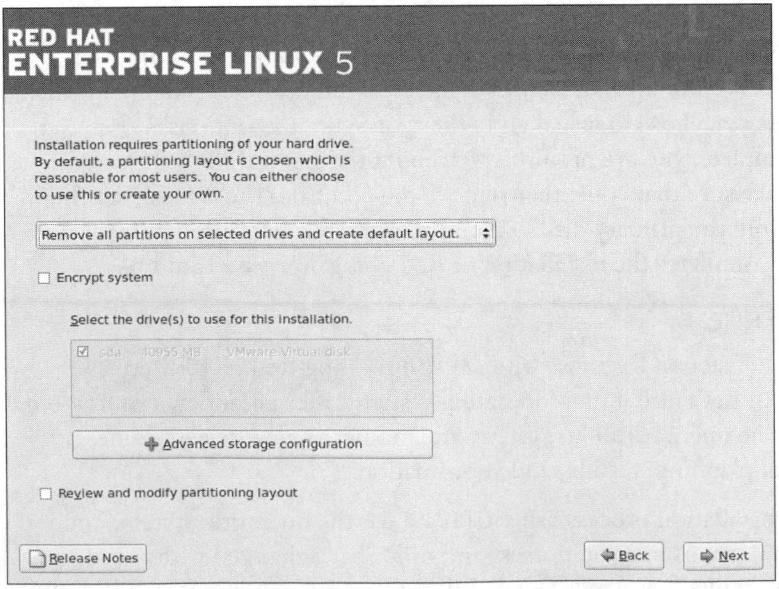

RED HAT
ENTERPRISE LINUX 5

Installation requires partitioning of your hard drive.
By default, a partitioning layout is chosen which is
reasonable for most users. You can either choose
to use this or create your own.

Remove all partitions on selected drives and create default layout.   ⬍

☐ Encrypt system

Select the drive(s) to use for this installation.

☑ sda   40955 MB   VMware Virtual disk

✦ Advanced storage configuration

☐ Review and modify partitioning layout

🗎 Release Notes   ⬅ Back   ➡ Next

Figure 1-6   Partition creation.

REAL-WORLD TIP

Many system administrators have their own way of creating partition layouts, and sometimes that is even dictated through company requirements. Due to individual taste, and the fact that I will start a war discussing the topic of "what should be laid out where," I do not describe how to create a custom partitioning scheme based on any standards. There are, however, two important points to know. One is that the /boot partition can never be part of an LVM layout. Second, you should spend time and plan ahead as to how you want your partitions laid out because a little planning now will save you from a big headache later.

Step 6. By choosing to proceed, you should get a warning message about your partitions not being initialized and that doing so will erase all data on the system (see Figure 1-7). This isn't a concern because there is nothing on the system currently.

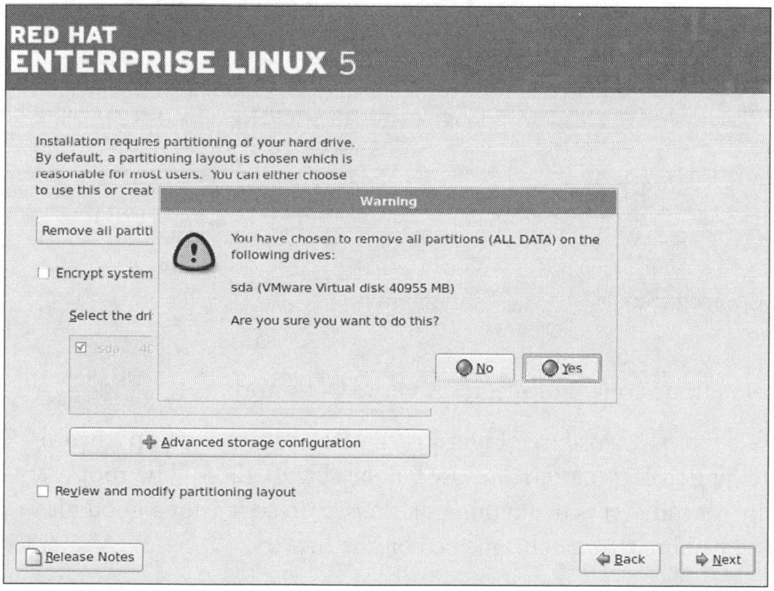

Figure 1-7 Partition warning.

WARNING

I should not have to say this, but I'll say it anyway: Initializing disk drives erases ALL DATA. If you are following along, there shouldn't be any data on your disk drives currently (because you are using a virtual machine); however, if you are building out a lab differently, make sure you make a backup of any data before installing, initializing, or formatting any disk drive!

Step 7.   Next on the list is setting up the network interfaces that you need for the system. For this installation, you'll set up two network interfaces. The first should be eth0, and it should get its IP address from a DHCP server; the second should be eth1 and have its IP address set statically (see Figure 1-8).

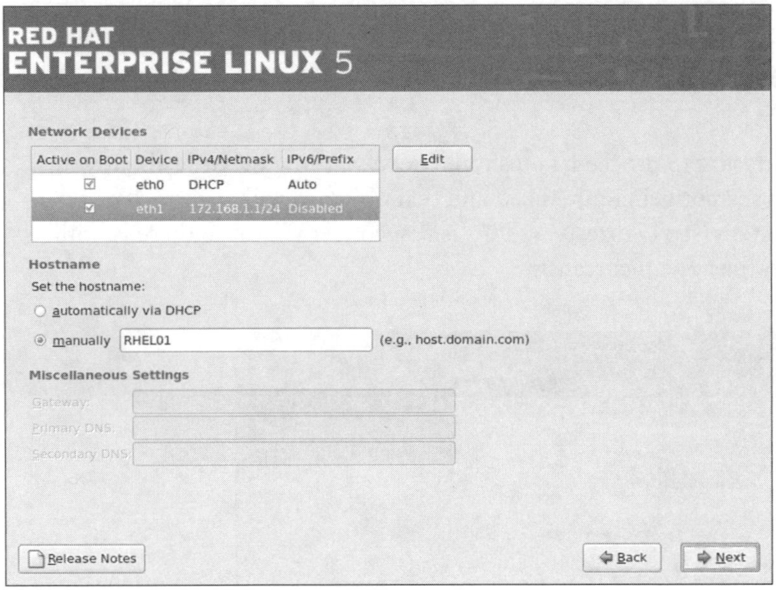

Figure 1-8   Add network interfaces.

Step 8.   Select your time zone. For me, it's America/New York.

Step 9.   Choose a root password (see Figure 1-9). Make sure that this password is something strong that no one else will be able to guess. The root user basically has full access to anything on the server, so it's not a good idea to use something that can be guessed on the first try.

REAL-WORLD TIP

There is big debate over whether choosing a strong password for the root user is necessary in a lab environment because it is usually cut off from production networks. Just remember that if you are working on a lab remotely, you had to get into it somehow, which means that someone else can too. If you are working on a local laptop (like I am on my laptop), the chances of someone breaking in decrease because there is no remote connection. Either way, the decision is up to you and which school of thought you'd like to follow.

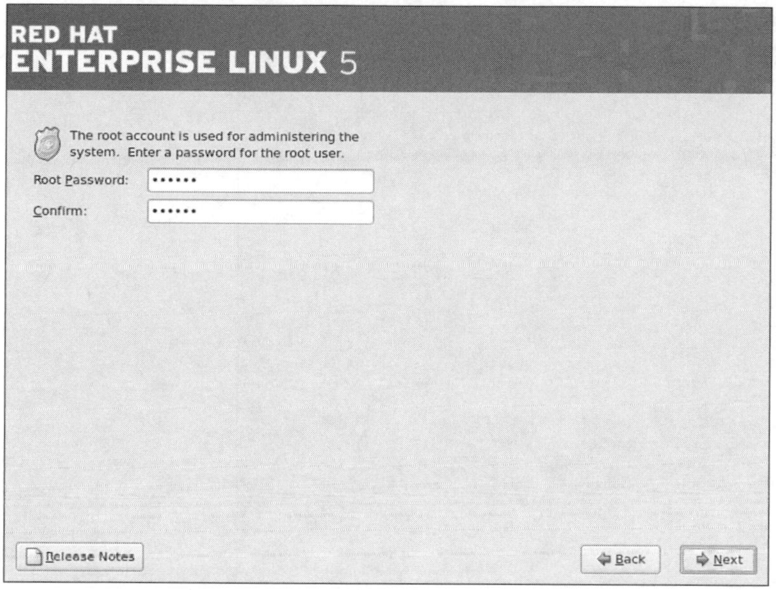

Figure 1-9   Choose a root password.

> **Step 10.** Now you are able to select which packages you want installed. This process can get very detailed because you can choose a package group and then individual packages within the group. For my install, I'm going to leave the defaults (which, as shown in Figure 1-10, install the base system plus the Gnome Desktop Manager). You need to know how to configure different packages and installations by hand, so allowing the system to install them now isn't going to help in the long run.

After you click Next, the installation of the operating system begins. This process can be fairly quick (10 minutes) or slightly longer (30 minutes) depending on which software packages you chose to install and other configuration options. When the installation is complete, you are prompted to reboot the system. When the system has rebooted, make sure that you either remove the CD from the drive or set the system to boot from the primary disk so as not to start the installation process all over again. Following the reboot, the system begins the firstboot process.

The Firstboot Process

The firstboot process we are going to follow here is a continuation from our RHEL5 installation. RHEL6 uses a text menu-driven process that is similar. The first thing you see during the firstboot process is the firewall configuration page, as shown in Figure 1-11.

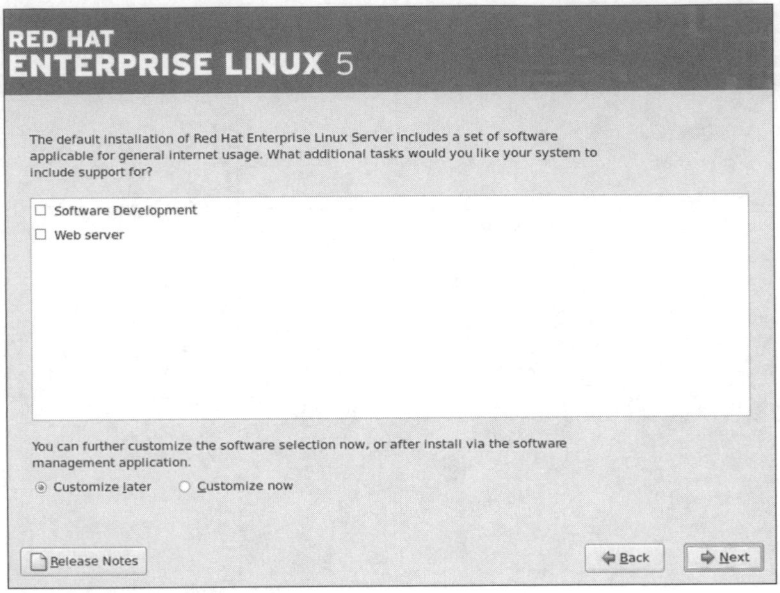

Figure 1-10   Package selection.

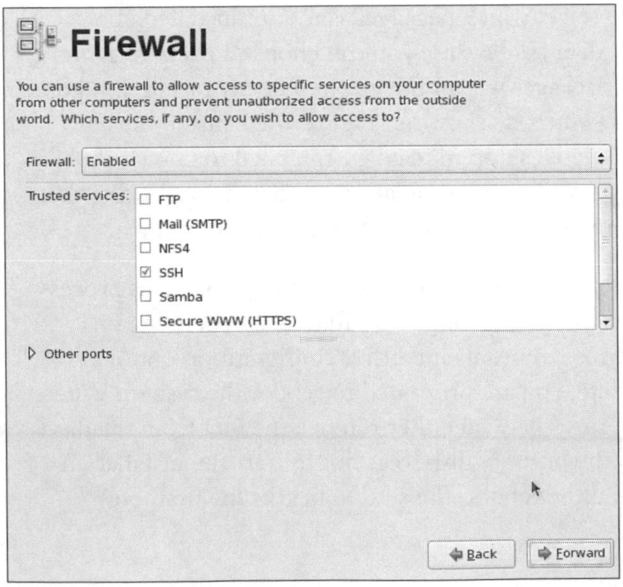

Figure 1-11   Select firewall ports.

Step 1.   Again, select the defaults for now, which allows incoming connections only to the SSH service (you can use SSH for remote management).

Step 2.   After the firewall is the next security utility, SELinux. The RHCSA requires that you know how to configure SELinux to work with different
services while in enforcing mode. To ensure that you practice that way,
choose Enforcing (see Figure 1-12) and select Forward.

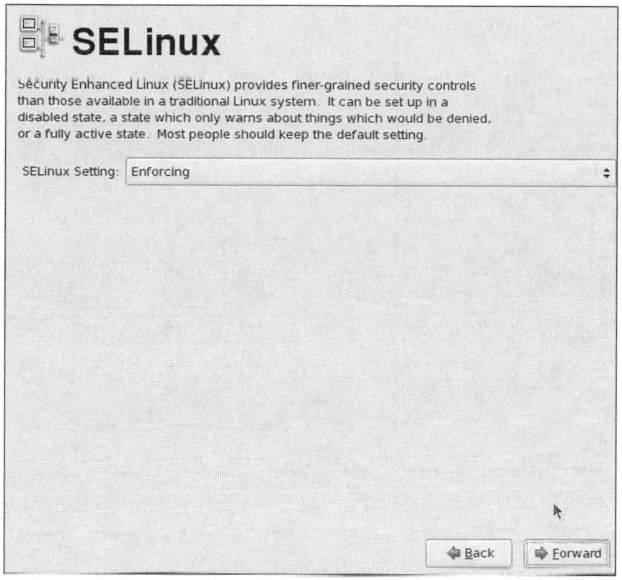

Figure 1-12   Set SELinux to Enforcing.

Step 3.   Choose the date and time, which should be detected automatically. Verify that they are correct, and continue with the firstboot process.

Step 4.   Create the first user that you will use to log in to the system (see
Figure 1-13). Don't forget to pick a good password for your user. I call
my user "user01" to keep things simple. Note that I will use this username throughout the book.

Step 5.   The last step here is to make sure that the sound card is working properly. When you click Next, you are allowed to install any additional software you may have. Because you don't have any further software to
install, you can finish the firstboot process and go to the login screen for
the first time. The installation process for Red Hat isn't that hard, but
understanding the different parts that go into it will help with troubleshooting the system later if you run into any problems.

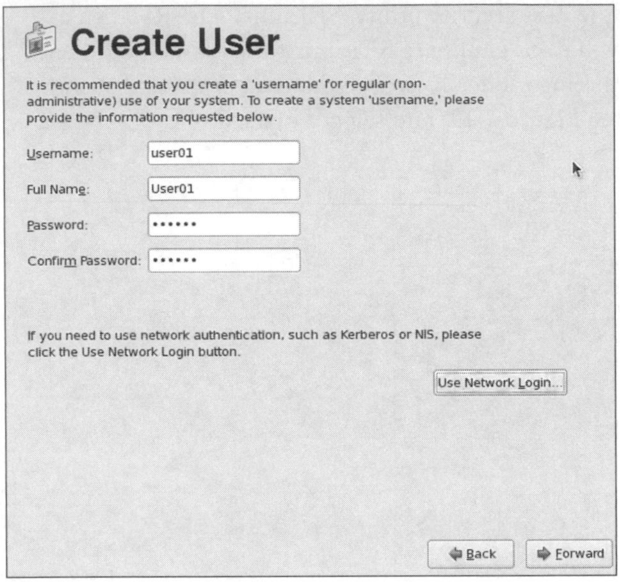

Figure 1-13 Create your first user.

Verifying the Installation

After installing Red Hat Enterprise Linux for the first time, you have to verify that everything went all right. You should log in to your virtual machine (RHEL01) for the first time and switch over to the root user (if you installed a Desktop Manager, go to Applications ☐ Accessories ☐ Terminal).

Switch to the root user:

```
[user01@RHEL01 ~]$ su -
Password: (Enter your root password that you made during install)
[root@RHEL01 ~]#
```
You can tell that you've become the root user because your prompt changes from $ to #. Throughout the entire book, I do everything as the root user.

Now you can look in the root user's home directory to find three log files that are created during the installation. These log files can provide you with valuable information should something go wrong.

```
# ls
anaconda-ks.cfg  install.log  install.log.syslog
```

The following list outlines what is contained in each file:

anaconda-ks.cfg	Provides a kickstart file of the installation
install.log	Lists all the installed packages during installation
install.log.syslog	Stores messages generated during the installation

The anaconda-ks.cfg file is actually a kickstart file created based on the details and selections made during installation. Later in the book, I talk about using the kickstart file to automate installation. The next file, install.log, lists all the packages that were installed during installation. When you want to customize your system and cut down on the number of packages being installed, this is a good place to start to see what is being installed in the first place. Finally, install.log.syslog holds messages generated during installation. In the /tmp directory, you can also find a set of anaconda.* log files that offer more information about events during the install process. Usually, if something goes wrong during installation of the system, you know about it right then and there. These files are good for troubleshooting, should you need them.

Summary

This chapter described the installation of Red Hat. Although installing a Red Hat system from CD is no longer part of the exam, it is important to understand the concepts discussed here. Partitioning, system setup and post-installation tasks affect how the system runs post-installation. You should have an understanding of how the system is installed and how to verify it was installed correctly. In the coming chapters, we discuss advanced partitioning such as RAID and LVM. Also in this chapter, we talked about viewing log files to verify that the installation was successful. In the next chapter, we dive deeper into how the boot process and system services work.

Review Questions

1. Red Hat Enterprise Linux 5 supports LUKS encryption. True or False?

2. In Red Hat Enterprise Linux 6, SELinux is set to Enforcing by default during the installation. True or False?

3. Which remote management service is installed by default? Can you name the port that it uses?

4. You can install software packages only after Red Hat Enterprise Linux is installed. True or False?

5. The default partition layout includes only basic partitions. True or False?

6. Which file contains all messages generated during installation that can be used for troubleshooting if the need arises?

Answers to Review Questions

1. False. Red Hat Enterprise Linux 6 is the only version that officially supports LUKS encryption.

2. True. In Red Hat Enterprise Linux 6, the default for SELinux is Enforcing during installation (which can be changed after the installation completes). For Red Hat Enterprise Linux 5, you were able to choose what mode you wanted SELinux to start in.

3. The SSH service is almost always installed by default in Red Hat. It uses TCP port 22, and this port is open on the default firewall rules.

4. False. The package selection screen allows you to install any software you want during the installation process as long as you have access to the correct packages or repositories.

5. False. The default partition layout for Red Hat Enterprise Linux 5 or 6 includes the use of LVM.

6. The install.log.syslog file contains messages that are generated during the installation. If you run into trouble during the installation, this is a good place to start.

Lab 1

Task 1 – The First Installation

Step 1. Erase your current instance of RHEL01.

Step 2. Create a new virtual machine in VirtualBox with the following settings:
- **a.** Assign the name RHEL01 to your new virtual machine.
- **b.** Set up the first NIC as a bridged adapter.
- **c.** Add a second NIC and set it up as an internal adapter on the inet network.
- **d.** Assign the primary hard drive to be 20GB in size.
- **e.** Create a second hard drive to be 8GB in size.
- **f.** Create a third hard drive to be 8GB in size.
- **g.** Create a fourth hard drive to be 8GB in size (this fourth drive must be created after the installation is complete because one slot must be left open for the CD-ROM drive).

Step 3. Start the installation of Red Hat Enterprise Linux 6 using the following settings:
- **a.** Assign drive 1 the default layout and leave the other drives empty.
- **b.** Set NIC 1 to obtain an IP address through DHCP.
- **c.** Set NIC 2 to have a static IP address of 172.168.1.1 /24.
- **d.** Assign the system a hostname of RHEL01.
- **e.** The time zone doesn't matter.
- **f.** Install only the base server packages (do not install any desktop package).

The task is complete when the system boots correctly, there are three blank drives (plus the primary), and you can log in to the system.

Task 2 – The Second Installation

Step 1. Create a new virtual machine in VirtualBox.

Step 2. During creation of the new machine, use the following settings:
- **a.** Assign the name RHEL02 to your new virtual machine.
- **b.** Set up the first NIC as an internal adapter on the inet network.
- **c.** Assign the primary hard drive to be 10GB in size.

Step 3.   Start the installation of Red Hat Enterprise Linux 6 using the following settings:

   a. Assign drive 1 the default layout.

   b. Set NIC 1 to have a static IP address of 172.168.1.2 /24.

   c. Assign the system a hostname of RHEL02.

   d. The time zone doesn't matter.

   e. Install only the base server packages (do not install any desktop package).

The task is complete when the system boots correctly and you can log in to the system.

Task 3 – The Third Installation

Step 1.   Create a new virtual machine with the following settings:

   a. Assign the name Client01 to your new virtual machine.

   b. Set up the first NIC as an internal adapter on the inet network.

   c. Assign the primary hard drive to be 10GB in size.

Step 2.   Start the installation of Red Hat Enterprise Linux 5 using the following settings:

   a. Assign drive 1 the default layout.

   b. Set NIC 1 to have a static IP address of 172.168.1.10 /24.

   c. Assign the system a hostname of Client01.

   d. The time zone doesn't matter.

   e. Install the base package and a desktop package (Gnome Desktop Manager).

   f. When asked to create a user, assign the name user01 to the user.

   g. Ensure that SELinux is set to Enforcing.

   h. Ensure that port 22 is left open on the firewall for SSH connections.

The task is complete when the system boots correctly and you can log in to the system.

Task 4 – The Fourth Installation

Step 1.   Create a new virtual machine with the following settings:
 a. Assign the name Client02 to your new virtual machine.
 b. Set up the first NIC as an internal adapter on the inet network.
 c. Assign the primary hard drive to be 10GB in size.

Step 2.   Start the installation of Red Hat Enterprise Linux 6 using the following settings:
 a. Assign drive 1 the default layout.
 b. Set NIC 1 to have a static IP address of 172.168.1.20 /24.
 c. Assign the system a hostname of Client02.
 d. The time zone doesn't matter.
 e. Install the base package and a desktop package (Gnome Desktop Manager).
 f. When asked to create a user, assign the name user02 to the user.

The task is complete when the system boots correctly and you can log in to the system.

This chapter covers the following subjects:

- **The Boot Process**—This section provides a high-level overview of the boot process and how it works.

- **Working with GRUB**—Here, you learn how to work with GRUB, the default bootloader for Red Hat.

- **Runlevels**—This section covers the different runlevels and how they work during the boot process.

- **Service Management**—This section explains how to manage system services during and after the boot process.

The following RHCSA exam objectives are covered:

- Boot, reboot, and shut down the system normally

- Boot systems into different runlevels manually

- Configure systems to boot into a specific runlevel automatically

- Use single-user mode to gain access to a system

- Start, stop, and check the status of network services

- Modify the system bootloader

- Configure network services to start automatically at boot

## CHAPTER 2

System Initialization

The boot process can be quite complex if you have never worked with it before. That being said, it is important to understand so that you can troubleshoot the system should it not boot properly. When a computer boots up, the BIOS is the first program that is run. After it is loaded, the BIOS begins to test the system through the Power On Self Test (POST) and then starts loading peripheral devices. The BIOS then looks for the boot device and passes control to it. The boot device contains the master boot record (MBR), which starts to boot the system via the bootloader. From here, the Grand Unified Bootloader (GRUB, the boot manager) looks to boot into the kernel that is labeled as the default. Finally, the kernel calls the init process (the first process to be spawned on a Linux system), which boots up the rest of the system. Aside from troubleshooting the boot process, you also need to understand how services are started and stopped, how to add system services to the boot process, and how to manage the bootloader itself.

The Boot Process

Let's look again at the boot process, but this time we can examine each area more in depth, starting with the GRUB bootloader. The Grand Unified Bootloader has become the default bootloader for Red Hat, Ubuntu, and many other versions of Linux as well. The bootloader can be used to boot into different operating systems (usually called a *multiboot system*), for system recovery, and to boot the kernel using special arguments. When GRUB loads, you are given a list of kernels and additional operating systems (if available) from which you can choose to boot (see Figure 2-1).

By default, there is a configurable 5-second timeout value that chooses the default kernel if you don't make a selection and the timeout threshold is reached.

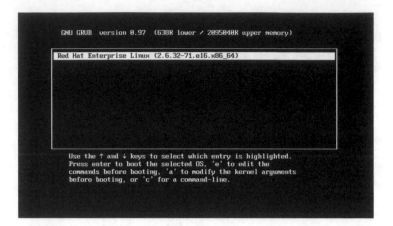

Figure 2-1   GRUB boot selection.

REAL-WORLD TIP

Although the default is 5 seconds, some older video cards take just 5 seconds to display the screen. I recommend that you set the default to at least 5 seconds and 10 for older systems.

After GRUB loads the kernel, it passes control over to the kernel, which in turn begins to initialize and configure the computer's hardware. Depending on how your GRUB configuration file is set up, you may or may not see anything during this process. There is a "quiet" option in GRUB that hides this process from the user (usually a graphic of some sort is shown in its place, such as the Red Hat logo). During the boot process, everything is logged to the /var/log/dmesg file. You can also use the dmesg command to query information about the boot process after the system has booted. When the system's drivers are in place, the kernel executes the /sbin/init program.

REAL-WORLD TIP

Although the Red Hat exams don't test on hardware, you can use the lsmod command to troubleshoot in the real world if you are having a hardware problem.

GENERAL INFO

In Red Hat 6, the boot process has been replaced by a new utility called *Upstart* instead of the traditional SysV Init style scripts. This utility decreases the time that it takes the system to boot and is already currently being used on other versions of Linux such as Ubuntu.

Things start to get tricky here. In Red Hat Enterprise Linux 6 (RHEL6), the boot sequence has changed to now use Upstart. Because many systems will still be using Red Hat Enterprise Linux 5 (RHEL5) for a while, you should also know how the traditional SysV Init boot process works. Understanding both can also help with migration issues. Let's continue for the moment with the traditional SysV Init scripts first and then look at the new implementation with Upstart.

The init program is the first process created by the kernel. It is responsible for the rest of the boot process and setting up the environment for the user. First, it consults the /etc/inittab file, which defines how the rest of the boot process will go. The /etc/inittab file lists the default runlevel to boot into and the system initialization script (/etc/rc.d/rc.sysinit). I describe what a runlevel is and how it is used later in this chapter. Let's look at the /etc/inittab file to see what the init process goes through:

```
# cat /etc/inittab
#
# inittab        This file describes how the INIT process should set up
#                the system in a certain run-level.
#
# Author.        Miquel van Smoorenburg, <miquels@drinkel.nl.mugnet.org>
#                Modified for RHS Linux by Marc Ewing and Donnie Barnes
#


# Default runlevel. The runlevels used by RHS are:
#    0 - halt (Do NOT set initdefault to this)
#    1 - Single user mode
#    2 - Multiuser, without NFS (The same as 3, if you do not have networking)
#    3 - Full multiuser mode
#    4 - unused
#    5 - X11
#    6 - reboot (Do NOT set initdefault to this)
#
id:5:initdefault:

# System initialization.
si::sysinit:/etc/rc.d/rc.sysinit

l0:0:wait:/etc/rc.d/rc 0
l1:1:wait:/etc/rc.d/rc 1
l2:2:wait:/etc/rc.d/rc 2
l3:3:wait:/etc/rc.d/rc 3
l4:4:wait:/etc/rc.d/rc 4
l5:5:wait:/etc/rc.d/rc 5
l6:6:wait:/etc/rc.d/rc 6
```

```
# Trap CTRL-ALT-DELETE
ca::ctrlaltdel:/sbin/shutdown -t3 -r now

# When our UPS tells us power has failed, assume we have a few minutes
# of power left. Schedule a shutdown for 2 minutes from now.
# This does, of course, assume you have power installed and your
# UPS connected and working correctly.
pf::powerfail:/sbin/shutdown -f -h +2 "Power Failure; System Shutting Down"

# If power was restored before the shutdown kicked in, cancel it.
pr:12345:powerokwait:/sbin/shutdown -c "Power Restored; Shutdown Cancelled"


# Run gettys in standard runlevels
1:2345:respawn:/sbin/mingetty tty1
2:2345:respawn:/sbin/mingetty tty2
3:2345:respawn:/sbin/mingetty tty3
4:2345:respawn:/sbin/mingetty tty4
5:2345:respawn:/sbin/mingetty tty5
6:2345:respawn:/sbin/mingetty tty6

# Run xdm in runlevel 5
x:5:respawn:/etc/X11/prefdm -nodaemon
```

From this file, you can see that the default runlevel is set to 5, although six different runlevels are listed. The /etc/inittab file also defines how to handle power failures and virtual terminals. After the init process is done consulting the /etc/inittab file, the /etc/rc.d/rc.sysinit script is run, which handles setting the system clock, networking, setting up the user environment, and more.

In Red Hat Enterprise Linux, the default runlevel is 5, as already noted from examining the /etc/inittab file. This default runlevel is passed to the /etc/rc.d/rc script, which calls all the programs in the /etc/rc.d/rc#.d directory. The last thing that you should see is the login prompt. If you have a desktop manager installed such as Gnome, you should see a GUI login screen where you can log in to the system; otherwise, you see a text mode login. This completes the boot process.

Now that you have seen what the boot process looks like on RHEL5, let's start over using the new Upstart program in RHEL6. Upstart is event based, so it doesn't require everything to be processed sequentially (unlike RHEL5). Each process is known to Upstart as a job and is defined within the /etc/init directory. The init process is still created first; however, it comes from an Upstart event. Instead of the rc.sysinit master script being called, which in turn calls each runlevel, Upstart's init takes a job from a directory to continue with the boot process. The /etc/inittab file is deprecated and is consulted for the default runlevel only as defined by the `initdefault` line. Each runlevel is still called; however, the services that need to be started or stopped are also processed by Upstart. Later in this chapter in the description of service management, we look at some Upstart jobs to see how exactly it controls services.

So now that we have covered the boot process and two different ways that it is done, you're an expert, right? Don't be thrown by all the information presented in this section. This is just a high-level overview, and the rest of this chapter deals with the in-depth details surrounding each part of the boot process. The best thing you can do when working with any part of the boot process is practice, lab, practice, and then lab again. The more hands-on exposure you get, the more comfortable you will feel when working with and troubleshooting the boot process.

Working with GRUB

The previous section described the boot process and how it works. The first part of that process deals with the bootloader, GRUB. In this section, we look at GRUB and its role in the boot process more in depth.

The GRUB bootloader is broken down into different stages. The code contained on the master boot record (MBR) is considered GRUB stage 1. It loads GRUB stage 1.5, which tries to identify the file system type (optional), or it can call GRUB stage 2 directly. Stage 2 is what calls the kernel and loads it into memory. In stage 1, GRUB needs to search the MBR looking for an active partition from which to boot the kernel. GRUB has its own format for looking through hard disks. The syntax of this format is

(xdn[,m])   where xd is the drive, n is the number of the disk, and m denotes the partition number.

This syntax is very useful when troubleshooting issues with GRUB because you need to know how GRUB searches for disk drives when trying to find the primary partition. When the primary partition is found, GRUB loads the kernel, which is where you move on to stage 2. Stage 2 is the place where you will tend to spend the most time troubleshooting boot issues with the system. As stage 2 starts, it presents you with a list of kernels that you can boot from, along with a listing of options that you can use to modify the parameters passed to the kernel during bootup (as you saw in Figure 2-1). Now let's look at how to edit those entries (see Figure 2-2).

Grub Boot Options:

e   Edit the commands before booting

a   Modify or append the kernel arguments before booting

c   Open the GRUB command line

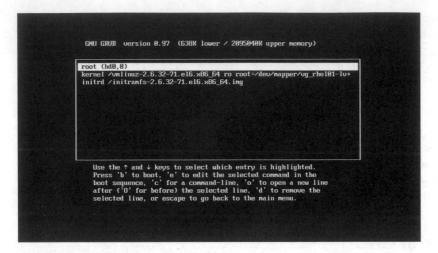

Figure 2-2   Editing a GRUB kernel entry.

You can use the a option to modify any parameters you want to pass to the kernel. This includes changing the runlevel that the system will boot into. Although you learn more about runlevels in the next section, for now you should know that each runlevel is a different "state" that the system can enter. After choosing the a option, you can pass a mode as a parameter to enter into that mode. Here are the different modes that you can boot into:

Single-User Mode	Used to perform maintenance tasks or if you forget the root password
Runlevel 2 or 3	Used to load only partial services during the boot process
Emergency Mode	Used to perform tasks on an unbootable system
Rescue Mode	Used to fix boot issues or reinstall GRUB

Aside from passing parameters to the kernel, you can also enter the GRUB command line to make changes. We're getting ahead of ourselves, though; first, we need to look at the config file for GRUB.

The Config File

GRUB has only a single config file, /boot/grub/grub.conf. Two other files actually have soft links to this main config file as well: /boot/grub/menu.lst and /etc/grub.conf. When GRUB starts, it reads its configuration from the main config file. You can make changes on the command line to test different features of GRUB. However, you need to make any permanent changes to the main config file; otherwise, they will be lost upon reboot. After the system has booted, you can view the config file, but this is one area where RHEL6 has changed. First, let's look at a version of the old grub.conf file:

```
# cat /boot/grub/grub.conf
default=0
timeout=5
splashimage=(hd0,0)/grub/splash.xpm.gz
hiddenmenu
title Red Hat Enterprise Linux Server (2.6.18-92.el5)
    root (hd0,0)
    kernel /vmlinuz-2.6.18-92.el5 ro root=/dev/VolGroup00/LogVol00 rhgb quiet
    initrd /initrd-2.6.18-92.el5.img
```

In the preceding example, you can see that there is a single option to boot from, as defined by the `title` entry. This is also known as entry 0, so it becomes the default kernel to boot from. You can also see the version of the kernel that you are using and the place where the root partition will be mounted from during the boot process. If you want to add additional options to boot into, you could append another `title` with options for a second boot choice. This grub.conf file contains everything you need to make sure the boot process works smoothly.

Now let's look at the new version of the grub.conf file for RHEL6:

```
# cat grub.conf
default=0
timeout=5
splashimage=(hd0,0)/grub/splash.xpm.gz
hiddenmenu
title Red Hat Enterprise Linux (2.6.32-71.el6.x86_64)
  root (hd0,0)
  kernel /vmlinuz-2.6.32-71.el6.x86_64 ro root=/dev/mapper/vg_rhel01-lv_root
rd_LVM_LV=vg_rhel01/lv_root rd_LVM_LV=vg_rhel01/lv_swap rd_NO_LUKS rd_NO_MD
rd_NO_DM LANG=en_US.UTF-8 SYSFONT=latarcyrheb-sun16 KEYBOARDTYPE=pc
KEYTABLE=us crashkernel=auto rhgb quiet
  initrd /initramfs-2.6.32-71.el6.x86_64.img
```

Notice that almost everything is the same except for the line containing the kernel boot parameters. This new version defines additional options such as encryption, RAID, and use of the /dev/mapper for LVM management. Again, it is important to take note of the new changes in RHEL6 because you need to be able to troubleshoot the grub.conf file should something go wrong with the system. In both versions of Red Hat, you can also edit the config file from within the GRUB command line as well. Using the c option to enter the GRUB command line, you can make changes to the config file, reinstall GRUB, or repair a broken config file.

REAL-WORLD TIP

In RHEL6, the version of GRUB being used is 0.97. The most current version of GRUB is 2.0, which has different features available. One notable feature if you upgrade to version 2.0 is that you can't edit the grub.conf file by hand (your changes will be overwritten). The differences in GRUB versions are outside the scope of this book, so just be aware that updating GRUB requires you to manage grub.conf differently.

The GRUB Command Line

One task that is common in the real world and also a possible exam question is how to repair a broken MBR. For this to happen, you need to make use of the rescue environment, which can be found by booting from the RHEL installation DVD. When you are in the rescue environment, you can repair your broken MBR.

Step 1. Load up the GRUB command line to find the disk and partition that contain the grub.conf file using the find command:

```
grub> find /grub/grub.conf
(hd0,0)
```

You could also run:

```
grub> root
 (hd0,0): Filesystem type is unknown, partition type 0x8e
```

Step 2. Install GRUB on the drive that is returned:

```
grub> setup (hd0)
 Checking if "/boot/grub/stage1" exists... no
 Checking if "/grub/stage1" exists... yes
 Checking if "/grub/stage2" exists... yes
 Checking if "/grub/e2fs_stage1_5" exists... yes
 Running "embed /grub/e2fs_stage1_5 (hd0)"... 26 sectors are
embedded.
 Running "install /grub/stage1 (hd0) (hd0)1+26 p
(hd0,0)/grub/stage2
/grub/grub.conf"... succeeded
Done.
```

Now that your MBR is fixed, you should be able to boot into the system once again. The preceding example also shows where the boot partition is located (partition 0 on disk 0), as well as the file system type. It is important that you also back up the grub.conf file in case something happens to your system; that way, you can easily restore it. Chapter 18, "DNS," covers more scenarios and issues that might appear on the exam dealing with troubleshooting GRUB and the system boot process.

Runlevels

When the system boots up, it queries for the default runlevel, which is defined in the /etc/inittab file. When that default runlevel is located, the system boots into that particular runlevel. The different runlevels are essentially "states," which allow services to be started or stopped depending on the runlevel you are in. There are six runlevels in total, which are shown in the /etc/inittab file. Each runlevel also has a directory called /etc/rc.d/rc#.d, where # is the runlevel (from 0 to 6). These different directories contain scripts to tell the system which services should be started or stopped at the particular runlevel. Let's look at the different runlevels:

0	Halt
1	Single-user mode
2	Multiuser with partial services
3	Full multiuser with networking (text mode)
4	Not used
5	Full multiuser graphical mode (provides a GUI desktop login)
6	Reboot

The easiest runlevels to understand are 0 and 6. These two runlevels are called by the same command with different input. In runlevel 0, essentially the system is off (the powered off "state" if you will). In runlevel 6, the system is restarting (the reboot "state"). Runlevel 1 is used to enter single-user mode, which you would enter if there are issues with the system and you'd like to perform maintenance. You can also reset the root user's password in this runlevel. The remaining runlevels—2, 3, and 5—provide various states for different services to run in. There is also a runlevel 4, but it is unused. The best way to get a feel for what is started in each of these runlevels is to look in the /etc/rc.d/rc#.d directory for each runlevel. These directories contain files that define whichservices should be started or stopped. These files are actually soft links to the service init scripts on the system. Don't forget that Upstart is the program that actually starts and stops services at each runlevel now. The /etc/init/rc.conf file shows how each set of scripts is called:

```
# cat rc.conf
# rc - System V runlevel compatibility
#
# This task runs the old sysv-rc runlevel scripts. It
# is usually started by the telinit compatibility wrapper.

start on runlevel [0123456]
```

```
stop on runlevel [!$RUNLEVEL]

task

export RUNLEVEL
console output
exec /etc/rc.d/rc $RUNLEVEL
```

Runlevel Utilities

Let's now look at the many system utilities that help you manage the system in different runlevels. These management commands include the following:

shutdown	Brings the system to a powered-off state or can reboot the system
halt	Powers down the system
reboot	Reboots the system
poweroff	Works the same as the halt command
chkconfig	Manages what runlevels services start and stop at
runlevel	Displays the current and previous runlevels
init	Changes runlevels
ntsysv	Works similarly to chkconfig in that it is a menu-driven service management utility

Let's start with management of the two easiest runlevels again: 0 and 6. To manage these two particular runlevels, you can use the shutdown command to bring the system to a powered-off state or reboot the system. The shutdown command also has options to alert users on the system when it is going down and to set up a shutdown at a particular time.

Syntax: shutdown [options] time

Options:

-k	Doesn't shut down; just warns
-h	Halts the system after shutdown
-r	Reboots instead of turning off the system
-F	Forces a file system check on reboot
-n	Kills all processes quickly (not recommended)
-t SECS	Sends a shutdown message but delays shutdown by x seconds

REAL-WORLD TIP

If you just use the `shutdown now` command, it actually brings the system into maintenance mode. To have the system actually shut down or reboot, you need to use the `-h` or `-r` option.

Let's look at some examples for a better understanding of how this works. Suppose you just want to turn off the system. You could then do the following:

```
# shutdown -h now
```

This time instead of a complete power off, reboot the system as follows:

```
# shutdown -r now
```

You could also use the `reboot` command to achieve the same effect:

```
# reboot
```

As a final example, delay the shutdown by 2 minutes:

```
# shutdown -h 120
```

These are just some examples of what you can do with the `shutdown` command. Unless you give permissions to your users, only the root user can issue the `shutdown` and `reboot` commands. Be careful about those users you allow to have access to these commands. You wouldn't want random users rebooting your system constantly to fix problems!

WARNING: In earlier versions of Red Hat, you could use the /etc/shutdown.allow file to control who was allowed to shut down the system. With the release of RHEL6 and the new Upstart utility, you can no longer use this file to control the shutdown process for individual users.

Similar to the `shutdown` command is the `halt` command. The `halt` command brings the system to a powered-off state like `shutdown`.

To turn off the system, you use this command:

```
# shutdown now
```

You could also use

```
# halt
```

Coinciding with the `halt` command are `poweroff` and `reboot`. The reason these commands all go hand in hand is that `poweroff` and `reboot` are actually both links to the `halt` command. You can verify this by using the following example:

```
# cd /sbin
# ll | grep halt
```

```
-rwxr-xr-x 1 root root        16152 Jan 21  2009 halt
lrwxrwxrwx 1 root root            4 Jul 22  2010 poweroff -> halt
lrwxrwxrwx 1 root root            4 Jul 22  2010 reboot -> halt
```

The difference is that each one calls the `halt` command with a different argument, yielding different results. The `poweroff` command, like `halt`, stops the system, whereas the `reboot` command restarts the system...obviously. With all this jumping around to different runlevels, how do you know which runlevel you are actually in? To check the current runlevel you're in, you can use the `runlevel` command (confusing, right?):

```
# runlevel
N 5
```

As an alternative, you can also use the `who` command to produce the same results:

```
# who -r
         run-level 5  2010-09-05 09:45                        last=S
```

You can also change the current runlevel you're in by using the `init` command. Before changing runlevels, however, you should check which runlevel you are in by using one of the two previous commands.

EXAM TIP

Make sure you note that the `runlevel` command displays the previous runlevel and then the current runlevel, but the `who` command displays them the other way around. My suggestion is to choose one of the two commands and use only that command so as not to confuse yourself in the middle of the exam or in the real world on a production environment system.

Now that you know how to view your current runlevel and how to change to runlevel 0 and 6, let's look at how to get to the remaining runlevels. Using the `init` command, you can change from one runlevel to another. Make sure that you check which runlevel you are currently in first. As already mentioned, runlevel 5 is the default for Red Hat. Suppose, though, that you would like to drop down to runlevel 3.

Step 1.   Check the runlevel you're in:

```
# runlevel
N 5
```

Step 2.   Because you are in runlevel 5, change over to runlevel 3:
```
# init 3
```

After a minute or so, you will be in runlevel 3. Notice the services that are stopped as you move into a lower runlevel.

Step 3.   Verify that you are indeed in runlevel 3:

```
# runlevel
N 3
```

Let's look a little more closely at the emergency runlevel.

Rescue and Recovery Runlevels

Sometimes things go wrong with the system to the point where it refuses to boot. For those users who are just starting out with Linux, this is a major red flag that throws them off their balance because they aren't quite sure how to handle such a system crash. At this point, you can use the lower runlevels for system rescue or recovery. If your system boots into runlevel 3, you can bring yourself into a recovery runlevel with

```
# init 1
```

If the system doesn't even get that far, you can boot up, enter a at the GRUB boot menu, and append the word single to the kernel that you want to boot into. This approach has the same effect as booting you into a recovery runlevel. After you get into the recovery runlevel, you can perform maintenance or repairs on your system (such as figuring out what is preventing the system from booting). For the exam, keep the following in mind about the recovery runlevel:

- You can reset or change the root user's password.

- You can adjust system files or partitions that are normally locked when the system is in use.

- You can repair system files by replacing them with working copies from a backup or the Red Hat installation CD.

After you finish making any changes or repairs, you can reboot the system and see whether it returns to its normal working state. If it doesn't, you can re-enter the recovery runlevel to try again. You can also access this rescue environment by booting the first Red Hat installation CD.

Now that you have an understanding of runlevels and how to move between them, we can shift focus to service management, which deals with different system services starting and stopping at the different runlevels.

Service Management

On any system it is important to manage the running services. Managing services enables you to ensure the stability and reliability that your system will offer. A service can range from something simple, such as providing your local system with the correct time, or something more complex, such as sharing a file system over the entire network for your users using NFS. Knowing how to manage services is a big part of the Red Hat exams (as defined by the Red Hat Prep Guide), but it is also a critical system administrator skill in the real world. In Linux, services can also be called *daemons*. The reason for this is that some services are actually composed of multiple daemons. One example of this is NFS, which you see in Chapter 15, "NFS." You can usually tell if something is a daemon because it (the service name) ends in a *d*. An example of this would be the SSH service (sshd) or the Apache web service (httpd).

Let's look again at the different runlevels and how they deal with services during the boot process. Because the preceding section ended by moving the system into runlevel 3, why don't we start by looking in the /etc/rc.d/rc3.d directory (which correlates to runlevel 3):

```
# ls /etc/rc.d/rc3.d/
K01dnsmasq          K50ibmasm           K89pand             S08iptables
K02avahi-dnsconfd   K50netconsole       K89rdisc            S08mcstrans
K02NetworkManager   K69rpcsvcgssd       K91capi             S09isdn
K02oddjobd          K73ypbind           K99readahead_later  S10network
K05conman           K74nscd             S00microcode_ctl    S11auditd
K05saslauthd        K85mdmpd            S02lvm2-monitor     S12restorecond
K10psacct           K87multipathd       S04readahead_early  S12syslog
K10tcsd             K88wpa_supplicant   S05kudzu            S13irqbalance
K20nfs              K89dund             S06cpuspeed         S13portmap
K24irda             K89netplugd         S08ip6tables        S14nfslock
```

You wouldn't know by looking at the output of this command, but these are all actually soft links to scripts on the system, usually within the /etc/rc.d/init.d directory. You can also see from the output that each link has an interesting syntax. The syntax is something like

```
[K|S]##ServiceName
```

The K stands for Kill and the S stands for Start. The ## are any number between 01 and 99, including duplicates. Finally, there is the name of the service. When you put all this together, you get a listing of every service that is either stopped (K) or started (S) when the system enters runlevel 3. The numbers indicate the order in which a service is stopped or started, with all Kills being processed first (in numerical order from 1 to 99) and then all Starts being processed second (in numerical order from 1 to 99). If the number order is the same, the alphabetical sort dictates the order. Now suppose you have the following three services listed in your directory:

- K15httpd
- S10network
- S55sshd

When the system moves to runlevel 3, the first thing to happen would be the system stopping the httpd service (httpd is the Apache Web Server). Next, the network service would be started, bringing up the network interfaces (this includes assigning the system an IP address). Finally, the sshd service would be started, providing you with an SSH server for remote management. This order should make sense because you can't connect to a server for remote management unless the network interfaces are up with an assigned IP address first!

EXAM TIP

As a troubleshooting tip, if you are making your own services or entries in the /etc/rc.d/rc#.d directories, make sure that you pay attention to the order in which you start and stop your service. Attempting to start or stop a service when there are other dependencies could have strange effects on the system or cause the service to just fail completely.

Now that you have an understanding of how the different services are stopped and started at different runlevels, we can look at the final management utilities, which provide a means for enabling and disabling services at each runlevel. Going back to the previous example with the three services, you would need to make an entry for each of these three services in each /etc/rc.d/rc[1-6].d directory. That comes out to 18 entries alone. Can you imagine how long that would take you for all the services on the system? To ease the management of services at each runlevel, you can use the chkconfig command.

Syntax: `chkconfig [option] service_name`

Options:

`--list [name]`	Shows the status of the service at each runlevel
`--add <name>`	Adds a service to be managed by the chkconfig command
`--del <name>`	Removes a service from being managed by the chkconfig command
`--level <levels>`	Enables or disables the service at the given levels
`<name> <on¦off¦reset>`	Enables or disables the service at levels 2–5

The options for this command are a little different than you would normally see for a utility. The easiest way to explain how to use this command is through examples.

Step 1. Check the status of the sshd service:

```
# chkconfig --list sshd
```

```
sshd          0:off   1:off   2:on    3:on    4:on    5:on    6:off
```

This should be fairly easy to understand. The sshd service will be started at runlevels 2, 3, 4, and 5. It will be stopped at runlevels 0, 1, and 6. Now say that you want the sshd service to be completely turned off at all runlevels.

Step 2.   Use the `off` option to disable the service at boot:

```
# chkconfig sshd off
```

Step 3.   Verify with the original command:

```
# chkconfig --list sshd
sshd          0:off   1:off   2:off   3:off   4:off   5:off   6:off
```

Now the sshd service will not start at all when the system boots. Because this is the service used for remote management, this result probably isn't desirable, so you should probably turn it back on.

Step 4.   Re-enable the SSH service:

```
# chkconfig sshd on
```

Step 5.   Verify again:

```
# chkconfig --list sshd
sshd          0:off   1:off   2:on    3:on    4:on    5:on    6:off
```

As you can see, it has now been restored. You could also turn off this service for runlevel 4, though, because this runlevel is unused. To edit just one (or multiple) runlevel, you can do this:

```
# chkconfig --level 4 sshd off
```

Step 6.   You should verify one last time:

```
# chkconfig --list sshd
sshd          0:off   1:off   2:on    3:on    4:off   5:on    6:off
```

Aside from using the `chkconfig` command, you can accomplish all the same tasks by using the `ntsysv` command. The only difference is that `ntsysv` is menu driven, making it more visually appealing. You can enable and disable different services just as you would with `chkconfig`. To manage the different runlevels, you just call the `ntsysv` command with the runlevel(s) you want to manage.

To edit all services at runlevel 2, enter the following. The resulting screen looks like that shown in Figure 2-3.

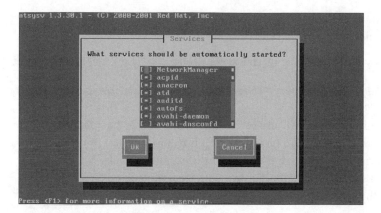

Figure 2-3 The **ntsysv** service management utility.

```
# ntsysv --level 2
```

I like using the chkconfig command because it is faster and easier to work with. As long as you know how to enable and disable services at different runlevels, the utility you use doesn't matter. Here is a question: What happens when the system boots and you want to start a service that you forgot to include in the startup services? Do you have to use the chkconfig command to add it and reboot the system? No. Aside from enabling and disabling services at system boot, you also can use the service command. You can use this to start, stop, and query the status of services on the system after it has already booted.

Syntax: service <--status-all | service_name CMD>

Step 1.   Usually, it is a good idea to always check the status of the service first:

```
# service ntpd status
ntpd is stopped
```

Step 2.   When you know that the service is stopped, you can start it:

```
# service ntpd start
Starting ntpd:                                          [  OK  ]
```

You always see an OK or Fail to indicate whether the service started successfully. Because this service was off when the system started, you should turn it back off for now.

Step 3.   Stop the NTP service:

```
# service ntpd stop
Shutting down ntpd:                                     [  OK  ]
```

You should make it a habit to verify the status of a service any time you make a change to it.

Step 4.   Verify that you stopped the service successfully:

```
# service ntpd status
ntpd is stopped
```

The Red Hat Prep Guide lists numerous services that you need to be able to manage at boot time and when the system has started, so it is key that you understand how to work with services and manage them at the different runlevels. Before moving on to the next section, you should move your system back into runlevel 5 or reboot to achieve the same effect.

The Upstart Conversion

As already discussed, the new Upstart program uses jobs and events to run different services. The biggest issue with using Upstart is that there is no standard currently in place for where to store files. Currently, you can find jobs located in the /etc/init directory, you can find events located in the /etc/event.d directory, and there are still the traditional SysV Init directories. With the release of RHEL6, a few services have been moved over to use the new Upstart utility exclusively (such as the Syslog service, which is responsible for system logs). Each job can include events that trigger additional jobs or system scripts. Let's look at a sample job:

```
# cat control-alt-delete.conf
# control-alt-delete - emergency keypress handling
#
# This task is run whenever the Control-Alt-Delete key combination is
# pressed. Usually used to shut down the machine.

start on control-alt-delete

exec /sbin/shutdown -r now "Control-Alt-Delete pressed"
```

You can see from the output that this job handles the pressing of the Control-Alt-Delete keys. exec defines the command executed when the key combination is pressed. Aside from jobs, you can also define events:

```
# cat ck-log-system-start
# Upstart event
# ck-log-system-start - write system start to log
#
```

```
start on stopped rcS

console output
exec /usr/sbin/ck-log-system-start
```

This event creates a log entry showing that the system started successfully. At this point, you might be wondering how you can call some of these events or jobs that exist. Using the `initctl` command, you can view, start, and stop jobs much like the `service` command does.

Syntax: `initctl [command]`

Options:

`start`	Starts a job
`stop`	Stops a job
`restart`	Restarts a job
`reload`	Sends a HUP signal to a job
`status`	Queries the status of a job
`list`	Lists known jobs
`emit`	Emits an event

Using the `initctl` command, you can view the currently running jobs on the system:

```
# initctl list
rc stop/waiting
tty (/dev/tty3) start/running, process 1465
tty (/dev/tty2) start/running, process 1463
tty (/dev/tty1) start/running, process 1461
tty (/dev/tty6) start/running, process 1471
tty (/dev/tty5) start/running, process 1469
tty (/dev/tty4) start/running, process 1467
plymouth-shutdown stop/waiting
control-alt-delete stop/waiting
readahead-collector stop/waiting
kexec-disable stop/waiting
quit-plymouth stop/waiting
rcS stop/waiting
prefdm stop/waiting
init-system-dbus stop/waiting
readahead stop/waiting
splash-manager stop/waiting
start-ttys stop/waiting
readahead-disable-services stop/waiting
```

```
rcS-sulogin stop/waiting
serial stop/waiting
```

You'll notice that `initctl` is similar to the `service` command, but you can call both jobs and events. There aren't many jobs or events on RHEL6 yet because the implementation of Upstart is new. I hope that with future releases, more and more services will be ported over to the Upstart program. If you'd like to beat the developers to the punch, writing Upstart jobs and events isn't too difficult, but it is outside the scope of this book. For more information, visit the following site:

http://upstart.ubuntu.com/

REAL-WORLD TIP

Another popular version of Linux is the Ubuntu operating system. Ubuntu has a more aggressive release schedule than Red Hat and therefore tends to have newer features implemented. At the time of this writing, Ubuntu is on version 10.10 and has ported almost all its services to the new Upstart utility. If you'd like more examples of Upstart jobs and events, you can download and try the Ubuntu operating system.

Summary

This chapter described the boot process, the GRUB, and service management during and after the boot process. Knowing how to troubleshoot boot issues through GRUB and service management during boot are listed in multiple places in the Red Hat Prep Guide; clearly, they are a good area on which to focus. You should now know how to move between runlevels, manage services, diagnose and fix common boot issues, and pass arguments to the kernel during the boot process. In the following chapters, we look at some more troubleshooting topics pertaining to the boot process and how to resolve them.

Review Questions

1. GRUB has three stages. Can you name them?

2. What option at the GRUB boot menu can you use to append something to a kernel?

3. The old SysInit scripts have been replaced in Red Hat Enterprise Linux 6 for what new boot utility?

4. Runlevel 0 reboots the system. True or False?

5. If your system crashes and becomes unbootable, you have to reinstall the whole operating system. True or False?

6. What command can you use to manage system services?

7. What command disables the SSH service from running when the system boots?

8. How can you list all services on the system to tell whether they will boot during startup?

9. What does S12rsyslog in the /etc/rc.d/rc2.d directory mean?

10. How can you verify the status of the SSH service after the system has booted?

11. What command and option can you use to enable a service to start on boot?

Answers to Review Questions

1. Stage 1: During this stage, the primary bootloader is read into memory by the BIOS from the MBR. Stage 1.5: During this stage, the bootloader is read into memory by the stage 1 bootloader (only if necessary). Stage 2: During this stage, the bootloader reads the operating system or kernel.

2. By entering the GRUB boot menu, you can choose the a option to append something to the kernel command-line options.

3. Upstart. The Upstart utility is now used in the boot process for Red Hat Enterprise Linux 6.

4. False. Runlevel 0 halts the system. Runlevel 6 reboots the system.

5. False. Most boot issues can be resolved by entering rescue mode and repairing the problem.

6. The `service` command is used to start, stop, and manage system services.

7. `chkconfig sshd off`

8. `chkconfig —list`

9. When the system enters into runlevel 2, the rsyslog service has a priority of 12 when starting. Anything with a lower number (or the same number and lower first letter) starts before the rsyslog service.

10. `service sshd statuts`

11. Use the `chkconfig` command to enable or disable services during the boot process. The `on` option enables the service and `off` disables it.

Lab 2

Task 1 – GRUB Setup

Step 1. On RHEL01, open the GRUB config file in any text editor.

Step 2. Add a new entry to the config file:
  a. The new entry should have the "title" Red Hat Recovery.
  b. The new entry should not be the default.
  c. The recovery entry should allow you to boot into recovery mode.

Step 3. Change the timeout of the boot selection to 10 seconds.

The task is complete when the system boots with both entries in the GRUB menu and they both work correctly.

Task 2 – Boot Issues

Step 1. Make sure you have your Red Hat installation CD available. On RHEL02, delete the /etc/inittab file and reboot the system. You will receive an error message that the system can't find the file.

Step 2. Boot from the Red Hat installation CD into recovery mode.

Step 3. Replace the file from the CD into the correct location on the system.

HINT: You may need to use the command `mount /dev/cd-rom /mnt` to access the CD drive.

The task is complete when the system boots up again.

Task 3 – System Services

Perform the following system service-related actions:

Step 1. On all systems in your lab, make sure that the SSH service (sshd) starts when the system boots.

Step 2. On Client01, prevent the YUM updater (yum-updatesd) service from starting when the system boots.

Step 3.   On Client01, prevent the Sendmail (sendmail) service from starting when the system boots.

Step 4.   On Client02, set the firewall (`iptables`) to start only in runlevels 2 and 3.

The task is complete when all services can be verified to meet the preceding requirements.

Task 4 – Lost Password

Step 1.   On your RHEL02 system, change the root password to something random.

Step 2.   Assuming you can't remember this newly generated random password, recover the root password.

The task is complete when you can log in to the system as the root user.

This chapter covers the following subjects:

- **Basic Partitions**—This section covers the setup of basic system partitions.
- **Logical Volume Manager**—This section describes more advanced partitioning with LVM.
- **Setting Up RAID**—This section covers a form of advanced partitioning called RAID that can be used for performance and redundancy.

The following RHCSA exam objectives are covered:

- List, create, delete, and set partition types for primary, extended, and logical partitions
- Create and remove physical volumes, assign physical volumes to volume groups, and create and delete logical volumes
- Add new partitions, logical volumes, and swap to a system nondestructively

## CHAPTER 3

Disks and Partitioning

Disk partitioning is one of the many steps you must take when preparing a system for use. In each system the physical disk drives are divided up logically into partitions that allow you to store data on them (after a file system has been created, of course, but that's in the next chapter). There are also special types of partitions such as RAID that allow for increased performance, redundancy, or both. LVM, like RAID, is an advanced form of partitioning that eases management of partitions and makes growing them for increased storage capacity simple. One of the key points to remember when working with partitions is to always plan ahead. Will your partitions need to be bigger in the future? How should your data be organized? Planning ahead will make you a better system administrator and also ease the pain of partition migration and management down the road.

Basic Partitions

Working with disks is an important part of maintaining storage space on your system. Partitions determine how your storage space is carved out for use later by the system and its users. When adding more storage or creating it for the first time, you should partition your disk space into a logical format for use later. Many installers come with an "automated" partitioning option for those that don't need a custom layout; however, most system administrators will probably want to lay out their own partitions. In the lab, RHEL01 is configured with four hard disks. You will use three of these drives (the smaller ones) to set up custom partitions. All drives are IDE (/dev/hdx) versus /dev/sdx for SCSI/SATA users. Before you begin partitioning, you should look at the drives currently available for use as well as the current partitions on any of these drives. You can use two different utilities when partitioning disks:

fdisk   Disk-partitioning utility

parted   Another disk-partitioning utility

While `fdisk` is more common, it is slowly being replaced by `parted`, which is more flexible. You can also use `cat` to check the output of various files on the /proc file system for information. The /proc file system is created by the kernel when the system boots and holds current information about the system (you learn more about the /proc file system in Chapter 10, "The Kernel").

To view information about the current partition layout, use the following command:

```
# cat /proc/partitions | grep hd
   8       0   20971520 hda
   8       1     512000 hda1
   8       2   20458496 hda2
   8      16    8388608 hdb
   8      32    8388608 hdc
   8      48    8388608 hdd
```

If you are using SCSI disks instead of IDE disks, you can just change the command to

```
# cat /proc/partitions | grep sd
```

As you can see from the output, you get a listing of four different disks: hda, hdb, hdc, and hdd.

NOTE: The first two letters represent whether the disk is a SCSI (sd) or IDE (hd) disk. The third letter represents which disk it actually is. If there is a number after the three letters, it is the number of the partition. For the lab, you can see that they are all hd disks, meaning they are IDE. There also are four physical drives: a, b, c, and d. Because no partitions are created yet on the last three disks (hdb, hdc, and hdd), there are no numbers. Meanwhile, you can see hda has three partitions.

In this case, you want to partition the last three disks, so you need to view their current partitions to see if any exist. You can use the `fdisk` command to accomplish this.

Syntax: `fdisk [options] [device]`

Options:

`-b`   Specifies the sector size of the disk

`-h`   Specifies the number of heads on the disk

`-l`   Lists current partition tables

To list the current partitions on all disks, use this command:

```
# fdisk -l

Disk /dev/hda: 21.5 GB, 21474836480 bytes
255 heads, 63 sectors/track, 2610 cylinders
Units = cylinders of 16065 * 512 = 8225280 bytes
Sector size (logical/physical): 512 bytes / 512 bytes
I/O size (minimum/optimal): 512 bytes / 512 bytes
Disk identifier: 0x00021654

   Device Boot      Start         End      Blocks   Id  System
/dev/hda1   *           1          64      512000   83  Linux
/dev/hda2              64        2611    20458496   8e  Linux LVM

Disk /dev/hdb: 8589 MB, 8589934592 bytes
255 heads, 63 sectors/track, 1044 cylinders
Units = cylinders of 16065 * 512 = 8225280 bytes
Sector size (logical/physical): 512 bytes / 512 bytes
I/O size (minimum/optimal): 512 bytes / 512 bytes
Disk identifier: 0x0004b72d

Disk /dev/hdb doesn't contain a valid partition table

Disk /dev/hdc: 8589 MB, 8589934592 bytes
255 heads, 63 sectors/track, 1044 cylinders
Units = cylinders of 16065 * 512 = 8225280 bytes
Sector size (logical/physical): 512 bytes / 512 bytes
I/O size (minimum/optimal): 512 bytes / 512 bytes
Disk identifier: 0x00000000

Disk /dev/hdc doesn't contain a valid partition table

Disk /dev/hdd: 8589 MB, 8589934592 bytes
255 heads, 63 sectors/track, 1044 cylinders
Units = cylinders of 16065 * 512 = 8225280 bytes
Sector size (logical/physical): 512 bytes / 512 bytes
I/O size (minimum/optimal): 512 bytes / 512 bytes
Disk identifier: 0x00079351

Disk /dev/hdd doesn't contain a valid partition table
```

You could also use the parted command to obtain the same information.

Syntax: parted [options] [device [command]]

Options:

-l   Lists all partition tables detected

-s   Never prompts for interaction (useful for scripting)

View all partitions using parted:

 # parted -l

```
Model: VBOX HARDDISK (ide)
Disk /dev/hda: 21.5GB
Sector size (logical/physical): 512B/512B
Partition Table: msdos

Number  Start   End     Size    Type     File system  Flags
1       1049kB  525MB   525MB   primary  ext4         boot
2       525MB   21.5GB  20.9GB  primary               lvm

Error: Unable to open /dev/hdb - unrecognised disk label.

Error: Unable to open /dev/hdc - unrecognised disk label.

Error: Unable to open /dev/hdd - unrecognised disk label.
```

The fdisk, parted, and cat commands all provide similar information. It is good, however, to know different ways in which you can retrieve information about your system. Based on the preceding current information, you can see a few things about the different disks on the system. The first line specifies the disk and the total amount of storage available (that is, Disk /dev/hda: 21.5 GB). Under the disk info, you can see the current partitions laid out for each disk. Notice the last line, Disk /dev/hdd. It gives information about the disk (it has 8GB of space), but there are currently no partitions on it. Using the fdisk and parted utilities, you can partition the hdb, hdc, and hdd disks.

MIGRATION TIP
Starting with RHEL6, Red Hat recommends using the parted utility over fdisk.

REAL-WORLD TIP
There are some limitations when it comes to working with partitions. You can have only four partitions to a physical disk—with one exception. If you want to make

more than the four, you need to create three primary partitions and one extended partition, although the primary partitions aren't required for extended partition creation. The extended partition can then hold 11 logical partitions (5–16) on it.

Creating a Partition

First, let's use fdisk to create a partition. The fdisk utility is driven by commands after you have chosen which disk you'd like to work with.

Step 1.   Choose the disk:

```
# fdisk /dev/hdb
```

MIGRATION TIP

In RHEL6, DOS-compatible partitions are deprecated. If you are still using MS-DOS partitions, you receive the following warning when using the fdisk utility:

```
WARNING: DOS-compatible mode is deprecated. It's strongly recommended to switch
off the mode (command 'c') and change display units to sectors (command 'u').
```

Step 2.   View all the options available to you:

```
Command (m for help): m
Command action
   a   toggle a bootable flag
   b   edit bsd disklabel
   c   toggle the dos compatibility flag
   d   delete a partition
   l   list known partition types
   m   print this menu
   n   add a new partition
   o   create a new empty DOS partition table
   p   print the partition table
   q   quit without saving changes
   s   create a new empty Sun disklabel
   t   change a partition's system id
   u   change display/entry units
   v   verify the partition table
   w   write table to disk and exit
   x   extra functionality (experts only)
```

You can see here that there are many different things you can do with the fdisk utility.

Step 3.   Use the p command to print out the current partition table (this shouldn't exist, but just verify):

```
Command (m for help): p
```

```
Disk /dev/hdb: 8589 MB, 8589934592 bytes
```

```
255 heads, 63 sectors/track, 1044 cylinders
Units = cylinders of 16065 * 512 = 8225280 bytes
Sector size (logical/physical): 512 bytes / 512 bytes
I/O size (minimum/optimal): 512 bytes / 512 bytes
Disk identifier: 0x0004b72d

   Device Boot       Start           End       Blocks   Id  System
```

As you can see, there is nothing here. However, you can see that you have 8,589MB of space to work with when dividing up the partitions on this disk. For ease of use, cut this disk directly in half. Create two partitions, each with half of the disk space available; verify they are correct; and then write the changes to the disk.

Step 4. Create a new partition:

```
Command (m for help): n
Command action
   e   extended
   p   primary partition (1-4)
p
Partition number (1-4): 1
First cylinder (1-1044, default 1):
Using default value 1
Last cylinder or +size or +sizeM or +sizeK (1-1044, default
1044): +4294M
```

Because you are cutting the disk in half based on the megabytes available, you use the +sizeM syntax (as shown here). You could divide the disk based on kilobytes (+sizeK) or cylinders (+size) if you want, but working in megabytes is much easier. With the first partition created, you can make the second.

Step 5. Create a second partition:

```
Command (m for help): n
Command action
   e   extended
   p   primary partition (1-4)
p
Partition number (1-4): 2
First cylinder (549-1044, default 549):
Using default value 549
Last cylinder or +size or +sizeM or +sizeK (8322-16644, default
16644):
Using default value 1044
```

For this partition, you don't need to specify a partition size because, by default, it will grow the partition to the size remaining on the disk. When you are asked what the size should be, pressing Enter just allocates the remaining disk space available.

Step 6.   Verify your newly created partitions:

```
Command (m for help): p

Disk /dev/hdb: 8589 MB, 8589934592 bytes
255 heads, 63 sectors/track, 1044 cylinders
Units = cylinders of 16065 * 512 = 8225280 bytes
Sector size (logical/physical): 512 bytes / 512 bytes
I/O size (minimum/optimal): 512 bytes / 512 bytes
Disk identifier: 0x0004b72d

   Device Boot      Start         End      Blocks   Id  System
/dev/hdb1               1         548     4401778+  83  Linux
/dev/hdb2             549        1044     3984120   83  Linux
```

You can see here the two partitions just created. Based on their block sizes, they are almost identical in size (there is some variation because of reserved space, superblocks, and other factors that we discuss later).

Step 7.   Write the changes to disk:

```
Command (m for help): w
The partition table has been altered!

Calling ioctl() to re-read partition table.
Syncing disks.
```

Now that two new partitions have been created and written to disk, you should verify their existence. Before doing that, however, you want the kernel to reread the partition table to make sure that it recognizes all disks and partitions correctly. To do this, you use the partprobe command.

Syntax: partprobe [OPTIONS] [DEVICE]

Options:

-d   Does not actually inform the operating system

-s   Prints a summary of contents

Step 8.   Call the partprobe command:

```
# partprobe /dev/hdb
```

This command has no output to it.

GENERAL INFO

Although you can check the partitions just created without running the partprobe command first, it is always a good idea to run this command first. Forcing a reread of the partition table ensures that you get the latest information from your system and that no strange errors or outdated information is returned.

Step 9.   Verify the partition creation one last time:

```
# fdisk -l

Disk /dev/hda: 21.5 GB, 21474836480 bytes
255 heads, 63 sectors/track, 2610 cylinders
Units = cylinders of 16065 * 512 = 8225280 bytes
Sector size (logical/physical): 512 bytes / 512 bytes
I/O size (minimum/optimal): 512 bytes / 512 bytes
Disk identifier: 0x00021654

   Device Boot      Start         End      Blocks   Id  System
/dev/hda1   *           1          64      512000   83  Linux
/dev/hda2              64        2611    20458496   8e  Linux LVM

Disk /dev/hdb: 8589 MB, 8589934592 bytes
255 heads, 63 sectors/track, 1044 cylinders
Units = cylinders of 16065 * 512 = 8225280 bytes
Sector size (logical/physical): 512 bytes / 512 bytes
I/O size (minimum/optimal): 512 bytes / 512 bytes
Disk identifier: 0x0004b72d

   Device Boot      Start         End      Blocks   Id  System
/dev/hdb1               1         548     4401778+  83  Linux
/dev/hdb2             549        1044     3984120   83  Linux

Disk /dev/hdc: 8589 MB, 8589934592 bytes
255 heads, 63 sectors/track, 1044 cylinders
Units = cylinders of 16065 * 512 = 8225280 bytes
Sector size (logical/physical): 512 bytes / 512 bytes
I/O size (minimum/optimal): 512 bytes / 512 bytes
Disk identifier: 0x00000000

Disk /dev/hdc doesn't contain a valid partition table

Disk /dev/hdd: 8589 MB, 8589934592 bytes
255 heads, 63 sectors/track, 1044 cylinders
Units = cylinders of 16065 * 512 = 8225280 bytes
Sector size (logical/physical): 512 bytes / 512 bytes
I/O size (minimum/optimal): 512 bytes / 512 bytes
Disk identifier: 0x00079351

Disk /dev/hdd doesn't contain a valid partition table
```

Now that you have created partitions with the fdisk utility, do it again using the parted command. Create the same two partitions, but this time use the third disk, /dev/hdc.

Step 1.   Start the parted utility the same way you used fdisk:
```
# parted /dev/hdc
```

Step 2.   Use parted, like fdisk, through a menu interface using subcommands:

```
(parted) help
  check NUMBER                             do a simple check on the
file
  cp [FROM-DEVICE] FROM-NUMBER TO-NUMBER   copy file system to
another
  help [COMMAND]                           prints general help, or
help on
  mklabel,mktable LABEL-TYPE               create a new disklabel
(partition)
  mkfs NUMBER FS-TYPE                       make a FS-TYPE file sys-
tem on
  mkpart PART-TYPE [FS-TYPE] START END     make a partition
  mkpartfs PART-TYPE FS-TYPE START END     make a partition with a
file system
  move NUMBER START END                    move partition NUMBER
  name NUMBER NAME                         name partition NUMBER as
NAME
  print [free|NUMBER|all]                  display the partition
table, or all
  quit                                     exit program
  rescue START END                         rescue a lost partition
near START
  resize NUMBER START END                  resize partition NUMBER
and its
  rm NUMBER                                delete partition NUMBER
  select DEVICE                            choose the device to
edit
  set NUMBER FLAG STATE                    change the FLAG on par-
tition NUMBER
  toggle [NUMBER [FLAG]]                    toggle the state of FLAG
on
  unit UNIT                                set the default unit to
UNIT
```

CAUTION: The process of creating a label for a drive using the parted utility initializes whatever disk you run the command on. Because it is being initialized as a new disk, all data is erased from the disk. DO NOT use parted to label a disk that contains data! As always, ensure that you have a backup of your data before making changes to your system.

Step 3.   Create your first partition in a similar manner to fdisk:

```
(parted) mkpart
Partition type? primary/extended? primary
File system type? [ext2]? ext4
Start? 0
End? 4294m
```

CAUTION: You may get an error message about the result partitions not being properly aligned for best performance. You can choose to ignore this message for now because you are just working in a lab and performance isn't a big concern.

Step 4.   Make your second partition:

```
(parted) mkpart
Partition type? primary/extended? primary
File system type? [ext2]? ext4
Start? 4294m
End? 8590m
```

Step 5.   Before writing changes to disk, you should verify that they have been created the way you want them:

```
(parted) print

Model: VBOX HARDDISK (ide)
Disk /dev/hdc: 8590MB
Sector size (logical/physical): 512B/512B
Partition Table: msdos

Number  Start    End      Size     Type      File system  Flags
1       512B     4294MB   4294MB   primary
2       4295MB   8590MB   4295MB   primary
```

Step 6.   Exit the program to save your changes:

```
(parted) quit
```

There are a few things you should notice here. First, you need to specify exactly where you want the start and end of the partition to be. If you don't plan this out ahead of time, you will end up with incorrect partition sizes. You should also take note of the fact that you don't have to write the changes to disk manually; this is done for you when you quit the parted program.

Step 7.   Again, you need to force the kernel to reread the partition table:

```
# partprobe
```

Step 8.   Once again, verify that your partitions have been created successfully:

```
# parted -l

Model: VBOX HARDDISK (ide)
Disk /dev/hda: 21.5GB
Sector size (logical/physical): 512B/512B
Partition Table: msdos

Number  Start    End      Size     Type      File system  Flags
1       1049kB   525MB    524MB    primary   ext4         boot
2       525MB    21.5GB   20.9GB   primary                lvm

Model: VBOX HARDDISK (ide)
Disk /dev/hdb: 8590MB
Sector size (logical/physical): 512B/512B
Partition Table: msdos
```

```
Number   Start   End     Size    Type      File system  Flags
1        32.3kB  4507MB  4507MB  primary
2        4507MB  8587MB  4080MB  primary

Model: VBOX HARDDISK (ide)
Disk /dev/hdc: 8590MB
Sector size (logical/physical): 512B/512B
Partition Table: msdos

Number   Start   End     Size    Type      File system  Flags
1        512B    4294MB  4294MB  primary
2        4295MB  8590MB  4295MB  primary

Error: Unable to open /dev/hdd - unrecognised disk label.
```

Making a Swap Partition

The system uses swap space as a type of "virtual memory" for when your physical memory begins to run low. It does this by using a piece of disk storage to swap files in and out of memory (hence, the term *swap*). This capability can be useful on systems that don't have large amounts of physical memory or when your system is running something that becomes memory intensive. Before you can create a swap, however (which is done in the next chapter), you need to partition space on your disk for it. This is also a little different from the partitions you have previously been creating because the partition type is different. Let's make a swap partition on /dev/hdd for the system.

Step 1. Like before, use the fdisk utility to start:

```
# fdisk /dev/hdd
```

Step 2. Create a new partition:

```
Command (m for help): n
Command action
   e   extended
   p   primary partition (1-4)
p
Partition number (1-4): 1
First cylinder (1-16644, default 1):
Using default value 1
Last cylinder or +size or +sizeM or +sizeK (1-16644, default
16644): +2048M
```

When you are creating partitions, by default, partition type 83 is chosen (Linux). For a swap partition, however, you need to change the type to 82 (Linux Swap). If you want a list of all the available partition types, you can use the l option.

Step 3. Change the type of the partition with the t option:

```
Command (m for help): t
Selected partition 1
Hex code (type L to list codes): 82
Changed system type of partition 1 to 82 (Linux swap / Solaris)
```

Step 4.   Verify that the partition is set up correctly:

```
Command (m for help): p


Disk /dev/hdd: 8589 MB, 8589934592 bytes
255 heads, 63 sectors/track, 1044 cylinders
Units = cylinders of 16065 * 512 = 8225280 bytes
Sector size (logical/physical): 512 bytes / 512 bytes
I/O size (minimum/optimal): 512 bytes / 512 bytes
Disk identifier: 0x00079351

   Device Boot   Start   End    Blocks    Id  System
/dev/hdd1              1     262   2104483+  82  Linux swap / Solaris
```

You can see that the swap partition is set up properly, but do not write the changes to disk! You can have only one swap partition per physical disk, and we still need to cover how to make a swap with the parted command, so don't save your changes here.

Step 5.   Quit without saving changes:

```
Command (m for help): q
```

As you can see, there isn't too much of a difference when creating a swap partition. Let's look again at how to create a swap partition, but this time you can use the parted utility instead.

Step 6.   Start by selecting the drive you'd like to use:

```
# parted /dev/hdd
```

Step 7.   Create the partition:

```
(parted) mkpart
Partition type? primary/extended? primary
File system type? [ext2]? linux-swap
Start? 0
End? 2048m
```

Notice here that you can specify a different partition type from the default while creating the new partition, unlike with the fdisk utility, where you need to change it after the partition is created.

Step 8.   Verify that the partition is set up correctly:

```
(parted) print


Model: VBOX HARDDISK (ide)
Disk /dev/hdd: 8590MB
Sector size (logical/physical): 512B/512B
Partition Table: msdos

Number  Start   End     Size    Type     File system  Flags
 1      512B    2048MB  2048MB  primary
```

Step 9.   Finally, you can exit the `parted` utility and reread the partition table:

```
# partprobe /dev/hdd
```

Deleting a Partition

In the next section, we discuss Logical Volume Manager (LVM), in which you use multiple drives and partitions. Because you have created a bunch of different partitions in this section, the last thing to discuss is deleting partitions so that you can clean off all your drives before beginning the section on LVM. Deleting a partition is much easier than creating one because you need to specify only the partition number that you want to delete.

Step 1.   Start the `fdisk` utility:
```
# fdisk /dev/hdb
```

Step 2.   Print out the current partition table:
```
Command (m for help): p

Disk /dev/hdb: 8589 MB, 8589934592 bytes
255 heads, 63 sectors/track, 1044 cylinders
Units = cylinders of 16065 * 512 = 8225280 bytes
Sector size (logical/physical): 512 bytes / 512 bytes
I/O size (minimum/optimal): 512 bytes / 512 bytes
Disk identifier: 0x0004b72d

   Device Boot      Start         End      Blocks   Id  System
/dev/hdb1               1         548     4401778+  83  Linux
/dev/hdb2             549        1044     3984120   83  Linux
```

You can see the two partitions created earlier. Delete them both using the d option and specifying the partition number you want to delete.

Step 3.   Delete the first partition:
```
Command (m for help): d
Partition number (1-4): 1
```

Step 4.   Delete the second partition:
```
Command (m for help): d
Selected partition 2
```

Step 5.   Write the changes to disk:
```
Command (m for help): w
The partition table has been altered!

Calling ioctl() to re-read partition table.
Syncing disks.
```

Step 6.   Don't forget to reread the partition table:

```
# partprobe /dev/hdb
```

You can also delete partitions with the parted utility.

Step 7.   Start the parted utility:

```
# parted /dev/hdc
```

Step 8.   Print out the current partition table:

```
(parted) print

Model: VBOX HARDDISK (ide)
Disk /dev/hdc: 8590MB
Sector size (logical/physical): 512B/512B
Partition Table: msdos

Number  Start    End      Size     Type      File system  Flags
 1      512B     4294MB   4294MB   primary
 2      4295MB   8590MB   4295MB   primary
```

Step 9.   Again, you can see the two partitions on this drive. Remove them both with the rm option:

```
(parted) rm 1
(parted) rm 2
```

Step 10.   Exit the parted program and reread the partition table:

```
(parted) quit
# partprobe /dev/hdc
```

Step 11.   Also remove the swap partition that you created as well:

```
# parted /dev/hdd
```

Step 12.   Remove the first partition:

```
(parted) rm 1
```

Step 13.   Exit the parted program and reread the partition table:

```
(parted) quit
# partprobe /dev/hdd
```

Step 14.   You can verify all the deletions to the different disks using fdisk or parted:

```
# fdisk -l

Disk /dev/hda: 21.5 GB, 21474836480 bytes
255 heads, 63 sectors/track, 2610 cylinders
Units = cylinders of 16065 * 512 = 8225280 bytes
Sector size (logical/physical): 512 bytes / 512 bytes
I/O size (minimum/optimal): 512 bytes / 512 bytes
Disk identifier: 0x00021654
```

```
   Device Boot        Start         End       Blocks    Id  System
/dev/hda1    *           1          64       512000    83  Linux
/dev/hda2               64        2611     20458496    8e  Linux LVM

Disk /dev/hdb: 8589 MB, 8589934592 bytes
255 heads, 63 sectors/track, 1044 cylinders
Units = cylinders of 16065 * 512 = 8225280 bytes
Sector size (logical/physical): 512 bytes / 512 bytes
I/O size (minimum/optimal): 512 bytes / 512 bytes
Disk identifier: 0x0004b72d

   Device Boot        Start         End       Blocks    Id  System

Disk /dev/hdc: 8589 MB, 8589934592 bytes
255 heads, 63 sectors/track, 1044 cylinders
Units = cylinders of 16065 * 512 = 8225280 bytes
Sector size (logical/physical): 512 bytes / 512 bytes
I/O size (minimum/optimal): 512 bytes / 512 bytes
Disk identifier: 0x000661e0

   Device Boot        Start         End       Blocks    Id  System

Disk /dev/hdd: 8589 MB, 8589934592 bytes
255 heads, 63 sectors/track, 1044 cylinders
Units = cylinders of 16065 * 512 = 8225280 bytes
Sector size (logical/physical): 512 bytes / 512 bytes
I/O size (minimum/optimal): 512 bytes / 512 bytes
Disk identifier: 0x00079351

   Device Boot        Start         End       Blocks    Id  System
```

Logical Volume Manager

LVM is a form of advanced partition management. The benefit to using LVM is ease of management due to the way disks are set up. Working with LVM, however, is one of the more complex topics to understand the first time you deal with it. After you have some practice, you will find that LVM just makes life easier. When you set up your system for the first time, you have a certain number of physical disks (the lab has four for this book). These physical disks are the base of the LVM structure and referred to as *physical volumes*. The next layer in the structure is *volume groups*, where physical volumes are combined into a single pool of storage. The final layer in the structure is *logical volumes*, which are the actual partitions on the system.

GENERAL INFO
Aside from physical disks, a partition can serve as a physical volume as well.

REAL-WORLD TIP
RAID arrays count as a physical volume because they are multiple disks combined to act as one physical disk.

Sometimes pictures help. Take a look at Figure 3-1.

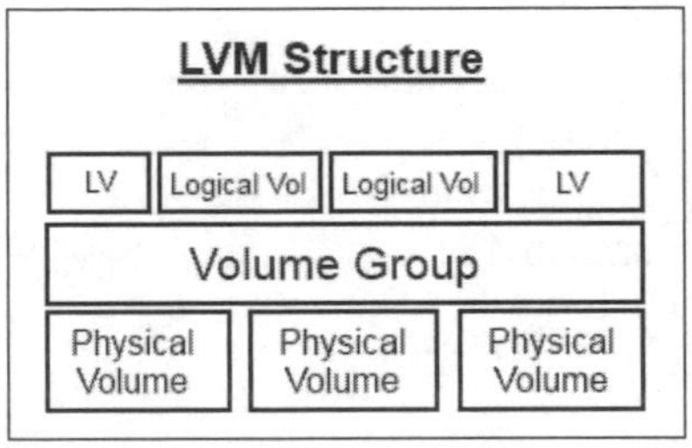

Figure 3-1   The LVM structure.

There are many commands and management utilities for working with LVM. Here is an overview of them:

pvs	Displays physical volumes
vgs	Displays volume groups
lvs	Displays logical volumes
pvdisplay	Displays detailed information on physical volumes
vgdisplay	Displays detailed information on volume groups
lvdisplay	Displays detailed information on logical volumes
pvcreate	Creates a new physical volume
vgcreate	Creates a new volume group
lvcreate	Creates a new logical volume
vgextend	Extends an existing volume group
lvextend	Extends a logical volume
lvresize	Resizes a logical volume
lvreduce	Reduces a logical volume
lvrename	Renames a logical volume
pvmove	Moves/migrates data from one physical volume to another

vgreduce	Reduces a volume group
pvremove	Removes a physical volume
vgremove	Removes a volume group
lvremove	Removes a logical volume

Due to the sheer volume of commands in this particular section, it is impossible to cover the syntax and options for all the LVM management commands. I do, however, show you how to use all of them and a majority of the options. Before getting in over your head in commands, first make sure that you install the package needed for LVM.

Step 1. Install the required packages:

```
# yum install -y lvm2
```

Step 2. Verify that it is installed:

```
# rpm -qa | grep lvm
lvm2-libs-2.02.72-8.el6.x86_64
lvm2-2.02.72-8.el6.x86_64
```

This package is usually installed by default, but verify that it is. Without this package, you are unable to use LVM on your system. Let's go through the model again, but this time make use of the management commands. First, let's look at the physical volumes.

Step 3. To view the physical volumes, use the pvs command:

```
# pvs
  PV          VG          Fmt   Attr PSize    PFree
  /dev/hda2   vg_rhel601  lvm2  a-   19.51g      0
```

MIGRATION TIP

In RHEL5, the default name for volume groups and logical volumes was VolGroup or LogVol. In RHEL6, the new naming convention uses the "vg_" or "lv_" prefix and then the hostname of the system.

Step 4. You could also get more detailed information about the physical volume with the pvdisplay command:

```
# pvdisplay
  -- Physical volume --
  PV Name               /dev/hda2
  VG Name               vg_rhel601
  PV Size               19.51 GiB / not usable 3.00 MiB
  Allocatable           yes (but full)
  PE Size               4.00 MiB
  Total PE              4994
  Free PE               0
```

```
        Allocated PE              4994
        PV UUID                   XI3mef-f2Qm-J5Ri-jiU9-qI8S-hBTI-No6tPn
```

By default, when Red Hat is installed, it uses LVM to manage the disks. The preceding output shows the physical volume created during the installation of Red Hat on the lab box. The next layer in the LVM structure would be the volume group.

Step 5.   To view information about the volume group, use the vgs command:

```
# vgs
  VG            #PV #LV #SN Attr   VSize  VFree
  vg_rhel601      1   2   0 wz—n- 19.51g     0
```

Step 6.   To get more detailed information about the volume group, use the vgdisplay command:

```
# vgdisplay
  -- Volume group --
  VG Name                 vg_rhel601
  System ID
  Format                  lvm2
  Metadata Areas          1
  Metadata Sequence No    3
  VG Access               read/write
  VG Status               resizable
  MAX LV                  0
  Cur LV                  2
  Open LV                 2
  Max PV                  0
  Cur PV                  1
  Act PV                  1
  VG Size                 19.51 GiB
  PE Size                 4.00 MiB
  Total PE                4994
  Alloc PE / Size         4994 / 19.51 GiB
  Free  PE / Size         0 / 0
  VG UUID                 pDycLd-SMos-RLeW-656R-xUZv-b45T-485S8D
```

Finally, you can look at the last layer, the logical volumes.

Step 7.   To view the logical volumes, use the lvs command:

```
# lvs
  LV        VG           Attr   LSize  Origin Snap%  Move Log
Copy%  Convert
  lv_root vg_rhel601 -wi-ao 15.57g
  lv_swap vg_rhel601 -wi-ao  3.94g
```

Step 8.   To get more detailed information about the logical volumes, use the lvdisplay command:

```
# lvdisplay
  -- Logical volume --
  LV Name                 /dev/vg_rhel601/lv_root
  VG Name                 vg_rhel601
```

```
        LV UUID               I1rLRo-T8Qu-uprj-FdIh-oCQi-6PgL-d0bGeC
        LV Write Access       read/write
        LV Status             available
        # open                1
        LV Size               15.57 GiB
        Current LE            3986
        Segments              1
        Allocation            inherit
        Read ahead sectors    auto
        - currently set to    256
        Block device          253:0

        -- Logical volume --
        LV Name               /dev/vg_rhel601/lv_swap
        VG Name               vg_rhel601
        LV UUID               JgOxey-h7Ih-mFgO-6mdt-uibZ-9W9H-I8tZKv
        LV Write Access       read/write
        LV Status             available
        # open                1
        LV Size               3.94 GiB
        Current LE            1008
        Segments              1
        Allocation            inherit
        Read ahead sectors    auto
        - currently set to    256
        Block device          253:1
```

By now, you should be able to view all the information available about the LVM.
You can also look in the /etc/lvm directory, which contains all the information
about each layer of the LVM structure. Because LVM is broken into different layers, there needs to be a unit by which to measure each layer. LVM has two such
units: physical extents and logical extents. *Physical extents* are used when dealing
with volume groups, and logical extents, with logical volumes. The *logical extents*
always map back to a physical extent.

Creating an LVM Partition

Let's use disk /dev/hdb for the LVM partition. First, you need to initialize the disk
to be used for a physical volume.

Step 1.   To initialize the disk, use the pvcreate command:

```
# pvcreate /dev/hdb
  Physical volume "/dev/hdb" successfully created
```

Step 2.   Verify that the physical volume was created successfully:

```
# pvdisplay /dev/hdb
  "/dev/hdb" is a new physical volume of "8.00 GiB"
  -- NEW Physical volume --
  PV Name               /dev/hdb
  VG Name
  PV Size               8.00 GiB
  Allocatable           NO
  PE Size (KByte)       0
  Total PE              0
  Free PE               0
```

```
Allocated PE          0
PV UUID               QlCLgF-esaN-5PvR-PWWV-D6jZ-O207-rHg90j
```

> **WARNING:** Physical volumes are limited to one physical disk or one partition of a physical disk per one physical volume.

With the disk initialized, you can next create a volume group and add the physical disk to it.

Step 3. To create the volume group, use the vgcreate command:

```
# vgcreate vg_group01 /dev/hdb
  Volume group "vg_group01" successfully created
```

Step 4. Verify that the volume group was created successfully:

```
# vgdisplay -v VolGroup01
    Using volume group(s) on command line
    Finding volume group "vg_group01"
  -- Volume group --
  VG Name               vg_group01
  System ID
  Format                lvm2
  Metadata Areas        1
  Metadata Sequence No  1
  VG Access             read/write
  VG Status             resizable
  MAX LV                0
  Cur LV                0
  Open LV               0
  Max PV                0
  Cur PV                1
  Act PV                1
  VG Size               8.00 GiB
  PE Size               4.00 MiB
  Total PE              2047
  Alloc PE / Size       0 / 0
  Free  PE / Size       2047 / 8.00 GiB
  VG UUID               IvjXga-898Y-1vCC-azRt-pszL-PeWR-E5athz

  -- Physical volumes --
  PV Name               /dev/sdb
  PV UUID               B0K2qH-0UF4-gphE-MLi3-RFXH-HEP9-9FMbA9
  PV Status             allocatable
  Total PE / Free PE    2047 / 2047
```

When volume groups are created and initialized, the physical volumes are broken down into physical extents (the unit of measurement for LVM). This is significant because you can adjust the size of how data is stored based on the size of each physical extent, defined when the volume group is created (the default is 4MB). Although you have added only one physical volume to the volume group, you still have created a pool of storage space. Now you can set up logical volumes that hold the partitions for the system. To create a logical volume, use the lvcreate command and specify the size of the partition that you'd like to create. The size can be specified in kilobytes, megabytes, gigabytes, or logical extents (LE). Like physical extents, logical extents are a unit of measure when dealing with logical volumes. They map directly to physical extents where the actual data is kept. Dealing with megabytes is probably the easiest here.

Step 5. Create a partition 3GB in size:

```
# lvcreate -L 3000 VolGroup01
  Logical volume "lvol0" created
```

EXAM TIP

If you don't specify a unit, megabytes is used as the default.

Step 6. Verify that the logical volume was created successfully:

```
# lvdisplay vg_group01
  -- Logical volume --
  LV Name              /dev/vg_group01/lvol0
  VG Name              vg_group01
  LV UUID              mk9dJM-3qt7-ypbC-nsks-I8Gh-9V3d-4BNE6s
  LV Write Access      read/write
  LV Status            available
  # open               0
  LV Size              2.93 GiB
  Current LE           750
  Segments             1
  Allocation           inherit
  Read ahead sectors   auto
  - currently set to   256
  Block device         253:2
```

Step 7. Use the vgdisplay command again and see whether the logical volume has been added to it:

```
# vgdisplay -v VolGroup01
    Using volume group(s) on command line
    Finding volume group "vg_group01"
  -- Volume group --
  VG Name              vg_group01
  System ID
  Format               lvm2
  Metadata Areas       1
  Metadata Sequence No 2
  VG Access            read/write
  VG Status            resizable
  MAX LV               0
  Cur LV               1
  Open LV              0
  Max PV               0
  Cur PV               1
  Act PV               1
  VG Size              8.00 GiB
```

```
PE Size                 4.00 MiB
Total PE                2047
Alloc PE / Size         750 / 2.93 GiB
Free  PE / Size         1297 / 5.07 GiB
VG UUID                 IvjXga-898Y-1vCC-azRt-pszL-PeWR-E5athz

-- Logical volume --
LV Name                 /dev/vg_group01/lvol0
VG Name                 vg_group01
LV UUID                 mk9dJM-3qt7-ypbC-nsks-I8Gh-9V3d-4BNE6s
LV Write Access         read/write
LV Status               available
# open                  0
LV Size                 2.93 GiB
Current LE              750
Segments                1
Allocation              inherit
Read ahead sectors      auto
- currently set to      256
Block device            253:2

-- Physical volumes --
PV Name                 /dev/sdb
PV UUID                 B0K2qH-0UF4-gphE-MLi3-RFXH-HEP9-9FMbA9
PV Status               allocatable
Total PE / Free PE      2047 / 1297
```

By default, all logical volumes take the name lvol#. You can change this and specify the name that you'd like to use for your logical volume partition with the lvcreate command (when you're creating your partition). Use the -n option to specify a name.

Step 8.   Alternatively, you could do the following:

```
# lvcreate -L 3000 -n SecretData vg_group01
```

This approach would have created the logical volume the same as before, but the name would be SecretData instead of lvol0. If you have already created your logical volume and you forgot to give it a name, you don't have to delete it and create it again. Using the lvrename command, you can change the name of a logical partition:

```
# lvrename /dev/vg_group01/lvol0 /dev/vg_group01/SecretData
Renamed "lvol0" to "SecretData" in volume group "vg_group01"
```

Step 9.   Verify with the following command:

```
# lvdisplay vg_group01
  -- Logical volume --
  LV Name               /dev/vg_group01/SecretData
  VG Name               vg_group01
  LV UUID               mk9dJM-3qt7-ypbC-nsks-I8Gh-9V3d-4BNE6s
  LV Write Access       read/write
  LV Status             available
  # open                0
  LV Size               2.93 GiB
```

```
Current LE              750
Segments                1
Allocation              inherit
Read ahead sectors      auto
- currently set to      256
Block device            253:2
```

Adjusting the Size of LVM Partitions

The single best feature of LVM is that you can reduce or expand your logical volumes and volume groups. If you are running out of room on a particular logical volume or volume group, you can add another physical volume to the volume group and then expand the logical volume to give you more room.

EXAM TIP

When you resize a logical volume that already contains a formatted file system, you need to grow the file system into the new space that becomes available. We discuss growing a file system in Chapter 4, "File Systems and Such," but you should make a mental note if you run into this on the exams.

To extend a logical volume, use the lvextend command.

Step 1.   Add 2GB more to the SecretData logical volume:

```
# lvextend -L +2000 /dev/vg_group01/SecretData
  Extending logical volume SecretData to 4.88 GB
  Logical volume SecretData successfully resized
```

Step 2.   You also could specify a new size instead of using the + to add:

```
# lvextend -L 6000 /dev/VolGroup01/SecretData
  Extending logical volume SecretData to 5.86 GB
  Logical volume SecretData successfully resized
```

Step 3.   Either of the preceding commands yields the same results. As a third alternative, you could also use the lvresize command:

```
# lvresize -L 7000 /dev/VolGroup01/SecretData
  Extending logical volume SecretData to 6.84 GB
  Logical volume SecretData successfully resized
```

Step 4.   Verify the change with the following command:

```
# lvdisplay vg_group01
    Using logical volume(s) on command line
    -- Logical volume --
    LV Name              /dev/vg_group01/SecretData
    VG Name              vg_group01
    LV UUID              mk9dJM-3qt7-ypbC-nsks-I8Gh-9V3d-4BNE6s
    LV Write Access      read/write
    LV Status            available
    # open               0
    LV Size              6.84 GiB
    Current LE           1750
```

```
Segments              1
Allocation            inherit
Read ahead sectors    auto
- currently set to    256
Block device          253:2
```

Suppose, though, that you want to add a new physical volume so that you can extend your volume group (possibly to add a new partition). You can use vgextend to expand your volume group.

Step 5.   Create a new physical volume somewhere:

```
# pvcreate /dev/hdc
  Physical volume "/dev/hdc" successfully created
```

Step 6.   Extend your volume group to incorporate that new physical volume:

```
# vgextend VolGroup01 /dev/hdc
  Volume group "vg_group01" successfully extended
```

Step 7.   Now view the details of the newly increased volume group:

```
# vgdisplay -v vg_group01
    Using volume group(s) on command line
    Finding volume group "vg_group01"
  -- Volume group --
  VG Name               vg_group01
  System ID
  Format                lvm2
  Metadata Areas        2
  Metadata Sequence No  9
  VG Access             read/write
  VG Status             resizable
  MAX LV                0
  Cur LV                1
  Open LV               0
  Max PV                0
  Cur PV                2
  Act PV                2
  VG Size               15.99 GiB
  PE Size               4.00 MiB
  Total PE              4094
  Alloc PE / Size       1750 / 6.84 GiB
  Free  PE / Size       2344 / 9.16 GiB
  VG UUID               IvjXga-898Y-1vCC-azRt-pszL-PeWR-E5athz

  -- Logical volume --
  LV Name               /dev/vg_group01/SecretData
  VG Name               vg_group01
  LV UUID               mk9dJM-3qt7-ypbC-nsks-I8Gh-9V3d-4BNE6s
  LV Write Access       read/write
  LV Status             available
  # open                0
  LV Size               6.84 GiB
  Current LE            1750
  Segments              1
  Allocation            inherit
  Read ahead sectors    auto
```

```
 - currently set to      256
Block device             253:2

-- Physical volumes --
PV Name                  /dev/sdb
PV UUID                  B0K2qH-0UF4-gphE-MLi3-RFXH-HEP9-9FMbA9
PV Status                allocatable
Total PE / Free PE       2047 / 297

PV Name                  /dev/sdc
PV UUID                  Wn52Tv-ZEJR-IkYb-2oi1-5lw7-2oN7-wHihl4
PV Status                allocatable
Total PE / Free PE       2047 / 2047
```

You can see that the VG Size has gone up to 15.99GB from 8GB earlier.
Just as you can use commands to increase or extend the LVM structures,
you can also reduce them. Although extension creates space that isn't
there, you need to be extra careful when removing space because doing
so could cause data loss. To decrease a logical volume, you use the
lvreduce command, which has a similar syntax to lvextend.

Step 8.   Reduce the SecretData logical volume to 2GB in size:

```
# lvresize -L 4000 /dev/vg_group01/SecretData
  WARNING: Reducing active logical volume to 3.91 GiB
  THIS MAY DESTROY YOUR DATA (filesystem etc.)
Do you really want to reduce SecretData? [y/n]: y
  Reducing logical volume SecretData to 3.91 GiB
  Logical volume SecretData successfully resized
```

Step 9.   You could also use the following command:

```
# lvresize -L 2000 /dev/vg_group01/SecretData
  WARNING: Reducing active logical volume to 1.95 GiB
  THIS MAY DESTROY YOUR DATA (filesystem etc.)
Do you really want to reduce SecretData? [y/n]: y
  Reducing logical volume SecretData to 1.95 GiB
  Logical volume SecretData successfully resized
```

Reducing a volume group works in the same manner.

Step 10.   To reduce the volume group to no longer include the physical volume
/dev/hdc, you can use the vgreduce command:

```
# vgreduce vg_group01 /dev/hdc
  Removed "/dev/hdc" from volume group "vg_group01"
```

Step 11.   Use the vgdisplay command to verify expansion or reduction of volume
groups and logical volumes:

```
# vgdisplay vg_group01
  -- Volume group --
  VG Name                  vg_group01
  System ID
  Format                   lvm2
  Metadata Areas           1
```

```
Metadata Sequence No    12
VG Access               read/write
VG Status               resizable
MAX LV                  0
Cur LV                  1
Open LV                 0
Max PV                  0
Cur PV                  1
Act PV                  1
VG Size                 8.00 GiB
PE Size                 4.00 MiB
Total PE                2047
Alloc PE / Size         500 / 1.95 GiB
Free  PE / Size         1547 / 6.04 GiB
VG UUID                 IvjXga-898Y-1vCC-azRt-pszL-PeWR-E5athz
```

Migrating Data

Suppose you have a drive that is old or dying and you'd like to remove it from the system. On a system with normal partitions, you would have to copy all the data from one disk to another while the disk is offline (because of file locks). Having LVM makes this easier because you can migrate your data from one disk to another, even while the disk is online! This capability is very useful when you need to replace a disk. If you want to replace /dev/hdb because it's failing, you can use the pvmove command to migrate the physical extents (which is really your data) to another physical volume (/dev/hdc). Because you removed /dev/hdc from the volume group in the previous section, you need to add it back.

Step 1.   Verify that you have two physical volumes inside the vg_group01 volume group:

```
# vgdisplay -v vg_group01
    Using volume group(s) on command line
    Finding volume group "vg_group01"
  -- Volume group --
  VG Name                 vg_group01
  System ID
  Format                  lvm2
  Metadata Areas          2
  Metadata Sequence No    14
  VG Access               read/write
  VG Status               resizable
  MAX LV                  0
  Cur LV                  2
  Open LV                 0
  Max PV                  0
  Cur PV                  2
  Act PV                  2
  VG Size                 15.99 GiB
  PE Size                 4.00 MiB
  Total PE                4094
  Alloc PE / Size         1750 / 6.84 GiB
  Free  PE / Size         2344 / 9.16 GiB
  VG UUID                 IvjXga-898Y-1vCC-azRt-pszL-PeWR-E5athz

  -- Logical volume --
```

```
LV Name                /dev/vg_group01/SecretData
VG Name                vg_group01
LV UUID                mk9dJM-3qt7-ypbC-nsks-I8Gh-9V3d-4BNE6s
LV Write Access        read/write
LV Status              available
# open                 0
LV Size                1.95 GiB
Current LE             500
Segments               1
Allocation             inherit
Read ahead sectors     auto
- currently set to     256
Block device           253:2

-- Physical volumes --
PV Name                /dev/sdb
PV UUID                B0K2qH-0UF4-gphE-MLi3-RFXH-HEP9-9FMbA9
PV Status              allocatable
Total PE / Free PE     2047 / 297
```

Step 2.   Because there is only a single physical disk, you need to add back /dev/hdc to the volume group:

```
# vgextend vg_group01 /dev/sdc
Volume group "vg_group01" successfully extended
```

Step 3.   Also create a logical volume to hold the migrated data:

```
# lvcreate -L 5000 vg_group01
Logical volume "lvol0" created
```

Step 4.   Verify all logical volumes are in place:

```
# lvdisplay vg_group01
-- Logical volume --
LV Name                /dev/vg_group01/SecretData
VG Name                vg_group01
LV UUID                mk9dJM-3qt7-ypbC-nsks-I8Gh-9V3d-4BNE6s
LV Write Access        read/write
LV Status              available
# open                 0
LV Size                1.95 GiB
Current LE             500
Segments               1
Allocation             inherit
Read ahead sectors     auto
- currently set to     256
Block device           253:2

-- Logical volume --
LV Name                /dev/vg_group01/lvol0
VG Name                vg_group01
LV UUID                6vsP79-Gu7W-PO4p-tCHg-OMqN-W8QN-QAIrhH
LV Write Access        read/write
LV Status              available
# open                 0
LV Size                4.88 GiB
Current LE             1250
Segments               1
```

```
         Allocation                inherit
         Read ahead sectors        auto
         - currently set to        256
         Block device              253:3
```

Step 5.   You should also verify that you now have two physical disks for the
vg_group01 volume group:

```
# vgdisplay -v vg_group01
    Using volume group(s) on command line
    Finding volume group "vg_group01"
  -- Volume group --
  VG Name                  vg_group01
  System ID
  Format                   lvm2
  Metadata Areas           2
  Metadata Sequence No     14
  VG Access                read/write
  VG Status                resizable
  MAX LV                   0
  Cur LV                   2
  Open LV                  0
  Max PV                   0
  Cur PV                   2
  Act PV                   2
  VG Size                  15.99 GiB
  PE Size                  4.00 MiB
  Total PE                 4094
  Alloc PE / Size          1750 / 6.84 GiB
  Free  PE / Size          2344 / 9.16 GiB
  VG UUID                  IvjXga-898Y-1vCC-azRt-pszL-PeWR-E5athz

  -- Logical volume --
  LV Name                  /dev/vg_group01/SecretData
  VG Name                  vg_group01
  LV UUID                  mk9dJM-3qt7-ypbC-nsks-I8Gh-9V3d-4BNE6s
  LV Write Access          read/write
  LV Status                available
  # open                   0
  LV Size                  1.95 GiB
  Current LE               500
  Segments                 1
  Allocation               inherit
  Read ahead sectors       auto
  - currently set to       256
  Block device             253:2

  -- Logical volume --
  LV Name                  /dev/vg_group01/lvol0
  VG Name                  vg_group01
  LV UUID                  6vsP79-Gu7W-PO4p-tCHg-OMqN-W8QN-QAIrhH
  LV Write Access          read/write
  LV Status                available
  # open                   0
  LV Size                  4.88 GiB
  Current LE               1250
  Segments                 1
  Allocation               inherit
  Read ahead sectors       auto
```

```
          - currently set to      256
          Block device            253:3

          -- Physical volumes --
          PV Name                 /dev/sdb
          PV UUID                 B0K2qH-0UF4-gphE-MLi3-RFXH-HEP9-9FMbA9
          PV Status               allocatable
          Total PE / Free PE      2047 / 297

          PV Name                 /dev/sdc
          PV UUID                 Wn52Tv-ZEJR-IkYb-2oi1-5Iw7-2oN7-wHihl4
          PV Status               allocatable
          Total PE / Free PE      2047 / 2047
```

Step 6.   Migrate the data from the "dying" drive:

```
# pvmove /dev/hdb /dev/hdc
/dev/sdb: Moved: 0.2%
/dev/sdb: Moved: 7.0%
/dev/sdb: Moved: 13.7%
/dev/sdb: Moved: 20.2%
/dev/sdb: Moved: 26.9%
/dev/sdb: Moved: 28.6%
/dev/sdb: Moved: 35.4%
/dev/sdb: Moved: 40.8%
/dev/sdb: Moved: 47.2%
/dev/sdb: Moved: 53.9%
/dev/sdb: Moved: 60.4%
/dev/sdb: Moved: 67.0%
/dev/sdb: Moved: 73.7%
/dev/sdb: Moved: 80.4%
/dev/sdb: Moved: 87.0%
/dev/sdb: Moved: 93.8%
/dev/sdb: Moved: 100.0%
```

Make sure that you have more than one physical volume; otherwise, there will be nowhere for the data to move.

Step 7.   Verify that the physical volume is empty:

```
# pvdisplay /dev/hdb
  -- Physical volume --
  PV Name                 /dev/sdb
  VG Name                 vg_group01
  PV Size                 8.00 GiB / not usable 4.00 MiB
  Allocatable             yes
  PE Size                 4.00 MiB
  Total PE                2047
  Free PE                 2047
  Allocated PE            0
  PV UUID                 B0K2qH-0UF4-gphE-MLi3-RFXH-HEP9-9FMbA9
```

Deleting an LVM Partition

It is just as important to understand how to delete LVM partitions as it is to create them. This is a common task when you are upgrading or redesigning a file system layout.

Step 1. To remove a logical volume, use the `lvremove` command:

```
# lvremove /dev/vg_group01/SecretData
Do you really want to remove active logical volume SecretData?
[y/n]: y
  Logical volume "SecretData" successfully removed
```

A nice feature about `lvremove` is that it has a `-t` option, which allows you to test the removal of a logical partition without actually deleting it. The commands to remove volume groups and physical volumes also support the `-t` option.

> **WARNING:**   Although this advice should be common sense, make sure you back up any data before deleting anything within the LVM structure. Removing logical volumes, volume groups, and physical volumes is destructive and results in all data loss for that object within the LVM structure. The deletion occurs even if there is data on any part of the LVM structure.

Going down the LVM layers, you could also remove the entire volume group if you want to.

Step 2. Use the `vgremove` command to remove the volume group:

```
# vgremove vg_group01
Do you really want to remove volume group "vg_group01" containing
1 logical volumes? [y/n]: y
Do you really want to remove active logical volume lvol0? [y/n]: y
  Logical volume "lvol0" successfully removed
  Volume group "vg_group01" successfully removed
```

You can also do both steps in one command by using the `-f` option with vgremove:

```
# vgremove -f VolGroup01
```

Step 3. Verify the changes:

```
# vgdisplay vg_group01
  Volume group "vg_group01" not found
```

You should no longer see vg_group01 (as displayed here). At the last layer are the physical volumes, which you can remove with the `pvremove` command. Using this command completely wipes all LVM metadata (essentially the whole disk drive).

Step 4. Wipe all the current physical volumes:

```
# pvremove /dev/hdb
  Labels on physical volume "/dev/hdb" successfully wiped

# pvremove /dev/hdc
  Labels on physical volume "/dev/hdc" successfully wiped
```

Setting Up RAID

So far, we have addressed basic partitions, including swap, and how to set them up. Now let's move on to the final type of advanced partitioning: RAID. RAID partitions allow for more advanced features such as redundancy and better performance. Before we describe how to implement RAID, let's look at the different types of RAID:

- **RAID 0** (Striping) disks are grouped together to form one large drive. This offers better performance at the cost of availability. Should any single disk in the RAID fail, the entire set of disks becomes unusable. Two disk minimum.

- **RAID 1** (Mirroring) disks are copied from one to another, allowing for redundancy. Should one disk fail, the other disk takes over, having an exact copy of data from the original disk. The downside here is slow write times. Two disk minimum.

- **RAID 5** (Striping with parity) disks are similar to RAID 0 and are join together to form one large drive. The difference here is that 25% of the disk is used for a parity bit, which allows the disks to be recovered should a single disk fail. Three disk minimum.

While RAID can be implemented at the hardware level, the Red Hat exams are not hardware based and therefore focus on the software implementation of RAID through the MD driver. Next, let's use the three free disk drives from the previous section (hdb, hdc, and hdd) to set up a RAID array.

Step 1.   Install the following package:

```
# yum install -y mdadm
```

Step 2.   Verify the install:

```
# rpm -qa | grep mdadm
mdadm-3.1.3-1.el6.x86_64
```

This package should have already been installed with the system, so you may be able to just verify its existence. To start, you first need to create partitions on the disk you want to use (yes, I know I had you erase them at the end of the previous section...think of it as practice). You start with a RAID 5 setup, so you need to make partitions on at least three different disks.

REAL-WORLD TIP

If you are just starting out with RAID, it is worth noting that you can create partitions on a single disk and then use them to create your RAID just to see how it is implemented. In the real world, however, making a RAID setup on a single disk completely defeats the purpose of the RAID because it exists for performance or redundancy, which you can't achieve with all your partitions on a single disk.

Creating a RAID Array

You should know how to create basic partitions by now, so creating a RAID array should be good practice for you. Create three partitions, one on each disk (hdb, hdc, hdd), allowing each partition to consume the whole disk.

Step 1.   Here are the results you should see when you're done:

```
# fdisk -l

Disk /dev/hda: 21.5 GB, 21474836480 bytes
255 heads, 63 sectors/track, 2610 cylinders
Units = cylinders of 16065 * 512 = 8225280 bytes
Sector size (logical/physical): 512 bytes / 512 bytes
I/O size (minimum/optimal): 512 bytes / 512 bytes
Disk identifier: 0x00021654

    Device Boot       Start          End      Blocks   Id  System
/dev/hda1    *            1           64      512000   83  Linux
Partition 1 does not end on cylinder boundary.
/dev/hda2                64         2611    20458496   8e  Linux LVM

Disk /dev/hdb: 8589 MB, 8589934592 bytes
255 heads, 63 sectors/track, 1044 cylinders
Units = cylinders of 16065 * 512 = 8225280 bytes
Sector size (logical/physical): 512 bytes / 512 bytes
I/O size (minimum/optimal): 512 bytes / 512 bytes
Disk identifier: 0x8f3fa89a

    Device Boot       Start          End      Blocks   Id  System
/dev/hdb1                1         1044     8385898+  83  Linux

Disk /dev/hdc: 8589 MB, 8589934592 bytes
255 heads, 63 sectors/track, 1044 cylinders
Units = cylinders of 16065 * 512 = 8225280 bytes
Sector size (logical/physical): 512 bytes / 512 bytes
I/O size (minimum/optimal): 512 bytes / 512 bytes
Disk identifier: 0x6004464d

    Device Boot       Start          End      Blocks   Id  System
/dev/hdc1                1         1044     8385898+  83  Linux

Disk /dev/hdd: 8589 MB, 8589934592 bytes
255 heads, 63 sectors/track, 1044 cylinders
Units = cylinders of 16065 * 512 = 8225280 bytes
Sector size (logical/physical): 512 bytes / 512 bytes
```

```
I/O size (minimum/optimal): 512 bytes / 512 bytes
Disk identifier: 0x00079351

    Device Boot      Start         End      Blocks   Id  System
/dev/hdd1                1        1044     8385898+   83  Linux
```

Now you can begin to set up the RAID 5 array with the three partitions in hand. You can use the mdadm command to create any RAID array.

Syntax: mdadm [options]

Options:

-a, xx	Adds a disk into a current array
-C, —create	Creates a new RAID array
-D, —detail	Prints the details of an array
-G, —grow	Changes the size or shape of an active array
-f, xx	Fails a disk in the array
-l, —level	Specifies level (type) of RAID array to create
-n, —raid-devices	Specifies the devices in the RAID array
-q, —quiet	Species not to show output
-S, —stop	Stops an array
-v, —verbose	Provides verbose output

Step 2. You should be able to tell from the following command that you created a new RAID array (/dev/md0), which is a RAID 5, and it contains three disks:

```
# mdadm -Cv /dev/md0 — level=5 -n3 /dev/hdb1 /dev/hdc1 /dev/hdd1
mdadm: Defaulting to version 1.2 metadata
mdadm: array /dev/md0 started.
```

Step 3. Use the mdadm command again to verify that the RAID array has been created successfully:

```
# mdadm -D /dev/md0
/dev/md0:
          Version : 1.2
    Creation Time : Thu Jan 27 14:09:23 2011
       Raid Level : raid5
       Array Size : 16769024 (15.99 GiB 17.17 GB)
    Used Dev Size : 8384512 (8.00 GiB 8.59 GB)
     Raid Devices : 3
    Total Devices : 3
      Persistence : Superblock is persistent
```

```
                Update Time : Thu Jan 27 14:15:27 2011
                      State : clean
             Active Devices : 3
            Working Devices : 3
             Failed Devices : 0
              Spare Devices : 0

                     Layout : left-symmetric
                 Chunk Size : 512K

                       Name : RHEL-01:0  (local to host RHEL-01)
                       UUID : a02fb98a:63a7cbbf:762c7a7f:e681a8ee
                     Events : 18

        Number   Major   Minor   RaidDevice State
           0       8       17         0       active sync   /dev/hdb1
           1       8       33         1       active sync   /dev/hdc1
           3       8       49         2       active sync   /dev/hdd1
```

In Chapter 10, you learn how to query the kernel for information as well (such as how to show current RAID arrays on the system). You can also cheat a little and query the kernel now for information.

Step 4. View the status of the newly created RAID array:

```
# cat /proc/mdstat
Personalities : [raid0] [raid6] [raid5] [raid4]
md0 : active raid5 hdd1[3] hdc1[1] hdb1[0]
      16769024 blocks super 1.2 level 5, 512k chunk, algorithm 2
[3/2] [UU_]
      [===>................]  recovery = 17.8% (6148864/8384512)
finish=2.9min speed=22072K/sec

unused devices: <none>
```

This output shows that you have an active RAID 5 array with three disks in it. The last few lines here show the state of each disk and partition in the RAID array. You can also see that the RAID is in "recovery" mode, or creating itself.

Step 5. If you wait the estimated 2.9 minutes and then query again, you see the following:

```
# cat /proc/mdstat
Personalities : [raid0] [raid6] [raid5] [raid4]
md0 : active raid5 hdd1[2] hdc1[1] hdb1[0]
      8001280 blocks level 5, 64k chunk, algorithm 2 [3/3] [UUU]

unused devices: <none>
```

You now see that the RAID is good to go as it has finished building itself.

What to Do When a Disk Fails

Suppose that a disk in the array failed. In that case, you need to remove that disk from the array and replace it with a working one. You do have extra disk drives, right? You can manually fail a disk to see what it would be like if a disk failed in the array.

Step 1. To fail a disk in the array, use this command:

```
# mdadm /dev/md0 -f /dev/hdd1
mdadm: set /dev/hdd1 faulty in /dev/md0
```

Step 2. Verify that the disk in the array has failed by looking at the details of the RAID array:

```
# mdadm -D /dev/md0
/dev/md0:
          Version : 1.2
    Creation Time : Thu Jan 27 14:09:23 2011
       Raid Level : raid5
       Array Size : 16769024 (15.99 GiB 17.17 GB)
    Used Dev Size : 8384512 (8.00 GiB 8.59 GB)
     Raid Devices : 3
    Total Devices : 3
      Persistence : Superblock is persistent

      Update Time : Thu Jan 27 14:28:55 2011
            State : clean, degraded
   Active Devices : 2
  Working Devices : 2
   Failed Devices : 1
    Spare Devices : 0

           Layout : left-symmetric
       Chunk Size : 512K

             Name : RHEL-01:0  (local to host RHEL-01)
             UUID : a02fb98a:63a7cbbf:762c7a7f:e681a8ee
           Events : 19

    Number   Major   Minor   RaidDevice State
       0       8       17        0      active sync   /dev/hdb1
       1       8       33        1      active sync   /dev/hdc1
       2       0        0        2      removed

       3       8       49        -      faulty spare
/dev/hdd1
```

Now that you know that the disk has failed, you need to remove it from the array so it can be replaced.

Step 3. To remove a disk from the array, use this command:

```
# mdadm /dev/md0 -r /dev/hdd1
mdadm: hot removed /dev/hdd1 from /dev/md0
```

Step 4.   Look at the last few lines of the RAID details again:

```
# mdadm -D /dev/md0
/dev/md0:
          Version : 1.2
    Creation Time : Thu Jan 27 14:09:23 2011
       Raid Level : raid5
       Array Size : 16769024 (15.99 GiB 17.17 GB)
    Used Dev Size : 8384512 (8.00 GiB 8.59 GB)
     Raid Devices : 3
    Total Devices : 2
      Persistence : Superblock is persistent

      Update Time : Thu Jan 27 14:31:23 2011
            State : clean, degraded
   Active Devices : 2
  Working Devices : 2
   Failed Devices : 0
    Spare Devices : 0

           Layout : left-symmetric
       Chunk Size : 512K

             Name : RHEL-01:0  (local to host RHEL-01)
             UUID : a02fb98a:63a7cbbf:762c7a7f:e681a8ee
           Events : 22

    Number   Major   Minor   RaidDevice State
       0       8      17         0      active sync   /dev/hdb1
       1       8      33         1      active sync   /dev/hdc1
       2       0       0         2      removed
```

You can see from the last line of the output that the disk has been "removed." If this were a real failure, you could take the disk out and replace it with a working one. In this situation, it is useful to have "hot-swap" disk drives.

> **EXAM TIP**
>
> If you want, you could combine the previous two commands to fail the disk and remove it from the array in one step. I broke them apart to make it easier to understand. If you want to use them together, you could use the following:
>
> ```
> # mdadm -v /dev/md0 -f /dev/hdd1 -r /dev/hdd1
> ```

When you have a new disk in place, you need to make it active in the array. First, you need to partition the disk like you did originally when setting up the RAID array.

Step 5.   When the disk is partitioned, you can add it back to the array as follows:

```
# mdadm /dev/md0 -a /dev/hdd1
mdadm: re-added /dev/hdd1
```

Step 6.   Verify that it has been added properly:

```
# mdadm -D /dev/md0
/dev/md0:
           Version : 1.2
     Creation Time : Thu Jan 27 14:09:23 2011
        Raid Level : raid5
        Array Size : 16769024 (15.99 GiB 17.17 GB)
     Used Dev Size : 8384512 (8.00 GiB 8.59 GB)
      Raid Devices : 3
     Total Devices : 3
       Persistence : Superblock is persistent

       Update Time : Thu Jan 27 14:34:21 2011
             State : clean, degraded, recovering
    Active Devices : 2
   Working Devices : 3
    Failed Devices : 0
     Spare Devices : 1

            Layout : left-symmetric
        Chunk Size : 512K

    Rebuild Status : 3% complete

              Name : RHEL-01:0  (local to host RHEL-01)
              UUID : a02fb98a:63a7cbbf:762c7a7f:e681a8ee
            Events : 20

    Number   Major   Minor   RaidDevice State
       0       8       17        0      active sync   /dev/hdb1
       1       8       33        1      active sync   /dev/hdc1
       3       8       49        2      spare rebuilding
/dev/hdd1
```

Notice that the state of the drive is "rebuilding." You can query the kernel again to find out how long the system thinks it will be before the spare has been rebuilt.

Step 7.   Query the kernel:

```
# cat /proc/mdstat
Personalities : [raid0] [raid6] [raid5] [raid4]
md0 : active raid5 hdd1[2] hdc1[1] hdb1[0]
      16769024 blocks super 1.2 level 5, 512k chunk, algorithm 2
[3/2] [UU_]
      [===>.................]  recovery = 17.4% (697276/4000640)
finish=3.9min speed=13843K/sec

unused devices: <none>
```

You can now see why I showed you how to get the details of the RAID array as well as how to query information from the kernel.

Step 8.   Should something go seriously wrong and you need to take the RAID array offline completely, you can use the following command:

```
# mdadm -vS /dev/md0
mdadm: stopped /dev/md0
```

You might also want to take an array offline to perform some maintenance on the file system. After you finish making all changes, you can bring the array back on-line. Now your array is ready for use just like any other disk. You can format it and create a file system just as you would a regular partition (except you point to /dev/md0 instead of a single partition).

Deleting a RAID Array

Now that you have successfully implemented a RAID array, you can take it apart by deleting the array.

Step 1.   To delete an array, first stop it:

```
# mdadm -vS /dev/md0
mdadm: stopped /dev/md0
```

Step 2.   Then remove the RAID array device:

```
# mdadm — remove /dev/md0
```

You should also remove the partitions created for the RAID array. If you forget how, refer to the section "Deleting a Partition," earlier in the chapter on how to delete partitions. Don't forget to use fdisk (or parted) to verify that the partitions have been removed successfully.

> **WARNING:**   When you are creating RAID arrays, there is only one restriction to them. The /boot partition that contains the files necessary to boot the system can be located only on a RAID 1 or basic partition. The reason is that the bootloader (GRUB) understands how to handle only RAID 1 and basic partitions. If you try to create the /boot partition on a RAID 5 array, you get an error message.

Summary

Creating partitions is a key part to system management. You need to understand how to plan ahead and create custom partition layouts on systems as well as how to create the partition scheme you have designed. It is also important to understand the usefulness of RAID and LVM, along with how to implement them properly. These can both be very powerful tools when used correctly. The next chapter explains how to create file systems on your partitions, which allow them to become usable to the rest of the system.

Review Questions

1. What option is used with both the `fdisk` and `parted` commands to display the current partition tables?

2. What does the `partprobe` command do?

3. Do you need to write changes to the disk when using the `parted` command? What about `fdisk`?

4. What are the three different types of RAID described in this chapter?

5. What command can you use to query information from the kernel about RAID arrays?

6. Can you put your /boot partition on a RAID 5 array?

7. What are the three items that make up LVM?

8. What are the side effects of shrinking a volume group or logical volume?

9. What is the biggest benefit to using LVM over basic partitions?

10. What command can you use to get information about logical volumes?

Answers to Review Questions

1. The `print` option is used with both the `fdisk` and `parted` commands to display the current partition tables.

2. The `partprobe` command forces the kernel to reread the partition table. You should always call it after making any changes to your system partitions.

3. When you exit the `parted` utility, all your changes are automatically written to disk. With the `fdisk` command, you need to manually write your changes to disk for them to take effect.

4. RAID 0 (Striping), RAID 1 (Mirror), and RAID 5 (Striping with parity).

5. `cat /proc/mdstat`

6. This is actually a trick question because the answer could go either way. In this chapter, we discussed only software RAID setups, in which case the answer is no. If, however, you were using a hardware RAID 5, the answer would be yes.

7. Physical volumes, volume groups, and logical volumes.

8. If you shrink a volume group or logical volume, there is a chance you could lose data depending on how much you shrink the volume.

9. You have the flexibility to resize and add new volumes on the fly. With basic partitions, any time that you want to make a change, you need to destroy the partition and create it again.

10. `lvdisplay`

Lab 3

Task 1 – The First Partition

Step 1.   Disk /dev/hdb on RHEL01 needs to be partitioned. Use the following guidelines while partitioning the disk:
   a. There should be three partitions on this disk.
   b. The first and second partitions should both be 2GB in size.
   c. The third partition should consume the rest of the disk space.
   d. There should be no swap partition on this disk.

The task is complete when the partitions have been created and can be verified.

Task 2 – RAID

Step 1.   Disk /dev/hdc on RHEL01 needs to be partitioned. Use the following guidelines while partitioning the disk:

a. There should be three equal-sized partitions that consume the whole disk.

b. The third partition should be a swap partition.

c. The first two partitions should be set up in a RAID 1 array

The task is complete when the partitions and RAID array have been created and can be verified.

Task 3 – LVM

Step 1.   Set up LVM on your system using the following guidelines:

a. Create a physical volume on /dev/hdd.

b. Create a volume group called VolGroup22.

c. Create two logical volumes within VolGroup22.

d. The first logical volume should have the default name.

e. The second logical volume should be named Company_Data.

f. Both logical volumes should be 2,048MB in size.

Step 2.   Make the following changes to your LVM structure:

a. Extend your LVM structure by adding /dev/hdb3 into the volume group (VolGroup22).

b. Grow your Company_Data volume to fill the rest of the volume group.

The task is complete when the logical volumes, volume groups, and physical volumes can all be verified.

This chapter covers the following subjects:

- **File System Setup**—This section covers the creation of file systems.

- **Encryption with LUKS**—This section looks at how to encrypt file systems with LUKS.

- **Managing File System Quotas**—To prevent file systems from filling up, this section covers how to implement quotas.

- **File System Security**—This section looks at how to enforce different types of security on file systems.

- **Using AutoFS**—This section covers how to automatically mount file systems with AutoFS.

The following RHCSA exam objectives are covered:

- Create, mount, unmount, and use ext2, ext3, and ext4 file systems

- Mount, unmount, and use LUKS-encrypted file systems

- Mount and unmount CIFS and NFS network file systems

- Configure systems to mount ext4, LUKS-encrypted, and network file systems automatically

- Extend existing unencrypted ext4 formatted logical volumes

- Create and configure set-GID directories for collaboration

- Create and manage access control lists (ACLs)

- Diagnose and correct file permission problems

- Create and configure LUKS-encrypted partitions and logical volumes to prompt for password and mount decrypted file system at boot

- Configure systems to mount file systems at boot by using Universally Unique ID (UUID) or labels

## CHAPTER 4

File Systems and Such

In the preceding chapter, we spent a lot of time working with partitions and setting up the layout of the different disks for the system. Now to be able to use these disks, we need to create a file system for each one, mount it somewhere on the file hierarchy, and set it so that it will always be available when the system boots up. This chapter also describes file permissions, access control lists (ACLs), and quotas. All these tools together help you manage your system and storage more efficiently.

File System Setup

In the preceding chapter, we set up different types of partitions for the system. The partitions are essentially the disk space carved out for you to use. Before the partitions can be used, however, you need to create a file system for each one. The default file system for RHEL5 is ext3 and has been changed to ext4 for RHEL6. Both of these file systems offer a journaling option, which has two main advantages. First, it can help speed up recovery if there is a disk failure because journaling file systems keep a "journal" of the file system's metadata. Second, it can check drives faster during the system boot process. The journaling feature isn't available on older file systems such as ext2. The creation of ext3 and ext4 file systems is exactly the same, so moving between the two shouldn't be a big deal. Because we made a mess with partitions in the preceding chapter, we need a new partition layout on which to create file systems. Create the partitions presented in Table 4-1 if they don't already exist.

Table 4-1 Partitions Needed

Partition	Size	Comment
/dev/hdb1	8GB	Normal partition
/dev/hdc1	4GB	Normal partition
/dev/hdc2	4GB	Swap partition
/dev/hdd*	5GB	Logical volume using LVM
/dev/hdd1	8GB	Normal partition

> **GENERAL INFO**
>
> There are many types of file systems, including ext2, ext3, ext4, ReiserFS, ZFS, XFS, and JFS.

Creating a File System

When you're creating a file system, there are many different ways to complete the same task. Following are the commands you can use to create and manage file systems:

mkfs	Creates an ext[2|3|4] partition
mkfs.ext2	Creates an ext2 partition
mkfs.ext3	Creates an ext3 partition
mkfs.ext4	Creates an ext4 partition

In the preceding chapter, we worked with basic partitions, RAID, and LVM. The creation of file systems on these different partitions all work the same way. For simplicity, let's stick with basic partitions and LVM. The first partition is hdb1, which takes up the whole disk (8GB in size). Let's create a new ext4 file system on this partition using the mkfs command.

Syntax: mkfs [options] DEVICE

Options:

-j	Creates a journal option (by default for ext4, used on ext2 only to upgrade)
-m	Specifies a reserved percentage of blocks on a file system
-L	Labels the volume

Step 1.   Create the first file system:

```
# mkfs.ext4 /dev/hdb1
mke2fs 1.41.12 (17-May-2010)
Filesystem label=
OS type: Linux
Block size=4096 (log=2)
Fragment size=4096 (log=2)
Stride=0 blocks, Stripe width=0 blocks
524288 inodes, 2096474 blocks
104823 blocks (5.00%) reserved for the super user
First data block=0
Maximum filesystem blocks=2147483648
64 block groups
32768 blocks per group, 32768 fragments per group
8192 inodes per group
```

```
        Superblock backups stored on blocks:
                32768, 98304, 163840, 229376, 294912, 819200, 884736,
        1605632

        Writing inode tables: done
        Creating journal (32768 blocks): done
        Writing superblocks and filesystem accounting information: done

        This filesystem will be automatically checked every 31 mounts or
        180 days, whichever comes first. Use tune2fs -c or -i to override.
```

Step 2.   You could also do the following:

```
# mkfs -t ext4 /dev/hdb1
mke2fs 1.41.12 (17-May-2010)
Filesystem label=
OS type: Linux
Block size=4096 (log=2)
Fragment size-4096 (log=2)
Stride=0 blocks, Stripe width=0 blocks
524288 inodes, 2096474 blocks
104823 blocks (5.00%) reserved for the super user
First data block=0
Maximum filesystem blocks=2147483648
64 block groups
32768 blocks per group, 32768 fragments per group
8192 inodes per group
Superblock backups stored on blocks:
        32768, 98304, 163840, 229376, 294912, 819200, 884736,
1605632

Writing inode tables: done
Creating journal (32768 blocks): done
Writing superblocks and filesystem accounting information: done

This filesystem will be automatically checked every 31 mounts or
180 days, whichever comes first. Use tune2fs -c or -i to override.
```

Both of these commands yield the same result.

Step 3.   You could also create a file system on an LVM partition in the same manner:

```
# mkfs.ext4 /dev/vg_group01/lvol0
```

One of the great things about the ext family file system is that you can upgrade from one file system type to another. For example, some older systems may be running ext2 file systems, which have no journal option. You could upgrade these to ext3 and get the added benefits from journaling.

NOTE: An amazing file system currently in the works is known as btrfs. Although there is no official release date at the time of writing, this new file system offers huge improvements over the current ext family. Some of these features include

- Snapshots

- Online file system maintenance

- The ability to roll back to ext file systems

- Improved performance

Let's make another partition with an ext2 file system and then upgrade it to see how this works.

Step 4.   Create an ext2 file system on the hdc1 partition, which is 4GB in size:

```
# mkfs.ext2 /dev/hdc1
mke2fs 1.41.12 (17-May-2010)
Filesystem label=
OS type: Linux
Block size=4096 (log=2)
Fragment size=4096 (log=2)
Stride=0 blocks, Stripe width=0 blocks
262944 inodes, 1050241 blocks
52512 blocks (5.00%) reserved for the super user
First data block=0
Maximum filesystem blocks=1077936128
33 block groups
32768 blocks per group, 32768 fragments per group
7968 inodes per group
Superblock backups stored on blocks:
        32768, 98304, 163840, 229376, 294912, 819200, 884736

Writing inode tables: done
Writing superblocks and filesystem accounting information: done

This filesystem will be automatically checked every 25 mounts or
180 days, whichever comes first. Use tune2fs -c or -i to override.
```

Now upgrade it to ext3 using the tune2fs command:

```
# tune2fs -j /dev/hdc1
tune2fs 1.41.12 (17-May-2010)
Creating journal inode: done
This filesystem will be automatically checked every 25 mounts or
180 days, whichever comes first. Use tune2fs -c or -i to override.
```

This command creates a journal on the ext2 file system, essentially converting it to ext3. We cover the tune2fs command more in the next section.

Creating a Swap

In Linux, a swap space is used as a "scratch space" for the system. When the system runs low on memory, it uses the swap space as a virtual memory area to swap items in and out of physical memory. Although it should not be used in place of physical memory because it is much slower, it's a critical piece of any system. There are two different types of swaps that you can have: file swap and partition swap. Following are the commands you use when working with a swap space:

mkswap	Creates a swap device
swapon	Enables a swap space
swapoff	Disables a swap space
dd	Wipes or zeroes out an area of the disk

First, create a partition swap with the remaining space on the hdc2 partition (don't forget that the swap partition is a different type from ext partitions). Use the mkswap command to create a swap space.

Syntax: swapon [options] DEVICE

Options:

-a	Enables all swap devices
-e	Silently skips devices that don't exist
-s	Verifies that the swap is running

Step 1.   Starting with the swapon command, check whether there are any current swap spaces on the system:

```
# swapon -s
Filename                Type            Size     Used    Priority
/dev/dm-1               partition       4128760  0       -1
```

Although a swap is displayed here, it is not one of the partitions that you created (this partition is from the original install on the system).

Syntax: mkswap [options] DEVICE

Options:

-c	Checks the device for bad blocks before creating the swap area

Step 2.   Create the swap space on /dev/hdc2:

```
# mkswap /dev/hdc2
Setting up swapspace version 1, size = 4184928 KiB
no label, UUID=aaf9b7ec-4e88-462b-a369-d63cf84ec626
```

After you create a swap space, you need to enable or activate it using the swapon command.

Step 3.   Enable the swap partition:

```
# swapon /dev/hdc2
```

Step 4.   Verify that the swap is running correctly:

```
# swapon -s
Filename                Type            Size      Used   Priority
/dev/dm-1               partition       4128760   0      -1
/dev/hdc2               partition       4184924   0      -2
```

Now that you have a partition swap set up, you can also set up a file swap. You can use the dd command to reserve space for another swap on the /dev/hdb1 partition. The dd command can be used for many different purposes and has a huge syntax, so I do not cover the whole thing here, just the specific options you use.

Step 5.   Reserve 1GB of space for the swap:

```
# dd if=/dev/zero of=/mnt/file_swap bs=1024 count=1000000
1000000+0 records in
1000000+0 records out
1024000000 bytes (1.0 GB) copied, 19.2931 seconds, 53.1 MB/s
```

Step 6.   Just as with partition swaps, you can now create a swap space specifying the device file just created:

```
# mkswap /mnt/file_swap
Setting up swapspace version 1, size = 999996 KiB
no label, UUID=e08a3e4d-8712-413d-9db7-c221cf5087a2
```

Step 7.   Enable the swap:

```
# swapon /mnt/file_swap
```

Step 8.   Again, you can verify that the swap is enabled:

```
# swapon -s
Filename                Type            Size      Used   Priority
/dev/dm-1               partition       4128760   0      -1
/dev/hdc2               partition       4184924   0      -2
/mnt/file_swap          file            999992    0      -3
```

If you want to turn off the swap, you can use the `swapoff` command. I do not show how to use it here because you just set up the swap space.

Syntax: `swapoff [options] DEVICE`

Options:

`-a`	Enables all swap devices
`-e`	Silently skips devices that don't exist
`-s`	Verifies that the swap is running

REAL-WORLD TIP

The big difference between the two swap types is that file swap is easier to manage because you can just move the swap file to another disk if you want. The swap partition would need to be removed, re-created, and so on. Although Red Hat recommends using a partition swap, file swaps are fast enough these days with less administrative overhead to not use them instead. One word of caution, though, is that you can use only one swap (of either type) per physical disk.

Mounting a File System

You have created your partitions and given them all a file system to use. Now you'd like to use them. No problem! Before you can use your new file systems, though, you need to connect them to the directory hierarchy through the use of the mount command. They can be mounted to any directory, which is referred to as a *mount point*. If you mount a file system on a directory that is not empty, everything within that directory becomes inaccessible. Therefore, you should create a new directory as a mount point for each of your file systems. There are only two commands for mounting file systems:

`mount`	Mounts a file system
`umount`	Unmounts a file system

So far, you have created a few file systems plus some swap partitions. Let's get these file systems mounted on the system.

Step 1. Start by going to the /opt directory, where you can make some directories to serve as mount points.

```
# cd /opt
# mkdir company_data
# mkdir backup
```

You have made two directories here that you can now use as mount points for the file systems. You can mount /dev/hdb1 to the company_data directory and /dev/hdc1 to the backup directory.

Syntax: `mount [options] DEVICE MOUNT_POINT`

Options:

`-r`	Mounts as read-only
`-w`	Mounts as read/write (the default)
`-L LABEL`	Mounts the file system with the name LABEL
`-v`	Provides verbose output

Step 2.   Mount the two file systems:

```
# mount /dev/hdb1 /opt/company_data
# mount /dev/hdc1 /opt/backup
```

Notice that you don't specify a file system type or any mount options. The reason is that the `mount` command automatically detects the file system type and mounts it for you. By default, the file system is also mounted with the `defaults` option. This is a good option to go with for most file systems because it covers many options you would normally want a file system mounted with. They include

`rw`	Mounts a file system as read/write
`suid`	Enables running setuid and setgid programs
`dev`	Interprets device files on the file system
`exec`	Permits binary file execution
`auto`	Mounts the file system when the -a option is specified
`nouser`	Disallows any normal user from (un)mounting the file system
`async`	Allows all file system I/O to occur asynchronously

With the file systems now mounted, you can use them as if they were a regular directory. Removing or unmounting a file system is a little more complex because users might be actively using that file system. You can use the `fuser` and `lsof` commands to check for open files and users that are currently using files on a file system that you are trying to unmount.

Syntax: `umount`

Options:

-f   Forces unmount

-v   Provides verbose output

Step 3.   Try to unmount the file system to see whether it is busy:

```
# umount /opt/backup
umount: /opt/backup: device is busy.
         (In some cases useful info about processes that use
          the device is found by lsof(8) or fuser(1))
```

You can see that the device is busy, so check out who is using it.

Syntax: `fuser [options] MOUNT_POINT | FILE SYSTEM`

Options:

-c   Checks the mounted file system

-k   Kills processes using the file system

-m   Shows all processes using the file system

-u   Displays user IDs

-v   Provides verbose output

Step 4.   Check to see what users are currently using the file system:

```
# fuser -cu /dev/hdc1
/opt/backup:           2337c(root)
```

You can also use the lsof command for more details. This is another command like dd that has a huge number of options that I can't possibly begin to cover in this book.

Step 5.   View all open files:

```
# lsof /dev/hdc1
COMMAND  PID USER   FD    TYPE DEVICE SIZE NODE NAME
bash    2337 root   cwd    DIR   22,1 4096    2 /opt/backup
lsof    4815 root   cwd    DIR   22,1 4096    2 /opt/backup
lsof    4816 root   cwd    DIR   22,1 4096    2 /opt/backup
```

You can either contact the users or terminate any open connections yourself.

Step 6.   To kill the open connections, you can use the fuser command again:

```
# fuser -ck /opt/backup
```

Step 7.   Now you should be able to unmount the file system:

```
# umount /opt/backup
```

> **WARNING:**   By killing all the open connections, you are essentially terminating anything that users have open. If they are working on something that has not been saved (such as a Word or PowerPoint document), all the changes are lost. It's good practice to send out notifications to your users to alert them when file system maintenance will occur; that way, they are responsible for saving and closing all their documents beforehand.

Now you know how to mount and unmount file systems, but there is something else you need to look at. If you reboot your system right now, all the file systems that you just mounted will no longer be available when the system comes back up. Why? The mount command is not persistent, so anything that is mounted with it will no longer be available across system reboots. I suppose you want to know how to fix that, right? The system looks at two config files. One deals with the mounting of file systems during the boot process, and the other keeps track of currently mounted file systems:

/etc/mtab   Contains a list of all currently mounted file systems

/etc/fstab   Mounts all listed file systems with given options at boot time

Let's look at the /etc/mtab file first. Every time you mount or unmount a file system, this file is updated to always reflect what is currently mounted on the system.

Step 1.   View the /etc/mtab file:

```
# cat /etc/mtab
/dev/mapper/vg_rhel01-lv_root / ext4 rw 0 0
proc /proc proc rw 0 0
sysfs /sys sysfs rw 0 0
devpts /dev/pts devpts rw,gid=5,mode=620 0 0
tmpfs /dev/shm tmpfs rw,rootcontext="system_u:object_r:tmpfs_t:s0"
0 0
/dev/hda1 /boot ext4 rw 0 0
none /proc/sys/fs/binfmt_misc binfmt_misc rw 0 0
sunrpc /var/lib/nfs/rpc_pipefs rpc_pipefs rw 0 0
/dev/hdb1 /opt/company_data ext4 rw 0 0
/dev/hdc1 /opt/backup ext3 rw 0 0
```

Step 2.   You can also query to check whether a particular file system is mounted with the grep command:

```
# cat /etc/mtab | grep backup
/dev/hdc1 /opt/backup ext3 rw 0 0
```

Step 3. Because you don't want to search this file or print it every time you need to view the mounted file systems, you can use the `mount` command with no options to also view the currently mounted file systems:

```
# mount
/dev/mapper/vg_rhel01-lv_root on / type ext4 (rw)
proc on /proc type proc (rw)
sysfs on /sys type sysfs (rw)
devpts on /dev/pts type devpts (rw,gid=5,mode=620)
tmpfs on /dev/shm type tmpfs
(rw,rootcontext="system_u:object_r:tmpfs_t:s0")
/dev/hda1 on /boot type ext4 (rw)
none on /proc/sys/fs/binfmt_misc type binfmt_misc (rw)
sunrpc on /var/lib/nfs/rpc_pipefs type rpc_pipefs (rw)
/dev/hdb1 on /opt/company_data type ext4 (rw)
/dev/hdc1 on /opt/backup type ext3 (rw)
```

Step 4. Go through the /etc/fstab file. The file follows this syntax:

```
<device>      <mount point>      <file system type> <mount options>
<write data during shutdown> <check sequence>
```

Step 5. View the /etc/fstab file:

```
# cat /etc/fstab
/dev/mapper/vg_rhel01-lv_root /                      ext4     defaults    1 1
UUID=5485df3d-7b48-42bf-b3dd-3dd84c6560fb /boot ext4      defaults    1 2
/dev/mapper/vg_rhel01-lv_swap swap                  swap     defaults    0 0
tmpfs                /dev/shm               tmpfs    defaults    0 0
devpts               /dev/pts    devpts               gid=5,mode=620  0 0
sysfs                /sys                   sysfs    defaults    0 0
proc                 /proc                  proc     defaults    0 0
```

The first three fields should be fairly obvious because you have been working with them throughout the chapter. The last three fields require some explaining, though. The fourth field defines the options that you can use to mount the file system. You have already seen that the `defaults` option actually includes many different options for the file system. Here is a complete list of all the options available:

rw   Mounts a file system as read/write

suid   Enables running setuid and setgid programs

dev   Interprets device files on the file system

exec   Permits binary file execution

auto   Mounts the file system when the -a option is specified

nouser   Disallows any normal user from (un)mounting the file system

async   Allows all file system I/O to occur asynchronously

The fifth field defines whether data should be backed up (also called *dumping*) before a system shutdown or reboot occurs. This field commonly uses a value of 1. A value of 0 might be used if the file system is a temporary storage space for files, such as /tmp. The last field defines the order in which file system checking should take place. For the root file system, the value should be 1; everything else should be 2. If you have a removable file system (such as a CD-ROM or external hard drive), you can define a value of 0 and skip the checking altogether. Because you want the two file systems created earlier to be mounted when the system boots, you can add two definitions for them here.

Step 6.   Open the /etc/fstab file for editing:

```
# nano /etc/fstab
```

Step 7.   Add the following line for the /dev/hdc1 file system:

```
/dev/hdc1    /opt/backup              ext3    defaults      0 0
```

While you have this file open, you should also define the swap file system as well (you don't think I forgot about that, do you?). You have one swap partition and one swap file. The order of the swap file matters because it indicates the order in which the devices are used by the system itself.

Step 8.   Add the following line for the swap:

```
/dev/hdc2    swap                     swap    defaults      0 0
```

Now you can save the file and exit. You don't even have to reboot to test it!

Step 9.   You can use the mount command with the -a option to remount all file systems defined in the /etc/fstab file:

```
# mount -a
```

Now all your file systems should be mounted and available for use.

> **NOTE:**   Although we have been talking a lot about file systems as they relate to disk drives, the mount command can be used to mount other types of file systems as well. For example, you usually have a /media directory off the root partition that is

commonly used to mount the CD/DVD-ROM drive. You can use the mount command with the o option. Mount the /dev/cd-rom device to the /media directory like this:

```
# mount -o loop /dev/cd-rom /media
```

Extra File System Commands

From time to time, you need to perform maintenance on your file systems to ensure reliability and optimal performance. Usually, for any maintenance purposes, you take the file system offline by unmounting it. Suppose your boss just came in and told you that you need to perform maintenance on the /dev/hdb1 file system this weekend.

Step 1. Take your file system offline:

```
# umount /dev/hdb1
```

Now let's look at some of the different maintenance tasks you can perform. Here are the file system maintenance commands you have to work with:

blkid	Displays block device attributes
df	Shows usage of the file system(s)
e2fsck	Checks ext file systems
e2label	Modifies the label on an ext file system
findfs	Allows you to locate a specific file system
resize2fs	Resizes an ext file system
tune2fs	Tunes ext file system attributes

First, you need to label the file system. Labels enable you to determine a specific file system more easily with a common name, instead of /dev/hdc1. An added benefit is the system's being able to keep its label even if the underlying disk is switched with a new one. To label a file system, use the e2label command.

Syntax: e2label DEVICE

Step 2. Let's label the file system CData to denote that it's the company data file system:

```
# e2label /dev/hdb1 CData
```

Step 3. You can use the same command to also verify:

```
# e2label /dev/hdb1
CData
```

At this point, you have only a handful of file systems, so it isn't too hard to find the one you're looking for. If this were not the case, you could use the `findfs` command to search through the labels of your file systems and return the one you are looking for.

Syntax: `findfs LABEL=<label>|UUID=<uuid>`

Step 4. Find the file system you just labeled:

```
# findfs LABEL=CData
/dev/hdb1
```

When you verify that the label exists and it is the file system that you are looking for, you can also query more information about the device using the `blkid` command.

Syntax: `blkid [options]`

Options:

`-s`	Shows specified tag(s)
`dev`	Specifies the device to probe

Step 5. Combine the `blkid` command with `grep` for specific results:

```
# blkid | grep CData
/dev/hdb1: LABEL="CData" UUID="2752ffb4-2bca-41c6-a569-
f3563f6e884d" TYPE="ext4"
```

Step 6. When you finish with your maintenance, you can remount the file system with the new label instead of the device path:

```
# mount LABEL=CData /opt/company_data
```

GENERAL INFO
In Red Hat, you use the `LABEL=` syntax. If you're using an Ubuntu or Debian system, however, you can use `-L` instead to achieve the same results.

You could even update the /etc/fstab file to use the label information instead of the device path. Don't remount your file system again just yet; you still have some more work to do. In the preceding chapter, we looked at the great benefits of using LVM for partitions, and the biggest benefit was being able to extend partitions. If you already have free space on your partition, you can extend your file system. However, if you don't have free space, you can add a new disk, extend your LVM partition, and then extend your file system. This benefit doesn't work on basic partitions. To make a basic partition larger, you have to actually destroy the whole partition, increase its size, and then re-create the file system. Because the /dev/hdd drive is set up with LVM, let's use it for this example. Use the resize2fs command to extend the file system. Before extending the file system, however, you should always ensure the integrity of the file system first with the e2fsck command.

Syntax: e2fsck [options] DEVICE

Options:

-p	Automatically repairs (no questions)
-n	Makes no changes to the file system
-y	Assumes "yes" to all questions
-f	Forces checking of the file system
-v	Provides verbose output

Step 7. Check the file system:

```
# e2fsck -f /dev/vg_group01/lvol0
e2fsck 1.41.12 (17-May-2010)
/dev/vg_group01/lvol0: clean, 11/320000 files, 55366/1280000 blocks
```

Syntax: resize2fs [options] DEVICE

Options:

-p	Prints percentage as task completes
-f	Forces the command to proceed

Step 8. Extend the underlying logical volume:

```
# lvextend -L 6000 /dev/vg_group01/lvol0
  Extending logical volume lvol0 to 5.86 GiB
  Logical volume lvol0 successfully resized
```

Step 9. Now you can extend the file system:

```
# resize2fs -p /dev/vg_group01/lvol0
resize2fs 1.41.12 (17-May-2010)
Resizing the filesystem on /dev/vg_group01/lvol0 to 1536000 (4k)
blocks.
Begin pass 1 (max = 7)
Extending the inode table
XXXXXXXXXXXXXXXXXXXXXXXXXXXXXXXXXXXXXXXXXXX
The filesystem on /dev/vg_group01/lvol0 is now 1536000 blocks long.
```

Step 10.   Now that your maintenance is complete, remount the file system:
```
# mount LABEL=CData /opt/company_data
```

Step 11.   You can use the mount command to verify it mounted successfully:

```
# mount
/dev/mapper/vg_rhel01-lv_root on / type ext4 (rw)
proc on /proc type proc (rw)
sysfs on /sys type sysfs (rw)
devpts on /dev/pts type devpts (rw,gid=5,mode=620)
tmpfs on /dev/shm type tmpfs
(rw,rootcontext="system_u:object_r:tmpfs_t:s0")
/dev/hda1 on /boot type ext4 (rw)
none on /proc/sys/fs/binfmt_misc type binfmt_misc (rw)
sunrpc on /var/lib/nfs/rpc_pipefs type rpc_pipefs (rw)
/dev/hdc1 on /opt/backup type ext3 (rw)
/dev/hdb1 on /opt/company_data type ext4 (rw)
```

You also can use the df command to view the usage information for your file systems. This should also reflect the additional space that you just added to the CData file system.

Syntax: df [options]

Options:

-h   Specifies human-readable format

-l   Indicates local file systems only

-T   Prints the file system type

Step 12.   Check how much free space you have available:
```
# df -h
Filesystem                     Size Used Avail Use% Mounted on
/dev/mapper/vg_rhel01-lv_root   16G 2.3G   13G  16% /
tmpfs                         1004M    0 1004M   0% /dev/shm
/dev/hda1                      485M  30M  430M   7% /boot
/dev/hdc1                      4.0G 137M  3.7G   4% /opt/backup
/dev/hdb1                      7.9G 146M  7.4G   2% /opt/company_data
```

Encryption with LUKS

Linux Unified Key Setup, or LUKS, is a disk encryption for Linux. LUKS uses block device encryption, which protects the system when it is off (particularly if the drive is removed or stolen). When installing RHEL6 for the first time, you come to the partition creation screen where you can also choose to use encryption on your partitions. If you select this option, you are required to enter a password. You will be prompted for this password every time the system boots to decrypt the partitions for use by the system.

> **WARNING:**   Do not lose this password! If you do, anything you have encrypted will be completely inaccessible.

Just because your partitions are encrypted with LUKS doesn't ensure that they are protected when the system is turned on. LUKS protects your system only when it is off (or if the partition isn't mounted as in single-user mode). When the system has booted and the partition is decrypted (which it has to do to make the data accessible), it is no longer protected by LUKS. You can use file-based encryption in combination with LUKS to provide additional security when the system is on. Later in this chapter, we discuss GnuPG, which is an open source file-based encryption using PGP.

Creating Encrypted Partitions

Even after you have installed Red Hat, you can still create encrypted partitions. By default, RHEL6 uses AES 128-bit encryption with 256SHA hashing. There are other ciphers available as well:

- AES
- Twofish
- Serpent
- Cast5
- Cast6

This section looks at how to encrypt a partition after the system has been installed and booted. For the example here, I have created a new virtual hard drive on RHEL02 that is 4GB in size (/dev/hdb1).

> **WARNING:**   Creating an encrypted partition erases all data on the partition. Make sure that you back up any data before proceeding.

Step 1.   On RHEL02, you need to boot into runlevel 1 to create the encrypted partition (similar to performing file system maintenance):
```
# telinit 1
```

Step 2.   After the system boots, make sure that the partition isn't mounted:
```
# umount /dev/hdb1
```

Step 3.   Verify that the partition is truly unmounted:

```
# mount | grep /dev/hdb1
```

Step 4.   Fill your partition with random data; this can take a long time to complete:

```
# dd if=/dev/urandom of=/dev/hdb1
```

Step 5.   After the random data is finished, you need to initialize your partition:

```
# cryptsetup — verbose — verify-passphrase luksFormat /dev/hdb1
```

```
WARNING!
========
This will overwrite data on /dev/hdb1 irrevocably.

Are you sure? (Type uppercase yes): YES
Enter LUKS passphrase:
Verify passphrase:
Command successful.
```

Step 6.   Open the newly encrypted device and give it a name (opt_data for the example here):

```
# cryptsetup luksOpen /dev/hdb1 opt_data
Enter passphrase for /dev/hdb1:
```

Step 7.   Verify that the encrypted partition is there:

```
# ls -l /dev/mapper | grep opt_data
lrwxrwxrwx. 1 root root       7 Jan 27 18:36 opt_data -> ../dm-2
```

Step 8.   Create a new file system:

```
# mkfs.ext4 /dev/mapper/opt_data
mke2fs 1.41.12 (17-May-2010)
Filesystem label=
OS type: Linux
Block size=4096 (log=2)
Fragment size=4096 (log=2)
Stride=0 blocks, Stripe width=0 blocks
524288 inodes, 2095962 blocks
104798 blocks (5.00%) reserved for the super user
First data block=0
Maximum filesystem blocks=2147483648
64 block groups
32768 blocks per group, 32768 fragments per group
8192 inodes per group
Superblock backups stored on blocks:
        32768, 98304, 163840, 229376, 294912, 819200, 884736,
1605632

Writing inode tables: done
Creating journal (32768 blocks): done
Writing superblocks and filesystem accounting information: done
```

```
This filesystem will be automatically checked every 25 mounts or
180 days, whichever comes first. Use tune2fs -c or -i to override.
```

Step 9. After the file system is created, you need to mount it again:

```
# mkdir /opt/opt_data
# mount /dev/mapper/opt_data /opt/opt_data
```

Step 10. You need to add this encrypted partition to the /etc/crypttab file:

```
# nano /etc/crypttab
opt_data /dev/hdb1 none
```

Step 11. Update your /etc/fstab file to reflect the changes:

```
# nano /etc/fstab
/dev/mapper/opt_data            /opt_data           ext4      defaults 1 2
```

Step 12. At this point, you should restore the default SELinux security contexts:
```
# /sbin/restorecon -v -R /opt_data
```

Step 13. Now that you are finished, reboot the system:

```
# shutdown -r now
```

You need to enter a lot of commands to create and set up an encrypted partition. Don't let this overwhelm you, though, because this process is actually not that difficult after you have created one or two encrypted partitions. The most important point is that you need to go through all the steps and ensure that everything is in place before rebooting the system. Because you have now added an entry to the /etc/crypttab file, the system asks you for the password to your encrypted partition. If you had created a backup, you could also restore it at this point.

REAL-WORLD TIP

You can use the following command to verify that the partition is, in fact, encrypted:

```
# cryptsetup isLuks /dev/hdb1 && echo Success
# cryptsetup luksDump /dev/hdb1
```

REAL-WORLD TIP

If you want to use a UUID to mount the partition in /etc/fstab (for stability), you can find the UUID of the encrypted device with the following:

```
# cryptsetup luksUUID /dev/hdb1
```

Mounting LUKS at Boot

As you have already seen, the /etc/fstab file is responsible for keeping track of which partitions are mounted during boot. When you are working with an encrypted partition, nothing really changes, except that you need to make an entry in the /etc/crypttab file as well. This /etc/crypttab file uses the following syntax:

```
<mount point>          <partition>          none
```

When the system boots, it checks the /etc/crypttab file to see whether it contains any entries. If it does, the system prompts you for a password to decrypt the partition during boot.

Managing File System Quotas

As you've done in all the sections so far, you need to install the required packages before you can use quotas on your system.

Step 1.   To install the quota package, use the following:

```
# yum install - y quota
```

Step 2.   Verify that the package was installed successfully:

```
# rpm -qa | grep quota
quota-3.17-10.el6.x86_64
```

Although Red Hat supports quotas in the kernel by default, it is always a good idea to verify things for yourself. Should you ever find yourself working on a system with a custom kernel, you will know how to verify whether the kernel supports quotas.

Step 3.   You can query quota support from the kernel with the following command:

```
# grep -i config_quota /boot/config-`uname -r`
CONFIG_QUOTA=y
CONFIG_QUOTACTL=y
```

You should see a y next to the options to show that the kernel does indeed support quotas. After verifying that the package is installed and that the kernel does support quotas, you can start configuring the system to use them. For a working example, you can configure quotas on the /opt/company_data file system so that you can limit the amount of data that users can store in the company's directory.

Setting Up Quotas

To start setting up quotas, let's look at some of the commands you can use with them:

quotaon	Turns on quota tracking
quotaoff	Turns off quota tracking

edquota	Edits the settings of a user's quota
quota	Allows each user to see his disk consumption
repquota	Generates a report of quota usage
quotacheck	Initializes a quota database

Now that you have a listing of the commands you can use, you first need to edit the /etc/fstab file to specify which file systems you want to utilize quotas. You can have quotas that limit users, groups, or both. For this chapter, you can enable both by adding the usrquota option and the grpquota option to the /detc/fstab file. You don't have to enable both, but it doesn't hurt to enable them both in case you find a need for the other later.

Step 1.   In the /etc/fstab file, edit the following line:
```
/dev/hdb1      /opt/company_data           ext4
defaults,usrquota,grpquota      1 2
```

Step 2.   Save and close the file.

> **WARNING:** When you're working on files in text editors, they often have a bad habit of wrapping the line you're working on. Make sure that this DOES NOT happen! If a line wraps in the /etc/fstab file, it will be read as two different lines. This makes your /etc/fstab file corrupt, and your system will not boot! This is a very common cause of issues when it comes to editing text files. You see this problem come to light again when dealing with kickstart files in Chapter 8, "Network Installs."

You now need to remount the /opt/company_data file system before the changes take effect.

Step 3.   You can accomplish this by using the mount command:
```
# mount -o remount /opt/company_data
```

Step 4.   You can verify that the mount and quota options took correctly by using the following:
```
# mount | grep company_data
/dev/hdb1 on /opt/company_data type ext4 (rw,usrquota,grpquota)
```

With the quota options now in place on the /opt/company_data file system, you can begin setting up quotas for users. There are two files that maintain quotas for users and groups:

| aquota.users | User quota file |
| aquota.group | Group quota file |

These two files are automatically created in the top-level directory of the file system where you are turning on quotas—in this case, the /opt/company_data file system. To start the quota system, you use the quotacheck command.

Syntax: `quotacheck [options] <partition>`

-c	Don't read existing quota files
-u	Checks only user quotas
-g	Checks only group quotas
-m	Doesn't remount the file system as read-only
-v	Provides verbose output

The quotacheck command shouldn't be run on file systems that are actively being used because it can cause corruption. Due to this logic, the quotacheck command tries to mount the file systems as read-only to prevent damage. Because you don't want the /opt/company_data partition to become read-only, you can use the -m option. You also know that there are no pre-existing quota files, so there is no chance that they might become corrupt.

Step 5.   Create the quota files:

```
# quotacheck -ugm /opt/company_data/
```

Step 6.   Verify that the quota files were created successfully:

```
# ls /opt/company_data/
aquota.group   aquota.user   lost+found
```

Enabling Quotas

Normally, you would have to call the quotaon and quotaoff commands to have the quota system enforced, but they are automatically called when the system boots up and shuts down. Also, the quotaon command can't be called until the quota files are created in the root directory of the quota file system.

Step 1.   Run the command manually the first time just to make sure that quotas are turned on:

```
# quotaon -v /opt/company_data/
/dev/hdb1 [/opt/company_data]: group quotas turned on
/dev/hdb1 [/opt/company_data]: user quotas turned on
```

Let's briefly discuss the two different limits you can have when dealing with quotas:

- **Soft Limit**—Has a grace period that acts as an alarm, signaling when you are reaching your limit. If your grace period expires, you are required to delete files until you are once again under your limit. If you don't specify a grace period, the soft limit is the maximum number of files you can have.

- **Hard Limit**—Required only when a grace period exists for soft limits. If the hard limit does exist, it is the maximum limit that you can hit before your grace period expires on the soft limit.

With these two limits in mind, you can begin creating limits for your users. First, you should create a quota for user01. Use the `edquota` command to set it up. Because users don't have access to this file system yet, they aren't taking up any space. To work with quotas for users and groups, you need to do some conversions in your head here. Each block is equal to 1KB. If you aren't good at the conversions, remember that 1,000KB = 1MB. So here you are taking up only 40KB worth of space. If you also want to restrict the number of files that user01 can create, you can set a soft and hard limit on the inodes side. For purposes of this example, let's create a limit only on space for user01 at 20MB. Also, let's set a hard limit of 25MB. Set the limits for user01 by using the `edquota` command.

NOTE: Although the users we describe in this section (user01, user02, and user03) may not yet exist on your system, you will create them later.

Syntax: `edquota [-u | -g] [username | groupname]`

Step 2.   Change the line for the /dev/hdb1 file system to look like the following:

```
# edquota -u user01
Disk quotas for user user01 (uid 500):
  Filesystem     blocks     soft     hard     inodes     soft     hard
  /dev/hdb1          0    20000    25000          0        0        0
```

Step 3.   Save your changes and close the file.

EXAM TIP

By default, the `edquota` command uses the `vi` text editor. If you're not familiar with it, you need to press `i` to enter insert mode. In insert mode, you can edit the text of the file. When finished, press Esc to leave insert mode. Then you need to press : (colon) to enter a command. You should enter wq and press Enter to write the changes to the file and quit the editor. If you make a mistake and don't want to save the changes, you can also press q!.

Now that user01 has a quota, you should also set a grace period for this user (because you specified a hard limit).

Step 4.   Again, you use the edquota command, but with a different option:

```
# edquota -t
Grace period before enforcing soft limits for users:
Time units may be: days, hours, minutes, or seconds
   Filesystem              Block grace period      Inode grace period
   /dev/hdb1                    7days                   7days
```

Here, the current value is seven days for the block grace period. You should not give your users that much time to get their act together, so drop that limit to two days.

Step 5.   Edit your line to look like the following:

```
Grace period before enforcing soft limits for users:
Time units may be: days, hours, minutes, or seconds
   Filesystem              Block grace period      Inode grace period
   /dev/hdb1                    2days                   2days
```

Step 6.   Save your changes and close the file.

Both user02 and user03 now have the exact same quota in place that user01 has.

WARNING: Notice there is no space between the number and time (days, hours, and so on). This is on purpose because this is the format of this file. Don't put a space in between them. On RHEL5 and RHEL6, any space is removed automatically, but on older systems, it isn't. To avoid causing any errors, you should get in the habit of not using spaces at all.

TIP: The edquota command offers a pretty cool feature. After you configure a quota and your limits for a single user, you can actually copy this over to other users as if it were a template. To do this, specify the user you want to use as a template first and call the edquota command with the -p option.

```
# edquota -up user01 user02 user03
```

Now with the quotas in place for users, let's start looking at some of the reporting options available to check on users.

Quota Usage Reports

You can use the repquota command to collect information about file system quotas.

Syntax: repquota [options] <partition>

Options:

-a   Reports on all non-NFS file systems with quotas turned on

-u   Reports on user quotas

-g   Reports on group quotas

-v   Provides verbose output

Step 1.   Use the repquota command to collect some information on the user quotas you have recently implemented:

```
# repquota -uv /opt/company_data/
*** Report for user quotas on device /dev/hdb1
Block grace time: 2days; Inode grace time: 2days
                                Block limits                    File limits
User            used    soft    hard   grace    used   soft
hard   grace
----------------------------------------------------------------
root       —   142656      0       0                4      0       0
user01     —        0   20000   25000                0      0       0

Statistics:
Total blocks: 7
Data blocks: 1
Entries: 2
Used average: 2.000000
```

Here, a nicely detailed report shows how quotas are doing for each individual user. Later, when we cover job automation, it might be helpful to set up a job for a daily or weekly report on user and group quota usage. This allows you, as an administrator, to keep an eye on your file systems and make sure that they aren't getting out of hand. If you are logged in as a user, you also have the option of running the quota command to view your individual usage on the file system.

File System Security

Linux, like most operating systems, has a standard set of file permissions. Aside from these, it also has a more refined set of permissions implemented through access control lists. This section covers both of these topics and how they are used to implement file system security for files, directories, and more. In Chapter 7, "User

Administration," we also look at how to use these permissions to allow group collaboration, which is an important part of any real-world network.

Setting Up ACLs

Now let's discuss ACLs.

Step 1.   As usual, begin by installing the required package:

```
# yum install -y acl
```

Step 2.   Verify the package installation:

```
# rpm -qa | grep acl
libacl-2.2.49-4.el6.x86_64
acl-2.2.49-4.el6.x86_64
```

Because we covered file permissions in the introduction, you should have a firm grasp on file permissions. In this section, you enable and set up access control lists. They are an extended set of permissions on files and directories that give more granular control when needed. Two commands control ACLs: getfacl and setfacl. When you use the ls -l or ll command, a plus sign (+) on the side of the permission indicates that an ACL has been set.

Step 3.   Before you can even use ACLs, however, you need to make sure that the file system has been mounted with the ACL parameter:

```
# mount | grep acl
```

Because nothing is returned, you know that all currently mounted file systems do not have ACLs set up to be used. Therefore, you need to fix this. Suppose you want /dev/hdc1 (/opt/backup) to be able to use ACLs so that you can make use of extended file permissions for your users. To mount the file system with the ACL option, you need to unmount it and then mount it again (also known as *remounting*).

Step 4.   You can accomplish this using the following:

```
# mount -t ext4 -o acl,remount /dev/hdc1 /opt/backup/
```

Step 5.   If your file system isn't already mounted, you could also use the following:

```
# mount -t ext4 -o acl /dev/hdc1 /opt/backup
```

Step 6.   To verify, you can use the previous command:

```
# mount | grep acl
/dev/hdc1 on /opt/backup type ext4 (rw,acl)
```

You can now see that this file system includes the ACL option. You might be wondering whether this ACL option will remain when the system reboots. If you recall, we talked about the /etc/fstab file at the beginning of this chapter. For the ACL option to always be available, you need to add it to the /etc/fstab file so that it is persistent across reboots.

Step 7. Adjust the following line in your /etc/fstab file:

```
/dev/hdc1      /opt/backup      ext4      defaults,acl      1 2
```

Step 8. Save and close the file.

Step 9. To make the changes take effect, you need to remount the file system:

```
# mount -o remount /opt/backup/
```

Step 10. You can now verify that your file system has the ACL option:

```
# mount | grep -i acl
/dev/hdc1 on /opt/backup type ext3 (rw,acl)
```

The file system is now mounted properly with the ACL option, so you can start to look at the management commands that pertain to ACLs:

getfacl   Obtains the ACL from a file or directory

setfacl   Sets or modifies an ACL

Step 1. Create a sample file on which you can test an ACL in the /opt/backup directory:

```
# cd /opt/backup
# touch file1
```

Now you can use the getfacl command to view the ACL currently associated with the file.

Syntax: getfacl [options] file

Options:

-d   Displays the default ACL

-R   Recurses into subdirectories

Step 2. Grab the default ACL information from the file you just created:

```
# getfacl file1
# file: file1
# owner: root
# group: root
user::rw-
```

```
group::r—
other::r—
```

There's nothing really exciting here other than the default permissions. You can use the `setfacl` command now to create some additional ACLs on this file.

Syntax: `setfacl [options] file`

Options:

`-m`	Modifies an ACL
`-x`	Removes an ACL
`-n`	Doesn't recalculate the mask
`-R`	Recurses into subdirectories

Step 3. Set the test file so that user01 also has access to this file:

```
# setfacl -m u:user01:rwx /opt/backup/file1
```

Step 4. Now check the ACL permissions again:

```
# getfacl file1
# file: file1
# owner: root
# group: root
user::rw-
user:user01:rwx
group::r—
mask::rwx
other::r—
```

You can see that user01 has now been added to the list as having read, write, and execute permissions on this file. Obviously, you need to take into account parent directory permissions before going into more complex setups with ACLs. Suppose you just terminated user01 and need to remove his permissions from this critical file that you had previously granted permission to.

Step 5. Use the `setfacl` command again to remove the ACL for user01:

```
# setfacl -x u:user01 /opt/backup/file1
```

Step 6. Verify that the ACL has been removed:

```
# getfacl file1
# file: file1
# owner: root
# group: root
user::rw-
group::r—
```

```
mask::r—
other::r—
```

Step 7.   If you have multiple ACLs set up on a single file, you can remove them all with the -b option instead of removing them one by one:

```
# setfacl -b testfile
```

File permissions and ACLs can get really complex if they aren't thought out ahead of time. Make sure that you understand normal file permissions well because they are a key part of being a system administrator. In the real world, using ACLs will help you manage files between users more effectively and will save you from a permissions headache later.

GnuPG

GnuPG is open source file-based encryption software that uses the PGP encryption. One common use for PGP encryption is sending email, allowing you to authenticate who you are. You can also use it to encrypt files for protection when the system is running. You can use the seahorse package to work with PGP encryption either at the command line or with a GUI.

Step 1.   Install the required package:

```
# yum install -y seahorse
```

Step 2.   Verify the package installation:

```
# rpm -qa | grep seahorse
seahorse-2.28.1-4.el6.x86_64
```

Before you can begin encrypting things, you need to create a private key, which is used to encrypt your documents. You also get a public key, which others can use to decrypt your documents.

Step 3.   Generate your private/public key pair:

```
# gpg —key-gen
```

When the key generation is complete, you can begin encrypting files with your newly created private key.

Using AutoFS

To make your life as a system administrator easier, you also can use AutoFS, which is an automated file system. The benefit of this is that remote resources can be mounted automatically and without the need for the root user to perform the mount. This is done through the use of a special config file called maps. There are two key files to know when working with AutoFS:

/etc/sysconfig/autofs   Main config file for the service

/etc/auto.master   Master map file

In the /etc/sysconfig/autofs file, you can define some default values for the service, including timeout, name of the maps file, logging, and more. Following is what the file should look like by default:

```
# cat /etc/sysconfig/autofs | grep -v ^#
TIMEOUT=300
BROWSE_MODE="no"
MOUNT_NFS_DEFAULT_PROTOCOL=4
USE_MISC_DEVICE="yes"
```

These values are good for the default configuration with comments and other options commented out within the file. You just need the basic service, which is what these default values provide. When you're working with AutoFS, four different map files are available:

master   Default master map file that contains other types of map files

special   Map file that allows for group mounts without defining each one

direct   Map file that requires a manual restart before mount changes are recognized

indirect Map file used to mount resources under a common parent directory

Here is what my /etc/auto.master file looks like:

```
# cat auto.master | grep -v ^#
/misc    /etc/auto.misc
/net     -hosts
+auto.master
```

The first entry here is an indirect map. The first part of the entry (/misc) defines the common parent directory under which you'd like to have all your resources mounted. Next, you specify the file that holds the actual resources, including their locations, permissions, and a name. The /etc/auto.misc already exists and contains some samples we can look at as well:

```
# cat /etc/auto.misc
#
# $Id: auto.misc,v 1.2 2003/09/29 08:22:35 raven Exp $
#
# This is an automounter map and it has the following format
# key [ -mount-options-separated-by-comma ] location
# Details may be found in the autofs(5) manpage
```

```
cd                    -fstype=iso9660,ro,nosuid,nodev :/dev/cdrom

# the following entries are samples to pique your imagination
#linux          -ro,soft,intr           ftp.example.org:/pub/linux
#boot           -fstype=ext2            :/dev/hda1
#floppy         -fstype=auto            :/dev/fd0
#floppy         -fstype=ext2            :/dev/fd0
#e2floppy       -fstype=ext2            :/dev/fd0
#jaz            -fstype=ext2            :/dev/hdc1
#removable      -fstype=ext2            :/dev/hdd
```

This file uses the following syntax when creating an entry:

```
[relative pathname]  [mount options]         [location]
```

You can see that although most things are commented out here, the CD-ROM drive is actually defined. This allows for the CD drive to be unmounted when it is not in use.

Step 1.   On the Client01 system, you can create the following entry in the /etc/auto.misc file:

```
company_data -rw,sync                    rhel01:/opt/company_data
```

Step 2.   Save the file and reload the autofs service:

```
# service autofs reload
Reloading maps
```

Now if you navigate to /misc, you see another directory called company_data. When this directory is accessed, it mounts the remote NFS share from RHEL01 automatically to /misc/company_data. As you can see, this capability is really convenient for you, as a system administrator, to make multiple resources available to your different clients.

NOTE: One point to note about using indirect maps is that they allow for the use of two wildcard characters. If you would like to mount user home directories, you can create the following entry in an indirect map file:

```
*   -rw,sync         &:/home/&
```

The system makes the correct replacement for the username and automatically searches all available NFS servers for the right resource. This allows for easier centralized management for home directories on NFS servers. Although there are no examples in the default /etc/auto.master file, direct maps are similar to indirect maps.

Step 3.   In the /etc/auto.master file, you would create an entry like the following:

```
/-    /etc/auto.direct_maps
```

This tells the /etc/auto.master file to reference /etc/auto.direct_maps for additional information on direct maps. When creating indirect maps, you specify the relative pathname for each map, but with direct maps, you just specify the absolute path for each map you'd like. For example, on the Client01 system, say you want to map the /opt/company_data directory from RHEL01 to the local /usr directory instead of /misc.

Step 4.   You need to create the /etc/auto.direct_maps file and add the following entry:

```
/usr/data       -rw,sync                 rhel01:/opt/company_data
```

Step 5.   Save the file and reload the `autofs` service:

```
# service autofs reload
Reloading maps
```

Now the local path /usr/data on Client01 automounts to /opt/company_data on RHEL01. Make sure that you understand the difference between direct and indirect maps when working with `autofs`.

Going back to the /etc/auto.master file one last time, look at the second entry, which is a special map. The special map looks for all NFS servers available on the network and mounts all resources available under the directory specified—/net in this case. This capability is useful if you want to map multiple NFS resources to a client without needing to create an individual mapping for each one, but this is not a good idea if you have multiple NFS servers with many resources. Using `autofs` isn't too hard but requires a little practice to make the mounts automated the way you'd like them to be.

Summary

In this chapter, we covered all sorts of topics pertaining to file systems and file security. We looked at using basic permissions, adding ACLs, and restricting user space with quotas. At this point, we have completed the setup of all disks, partitions, and file systems, so in the next chapter we move on to other core parts of the operating system, such as networking. You should make sure you are comfortable working with file systems and file security before moving on from this chapter.

Review Questions

1. What is the difference between an ext2 and ext3 file system?

2. What command can you use to create a file system?

3. Can you grow a file system?

4. What is the superblock used for?

5. What is a swap? Is it created as a partition or device file?

6. How can you check the currently mounted file systems?

7. What file needs to be edited so that the system will mount a file system at boot time?

8. Before you work with quotas, what do you need to do to the file system?

9. What command do you use to change the permissions on a file or directory? To change ownership?

10. Explain the difference between soft and hard limits in quotas.

11. What command do you use to report information on quota usage?

12. Before you work with ACLs, what do you need to do to the file system?

13. What command can you use to view the current ACL on a file?

Answers to Review Questions

1. An ext3 file system has journaling built in to it, whereas the ext2 file system doesn't.

2. `mkfs.ext4`

3. Yes. Use the `resize2fs` command to grow a file system.

4. The superblock is a structure that contains metadata of the file system. If this becomes corrupt, you are in trouble.

5. A swap is scratch space on your file system used as virtual memory. A swap can be created as a partition or a device file.

6. The `mount` command lists all currently mounted file systems.

7. The /etc/fstab file.

8. The file system where quotas will be implemented must be mounted with the `usrquota` and `grpquota` options before quotas will work properly.

9. The `chmod` command is used to change the permissions of files and directories. The `chown` command is used to change the ownership of files and directories.

10. A soft limit acts like an alarm, signaling you when you are reaching your limit. If you don't specify a grace period, the soft limit is the max. A hard limit is required only when a grace period exists. It is the max limit you can hit before your grace period expires.

11. `repquota`

12. The file system where ACLs will be implemented must be mounted with the
`acl` option before ACLs will work properly.

13. `getfacl`

Lab 4

Task 1 – Creating a File System

Step 1.   Erase all existing partitions on /dev/hdb, /dev/hdc, and /dev/hdd.

Step 2.   Create the following layout on /dev/hdb:
  a. Create two partitions on disk /dev/hdb.
  b. Each partition should be 3GB in size.
  c. Create an ext4 file system on each partition.

Step 3.   Create the following layout on /dev/hdc:
  a. Create a single partition on disk /dev/hdc.
  b. The partition should take up the whole disk.
  c. Create an ext2 file system on the partition.
  d. Upgrade the partition to ext3.

Step 4.   Create the following layout on /dev/hdd:
  a. Create a single partition on disk /dev/hdd.
  b. The partition should be 2GB in size.
  c. Create a swap file system on the partition.
  d. Enable the swap.
  e. Edit the /etc/fstab file so that the swap is available during boot.

The task is complete when all partitions, file systems, and swap space can be verified. All file systems and swap space must survive a system reboot.

Task 2 – Is Your File System There?

Step 1.   Create the following directories on your system:
   a. /opt/weekly_backups
   b. /opt/home_drives
   c. /opt/storage01

Step 2.   Mount the following file system to the locations just created:
   a. Mount /dev/hdb1 on /opt/home_drives.
   b. Mount /dev/hdb2 on /opt/weekly_backups.
   c. Mount /dev/hdc1 on /opt/storage01.

All file systems and mount points must exist and be available when the system boots. The task is complete when the mount points and file systems can be verified after a system reboot.

Task 3 – User Quotas

Step 1.   Create a quota with the following guidelines:
   a. Only user quotas are required.
   b. Quotas should be active on the /dev/hdb1 file system only.
   c. Set a soft limit of 50MB for user01.
   d. Set a hard limit of 50MB for user01.

The task is complete when the quota can be verified.

This chapter covers the following subjects:

- **Setting Up Networking**—This section covers the basics of networking.

- **Troubleshooting Network Connections**—This section describes the utilities and steps to troubleshoot network connections.

- **Advanced Networking**—This section looks at advanced networking features such as NIC bonding.

- **Client DNS Troubleshooting**—This section covers client-side DNS issues and ways to resolve them.

The following RHCSA exam objective is covered:

- Configure network and hostname resolution statically or dynamically

The following RHCE exam objective is covered:

- Route IP traffic and create static routes

## CHAPTER 5

Networking

One of the key elements of connecting to different systems is the network configuration involved. In this chapter, we look at how to configure both DHCP and static IP addresses, troubleshoot network issues, and resolve client DNS problems. Networking is an important foundation because without it, you aren't able to communicate with the outside world or the rest of your network, or share files with your users. This book is not a primer on networking, so an understanding of subnetting, default gateways, and other basic networking concepts is vital before reading this chapter.

Setting Up Networking

Network management is fairly easy when it comes to Red Hat. Most of the network configuration is kept in files; therefore, adjusting these settings is simple. To start, you can use three management commands:

`ifconfig`	Displays the IP address and other interface-related information
`route`	Enables you to view or change the routing information on the system
`system-config-network-tui`	Provides a menu-driven utility for network configuration

When you're working with network interfaces, there are two additional files you need to know:

`/etc/sysconfig/network`	This file contains gateway and hostname information.
`/etc/sysconfig/network-scripts`	This directory contains all the interface config files for your system.

Let's start by looking at the hostname and networking information:

```
# cat /etc/sysconfig/network
NETWORKING=yes
```

```
NETWORKING_IPV6=yes
HOSTNAME=RHEL01
```

The output here should be reasonably straightforward. The first two lines tell the system whether or not to enable networking for IPv4 and IPv6. By default, they are both enabled and can remain that way unless otherwise noted. I prefer to disable IPv6 if it is not in use so as not to add extra traffic to the network. The third option defines what the system hostname is going to be. One additional option not listed here is GATEWAY. This option tells the system what the IP address of the gateway is. The reason that it doesn't appear on the system here (or may not on yours) is that the option is set by the DHCP server, in which case it doesn't appear. If you have a static IP address, you see the GATEWAY option listed here. You may also define the option yourself to override any other gateway settings.

EXAM TIP

When you change the hostname of your computer, you don't have to reboot. If you do not reboot, however, there are numerous places that you need to change the hostname. If the system is not mission critical (or you have extra time on the Red Hat exam), you should restart the system and allow it to make all the adjustments for you.

Next, let's jump over to the /etc/sysconfig/network-scripts directory, where we find the remaining important files that deal with networking. Each network interface has its own config file in this directory that follows the format ifcfg-ethX, where X is the number of the network card. For example, my primary network card contains the following in its config file:

```
# cat /etc/sysconfig/network-scripts/ifcfg-eth0
DEVICE=eth0
BOOTPROTO=dhcp
HWADDR=08:00:27:30:74:AA
ONBOOT=yes
DHCP_HOSTNAME=RHEL01
TYPE=Ethernet
```

There are two important elements to note in this file. The first is the DEVICE option, which specifies which interface you are working with. Here, the first interface is specified, and by looking at the next line, you can see the protocol in use. This interface uses the DHCP protocol, which means that the IP address is leased from a DHCP server on the network (automatically during boot). Suppose you want to change this to a static IP address? You could edit this file by hand, but for basic configuration, there is a faster method.

EXAM TIP

If you edit the network interface files by hand, you have more options available to work with. You can customize the options that you want to use; however, customizing them takes time and is not required for the Red Hat exams.

Static IP Addresses

A fast way for you to configure network interfaces is to use the `system-config-network-tui` command. It starts the menu-driven interface that allows you to configure your interfaces on-the-fly. Let's change the second interface (eth1) to have a static IP address with this utility.

Step 1.   Launch the utility:
```
# system-config-network-tui
```

Step 2.   Select which network interface you want to edit (see Figure 5-1).

Figure 5-1   Network interface choices to edit.

Step 3.   Edit the details of the interface (see Figure 5-2).

Step 4.   Save and quit when you are finished.

Here, you can see that you can make any change you need to the interface, including setting it to a static IP address instead of using the DHCP protocol. Now that you've made changes to the network interfaces, you need to restart the network service for the changes to take effect. Instead of bringing down all the interfaces on the system by restarting the network service, you could also just bring down a single interface to which you have made changes. Because you made a change only to eth1, you can just bring down that one interface. To do this, you use the `ifdown` and `ifup` commands. These two commands are really the `ifconfig` command, but in a shorthand format.

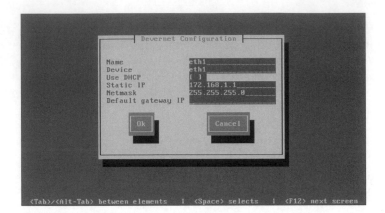

Figure 5-2   Interface details can be edited.

Step 1.   To bring the single interface down, use `ifdown`:

```
# ifdown eth1
```

Step 2.   To restore the interface that you just brought down, use `ifup`:

```
# ifup eth1
```

If the interface is static, there should be no output. If the interface is configured to use DHCP, you see just one line letting you know that the interface is getting the necessary information from the DHCP server. As with anything that you do, you should verify your work. Use the `ifconfig` command to display your current IP address and make sure that it is set correctly.

Syntax: `ifconfig [options] [interface]`

Options:

`netmask MASK`	Specifies the netmask for the interface
`hw ADDRESS`	Sets the MAC address of the interface
`up`	Brings up the interface
`down`	Bring down the interface

To view the current IP address of the eth0 interface, use the following command:

```
# ifconfig eth1
Eth1      Link encap:Ethernet  HWaddr 08:00:27:DB:D0:F5
          inet addr:172.168.1.1  Bcast:172.168.1.255  Mask:255.255.255.0
          inet6 addr: fe80::a00:27ff:fedb:d0f5/64 Scope:Link
          UP BROADCAST RUNNING MULTICAST  MTU:1500  Metric:1
          RX packets:0 errors:0 dropped:0 overruns:0 frame:0
          TX packets:202 errors:0 dropped:0 overruns:0 carrier:0
```

```
        collisions:0 txqueuelen:1000
        RX bytes:0 (0.0 b)  TX bytes:21322 (20.8 KiB)
        Interrupt:9 Base address:0xd240
```

The ifconfig command displays information about the interface along with its IP address. You could also check the output of the interface config file to see the changes:

```
# cat /etc/sysconfig/network-scripts/ifcfg-eth1
# Advanced Micro Devices [AMD] 79c970 [PCnet32 LANCE]
DEVICE=eth1
BOOTPROTO=none
HWADDR=00:0c:29:e8:c3:80
ONBOOT=yes
DHCP_HOSTNAME=RHEL01
IPADDR=172.168.1.1
NETMASK=255.255.255.0
TYPE=Ethernet
```

Now that you have verified that the IP address is set correctly, you should look at the IP address of any other interfaces on your system. Using the ifconfig command with no parameters displays all interfaces on the system and their current details. Now use the ifconfig command again to display all the interfaces on the system:

```
# ifconfig
eth0      Link encap:Ethernet   HWaddr 08:00:27:30:74:AA
          inet addr:192.168.1.5  Bcast:192.168.1.255  Mask:255.255.255.0
          inet6 addr: fe80::a00:27ff:fe30:74aa/64 Scope:Link
          UP BROADCAST RUNNING MULTICAST  MTU:1500  Metric:1
          RX packets:4140 errors:1 dropped:0 overruns:0 frame:0
          TX packets:705 errors:0 dropped:0 overruns:0 carrier:0
          collisions:0 txqueuelen:1000
          RX bytes:954993 (932.6 KiB)  TX bytes:88056 (85.9 KiB)
          Interrupt:10 Base address:0xd020

eth1      Link encap:Ethernet   HWaddr 08:00:27:DB:D0:F5
          inet addr:172.168.1.1  Bcast:172.168.1.255  Mask:255.255.255.0
          inet6 addr: fe80::a00:27ff:fedb:d0f5/64 Scope:Link
          UP BROADCAST RUNNING MULTICAST  MTU:1500  Metric:1
          RX packets:0 errors:0 dropped:0 overruns:0 frame:0
          TX packets:243 errors:0 dropped:0 overruns:0 carrier:0
          collisions:0 txqueuelen:1000
          RX bytes:0 (0.0 b)  TX bytes:16152 (15.7 KiB)
          Interrupt:9 Base address:0xd240

lo        Link encap:Local Loopback
```

```
inet addr:127.0.0.1  Mask:255.0.0.0
inet6 addr: ::1/128 Scope:Host
UP LOOPBACK RUNNING  MTU:16436  Metric:1
RX packets:2735 errors:0 dropped:0 overruns:0 frame:0
TX packets:2735 errors:0 dropped:0 overruns:0 carrier:0
collisions:0 txqueuelen:0
RX bytes:4258081 (4.0 MiB)  TX bytes:4258081 (4.0 MiB)
```

Here, you see that there are three interfaces: eth0; eth1; and lo, the loopback adapter. Any time you make a change to an interface's settings, you need to bring down that interface and then bring it back up again. If multiple interfaces have been edited, you could also just restart the entire networking service.

> **WARNING:** Restarting the network service interrupts all network connections and any client that is currently connected.

Restart the network service as follows:

```
# service network restart
Shutting down interface eth0:                          [  OK  ]
Shutting down interface eth1:                          [  OK  ]
Shutting down loopback interface:                      [  OK  ]
Bringing up loopback interface:                        [  OK  ]
Bringing up interface eth0:
Determining IP information for eth0... done.
                                                       [  OK  ]
Bringing up interface eth1:                            [  OK  ]
```

From this output, you can tell that eth0 is configured to use the DHCP protocol because it has to determine its IP address.

There is one other method that you can use to set an IP address. The ifconfig command, aside from displaying information about the network interface, can also be used to set the IP address. Suppose you want to set the IP address of the eth1 interface to something static. Because you want the IP address to remain the same, just set the same static IP address again with the ifconfig command:

```
# ifconfig eth0 172.168.1.1 netmask 255.255.255.0
```

This command gets you the same results as using the menu-driven option. Don't forget to bring the network interface down and then bring it back up again (or restart the network service). Make sure that you always use the ifconfig command to verify that your IP addresses have been set properly.

> **WARNING:**   For many commands and changes on Linux, there are multiple ways to achieve the same results. Make sure you choose the method that you are most comfortable with to save time on the exam.

Routing

When you have a system that has two or more network interfaces (such as the RHEL01 host), they are called *dual-homed* or *multihomed* systems. You need to make sure that each interface has a gateway that it can route through. Using the `route` command, you can display the current routes the system has and add additional routes if you need to.

Syntax: `route [options]`

Options:

add	Adds a net route
del	Deletes an existing route
flush	Flushes any temporary routes

> **WARNING:**   As a good troubleshooting tip, watch for keywords to detect gateway or routing issues. If you receive an error message about being unable to contact a host or particular domain, you should always check that the default gateway is set properly.

Let's look at the current routes on the system:

```
# route
Kernel IP routing table
Destination     Gateway         Genmask         Flags Metric Ref    Use Iface
192.168.1.0     *               255.255.255.0   U     0      0        0 eth0
172.168.1.0     *               255.255.255.0   U     0      0        0 eth1
169.254.0.0     *               255.255.0.0     U     0      0        0 eth1
default         192.168.1.1     0.0.0.0         UG    0      0        0 eth0
```

The preceding output shows that the home router is actually the default gateway for this system (refer to the lab layout in the introduction if you need further clarification). If you don't have a default gateway set, you can again use the `route` command to choose a default gateway.

Step 1.   Assuming that the default gateway has not yet been set, you can use the following to set it for the RHEL01 host:
```
# route add default gw 192.168.1.1 eth0
```

Step 2.   You can now verify the new default gateway you added by calling the route command again:

```
# route
Kernel IP routing table
Destination     Gateway          Genmask          Flags Metric Ref
Use Iface
192.168.1.0     *                255.255.255.0    U     0      0
0 eth0
172.168.1.0     *                255.255.255.0    U     0      0
0 eth1
169.254.0.0     *                255.255.0.0      U     0      0
0 eth1
default         192.168.1.1      0.0.0.0          UG    0      0
0 eth0
```

You get the same output here because the default gateway already existed. Setting up network interfaces and gateways requires you to have a good understanding of how networks work. As already mentioned, it is critical that you understand subnetting to make sure you are settings up networks and routes correctly. You should also be very comfortable with troubleshooting network interfaces, a topic covered in the next section.

> **NOTE:**   You may have noticed that the system has a 172.168.1.0 network with no specific default gateway defined. The reason is that this system will become the default gateway for this network later when we reach Chapter 15, "NFS," and talk about NAT.

Creating Static Routes

At some point, you might need to use a specific path to reach a network. To ensure that this happens, you can set up static routes that direct particular network traffic to a specified default gateway or network. To create a static route, you add entries to the /etc/sysconfig/network-scripts/route-<interface> file. Let's see what an example of this file might look like:

```
Default 192.168.1.1 dev eth0
172.168.1.0/24 via 172.168.1.1 eth1
```

This sets the default gateway to 192.168.1.1, and any traffic that is destined for the 172.168.1.1/24 network will go over the eth1 interface (to the internal network).

Troubleshooting Network Connections

A key component to network troubleshooting is making sure that everything is working smoothly and that your network is functioning properly. There are quite a few commands that you can use to help you when troubleshooting network problems.

ping	Tests the connectivity between two hosts
traceroute	Looks for latency in the path from host to host
netstat	Shows information about connections (open, closed, and listening)
route	Shows routing information

Up to this point, we have been working on only one of the four systems in the lab. The reason is primarily that everything else in the lab is on a private network and has no outside network access. For now, this is fine, but because the RHEL01 host has two interfaces, allowing it to exist in two networks, we can look at how it interacts with other hosts on the private network.

Networking Utilities

Let's start with the ping command, which you can use to verify that you can talk to other hosts on the network.

Syntax: ping DESTINATION

When you ping something on a Linux host, unlike in Windows, the ping continues until you cancel it. You can limit the number of ping requests sent by prefixing -c number_count in front of the destination host.

Step 1.   On RHEL01, verify that you can see RHEL02 on the internal network:

```
# ping -c 2 172.168.1.2
PING 172.168.1.2 (172.168.1.2) 56(84) bytes of data.
64 bytes from 172.168.1.2: icmp_seq=1 ttl=64 time=0.055 ms
64 bytes from 172.168.1.2: icmp_seq=2 ttl=64 time=0.074 ms
```

Step 2.   Now verify that you can see the router on the external network:

```
# ping -c 2 192.168.1.1
PING 192.168.1.1 (192.168.1.1) 56(84) bytes of data.
64 bytes from 192.168.1.1: icmp_seq=1 ttl=64 time=0.055 ms
64 bytes from 192.168.1.1: icmp_seq=2 ttl=64 time=0.074 ms
```

Communication is a two-way street in the networking world, so you also need to make sure that RHEL02 can talk to RHEL01.

Step 1.   On RHEL02, use the following:

```
# ping -c 2 172.168.1.1
PING 172.168.1.1 (172.168.1.1) 56(84) bytes of data.
64 bytes from 172.168.1.1: icmp_seq=1 ttl=64 time=0.055 ms
64 bytes from 172.168.1.1: icmp_seq=2 ttl=64 time=0.074 ms
```

As you can see, the two servers can talk to each other, and RHEL01 can talk to the outside world (via the 192.168.1.0 network). What would happen if you tried to contact the 192.168.1.0 network from RHEL02?

Step 2.   On RHEL02, use the following:

```
# ping -c 2 192.168.1.1
PING 192.168.1.1 (192.168.1.1) 56(84) bytes of data.
From 172.168.1.1 icmp_seq=2 Destination Host Unreachable
From 172.168.1.1 icmp_seq=3 Destination Host Unreachable
```

Here, you can't reach the 192.168.1.0 network, and you are told so by the
`Destination Host Unreachable` message. The reason you get this message is that
there is no route from RHEL02 to the 192.168.1.0 network. What routes are
available? Let's look at the `route` command again to find out.

On RHEL02, use the `route` command to view available networks:

```
# route
Kernel IP routing table
Destination     Gateway        Genmask         Flags Metric Ref   Use Iface
172.168.1.0     *              255.255.255.0   U     0      0       0 eth0
169.254.0.0     *              255.255.0.0     U     0      0       0 eth0
```

You can see that you can reach 172.168.1.0 only, which explains why you can't
reach the 192.168.1.0 network.

Now that you know how to check the interfaces and routes, you should also look at
how you can view listening or established ports using the `netstat` command. You
can also use the `netstat` command to obtain information on routing tables, listening sockets, and established connections.

Syntax: `netstat [options]`

Options:

-r	Displays the routing table
-I	Displays interface statistics
-t	Shows tcp connections
-u	Shows udp connections
-a	Displays all sockets (tcp, udp, or local)
-p	Displays process IDs
-e	Displays extended information

As an example, suppose you want to check that the SSH server is listening correctly on port 22. You could use `netstat` to check that the connection is available
for your clients:

```
# netstat -tuape | grep ssh
```

```
tcp        0      0 *:ssh      *:*       LISTEN     root    8627
2674/sshd
```

If nothing is returned, there is a good chance the service isn't running or listening correctly on that port. You can, however, see here that the SSH service is listening correctly (as denoted by `*:ssh` in the output).

The commands we have covered so far should help you when troubleshooting network connectivity issues. You should be able to handle any network troubleshooting problem, including routing issues, network interface issues, and connectivity problems. Before we move on to client-side DNS troubleshooting, make sure you know how to configure and troubleshoot any network connections you already have.

Network Monitoring and Analysis

Sometimes you may run into a problem on your network where the system just isn't giving you enough information. When you really need to see the fine details of what is going on behind the scenes, you can use a packet capture utility to view all the raw data being sent across the interfaces on your machine. To help out, you can use the `tcpdump` utility.

Syntax: `tcpdump [options]`

Options:

`-i INTERFACE`	Specifies which interface to listen on
`-r FILE`	Specifies a packet capture file to read
`-w FILE`	Defines a file to write output to instead of the console

As an example, suppose you want to know whether your system is leasing a DHCP address properly. You can monitor the connection on the eth0 interface to make sure that the DHCP server is responding properly.

Step 1. Start the `tcpdump` program and specify the interface that you want it to listen on as well as the file that you'd like it to dump the information to so that you can review it:

    `# tcpdump -i eth0 -w pkt_capture`

Step 2. While the packet capture is running, you need to obtain access to another console. Call the `dhclient` utility, which pulls down a new IP address for you from the DHCP server:

    `# dhclient`

Step 3.   When the system finishes determining its IP address, return to the first console and stop the `tcpdump` program by pressing Ctrl+C. To review the information you've captured, call the `tcpdump` program again:

```
# tcpdump -r pkt_capture | less
```

Although being able to monitor your network and see what is really happening can be very helpful in troubleshooting, it can also further complicate things. Much of the data captured from `tcpdump` is in raw format, making it hard to read. Usually, you also need a good understanding of network protocols for the data to be useful.

Advanced Networking

We have already looked at some of the basic steps to configuring networking. As mentioned previously, you can edit the network interface config files by hand to fine-tune the network settings (such as adjusting speed, duplexing, and more). One advanced networking topic we look at here is Ethernet bonding.

Ethernet Bonding

Ethernet bonding is used to combine multiple interfaces into one, creating an increase in available bandwidth and redundancy. This is done by creating a special network interface file called a *channel bonding interface*. Because you are in a lab environment and using virtual network interfaces, there really isn't any additional bandwidth benefit, but redundancy is always good. You need to create a third network interface on your RHEL01 virtual system before you can create your bonded interfaces.

Step 1.   Enable the bonding kernel module:

```
# nano /etc/modprobe.d/bond.conf
Alias bond0 bonding
```

Step 2.   Create the channel bond interface file in the /etc/sysconfig/network-scripts directory:

```
# nano /etc/sysconfig/network-scripts/ifcfg-bond0
DEVICE="eth0"
IPADDR=172.168.1.1
NETMASK=255.255.255.0
ONBOOT=yes
BOOTPROTO=none
USERCTL=no
BONDING_OPTS="primary=eth1"
```

Now that the bond interface is set up and the kernel module is loaded, you need to assign which interfaces will be added to the bond interface (in this case, eth1 and eth2).

Step 3.   Edit the eth1 interface to look like the following:

```
DEVICE=eth1
BOOTPROTO=none
ONBOOT=yes
MASTER=bond0
SALVE=yes
USERCTL=no
```

Step 4.   Edit the eth2 interface to look like the following:

```
DEVICE=eth2
BOOTPROTO=none
ONBOOT=yes
MASTER=bond0
SALVE=yes
USERCTL=no
```

Step 5.   You can now bring up the bonded interface:

```
# ifconfig bond0 up
```

With the bonded interface in place, you now have two interfaces acting as one, again providing redundancy. Interface bonding might be something commonly seen in a smaller network to provide link redundancy to servers; however, in a large-scale network, you might be more likely to see bonding on the switch level.

Client DNS Troubleshooting

Although working with IP addresses and assigning them to servers is great, it becomes highly impractical after you start managing a large number of servers and clients. Instead, you can use hostnames (the name of the system), which can be used in place of an IP address. The lookup and translation of an IP address to a hostname happen automatically via a DNS server on your network. Although this section doesn't cover DNS in its entirety, it describes client-side DNS issues and ways to troubleshoot them. There are some key files that make name resolution occur on the system. Let's look at those files first:

/etc/sysconfig/network	Contains the hostname of the system
/etc/resolv.conf	Contains the IP addresses of the DNS servers
/etc/hosts	Contains the local IP to hostname mappings
/etc/nsswitch.conf	Contains the order in which the local versus DNS server is queried for information

Aside from these key files, there are also a few client-side commands that you can use as well:

hostname	Sets or returns the hostname of the system

`nslookup`	Queries or looks up a domain name or system
`ping`	Tests connectivity between two systems

When dealing with DNS issues, you usually know right away due to key phrases in the error message, such as `Can't be resolved` or `Unable to lookup`. Although this isn't always the case, having trouble contacting anything in the outside world or systems by their hostnames is usually also a good indicator.

To start, let's look at the `hostname` command. This command pulls information from the /etc/sysconfig/network file, where the hostname is set during the boot process.

To view the current hostname, do the following:

```
# hostname
RHEL01
```

You can also view the hostname information in the /etc/sysconfig/network file as shown earlier:

```
# cat /etc/sysconfig/network
NETWORKING=yes
NETWORKING_IPV6=no
HOSTNAME=RHEL01
```

You can edit this file if you'd like to change the hostname of the system. If you intend to use a fully qualified domain name (FQDN), you can also specify that here. You could use RHEL01.example.com as an FQDN instead of RHEL01, for example. When you know the hostname of the system, you should determine where the server will query when trying to look up the name of another host. Two files contain the information for DNS lookups. The first file is /etc/hosts, which is local to the system.

Syntax of the /etc/hosts file:

```
<ip> <fqdn>  <alias>
```

Let's look at current entries in the file:

```
# cat /etc/hosts
# Do not remove the following line, or various programs
# that require network functionality will fail.
127.0.0.1          RHEL01 RHEL01 localhost.localdomain localhost
::1                localhost6.localdomain6 localhost6
```

As you can see, there is nothing in this hosts file other than a localhost entry (localhost is the local loopback). When you run a small (and I'm talking five or fewer machines here) environment, using host files is a feasible task. You would need to make entries in the hosts file on every server (remember the hosts file is local to the server). You can see, however, that this approach would quickly get out of hand from a management perspective when the number of machines to update and keep track of grows quickly. As I'm sure you could have guessed, the next logical step is to let the system query a DNS server instead of the local hosts file. The /etc/resolv.conf file contains the IP address of the DNS server. This allows your systems to rely on DNS queries instead of a local lookup in the hosts file.

Let's look at what is currently in the /etc/resolv.conf file:

```
# cat /etc/resolv.conf
; generated by /sbin/dhclient-script
nameserver 172.168.1.1
```

This output shows that the server you are on (RHEL01) sends all DNS queries to the DNS server 172.168.1.1 (which happens to be RHEL01). Although you don't have a DNS server installed (yet), this example shows how to troubleshoot incorrect settings on clients. You could also have a /etc/resolv.conf file that looks like this:

```
# cat /etc/resolv.conf
search example.com
nameserver 192.168.1.1
nameserver 172.168.1.1
```

The search option is the name of the domain that will be searched by default. If your client is trying to access a hostname that is not fully qualified (such as RHEL01.example.com), and the DNS server returns an error that it can't find the specified host, try adding the search <domain> option. This is a common setup when clients and servers belong to a domain. The second listing of the nameserver option just specifies a secondary DNS server in case the first is not available.

All right, so you have configured a hosts file and a resolv.conf file. Now, I'm sure someone is asking, which one gets queried first? Naturally, there is a third file that contains a single line defining the search order. This third file can be one of the following two, although it is usually the latter.

Older File:

```
# cat /etc/host.conf
order hosts,bind
```

Newer File:

```
# cat /etc/nsswitch.conf | grep hosts
hosts:      files dns
```

This nsswitch file is the default—and with good reason. Sometimes you want a specific system to look up a specific host. Instead of making a DNS entry where multiple systems would see it, you could define an entry in a system's local /etc/hosts file. Because you usually don't have anything in your hosts file, however, the system defaults to the DNS server next. When you know that all files are configured properly, you can begin testing that name resolution. You can do this one of two ways. First, you could use the ping command to ping a host by its hostname to see if it responds. Second, you could use the nslookup command to query the IP address associated with a hostname. Make sure that you test different ways to verify each issue.

To ping a system by hostname, do the following:

```
# ping RHEL02
```

If you want to look up a hostname, use this command:

```
# nslookup RHEL02
```

The dig command can be used to gain a larger look at IP addresses and hostnames. We look at dig, nslookup, and ping in more depth in Chapter 18, "DNS." At this point, you should now be able to troubleshoot client-side issues pertaining to DNS. A good methodology would be to follow the order presented here when troubleshooting:

Step 1.   Is the hostname set correctly?

Step 2.   In what order are the files queried?

Step 3.   Are the settings for the hosts file and resolv.conf file correct?

Summary

Network troubleshooting can be a torturous process if you don't know what you're looking for or don't have a strong understanding of how networking works. For the Red Hat exams, you need to be able to understand IP addressing, subnets, and routing. These are also big real-world concepts that allow system administrators to troubleshoot and resolve problems on their networks. This chapter covered how to troubleshoot and set up network interfaces as well as how to perform some client-side DNS troubleshooting.

Review Questions

1. What command displays your current interfaces and IP address?

2. What does `ifconfig 172.168.1.100 netmask 255.255.255.0 eth1` do?

3. What command can you use to test connectivity to another host?

4. What does it mean if you ping a host and you receive the response `Destination Unreachable`?

5. What is a gateway used for on a network?

6. How would you go about creating a static route?

7. What command can you use to monitor and troubleshoot network connections?

8. Can you name three utilities that can be used for network or DNS client troubleshooting?

9. What is the /etc/hosts file used for?

Answers to Review Questions

1. `ifconfig`

2. This command sets the eth1 interface to have a static IP address of 172.168.1.100 with a netmask of 255.255.255.0.

3. The `ping` command can be used to verify connectivity to another host.

4. The gateway is incorrectly set, and the subnet of the host you are trying to reach is inaccessible.

5. A gateway is used as an entry and exit point for a subnet on a network. To contact hosts outside your subnet, you need to pass through a gateway.

6. Use the `route` command with the `add` option to create a static route.

7. The `tcpdump` command is used to monitor network connections on different interfaces.

8. The three utilities are: `route`, `ping`, and `nslookup`.

9. The /etc/hosts file is a local lookup file used to map IP addresses to hostnames if a DNS server isn't available.

Lab 5

Task 1 – Static Interfaces

Step 1.   Set up a static IP address for your eth1 interface on Client01 with the following guidelines:

a. The IP address should be 172.168.1.10.

b. The netmask should be 255.255.255.0.

c. The gateway should be set to 172.168.1.1

The task is complete when all interfaces can be pinged successfully.

Task 2 – Client DNS

Step 1.   Set up RHEL01 with the following guidelines:

a. Your DNS server should be 192.168.1.1.

b. Set the secondary DNS server to a public DNS server (you can find many online).

The task is complete when all sites and hosts resolve successfully.

Task 3 – Packet Capture

Step 1.   Using the tcpdump utility on any system, perform the following actions:

a. Set up tcpdump to capture packets (they must be written to a file).

b. Ping any host on the local subnet until you get a reply.

c. Close the tcpdump program.

The task is complete when you have a packet capture file that contains the ping going across the local subnet.

This chapter covers the following subjects:

- **Working with RPM**—This section covers how to install, update, and query packages on the system.

- **Doing It Again with Yum**—This section covers how to install, update, and query packages again using the Yum utility.

- **Making Your Own RPM**—This section describes the process of building a simple RPM package.

- **Creating Your Own Repository**—This section looks at how you can build your own private package repository.

- **The Red Hat Network**—This section covers the Red Hat network and how to register your system.

The following RHCSA exam objective is covered:

- Install and update software packages from the Red Hat Network, a remote repository, or the local file system

The following RHCE exam objective is covered:

- Build a simple RPM that packages a single file

## CHAPTER 6

Package Management

Software is the basis of any operating system, allowing you to install and use different utilities. In Linux, software is distributed through the use of packages, which contain the actual software files. Each distribution of Linux has its own package management system. For Red Hat, there are two package management systems: RPM and Yum. In this chapter, we look at package management and how to handle software for the Red Hat system.

Working with RPM

A package contains a directory structure that is composed of files to make up the software application. In Red Hat, packages have the .rpm extension and can be installed through different means. Before diving into package management, let's look at the naming convention used by the system to describe packages.

Package Syntax: `package_name-version-release.arch.rpm`

As an example, let's look at the `postfix` package, which is used to install an SMTP mail server:

`postfix-2.6.6-2.el6.x86_64.rpm`

You can see from the preceding that the name of this package is `postfix`, the version number is 2.6.6, and it is meant for a 64-bit operating system. The `-2` is the release, and the `el6` is something you find only in Red Hat packages because it specifies an internal version number for the Red Hat release. Being able to read a package and understand its version information is important for a system administrator. This helps in determining whether your packages are out-of-date or whether you are vulnerable to certain security risks in different versions of software. Sometimes when you install one package, it requires that you install another as well; this is known as a *dependency*. Certain packages require certain versions to make sure that their dependencies don't break when upgrading. You can see why being able to get version information from packages is a necessary skill. All packages are held within a repository somewhere, depending on who produces the package. Red Hat has its own software repositories, which hold the packages for the Red Hat operating system. When you update your packages, they are compared to the version of the package in the repository to see if

there is a newer version. You can also have new versions of packages outside repositories too, but these require a slightly different installation method. In the first half
of this chapter, we look at packages outside repositories.

Installing and Removing Packages

The first package management utility we look at is RPM. This utility is used to
manage individual packages outside the repositories. This means you can use the `yum`
command to query packages in the repositories and install them, whereas you use
the RPM utility to install .rpm packages that you download (either manually from
the repositories or the Web). For both RPM and Yum, the syntax and options are
monstrous. Until you become accustomed to working with them, you can refer to
their help menus for a listing of all the options. This section includes only the most
common options that you will need. An example should help to clear things up.

Syntax: `rpm [options]`

The options for `rpm` are divided into three different sections (modes): install/
upgrade/erase, query, and verify.

Install/Upgrade/Erase Options:

`-e`	Removes a given package
`-i`	Installs a given package
`-h`	Shows hash progress when installing
`-U`	Upgrades a given package
`-v`	Provides verbose output

Query Options (with `-q`):

`-c`	Lists all config files
`-d`	Lists all documentation files
`-i`	Displays information about the package
`-l`	Lists the files in a package

Verify Options (with `-v`):

`-a`	Queries all packages
`-f`	Displays information about the specified file

As you can see, there is a multitude of options to choose from, and these are really
only the common options! Let's grab a package from the Web to demonstrate an

install with the rpm command. To download something from the command line, you can use the wget command.

Step 1.   Download the nano package from the Web:

```
# wget http://www.nano-editor.org/dist/v2.2/RPMS/nano-2.2.6-1.x86_64.rpm
--2010-09-06 08:30:26--  http://www.nano-
editor.org/dist/v2.2/RPMS/nano-2.2.6-
1.x86_64.rpm
Resolving www.nano-editor.org... 207.192.74.17
Connecting to www.nano-editor.org|207.192.74.17|:80... connected.
HTTP request sent, awaiting response... 200 OK
Length: 586766 (573K) [application/x-redhat-package-manager]
Saving to: `nano-2.2.6-1.x86_64.rpm'

100%[====================================================================
=>]
586,766      1.75M/s   in 0.3s

2010-09-06 08:30:27 (1.75 MB/s) - `nano-2.2.6-1.x86_64.rpm' saved
[586766/586766]
```

EXAM TIP
You can also use the wget command to pull packages from local or remote repositories. On the exam, you have no Internet access, but if you need to grab a remote RPM package, you can still use the wget utility.

Step 2.   When the download is finished, the package is in the present working directory. You can now install it with the rpm command:

```
# rpm -ivh nano-2.2.6-1.x86_64.rpm
Preparing...
######################################### [100%]
    1:nano
######################################### [100%]
```

Here, you use the install feature of the rpm command. You are telling it to install the package (-i), be verbose in the output (-v), and print a hash showing the progress of installation (-h). One of the downsides to using the rpm command is that if this package has any dependencies, the rpm command fails with an error message. You have to install any required dependencies by hand first.

NOTE: You may get an error regarding the package you are trying to install saying it conflicts with a current version of the software already on the system. If this is the case, keep reading to learn how to remove the old package first and then try the installation again.

If you want to upgrade this package (because you know that it is already installed), you can substitute the `-i` option for `-U`. This command upgrades the package or installs it if the package isn't already installed:

```
# rpm -Uvh nano-2.2.6-1.x86_64.rpm
Preparing...                ########################################### [100%]
   1:nano                   ########################################### [100%]
```

You might decide that you no longer want the package installed. In that case, you can use the `-e` option to remove it:

```
# rpm -e nano
```

You can always reinstall the package at a later date if you keep the .rpm file on your system (or you can always download it again).

> **REAL-WORLD TIP**
>
> A common situation to run into on the job is having to install a package that is already installed. You don't have to go through the trouble of uninstalling the package first only to reinstall it. You can use the `--replacepkgs` option alongside the regular install options to overwrite an existing installation:
>
> ```
> # rpm -ivh --replacepkgs  nano-2.2.6-1.x86_64.rpm
> ```

Querying and Verifying Packages

You just installed the latest version of a package and want to make sure that it installed properly. How do you check? You can use the query and verification options for the `rpm` command, of course. Let's jump back to the installation of nano for a second. This time, before you install the package, you can query the currently installed system packages to verify whether nano is already installed. If you already installed the newer version of nano, your output might look slightly different from mine.

Query the installed system packages for nano:

```
# rpm -qa | grep nano
nano-1.3.12-1.1.el6.x86_64
```

The `-q` option tells `rpm` that you are querying for something, and the `-a` option tells `rpm` to query all packages installed on the system. You don't want to list every single package, however, so you can use the `grep` command to pick out only the package(s) you are hunting for. The benefit to using `grep` is that it is actually a pattern match utility, so it returns multiple results matching what you are looking for (giving you all the installed packages on the system relating to nano or whatever you are hunting for). If the package doesn't exist, no results are returned. As you can see here, the package does exist and it is at version 1.3.12.

Now let's install the new version downloaded from the Web:

```
# rpm -ivh nano-2.2.6-1.x86_64.rpm
Preparing...                ########################################### [100%]
   1:nano                    ########################################### [100%]
```

Again, you can query for the package to see that the version has changed, indicating that the package has been updated:

```
# rpm -qa | grep nano
nano-2.2.6-1.el6.x86_64
```

REAL-WORLD TIP

If you have worked with package management before, you might be wondering why I don't suggest using the single -q option to query for the package:

```
# rpm -q nano
```

The reason I stay away from this is that you get results only if you know the exact name of the package. For example, say you query to see whether the text editor vim is installed:

```
# rpm -q vim
```

You get no results, making you think that the package is not installed. Now query the other way:

```
# rpm -qa | grep vim
vim-enhanced-7.0.109-6.el6.x86_64
vim-common-7.0.109-6.el6.x86_64
vim-minimal-7.0.109-6.el6.x86_64
```

You can see that it is, in fact, installed and that the package is named something other than what you thought it was. The grep command uses regex to check among all installed packages, giving you more accurate results.

Let's take a step back for a second. What if your boss told you that he just installed the postfix package from site *xyz* that you had never heard of before? You can query information that is provided by the package, providing details of what the package does. This way, you don't have to ask your boss and can see some detailed information on the package as well. Be wary of packages that don't provide details.

Query the information from the nano package:

```
# rpm -qi nano
Name        : nano                         Relocations: (not relocatable)
Version     : 2.2.6                              Vendor: (none)
Release     : 1                               Build Date: Thu 05 Aug 2010
11:08:24 PM EDT
Install Date: Mon 06 Sep 2010 08:35:32 AM EDT      Build Host: 012.redhat.com
```

```
Group        : Applications/Editors      Source RPM: nano-2.2.6-1.src.rpm
Size         : 1554146                    License: GPL
Signature    : (none)
URL          : http://www.nano-editor.org/
Summary      : A small text editor
Description :
GNU nano is a small and friendly text editor.
```

As you can see, there is basically everything you would ever want to know about this package. You get the current version, the date the package was built, the size of the package, and a description.

Now that you know how to install, update, and query for different packages, let's move on and look at some other options you can use when working with packages. Suppose you are looking around on your new Red Hat installation and find a file but aren't sure what it does. You can use the -f option to query the package that the file belongs to, possibly giving you a better idea of what that file might be used for. Find out where the /etc/rsyslog.conf file came from by doing the following:

```
# rpm -qf /etc/rsyslog.conf
rsyslog-4.6.2-2.el6.x86_64
```

The query tells you that this file belongs to the rsyslog package, which provides you with the rsyslog service (in case you couldn't guess that). What else does the rsyslog package provide you with? Are there other config files? Now that you know the name of the config file, you can query in reverse using the package name to find out all files associated with that particular package.

Use the -c option to find all config files:

```
# rpm -qc rsyslog
/etc/logrotate.d/syslog
/etc/rsyslog.conf
/etc/sysconfig/rsyslog
```

Aside from the -c option, you can also use -d to find the documentation files for a given package:

```
# rpm -qd rsyslog
/usr/share/doc/rsyslog-4.6.2/AUTHORS
/usr/share/doc/rsyslog-4.6.2/COPYING
/usr/share/doc/rsyslog-4.6.2/NEWS
/usr/share/doc/rsyslog-4.6.2/README
/usr/share/doc/rsyslog-4.6.2/bugs.html
/usr/share/doc/rsyslog-4.6.2/build_from_repo.html
/usr/share/doc/rsyslog-4.6.2/contributors.html
/usr/share/doc/rsyslog-4.6.2/debug.html
```

```
/usr/share/doc/rsyslog-4.6.2/dev_queue.html
/usr/share/doc/rsyslog-4.6.2/droppriv.html
/usr/share/doc/rsyslog-4.6.2/expression.html
/usr/share/doc/rsyslog-4.6.2/features.html
/usr/share/doc/rsyslog-4.6.2/syslog_parsing.html
/usr/share/doc/rsyslog-4.6.2/syslog_protocol.html
/usr/share/doc/rsyslog-4.6.2/tls_cert_ca.html
/usr/share/doc/rsyslog-4.6.2/tls_cert_client.html
/usr/share/doc/rsyslog-4.6.2/tls_cert_errmsgs.html
/usr/share/doc/rsyslog-4.6.2/tls_cert_machine.html
/usr/share/doc/rsyslog-4.6.2/tls_cert_scenario.html
/usr/share/doc/rsyslog-4.6.2/tls_cert_server.html
/usr/share/doc/rsyslog-4.6.2/tls_cert_summary.html
/usr/share/doc/rsyslog-4.6.2/tls_cert_udp_relay.html
/usr/share/doc/rsyslog-4.6.2/troubleshoot.html
/usr/share/doc/rsyslog-4.6.2/v3compatibility.html
/usr/share/doc/rsyslog-4.6.2/v4compatibility.html
/usr/share/doc/rsyslog-4.6.2/version_naming.html
/usr/share/man/man5/rsyslog.conf.5.gz
/usr/share/man/man8/rsyslogd.8.gz
[output truncated]
```

If neither -c nor -d provides you with what you're looking for, you can fall back on -l, which provides a listing of all files that come with the package:

```
# rpm -ql rsyslog
/etc/logrotate.d/syslog
/etc/rc.d/init.d/rsyslog
/etc/rsyslog.conf
/etc/sysconfig/rsyslog
/lib64/rsyslog
/lib64/rsyslog/imfile.so
/lib64/rsyslog/imklog.so
/lib64/rsyslog/immark.so
/lib64/rsyslog/imtcp.so
/lib64/rsyslog/imudp.so
/lib64/rsyslog/imuxsock.so
/lib64/rsyslog/lmnet.so
/lib64/rsyslog/lmnetstrms.so
/lib64/rsyslog/lmnsd_ptcp.so
/lib64/rsyslog/lmregexp.so
/lib64/rsyslog/lmstrmsrv.so
/lib64/rsyslog/lmtcpclt.so
/lib64/rsyslog/lmtcpsrv.so
/lib64/rsyslog/lmzlibw.so
/lib64/rsyslog/omtesting.so
```

```
/sbin/rsyslogd
/usr/share/doc/rsyslog-4.6.2
/usr/share/doc/rsyslog-4.6.2/AUTHORS
/usr/share/doc/rsyslog-4.6.2/COPYING
/usr/share/doc/rsyslog-4.6.2/NEWS
/usr/share/doc/rsyslog-4.6.2/README
/usr/share/doc/rsyslog-4.6.2/bugs.html
[output truncated]
```

Earlier, we described package dependencies and how you'd need to take care of those yourself with the rpm command. You can use the -R option to find out whether a package has any dependencies:

```
# rpm -qR rsyslog
/bin/bash
/bin/sh
/bin/sh
/bin/sh
/bin/sh
/sbin/chkconfig
/sbin/chkconfig
/sbin/service
/sbin/service
bash >= 2.0
config(rsyslog) = 4.6.2-2.el6
coreutils
libc.so.6()(64bit)
libc.so.6(GLIBC_2.2.5)(64bit)
libc.so.6(GLIBC_2.3)(64bit)
libc.so.6(GLIBC_2.3.4)(64bit)
libc.so.6(GLIBC_2.4)(64bit)
libdl.so.2()(64bit)
libdl.so.2(GLIBC_2.2.5)(64bit)
libgcc_s.so.1()(64bit)
libgcc_s.so.1(GCC_3.0)(64bit)
libgcc_s.so.1(GCC_3.3.1)(64bit)
libpthread.so.0()(64bit)
libpthread.so.0(GLIBC_2.2.5)(64bit)
libpthread.so.0(GLIBC_2.3.2)(64bit)
librt.so.1()(64bit)
librt.so.1(GLIBC_2.2.5)(64bit)
libz.so.1()(64bit)
logrotate >= 3.5.2
rpmlib(CompressedFileNames) <= 3.0.4-1
rpmlib(FileDigests) <= 4.6.0-1
rpmlib(PayloadFilesHavePrefix) <= 4.0-1
```

```
rtld(GNU_HASH)
rpmlib(PayloadIsXz) <= 5.2-1
```

Finally, you should also know how to look through the documentation for a given package. This documentation is known as a package's *man pages*, and most packages come with them. To access the man pages, use the man command:

man nano

Scroll up and down to view the documentation and press q to quit. Usually, the man pages provide in-depth details, usage, and examples for any given package. Working with the man pages is very important, especially for the Red Hat exams. You will not be able to remember every command option or every aspect of the syntax, and being able to find what you're looking for through the use of the man pages is very helpful.

REAL-WORLD TIP

For the curious, you can also take RPM packages apart to obtain individual files from within them. To extract the contents of an RPM package, use the rpm2cpio command:

```
# rpm2cpio <package> | cpio -id
```

This capability is useful if a single file is corrupted, and you need to replace it but don't want to install/uninstall/reinstall the entire package.

Doing It Again with Yum

In the previous section, we discussed software and package management with the rpm command. In this section, we look at the exact same tasks, except this time we use the more flexible Yum utility. The yum command has access to repositories where tons of packages are kept and can install, upgrade, or remove them for you automatically. Yum also takes care of resolving and installing any dependencies for you, which the rpm command can't do. We go through all the same commands using yum that we did with rpm.

Syntax: yum [options] command

Options:

-c   Specifies the location of the config file

-q   Specifies quiet, no output

-y   Indicates to always answer yes to prompts

-v   Provides verbose output

Commands:

`clean`	Removes cached data
`erase`	Removes a package from the system
`grouplist`	Displays available package groups
`groupinstall`	Installs the packages within a group
`info`	Displays information about a package
`install`	Installs a package on the system
`search`	Enables you to search for a package
`update`	Updates a package

Yum also has a config file located at /etc/yum.conf that contains some basic settings for how Yum will behave. These options include where Yum will locally cache packages as it installs them, how much output it will generate for log files, and the location of the log file. Usually, the default settings are good, but you should know where this file is located in case you ever want to tune the settings for Yum.

Installing and Removing Packages

Let's start by grabbing the `postfix` package. You install this directly from the Red Hat repositories:

```
# yum install -y postfix
Loaded plugins: fastestmirror
Loading mirror speeds from cached hostfile
 * addons: mirrors.bluehost.com
 * base: mirror.cisp.com
 * extras: mirror.5ninesolutions.com
 * updates: mirror.steadfast.net
Setting up Install Process
Resolving Dependencies
—> Running transaction check
—-> Package postfix.x86_64 2:2.6.6-2.el6 set to be updated
—> Finished Dependency Resolution

Dependencies Resolved

===============================================================================
 Package          Arch         Version            Repository         Size
===============================================================================
Installing:
 postfix          x86_64       2:2.6.6-2.el6      base               2.0 M
```

```
Transaction Summary
================================================================================
Install      1 Package(s)
Update       0 Package(s)
Remove       0 Package(s)

Total download size: 2.0 M
Downloading Packages:
postfix x86_64 2:2 6 6-2 el6 rpm                          | 3.6 MB      00:02
Running rpm_check_debug
Running Transaction Test
Finished Transaction Test
Transaction Test Succeeded
Running Transaction
  Installing      : postfix-2.6.6-2.el6.x64_86                            1/1

Installed:
  postfix.x86_64 2:2.6.6-2.el6
```

Complete!

You could also update the postfix package. Just change the command from install to update:

```
# yum update -y postfix
```

In the output, you see a section where dependencies are checked as the package is being installed. Because you aren't setting up an SMTP server just yet, you can remove that package from the system. As with the RPM utility, you can also remove packages using yum. However, there are two different removal options. You can use the erase or remove command with yum. The difference is that erase removes all packages but saves the config files for those packages in case you ever want to reinstall them. The remove command deletes everything from the package.

Use remove here because you don't want anything lingering around at the moment:

```
# yum remove -y postfix
Loaded plugins: fastestmirror
Setting up Remove Process
Resolving Dependencies
--> Running transaction check
---> Package postfix.x86_64 2:2.6.6-2.el6 set to be erased
--> Finished Dependency Resolution

Dependencies Resolved

================================================================================
```

```
Package              Arch          Version                Repository          Size
================================================================================
Removing:
postfix              x86_64        2:2.6.6-2.el6          installed           9.7 M

Transaction Summary
================================================================================
Install      0 Package(s)
Update       0 Package(s)
Remove       1 Package(s)

Downloading Packages:
Running rpm_check_debug
Running Transaction Test
Finished Transaction Test
Transaction Test Succeeded
Running Transaction
  Erasing        : 2:postfix-2.6.6-2.el6.x86_64                              1/1

Removed:
  postfix.x86_64 2:2.6.6-2.el6

Complete!
```

One great feature about yum is that instead of updating a single package, you can list all updates that need to be installed for the system:

```
# yum list updates
Loaded plugins: fastestmirror
Loading mirror speeds from cached hostfile
 * addons: mirrors.bluehost.com
 * base: mirror.cisp.com
 * extras: mirror.5ninesolutions.com
 * updates: mirror.steadfast.net
Updated Packages
NetworkManager.x86_64               1:0.7.0-10.el6_5.1          updates
NetworkManager-glib.x86_64          1:0.7.0-10.el6_5.1          updates
acl.x86_64                          2.2.39-6.el6               base
acpid.x86_64                        1.0.4-9.el6_4.2            base
at.x86_64                           3.1.8-84.el6              base

[output truncated]
```

From this list, you can choose to update packages individually or as a whole. If you want to install all the updates, you can use the following:

```
# yum update
```

REAL-WORLD TIP

If you have some scripting skills, you could set up a small script to run the Yum list updates and output them to a text file. The text file could then be emailed to you as a "Weekly Updates Summary" so you can see what patches you'd like to apply to your system. This is a common task you'd see as a system administrator.

The Yum utility also keeps a list of "groups" that contain a set of packages, making it easier to install sets of packages together. The most common example would be if you wanted to install an X server package so that your system has a GUI. You can use the `grouplist` command to get a listing of all available "groups":

```
# yum grouplist
Installed Groups:
    Administration Tools
    DNS Name Server
    Dialup Networking Support
    Editors
    GNOME Desktop Environment
    Games and Entertainment
    Graphical Internet
    Graphics

[output truncated]

Available Groups:
    Authoring and Publishing
    Base
    Beagle
    Cluster Storage
    Clustering
    Development Libraries
    Development Tools
    Emacs

[output truncated]
```

You can then install that "group" with the `groupinstall` command. For this section, install the `Emacs` group, which contains some text editors:

```
# yum groupinstall Emacs
```

The `groupinstall` command can save you large amounts of time so that you don't end up trying to hunt down all the needed packages to get something up and running.

> **WARNING:**   Don't forget that Linux doesn't handle whitespace the way that Windows does. If you specify a group name that you'd like to install but that name contains spaces, you need to enclose it in quotation marks (" "). For example, you could use the following:
>
> ```
> # yum groupinstall "Development Tools"
> ```

Searching for Packages

Unlike the RPM utility, the yum command gives you access to the repositories from which you can install software (like you just did). Now let's look at how to find software that you want to install. You can use the search command to query software packages from the repositories.

Find the postfix package to install:

```
# yum search postfix
Loaded plugins: fastestmirror
Loading mirror speeds from cached hostfile
 * addons: mirrors.bluehost.com
 * base: mirror.cisp.com
 * extras: mirror.5ninesolutions.com
 * updates: mirror.steadfast.net
============================= Matched: postfix ================================
postfix.x86_64 : Postfix Mail Transport Agent
spamassassin.x86_64 : Spam filter for email which can be invoked from mail
delivery agents
```

Here, you see that three matches were returned from the repositories along with a short description of what each package does. You can use the search option to look through the repositories for any package; however, keep in mind that there could be multiple matches depending on your search parameters. If you want more information than what is provided from the short description in the search command, you can use the info command to get more details.

To find out more information about the postfix package, use the following command:

```
# yum info postfix
Loaded plugins: fastestmirror
Repository spacewalk is listed more than once in the configuration
Loading mirror speeds from cached hostfile
 * addons: centos.aol.com
 * base: mirror.rackspace.com
 * extras: mirror.atlanticmetro.net
Available Packages
```

```
Name        : postfix
Arch        : x86_64
Epoch       : 2
Version     : 2.6.6
Release     : 2.el6
Size        : 9.7 M
Repo        : base
Summary     : Postfix Mail Transport Agent
URL         : http://www.postfix.org
License     : IBM Public License
Description : Postfix is a Mail Transport Agent (MTA), supporting LDAP, SMTP
AUTH (SASL),
            : TLS
```

One additional command that you can use with yum (rpm doesn't have an equivalent option) is the clean command. It wipes the yum cache and forces it to sync with the Red Hat repositories, giving you the most updated package information.

To flush the cache, do the following:

```
# yum clean all
Loaded plugins: fastestmirror
Cleaning up Everything
Cleaning up list of fastest mirrors
```

I find that yum is a very efficient tool for package management when it comes to adding, updating, and removing software. I do find, however, that the rpm command and its options provide greater functionality when I want to query a package on the system. Knowing when to use which command or when to switch between them will help you become a better system administrator.

Configuring Additional Repositories

Sometimes you might want to install a package that isn't in the repositories that come preconfigured with Red Hat. If the package is available in someone else's repository, you can add that person's repository to your yum config file.

WARNING: I can't begin to stress enough that you should NEVER download or install packages from random repositories or any location that you can't verify is a legitimate source. Make sure that you fully trust the repositories from which you are installing packages because this would be the easiest way for an attacker to get you to install harmful packages.

You can either add your own custom repositories to the main config file /etc/yum.conf or create a .repo file in the /etc/yum.repos.d directory, which will be added automatically. Here is what a sample entry for a custom repository looks like:

```
[unique title]
name=My Custom Yum Repository
baseurl=ftp://rhel01/opt/yum/myrepos
enabled=1
gpgcheck=1
gpgkey=file:///etc/pki/rpm-gpg/RPM-GPG-KEY-redhat-release
```

This entry defines a name, a location, and whether or not the repository is enabled. You can save this entry as a test.repo file in /etc/yum.repos.d, and you will have access to any of the packages in the /opt/yum/myrepos repository on the RHEL01 system. Currently, there is nothing there, so let's change that.

Making Your Own RPM

A key skill for a system administrator is being able to deploy your own custom software. However, you first need to build an RPM package that contains your custom software. This can seem like a large undertaking at first, but after a few times the process is pretty simple. To build an RPM, you must do the following:

Step 1.　Create a directory hierarchy.

Step 2.　Copy or create your source code into the directory hierarchy.

Step 3.　Create a spec file.

Step 4.　Build the RPM.

The hierarchy that you create must meet the rpmbuild specification, which is composed of the following directories:

BUILD	Contains scratch space used to compile software
RPMS	Contains the binary RPM that is built
SOURCES	Holds the source code for the RPM
SPECS	Contains the spec file(s) (one per RPM)
SRPMS	Contains the source RPM built during the process

REAL-WORLD TIP

Notice that the directory names are shown in uppercase. This is a standard that you should follow when creating the directory hierarchy.

Aside from the directories we have covered, you also need to install a few packages. Okay, enough with the theory; let's get started.

Creating an RPM

Create an RPM by following these steps:

Step 1. Install the required packages to build an RPM package:

```
# yum install -y rpm-build make
```

Step 2. Verify the packages are installed correctly:

```
# rpm -qa | grep rpm-build
rpm-build-4.8.0-12.el6.x86_64
# rpm -qa | grep make
make-3.81-19.el6.x86_64
```

Create the directory hierarchy you need to build in the /usr/src/redhat directory (this is a personal preference to build packages under the /usr/src directory).

Step 3. Create the required directories:

```
# mkdir -p /usr/src/redhat/{BUILD,RPMS,SOURCES,SPECS,SRPMS,tmp}
```

The tmp directory is used as a temporary build directory as well. When building a package, you need some additional items. In the SOURCES directory is a compressed file (.tar.gz) that contains the source files of the software from which you want to create a package. Note that the Red Hat exams require you to be able to build only a single-file RPM, so you don't need a full software source to make this work.

Step 4. Create a directory with some sample files that you'd like in the package:

```
# mkdir /usr/src/redhat/mysample
# cd /usr/src/redhat/mysample
# touch first_file second_file keys config_file
```

Step 5. Create an archive file based on your sample source:

```
# cd /usr/src/redhat
# tar cf mysample.tar.gz mysample
# mv mysample.tar.gz SOURCES/
```

Step 6. One final step before package creation involves the creation of a spec file. The spec file is the set of instructions used to create the actual package itself. If you couldn't guess, this file must be located in the SPECS directory. Here is a sample spec file to use for this package:

```
Summary: This package is a sample for the Red Hat exams.
Name: mysample
Version: 1.0
Release: 0
```

```
License: GPL
Packager: Joe Tester
Group: Development/Tools
Source: %{name}.tar.gz
BuildRoot: /usr/src/redhat/tmp/%{name}-%{version}

%description
This package is just a sample for the Red Hat exams.

%prep
%setup -n mysample

%install
mkdir -p "$RPM_BUILD_ROOT/opt/sample_pkge"
cp -R * "$RPM_BUILD_ROOT/opt/sample_pkge"

%files
/opt/sample_pkge

%clean
rm -rf "$RPM_BUILD_ROOT"

%post
chown user01:user01 -R /opt/sample_pkge
chmod 775 -R /opt/sample_pkge
```

This file definitely needs some explaining. The first main section is all information required for a package, which you already saw in this chapter when you queried information from a package. The Source and BuildRoot are both significant because they play a role in how the package is built. The Source is the archive file that the package will use; in this case it is named after the mysample.tar.gz file created and moved into the SOURCES directory. BuildRoot is the directory that will be used to actually build the software (you could use the BUILD directory as well).

The rest of the spec file contains sections defined with a %. First up is the %description section, which provides a description for the package that you are trying to build (as I'm sure you guessed). The %prep and %setup sections both move the SOURCE into the BUILD directory and decompress the file archive. The -n option specifies the name of the directory that will be entered into upon decompression. The %install section is normally the place where your software is compiled and installed on your current system. When it is installed, the files need to be collected so that they can be deployed via the package you are building, which leads us to the %files section. Here, you need to include any file that you want included in your package. Any directory that you specify here also includes all files and subdirectories below it as well. Because you are building a package with only a few files, you can just specify the directory previously created (/opt/sample_pkge) in the %install section.

The last two sections aren't required but are useful, so I have included them here. The %clean section is responsible for cleaning up a mess created when the package is created. In this case, the removal of $RPM_BUILD_ROOT should suffice, as shown by the single line in this section. Using %post enables you to run any additional scripts or commands as the package is completing installation. In the example, you are setting the permissions on the files you are creating. Notice, however, that this would fail on any system that doesn't have a user01 account. There are ways to enforce requirements, but they are beyond the scope of this book. Finally, you can run the rpmbuild command to create the package.

Step 7. Build the package with the rpmbuild command:

```
# rpmbuild -v -bb /usr/src/redhat/SPECS/sample.spec
Executing(%prep): /bin/sh -e /var/tmp/rpm-tmp.48604
+ umask 022
+ cd /usr/src/redhat/BUILD
+ cd /usr/src/redhat/BUILD
+ rm -rf mysample
+ tar -xvvf /usr/src/redhat/SOURCES/mysample.tar.gz
drwxr-xr-x root/root         0 2010-12-02 11:25:44 mysample/
-rw-r--r-- root/root         0 2010-12-02 11:25:44 mysample/con-
fig_file
-rw-r--r-- root/root         0 2010-12-02 11:25:44
mysample/first_file
-rw-r--r-- root/root         0 2010-12-02 11:25:44
mysample/second_file
-rw-r--r-- root/root         0 2010-12-02 11:25:44 mysample/keys
+ cd mysample
++ /usr/bin/id -u
+ '[' 0 = 0 ']'
+ /bin/chown -Rhf root .
++ /usr/bin/id -u
+ '[' 0 = 0 ']'
+ /bin/chgrp -Rhf root .
+ /bin/chmod -Rf a+rX,u+w,g-w,o-w .
+ exit 0
Executing(%install): /bin/sh -e /var/tmp/rpm-tmp.48604
+ umask 022
+ cd /usr/src/redhat/BUILD
+ cd mysample
+ mkdir -p /usr/src/redhat/tmp/mysample-1.0/opt/sample_pkge
+ cp -R config_file first_file keys second_file
/usr/src/redhat/tmp/mysample-
1.0/opt/sample_pkge
+ /usr/lib/rpm/brp-compress
+ /usr/lib/rpm/brp-strip
+ /usr/lib/rpm/brp-strip-static-archive
+ /usr/lib/rpm/brp-strip-comment-note
Processing files: mysample-1.0-0
Requires(interp): /bin/sh
Requires(rpmlib): rpmlib(CompressedFileNames) <= 3.0.4-1
rpmlib(PayloadFilesHavePrefix) <= 4.0-1
Requires(post): /bin/sh
```

```
Checking for unpackaged file(s): /usr/lib/rpm/check-files
/usr/src/redhat/tmp/mysample-1.0
Wrote: /usr/src/redhat/RPMS/x86_64/mysample-1.0-0.x86_64.rpm
Executing(%clean): /bin/sh -e /var/tmp/rpm-tmp.48604
+ umask 022
+ cd /usr/src/redhat/BUILD
+ cd mysample
+ rm -rf /usr/src/redhat/tmp/mysample-1.0
+ exit 0
```

Looking through this output, you can see all the commands executed to create the package. They should all be in line with what we have discussed so far. If everything went all right, you should now have your new RPM package in the RPMS directory.

Step 8.   View the new RPM package:

```
# ls /usr/src/redhat/RPMS/x86_64/
mysample-1.0-0.x86_64.rpm   QA-Keys-1.0-0.x86_64.rpm
```

Step 9.   Install the new package to ensure that it works properly:

```
# cd /usr/src/redhat/RPMS/x86_64
# rpm -ivh mysample-1.0-0.x86_64.rpm
Preparing...        ######################################### [100%]
   1:mysample        ######################################### [100%]
```

Because there were no errors, the package should have installed correctly.

Step 10.   As always, verify the installation:

```
# rpm -qa | grep mysample
mysample-1.0-0
```

Step 11.   You can also check the directory and files themselves to ensure installation:

```
# ls/opt/sample_pkge/
config_file  first_file   keys   second_file
```

Building a package can become very involved and requires practice. Luckily, the Red Hat exams don't require you to package more than a single file, so everything we have covered here should work just fine for the exams. With the newly created package in hand, let's add it to your private repository.

Creating Your Own Repository

On large networks, it is common for system administrators to create their own repositories where they keep not only a copy of Red Hat packages, but also their own custom software packages. Now let's set up a repository where you can keep your own software packages. First, you need to install a package that will help with the setup of the repository.

Step 1.   Install the required package:

```
# yum install -y createrepo
```

Step 2.   Make a directory where you will house all your packages:

```
# mkdir -p /opt/yum/myrepos
# cd /opt/yum/myrepos
```

Now you need to copy all the packages you want to maintain into your newly created directory. You can use the nano package that you downloaded in the beginning of this chapter. When you used the wget command originally, the package was saved in the home directory.

Step 3.   Copy the package over to the newly created repository directory:

```
# cp ~/nano-2.2.6-1.x86_64.rpm /opt/yum/myrepos
```

Next, you can use the createrepo command to set up the repository based on the directory you created (and moved packages into).

Step 4.   Specify which directory you created and call the createrepo command:

```
# createrepo /opt/yum/myrepos
1/1 - nano-2.2.6-1.x86_64.rpm
Saving Primary metadata
Saving file lists metadata
Saving other metadata
```

You should now see a directory called repodata that contains all your packages unzipped and an XML file that details the repository. In the config directory for yum, you need to create a .repo file to hold the repository information so that you can access the newly created repository. The repository files are kept in the /etc/yum.repos.d directory. This .repo file is just like what you created in the previous section.

Step 5.   Go to the repo directory and create a .repo file for your newly created repository:

```
# cd /etc/yum.repos.d
# nano myrepo.repo
```

Use the following for your myrepo.repo file:

```
[base]
name=My Custom Yum Repository
baseurl=ftp://rhel01/opt/yum/myrepos
enabled=1
gpgcheck=1
gpgkey=file:///etc/pki/rpm-gpg/RPM-GPG-KEY-redhat-release
```

When you're finished, save your file and exit. You should now be able to use yum to search and install packages from your repository. One neat trick that you can do is to create a repository based on an ISO. This trick can be useful in an environment where there is no Internet access and you'd like to install packages from the Red Hat DVD.

Step 1.   Create a folder for the temporary mount:

```
# mkdir /mnt/cd
```

Step 2.   Mount the CD or ISO:

```
# mount -o loop /dev/cdrom /mnt/cd
```

Step 3.   Create a repository in the temporary directory:

```
# cd /mnt
# createrepo .
```

This creates an XML file of all the packages from the mounted CD.

Step 4.   You also need to clean the current repository cache:

```
# yum clean all
```

Step 5.   Create a .repo file for your temporary repository:

```
# nano /etc/yum.repos.d/iso.repo
[ISO Repo]
Baseurl=file:///mnt/cd
enabled=1
```

Now when you use the yum command, you also query packages from the mounted Red Hat DVD.

Adding Your Custom Packages

Just as you have already created two different types of custom repositories, you can add packages you have created to them as well. In a previous section, you created your own RPM package called mysample-1.0-0.x86_64.rpm.

Step 1.   Copy this file over to your private directory:

```
# cp /usr/src/redhat/RPMS/x86_64/ mysample-1.0-0.x86_64.rpm
/opt/yum/myrepos
```

Step 2.   Update the repository to recognize your new package:

```
# createrepo -update
```

Now you should be able to search for your package in your private repository along with other software.

The Red Hat Network

The Red Hat Network is the web interface through which customers can subscribe to and manage their systems, software, and installs. For you to utilize the Red Hat Network for your systems, you need to register each system to the network. The biggest benefit to using the Red Hat Network is that it provides a central place to manage all your systems with ease. Each system that you register polls the network every four hours by default, although this setting can be changed. When it notices updates, it automatically adjusts to what has been configured for it through the web interface. This can also be a great help when you have satellite offices that are hard to get to or manage.

Registering Your System

To register your system to the Red Hat Network, you must have an active subscription with Red Hat. You can register during the installation of your system or manually after the system has already been installed. Use the rhn_register command to begin the registration process. After you finish, you can visit http://rhn.redhat.com to start managing your system(s) through the Web. You need to make sure that the rhnsd daemon is running in order for it to be managed.

Step 1.   Set the daemon to boot on system start:

```
# chkconfig rhnsd on
```

Step 2.   You should verify whether the service is currently running:

```
# service rhnsd status
rhnsd (pid  1985) is running...
```

Step 3.   If it is, you are all set; otherwise, start the service manually:

```
# service rhnsd start
Starting rhnsd:
[  OK  ]
```

Summary

Learning to work with software is important because the rest of this book and the Red Hat exams require you to install and configure different software packages. You also need to be able to verify that packages have been installed successfully and fix them when they are not. The package management process isn't difficult and can be very useful for keeping your systems in order. As you become more skilled with package management, you will start to get a feel for what packages can also be safely removed from your system to prevent security attacks (this is called *system hardening*). When we get to network installs, you can also pick and choose specific packages through config files, making the install process much faster on your system.

Review Questions

1. What two commands are used for package management?

2. What are the three modes in which the `rpm` command can operate?

3. What option would you use to query an installed package using the `rpm` command?

4. How would you install a group of packages all at a single time?

5. What options with the `yum` command would you use to remove a package?

6. Where are Yum repository config files located?

7. What command can you use to create your own repositories?

8. What command is used to create an RPM package?

9. What are the five required directories when building RPMS?

10. If a package is built on an RHEL6 system and deployed to a custom RHEL5 repository, are RHEL5 systems able to use it?

Answers to Review Questions

1. The `yum` and `rpm` commands are used for package management.

2. The `rpm` command can operate in install, query, or verify modes.

3. You can use the `-q` option to query an installed package. Combining `grep` and the `-qa` options, you can search among all installed packages on the system.

4. Use the `yum groupinstall` command to install multiple packages in a single group at once.

5. You can use the `remove` or `erase` options with yum to remove a package.

6. Yum repository config files (.repo files) are located in the /etc/yum.repos.d directory. You can also make direct entries into the main /etc/yum.conf file.

7. `createrepo`

8. `rpmbuild`

9. The five directories are BUILD, RPMS, SOURCES, SPECS, and SRPMS.

10. No. Red Hat Enterprise Linux 6 uses a different key to sign its packages.

Lab 6

Task 1 – Software Installation

Step 1.   Install the following packages on RHEL02:
emacs
php
perl

Step 2.   Remove the following packages on Client01:
wireless-tools
ypbind

Step 3.   Update all packages on RHEL01.

The task is complete when all packages can be verified as installed, removed, or upgraded.

Task 2 – Web Packages

Step 1.   Download the latest version of the nano package from the Web (also available from http://sourceforge.net/projects/rhcelabscripts/files/).

Step 2.   Remove any currently installed version of nano from RHEL02.

Step 3.   Install the newly downloaded version of nano with the rpm command.

The task is complete when the upgraded version of nano can be verified.

Task 3 – Your Very Own Package

Step 1.   Download the SourceFiles.tar.gz file from http://sourceforge.net/projects/rhcelabscripts/files/.

Step 2.   Install the rpm-build package.

Step 3.   Create an RPM package called SamplePackage using the SourceFiles.tar.gz.

The task is complete when the SamplePackage.rpm is installable on RHEL02.

This chapter covers the following subjects:

- **Users and Groups**—This section covers user and group creation, management, and passwords.

- **User Account Initialization**—This section covers global and specific user initialization and setup.

- **Group Collaboration**—This section covers how to set up files and directories for multiuser collaboration.

- **Network User Authentication**—This section covers client network authentication.

The following RHCSA exam objectives are covered:

- Log in and switch users in multiuser runlevels

- Create, delete, and modify local user accounts

- Change passwords and adjust password aging for local user accounts

- Create, delete, and modify local groups and group memberships

- Configure a system to use an existing LDAP directory service for user and group information

The following RHCE exam objective is covered:

- Configure a system to authenticate using Kerberos

## CHAPTER 7

User Administration

Every system comes with a way to add users, giving each person the ability to sign in to the system and work productively. This chapter looks at ways you can create users and groups in Red Hat and reasons you would want specific users and groups; in addition, it covers system accounts used to run services and special applications. Aside from normal and service users, there is also the root user, which is the main administrator account for Linux systems.

As a system administrator, you will spend a fair amount of time managing user and group accounts, particularly because those accounts determine what files and directories users or groups have access to. You could also add a bunch of different users to groups to allow for project collaboration. When users are created, they are also given a standard set of files. These files can be customized to deliver particular documents or notices to your end users upon creating their accounts. A lot goes into creating a user account, so many system administrators tend to script account creation, automating the process. Although it's good to create user accounts and groups, what happens if you have more than one server? All your accounts and groups are local to your system, so how will your users access other network hosts? Will you have to create all those accounts and groups all over again? To solve this problem, you can add your system to a domain, which contains all user accounts and groups in a centralized database, making administration easier.

Users and Groups

In Red Hat, there are three different types of user accounts: root, normal user, and system (or what some people like to call "pseudo-user") accounts. The root account is the equivalent of the Administrator or Enterprise Admin account in the Windows world. It is the most powerful account on the system and has access to everything. You should already realize that because of the power this account has, you should never use it. Ever!

When Red Hat is installed for the first time, you are asked to create the first user account (if you install a desktop manager). If you installed your system through an automated process (such as a network install) or without a desktop manager package, you need to create such an account for yourself. Either way, you should have a normal user account for yourself that has permissions to perform the actions you need to accomplish as a system administrator.

Later in this chapter, you see how you can delegate controls of the system to this user or any other users by allowing them to perform actions as if they were the root user. This not only makes your system more secure, but also makes it easier to detect break-in attempts and forces accountability of all users through their individual user accounts. Normal user accounts have no write access to anything on the system except their home directory (they can read and explore much of the system, however), which is created when the user account is added. As an administrator, you can assign access rights to different files and directories, allowing your users to gain access to different areas of the system (outside their home directory).

A system account is similar to a normal user account. The main difference is that system users normally don't have a home directory and can't log in the way normal users do. Many system users are created or associated with applications or services to help run them more securely. Think of the situation this way: If a system user is created for the Apache service (the web server), and the account becomes compromised, the attacker will have access only to the web server and its config files. This could be worse if the Apache service were running as the root user; in that case, the attacker would have full access to the system. These are just some additional reasons why you should never truly need the root account unless there is a problem with the system.

Users

When dealing with users, you need to create their accounts, give them passwords (and manage password settings), modify their account settings, and delete their accounts when they are no longer needed. To manage user accounts, you can use the following commands:

useradd	Creates user or system accounts
usermod	Modifies user accounts
userdel	Removes a user or system account

Imagine a user walks up to you in the office and says he'd like to log in to one of the servers so that he can install some new software and try it out. You can't give him your credentials because you are the administrator, and giving out the root credentials is also out of the question. Clearly, you need some user accounts. Let's start by making a few users for the sample system and looking at the different options you can use when creating a user account. To create a user account, you can use the useradd command.

Syntax: useradd [options] LOGIN

Options:

-b	Sets the base directory for the new user account home directory
-c COMMENT	Creates a description/label for the user account
-e EXPIRE_DATE	Sets the date when the account will expire
-m	Creates a home directory for the new user account
-r	Creates a system account
-s SHELL	Defines what shell the user will log in to
-u UID	Forces the use of the UID for the new user account

To make the first user account, you can use the following:

```
# useradd -c "Avg Joe" -m -s /bin/bash user02
```

This command creates a user account named user02 and a home directory for the user, sets the user's shell to BASH, and adds a description to the user's account called Avg Joe. There is more actually going on in the background as well. All users have a unique ID that defines them (this is known as the UID) and a group ID (this is known as the GID). In Red Hat, UIDs start at 500 for normal users and can extend into the thousands. For system users, the UID starts at 1 and goes to 499. Red Hat also uses a policy called User Private Groups that assigns the UID to be the same as the username. Although the GID doesn't have to match, it frequently does. This ensures that all users maintain security over their own files. Aside from the UID/GID being assigned, a home directory named after the user is created in the /home directory. You can check to see the new user's home directory by using the following:

```
# ls /home
user01   user02
```

Now create another user named user03 with a home directory:

```
# useradd -m user03
```

REAL-WORLD TIP

As a good practice, you should provide a label or some description for each account; otherwise, after time, you will forget what it is for.

Now that the user is created, suppose you want to make an adjustment to the user account. Let's add a description to the user account you just created. Because the user already exists, you can use the usermod command to modify the account information.

Syntax: `usermod [options] LOGIN`

Options:

`-c COMMENT`	Specifies the new value of the GECOS field
`-d HOME_DIR`	Identifies the new home directory for the user account
`-g GROUP`	Uses GROUP as the new primary group
`-G GROUPS`	Specifies a new list of supplementary GROUPS
`-l NEW_LOGIN`	Provides a new value for the login name
`-L`	Locks the user account
`-s SHELL`	Opens a new login shell for the user account
`-u UID`	Specifies a new UID for the user account
`-U`	Unlocks the user account

Add a description to the user's account:

```
# usermod -c "Third User" user03
```

The last user-related task we need to look at is how to delete users. This area can be somewhat tricky because user deletion doesn't function in the way you would expect. Create a dummy user named user05 to test:

```
# useradd user05
```

To delete this user, you use the `userdel` command:

Syntax: `userdel [options] LOGIN`

Options:

`-f`	Forces deletion of the user even if he's still logged in
`-r`	Removes the user's home directory and mail spool

Delete the user:

```
# userdel user05
```

Now if you go over to the /home directory and output its contents, you will notice that user05's home directory is still there!

```
# ls /home
user01  user02  user05
```

Didn't you just delete him? You did, but you didn't specify the `-r` option, which removes all the user's files (and with good reason).

Knowing how to delete users (and their home directories) may be essential for the exam, but this is not even close to real-world practice. Many companies have a strict policy about retention of files, so it goes without saying that 99% of the time you will want to delete the users but keep their files. As a best practice, you should have root take ownership of the files and make them read-only to everyone but the root user, essentially denying everyone else access. This way, if you ever need to recall anything from this user's directory or if you get audited, you can recall the user's files quickly.

REAL-WORLD TIP

Although you might like to think that users will stay organized and keep their files in their home directories, seasoned system administrators know that this is not the case. Users love to create files and put them in all sorts of places on the system. To combat this issue, you can search for all files that belong to a user before you delete her. You can lock her account so no one can gain access to it (you learn how shortly); then you can use the following command to search for all files that belong to the user you want to delete:

```
# find / -user user05
```

You can then move these files to a single location and change the permissions on them, as already discussed, for safekeeping.

Passwords

You may have noticed by now that no password was specified for any of the users created so far. Does this mean that each user's password is blank and anyone can log in with a user's account? Actually no. By default, an account is locked until a password is assigned to it. For password management, you can use the following commands:

passwd	Sets a password or resets a password for a user account
chage	Enables you to modify the parameters surrounding passwords (complexity, age, expiration)
pwck	Verifies the consistency of passwords across database files

When you create a user account, you can use the -p option to set a password; however, this requires you to type the password for the user in clear-text on the screen, and anyone walking by can see it. A better method for password creation/ assignment is to use the passwd command, which allows you to change (or, in this case, set) the user's password.

Syntax: passwd [options] LOGIN

Options:

-l   Locks a user's account

-u   Unlocks a user's account

-s   Sets status of the password on the account

Let's set a new user's password:

```
# passwd user02
Changing password for user user02.
New UNIX password:
Retype new UNIX password:
passwd: all authentication tokens updated successfully.
```

Now that the user has a username (user02) and a password (whatever you set it to), you can give these credentials to the user who asked to log in to the system. It is important to understand that this account is local to the system where you created it! If your user wants to log in to a different server, you need to create a user account on that system as well.

REAL-WORLD TIP

Some software packages (such as OpenLDAP and Red Hat Directory Server) allow you to create a centralized database for your users. This allows them to log in to any server on your network without having to create their accounts on every system within your network. The configuration and setup of such software can become complex, and it is a whole topic on its own. You can try setting up an OpenLDAP server on your own, but Red Hat also offers an advanced training course on Red Hat Directory Server if you want to utilize this technology.

We cover how to attach the system to a centralized server later in this chapter. Although you don't need to be able to set up a centralized authentication server for the Red Hat exams, you do need to be able to attach the client system. The good news, though, is that the user account you created can be used for services other than just logging in to the system. The same credentials are used if you have an FTP server or an SSH server running on the system as well. This makes it slightly easier to create accounts once and not have to make a user account for each individual service. If you're coming from a Windows world, you are likely familiar with this concept because many services allow you to pass your domain credentials for authentication to different services. Now that you know how to create users and their passwords, let's look at how the password files work.

The Password File

Syntax of /etc/passwd:

```
<username>:<password placeholder>:<UID>:<GID>:<comments>:<home dir>:<shell>
```

To view the user you just created, use the following command:

```
# cat /etc/passwd | grep user02
user02:x:501:501:Avg Joe:/home/user02:/bin/bash
```

When making users, including system users, you can always check this file to ensure they have been created properly. You can see that all the options specified during user creation are present here. The password field is actually just a placeholder (with an x). The reason is that the passwords are actually stored in a different file, /etc/shadow.

The Shadow File

Syntax of /etc/shadow:

```
<username>:<encrypted password>:<last passwd
change>:<min>:<max>:<warn>:<inactive>:<expires>:<not used>
```

With the exception of the username and password fields, all values are in days.

To view the information about the user you just created, use the following:

```
# cat /etc/shadow | grep user02
user02:$1$cMT6t6Ld$UXCCg5Pm2V2/YXxEjmz901:14767:0:99999:7:::
```

You can see here the username and encrypted password. The next field, 14767, is the number of days since the password has been changed. Well, you just made this user account, so where did that large number come from? This number is actually based on the number of days since epoch time (January 1, 1970), which is a standard for keeping track of how long it's been since something has elapsed. Also, notice that the next two fields show the minimum number of days before you can change your password (0) and the number of days your password is valid (the 99999 is basically forever, so the password won't expire). The difference between the max days field and expires field is that max days requires you to change your password, whereas the expires field disables, or expires, your account. You can edit and manage the password expiration details with the chage command.

Syntax: chage [options] USER

Options:

-d LAST_DAY	Indicates the day the password was last changed
-E EXPIRE_DATE	Sets the account expiration date
-I INACTIVE	Changes the password in an inactive state after the account expires
-l	Shows account aging information
-m MIN_DAYS	Sets the minimum number of days between password changes

-M MAX_DAYS	Sets the maximum number of days a password is valid
-W WARN_DAYS	Sets the number of days to warn before the password expires

Let's run through an example:

Step 1.   Find the user's password information:

```
# chage -l user03
Last password change                               : Oct
26, 2010
Password expires                                   : never
Password inactive                                  : never
Account expires                                    : never
Minimum number of days between password change     : 0
Maximum number of days between password change     : 99999
Number of days of warning before password expires  : 7
```

Step 2.   Set user03's account to expire in one week (say today's date is 10-22-2011):

```
# chage -E 2011-10-28 user03
```

Step 3.   Verify that the user's account is now set to expire on the 28th of this month:

```
# chage -l user03
Last password change                               : Oct
26, 2011
Password expires                                   : never
Password inactive                                  : never
Account expires                                    : Oct
28, 2011
Minimum number of days between password change     : 0
Maximum number of days between password change     : 99999
Number of days of warning before password expires  : 7
```

You can see that the fourth line shows the account expiry date.

REAL-WORLD TIP

It is a good practice to set an account to expire on all employees who aren't considered permanent. It's usually common for companies to hire contract employees or additional help when working on projects, but the hired help won't be around forever. It is better to set their accounts to expire after a certain period of time to prevent a security breach from stale accounts.

EXAM TIP

If you are using the chage command to set specifics on an account, do not reset the password with the passwd command because doing so erases any changes to the account expiring.

When you create or delete users, sometimes things don't always work out properly. This can cause the password files to become inconsistent. You can use the pwck command to verify the consistency between the /etc/passwd file and the /etc/shadow file:

```
# pwck
user adm: directory /var/adm does not exist
user news: directory /etc/news does not exist
user uucp: directory /var/spool/uucp does not exist
pwck: no changes
```

One other topic along the lines of passwords is locking and unlocking user accounts. This is done by manipulating users' passwords in the /etc/shadow file (usually through the usermod command, not by hand). As a real-world example, suppose you are hiring two new people next week. The boss says, "I want two accounts created for these two new people so that they are ready to go and don't have to wait on anything to be set up." You should already know that creating user accounts with no passwords is not an option, and sometimes administrators are obsessive with security and don't like to leave open accounts that have default passwords. In this case, you can create the two new users as you normally would with a standard default password (usually defined by policy) and then lock their accounts.

Step 1. Create a user account:

```
# useradd -c "New User" user06
```

Step 2. Set the user's default password:

```
# passwd user06
Changing password for user user06.
New UNIX password:
Retype new UNIX password:
passwd: all authentication tokens updated successfully.
```

Step 3. Now lock the user's account:

```
# usermod -L user06
```

Locked accounts have passwords that start with an exclamation point (!) in the /etc/shadow file.

Step 4. Verify that the account is locked:

```
# cat /etc/shadow | grep user06
user06:!$1$t9WeO2v2$MQb3YrqtNPp6n96ALudti0:14805:0:99999:7:::
```

Now when the user starts working Monday morning, you can simply unlock the user's account and she is up and running.

Step 5. Unlock the account:

```
# usermod -U user06
```

Step 6.   Verify:

```
# cat /etc/shadow | grep user06
user06:$1$t9WeO2v2$MQb3YrqtNPp6n96ALudti0:14805:0:99999:7:::
```

Notice the ! leading in the password field is now gone. The user should be able to log in with no problems. As you see in Chapter 9, "System Logging, Monitoring, and Automation," you can use cron or at to schedule jobs on a system. If you know the start date of your new users, you can simply set up a job to execute early Monday morning to unlock the user accounts for you.

Groups

Now that you have some users and they have passwords, let's create some groups to put some of the users in. Creating a group is similar to creating a user. Here are the commands for group creation and management:

id	Shows UID/GID for the group of a given user
groupadd	Creates a group
groupmod	Modifies the properties of a group
groupdel	Deletes a group

You can use the groupadd command to create a group.

Syntax: groupadd [options] GROUP

Options:

-r	Creates a system group
-g GID	Uses the GID specified for the group

That pesky user from the first section is back, and now he wants a group called Sales to start putting all his sales people in. Let's create a group called Sales for him:

```
# groupadd Sales
```

That's really all there is to it.

Much like users are contained within the /etc/passwd file, groups are maintained within the /etc/group file.

The Group File

Syntax of /etc/group:

```
<group name>:<password placeholder>:<GID>:<members>
```

You can verify that your group was added successfully by checking this file for the new group's existence.

```
# cat /etc/group | grep sales
sales:x:503:
```

Notice that there is an x placeholder as in the user's file, but this field is not typically used with groups. Now that you have the Sales group, why don't you add some of the users to that group:

```
# usermod -G Sales user02
```

This adds user02 to the Sales group. Verify with

```
# cat /etc/group | grep Sales
Sales:x:503:user02
```

Here, you can see the group named Sales and the last field, which shows a list of members for the group. Next, add another user to the Sales group.

```
# usermod -G Sales user03
```

Now if you verify, you should see two user accounts in the last field:

```
# cat /etc/group | grep Sales
Sales:x:503:user02,user03
```

Another way you can verify what groups a user belongs to is to use the id command:

Syntax: id [options] [username]

Options:

-G   Shows the GID

-n   Shows the name instead of the ID

-u   Shows the UID

Let's check out the groups to which user02 belongs:

```
# id -Gn user02
user02 Sales
```

If the id command is called without any options, you can also see what UID and GID the user has:

```
# id user02
uid=501(user02) gid=501(user02) groups=500(user02)
context=user_u:system_r:unconfined_t
```

You could also look at other users' information:

```
# id user03
uid=502(user03) gid=502(user03) groups=501(user03)
context=user_u:system_r:unconfined_t
```

One command that we haven't talked about yet is `groupdel`. This command is very straightforward in that it has no options; it simply deletes a group. As you know, Linux is case sensitive, so say you named your Sales group with a lowercase *s* and the boss doesn't like that (he is a stickler for capitalization):

```
# groupadd sales
```

Verify that the incorrectly spelled group is there:

```
# cat /etc/group | grep sales
sales:x:1005:
```

To remove this group, you can simply use this command:

```
# groupdel sales
```

Now if you try to verify again, you will come up with nothing because the group no longer exists.

Switching Accounts

With all these user accounts floating around, someone is bound to run into a problem sooner or later. Being able to switch accounts is most useful when you're troubleshooting some specific problem a user has or if you want to show a user how to do something. The commands you have available are as follows:

su   Enables you to run a command as another user or switch user accounts

sudo   Enables you to run a command as the root user

Suppose you are logged in as user02, but user03 is having trouble executing a command. You can switch over to user03's account to check that the command is able to be run and that the problem is not just a user error.

To switch accounts, use this command:

```
# su user03
Password:
```

Enter the password for user03, and you are logged in as that user. When you are finished, you can use the `exit` command to leave user03's account and return to your own account. If your user account is authorized, you can also log in as the root user using the `su` command:

```
# su -
Password:
```

REAL-WORLD TIP

You can log in to the root user account using the su command with no parameters. So what is the difference between using su and su -? The su command moves you into the root user's account without initializing any of root's path or shell variables. When you use su -, everything is initialized as if you were logging in from the console.

After you enter the root password, you are logged in as the root user.

Suppose, however, that you don't want to become the root user, but you need to run a command with elevated privileges for it to work. You can use the sudo command to run a single command as root. For example, only the root user can create users. To create a new user with a normal user account, you can use the following command:

```
# sudo useradd user09
```

To help determine which user you are logged in as, look at the command prompt. You can always tell that you are the root user if the command prompt starts with a # instead of $, which means you're a normal user.

By now, you should be an expert in user management! We have covered user creation, modification, and deletion. User management is crucial to working with Red Hat or any Linux distribution for that matter. Make sure you are comfortable working with users and groups for the Red Hat exams. Many system administrators create scripts for user creation because this process requires customization and usually follows a standard.

User Account Initialization

In the previous section, we discussed creating users and groups. Now let's look a little deeper at what happens during this creation process and how it can be customized. When a user is created, everything from the /etc/skel directory is copied to the user's newly created home directory (usually /home/<username>). You can modify these "skeleton" files or can add your own custom files. The benefit here is that user creation becomes standardized, ensuring that policies are adhered to. The customizable files are broken down into two different sections: user-specific files and system-wide settings.

User-Specific Files

After a user is created and his home directory is populated, that user can now customize those files to fit his own personal needs. For example, the user might like to have certain PATH values or specific environment variables set. The following three files allow a user to customize the login experience to his own style:

~/.bashrc   Defines functions and aliases

~/.bash_profile   Sets environment variables

~/.bash_logout   Defines any commands that should be executed before the user logs out

Editing these files allows each user to be unique in the way he operates. Because each file is stored in the user's home directory, that file is limited to use by that single user. What happens, though, if there is a standard that you'd like set when users start out? Glad you asked.

Global User Configuration

Just as in the /etc/skel directory, you can edit the following three additional files to provide a more standardized format for your users:

/etc/bashrc   Defines functions and aliases

/etc/profile   Sets environment variables

/etc/profile.d   Specifies a directory that contains scripts that are called by the /etc/profile file

These files help you make sure that your users receive everything they need when they get started. If you require that settings be changed for your users, customizing these files is the way to go. Just make sure that when you're editing files for distribution, you make sure you're editing system-wide config files and not the config files within a user's home directory.

One last file to look at is /etc/login.defs. This file controls specifics relating to system-wide user logins and passwords:

```
# grep -v ^# /etc/login.defs
MAIL_DIR          /var/spool/mail

PASS_MAX_DAYS     99999
PASS_MIN_DAYS     0
PASS_MIN_LEN      5
PASS_WARN_AGE     7

UID_MIN                        500
UID_MAX                        60000

GID_MIN                        500
GID_MAX                        60000
```

```
CREATE_HOME        yes

UMASK              077

USERGROUPS_ENAB yes

MD5_CRYPT_ENAB yes
```

These values should all be self-explanatory. You can edit them if you don't like the given defaults, but make sure you remember that these are local to this system and don't apply on other systems on your network unless you change them there as well. Initialization files can save you a great deal of time so that you don't have to create custom profiles and scripts for individual users every time they are created. This process does take some planning ahead, however, and making sure that your files and custom scripts are distributed to all users (even if they have already been created).

Group Collaboration

Group collaboration is an essential part of any business and for any system administrator who deals with users. Knowing how to set up group collaboration is definitely a key skill to have. Here, we look at three key features about file and directory permissions, which allow you to let users work together:

setuid   This flag is used to allow multiuser access.

setgid   This flag is used to allow multigroup access.

sticky bit   This flag prevents accidental delete by users or groups.

For group collaboration, you need two key commands as well:

chmod   Changes permissions on files and directories

chown   Changes ownership of files and directories

The first feature is setuid, which is set on files at the owner level with the chmod command. This allows executables to be run with the privileges of the file's owner. For example, if you have a script that generates reports for your company, but the script must be run as user01 to succeed, you can set the setuid bit to enable other users to run this command as though they were user01.

Create a file to hold the report script:

```
# touch reporting_script
```

Next, set the `setuid` bit:

```
# chmod 4755 reporting_script
```

You could also use the following:

```
# chmod u+s reporting_script
```

Now view the permissions of the file:

```
# ll
total 12
-rwsr-xr-x 1 user01 user01    0 Jun  8 17:20 reporting_script.sh
```

In the file's owner permissions, notice that there is an s in place of the x. This shows that this file has the `setuid` flag set. Now even if you're logged in as user02, you can still run this command as though you are user01.

REAL-WORLD TIP

Although the example we just looked at works properly, you can't use the `setuid` flag on scripts owned by the root user. You can, however, use it on binaries owned by the root user.

REAL-WORLD TIP

As a security tip, you can search your entire system for all files with the `setuid` bit to see what your users have access to run as another user.

To find all setuid files, use the following:

```
# find / -perm 4000
```

Next, let's look at `setgid`, which is similar to `setuid` but set at the group level instead. With this bit set, all users of the group are able to execute the file instead of just the user who owns it. The `setgid` bit allows users to collaborate on files. Let's create a directory for users to share and then assign it the correct permissions.

Step 1. As root, create the directory:

```
# mkdir /tmp/Sales
```

Step 2. Create the group and add users to it:

```
# groupadd Sales
# usermod -G Sales user02
# usermod -G Sales user03
```

Step 3. Assign the permissions for collaboration:

```
# chown nobody:Sales Sales/
# chmod 2770 /tmp/Sales
```

Step 4.   Verify:

```
# ll
total 16
drwxrws—- 2 nobody Sales   4096 Jun   8 18:11 Sales
```

Now all members of the Sales group are able to read/write to files within this folder. Also, notice that access to this folder is denied for anyone who isn't a member of the Sales group. If you log in as user01, you are not even able to get into the directory. All files created within this directory are owned by the user who creates them, but the group permissions allow for other users in the group to read and write to the files in the directory.

Finally, let's look at the sticky bit. It is used to prevent anyone from deleting files, and it is usually set on directories.

Step 1.   Set the sticky bit on the /tmp directory:

```
# chmod 1777 /tmp
```

Step 2.   Verify:

```
# ll
total 16
drwxrwxrwt   3 root root   4096 Jun   8 18:11 tmp
```

For the sticky bit, there is a t on the end of the permissions listed. Now other users are not able to delete your files; only you can. This feature might be helpful when you're sharing files and there are particular files you don't want other users to delete. Setting permissions for sharing files and group collaboration is important so that your users can work together, and it allows them to be more productive.

Network User Authentication

As mentioned at the beginning of this chapter, there are services like LDAP that allow you to store your users and passwords in a central location. The current exams require only that you are able to connect clients (servers or desktops) to a network directory service for network authentication to occur. This is easy because the servers will already be in place for you to connect to. There are a few ways that you can go about connecting to a network directory, and there are two types of servers to connect to. As far as commands go, you need to know only two:

`authconfig-tui`   A menu-based configuration utility for network authentication clients

`authconfig`   A command-line based version of authconfig-tui

Here, we cover only the `authconfig-tui` utility because it is faster to use and time is limited on the exam. If you're interested in scripting or adjusting more options, you can look further into the `authconfig` command on your own.

Before using the `authconfig-tui` tool, we cover how to manually set up and configure both NIS and LDAP, the two client network authentication methods. Although NIS is no longer a requirement for either exam, it might come in handy for legacy purposes.

The first type of network authentication is NIS, which requires the following two packages for client authentication to work:

ypbind   The actual service that binds an NIS client to an NIS server

portmap   A package used for security on NIS clients

Start by installing the required packages on the system:

```
# yum install -y ypbind portmap
```

After the packages are installed, you need to configure the /etc/yp.conf file and define your client settings. Specifically, you need to define the IP address of the NIS server and the domain name:

```
# nano /etc/yp.conf
```

Uncomment the following line:

```
domain NISDOMAIN server HOSTNAME
```

For the lab setup, you can use example.com as the domain name, and the IP address of the NIS server is 172.168.1.1. Your line in the config file therefore should be

```
domain example.com server 172.168.1.1
```

Save and close the file when finished. Next, you need to start the service:

```
# service ypbind start
Starting ypbind:                                          [  OK  ]
# service portmap start
Starting portmap:                                         [  OK  ]
```

On the exam, you also need to make sure that any changes are persistent across a reboot. Enable both services to start at boot time:

```
# chkconfig ypbind on
# chkconfig portmap on
```

Finally, you just need to edit the /etc/nsswitch.conf file and specify that you want your users and groups to be authenticated against the NIS domain, and if that isn't available, then check locally. Open the file for editing:

```
# nano /etc/nsswitch.conf
```

Edit the following lines to look like this:

```
passwd:                nis files
```

```
shadow:                    nis files
group:                     nis files
```

Now that you've gone through all the trouble of setting up the config files, let's look at an alternate way to configure an NIS client. Run the `authconfig-tui` command to view the menu-driven client configuration tool:

`authconfig-tui`

Choose NIS authentication (see Figure 7-1).

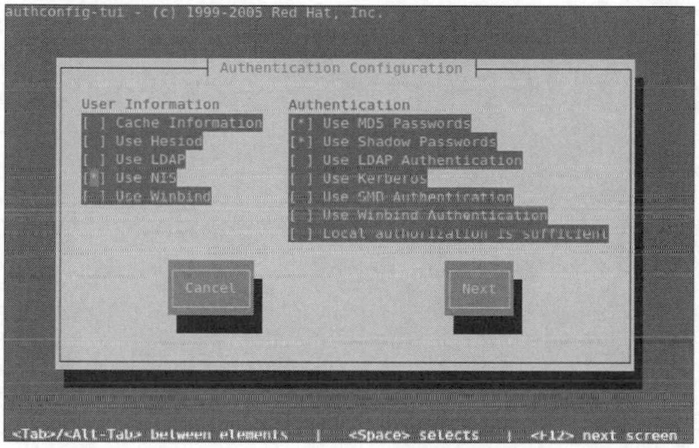

Figure 7-1   Choose NIS authentication from the menu.

Specify the correct domain settings (see Figure 7-2).

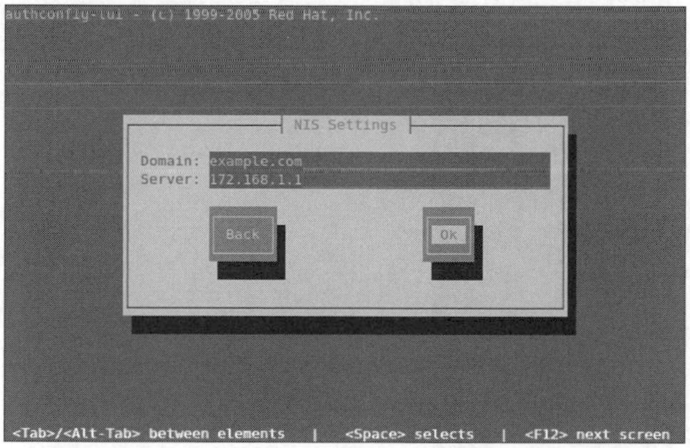

Figure 7-2   Enter the correct domain settings.

This utility automatically edits the /etc/nsswitch.conf and /etc/yp.conf file for you. Simpler, right? Your users should now be able to log in using network credentials as opposed to the local machine.

The second type of network authentication is with LDAP. LDAP is similar to NIS in setup; it just uses a different set of packages. First, install the two necessary packages:

```
# yum install -y openldap nss_ldap
```

As with NIS, you could also add the config file by hand, but now that you have seen how useful the authconfig-tui utility is, you can use that instead:

```
# authconfig-tui
```

Choose LDAP authentication (see Figure 7-3).

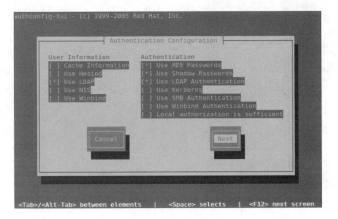

Figure 7-3   Choose the Use LDAP setting and authentication.

Specify the correct domain settings (see Figure 7-4).

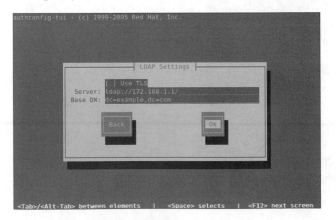

Figure 7-4   Enter the correct domain settings.

Again, the /etc/nsswitch.conf file is automatically edited for you as well as the /etc/ldap.conf file. There is no LDAP client service that needs to be started as with NIS. Notice in Figure 7-3 that you can also use Kerberos for your authentication method. You should also practice connecting a client with Kerberos authentication as well as shadow passwords. When the config file is in place, you are all set to start authenticating via the network. When troubleshooting network client authentication, check the /var/log/secure file for errors. Any time the client can't contact the central server or has other trouble logging in, all errors are logged to this file.

Summary

At this point, you should be a guru at creating users and groups...well, maybe. User administration is an important task, and we covered a lot of material in this chapter. You might want to come up with policies for creating accounts, such as using a first initial and last name, and ways to handle duplicate accounts; in addition, you might want to automate the account creation process. Although every situation is different, the fundamentals of creating users and groups do not change much. By now, you should also be comfortable setting up folders and files for users to share. Enabling collaboration between users is a real-world task that comes into play constantly.

Review Questions

1. What command (and options) can be used to create a user named JSmith with the description "Jr Admin"?

2. What is the format of the /etc/shadow file?

3. What command would you use to create a group? How about to add the user JSmith to the group?

4. How do you run a command with elevated privileges?

5. Is it possible to share files among groups? What permissions would you set on the directory to accomplish file sharing if possible?

6. If you want a specific action to take place when user01 logs in to the system, which file would you edit?

7. You can add files to a user's home directory during creation. True or False?

8. By default, what is the path to a user's home directory?

9. What is the benefit to using centralized authentication?

10. What commands can you use to add a client machine to an LDAP server?

Answers to Review Questions

1. `useradd -c "Jr Admin" JSmith`

2. The format of the /etc/shadow file is `<username>:<encrypted password>:<last passwd change>:<min>:<max>:<warn>:<inactive>:<expires>:<not used>`.

3. Use the `groupadd` command to create a group. You can then add user JSmith with the following: `usermod -G <group name> JSmith`

4. You can use the `sudo` command to run a command with elevated privileges provided you have the rights in the /etc/sudoers file.

5. Yes. You can use the `setgid` flag to create the appropriate permissions (`chmod 2770`).

6. You add your action to the end of the /home/user01/.bashrc file.

7. True. Place all files you want added to a user's home directory in the /etc/skel directory.

8. A user's home directory is created under the /home directory.

9. By using centralized authentication, you don't need to re-create or maintain multiple accounts across every system in your organization.

10. You can use the `authconfig-tui` command or the `authconfig` command.

Lab 7

Task 1 – Profile Customization

Step 1. On RHEL01, create a file with the following information in it:
Human Resources Notice
All employees are subject to random drug tests.
Sincerely,
HR

Step 2. Save the file as hr_notice.txt.

Step 3. Set up the hr_notice.txt file so that all new users created on the system receive a copy of this notice in their home directories.

The task is complete when a created user has the correct file in his home directory.

Task 2 – User and Group Management

Step 1.   Create the following groups on RHEL01:
   a. sales
   b. engineering
   c. developers

Step 2.   Create a new user on RHEL01. Use the following requirements:
   a. Username: user01
   b. Password: password
   c. Home Directory: /home/user01
   d. Shell: BASH
   e. Description: Normal User
   f. UID: 500
   g. GID: 500
   h. user01 should be a member of the sales group

Step 3.   Create a new user on RHEL01. Use the following requirements:
   a. Username: user02
   b. Password: secret
   c. Home Directory: /var/log
   d. Shell: BASH
   e. Description: Auditor
   f. UID: 600
   g. GID: 600
   h. user02 should be a member of the sales group

Step 4.   Create a new user on RHEL01. Use the following requirements:
   a. Username: user03
   b. Password: supercool
   c. Home Directory: none
   d. Shell: none
   e. Description: Fake Account
   f. UID: 501
   g. GID: 501
   h. user03 should be a member of the engineering group

Step 5. Create a new user on RHEL01. Use the following requirements:
  a. Username: user04
  b. Password: CheaperThanFree
  c. Home Directory: /home/user04
  d. Shell: Korn
  e. Description: Developer
  f. UID: 502
  g. GID: 502
  h. user04 should be a member of the developers group.

Step 6. Create a new user on RHEL01. Use the following requirements:
  a. Username: user05
  b. Password: S3cuReP@ssWorD
  c. Home Directory: none
  d. Shell: none
  e. Description: Security User
  f. user05 should be created as a system user.

The task is complete when all users, groups, files, and objectives can be verified.

Task 3 – Group Collaboration

Step 1. Create the following directories on RHEL01:
  a. /opt/Sales
  b. /opt/Sales/East_Coast
  c. /opt/Sales/West_Coast
  d. /opt/Marketing
  e. /opt/Audit
  f. /opt/Developers

Step 2. Set up the following permissions on the directories created in step 1:

    a. All members of the sales group should have access to all sales directories and subdirectories.

    b. All members of the marketing group should have access to the marketing directories.

    c. All members of the audit group should have access to the audit directory.

    d. No user outside a group should have access to a directory (that is, all non-sales users should not have access to the sales directory).

    e. As an exception to the rule above, the audit group should have read-only access to all directories within /opt.

Step 3. Create a new user on RHEL01. Use the following requirements:

    a. Log in as user01 and create two blank files with the East_Coast directory (the name of the files doesn't matter).

    b. Log out as user01.

    c. Log in as user02 and create two blank files within the Audit directory (the name of the files doesn't matter).

    d. Log out as user02.

The task is complete when all groups, files, and objectives can be verified.

This chapter covers the following subjects:

■ **Kickstart Server Setup**—This section covers how to build a basic kickstart server.

■ **Mastering Kickstart Config Files**—This section describes the kickstart config files in detail.

■ **Automating Kickstart**—This section describes how to automate the kickstart server by combining it with a DHCP server.

■ **Other Network Installs**—This section looks at other ways to perform network installs.

The following RHCSA exam objective is covered:

■ Install Red Hat Enterprise Linux automatically using kickstart

## CHAPTER 8

Network Installs

Installing Red Hat Enterprise Linux is an important topic, even though it is no longer included on the Red Hat exams. Network installations are still included, however, and knowing which method to use when can help you by saving time on installations. Using kickstart is also key in deploying RHEL in the real world because it is a heavily used technology. This chapter covers kickstart installations in depth and wraps up by looking at other types of network installation methods.

Kickstart Server Setup

The most widely used network installation setup for Red Hat is done through a kickstart server. It enables you to perform network installations with flexible options such as pre- and post-package customization, custom scripts, logging, and more. It also has the benefit of being fully automated. This section covers the basics for setting up a kickstart server and performing a simple network install.

Kickstart enables you to install Red Hat over the network via the HTTP, FTP, or NFS protocols. I chose to use the HTTP protocol here because it was the quickest to set up and slightly easier than the other two protocols. An HTTP kickstart server also has fewer configuration steps, for those attempting this for the first time.

Step 1. To start, you need to install the Apache web server:
```
# yum install -y httpd
```

Step 2. Verify the package was installed:
```
# rpm -qa | grep httpd
httpd-2.2.15-5.el6.x86_64
httpd-tools-2.2.15-5.el6.x86_64
```

Because this chapter isn't about the Apache web server, I don't want to go into specifics here, except to say that I'm pretty much using all the defaults provided with Apache.

Step 3.   Start the Apache service:

```
# service httpd start
Starting httpd:                                              [  OK  ]
```

> **WARNING:** You may get a warning about the ServerName not being set. Just ignore it for now.

Step 4.   Enable the service to start on boot:

```
# chkconfig httpd on
```

Step 5.   Verify:

```
# chkconfig httpd — list
httpd            0:off   1:off   2:on    3:on    4:on    5:on
6:off
```

Now that the HTTP server is running, you need to create a directory structure that will hold the files you need to serve up to the clients for installation.

Step 6.   Create the following directory:

```
# mkdir /var/www/pub
```

The /var/www directory is the default location where Apache stores files that clients can access. It is within that directory that you create a "pub" directory, which really is just used to hold the contents of the Red Hat CD that will later be installed on the client.

Step 7.   You should ensure that the Red Hat CD is mounted in the CD drive:

```
# mount /dev/cd-rom /mnt
```

Step 8.   Now copy the files from the CD to the directory previously created:

```
# cp -vR /mnt/* /var/www/pub/
```

This copy process takes some time because you are copying the entire contents of the Red Hat CD, which is quite large.

Step 9.   When the install files are in place, you need to make one last directory:

```
# mkdir /var/www/pub/kickstart
```

Step 10.   Verify that you now have a directory structure that looks like the following:

```
# tree /var/www/pub
/var/www/pub
|-- EFI
|    |-- BOOT
|    |    |-- BOOTX64.conf
|    |    |-- TRANS.TBL
```

```
|    |     `-- splash.xpm.gz
|    `-- TRANS.TBL
|-- EULA
|-- GPL
|-- HighAvailablility
|-- LoadBalancer
|-- Packages
|-- README
|-- ResilientStorage
|-- ScalableFileSystem
|-- Server
|-- images
|    |-- README
|    |-- TRANS.TBL
|    |-- efiboot.img
|    |-- efidisk.img
|    |-- install.img
|    |-- product.img
|    `-- pxeboot
|         |-- initrd.img
|         `-- vmlinuz
|-- isolinux
|    |-- boot.cat
|    |-- boot.msg
|    |-- grub.conf
|    |-- initrd.img
|    |-- isolinux.bin
|    |   ioolinux.cfg
|    |-- memtest
|    |-- splash.jpg
|    |-- vesamenu.c32
|    `-- vmlinuz
|-- kickstart
|    `-- redhat-base.cfg
|-- media.repo
`-- repodata
```

WARNING: You might need to install the tree command before using it. Depending on which packages you installed during the installation process, the tree package may or may not be installed.

WARNING: If you use the tree command, you get a huge listing of files that will look slightly different from mine. I created my directories by hand with no files to show you what the directory structure looks like. Your tree structure should be filled with all the files from the Red Hat CD.

MIGRATION TIP
In RHEL6, there is a completely different layout to the DVD, so the directories are completely different from those in RHEL5.

Step 11.   At this point, you would normally create your kickstart file, but we look at that in the next section, so for now just create a placeholder:

```
# touch /var/www/pub/kickstart/redhat-base.cfg
```

Firewall and SELinux Configuration

To complete the kickstart server setup, you just need to make a few adjustments to the security settings of the system. Because we haven't covered `iptables` or firewall rules yet, this section just shows you the commands you need for now. We cover firewall rules in Chapter 12.

You need to open TCP port 80 for the HTTP service to function properly. One security benefit of using the HTTP protocol for kickstart is that it requires only a single port open on the firewall.

Step 1.   Use the `iptables` command to create your firewall rule:

```
# iptables -I INPUT 5 -p tcp -m tcp --dport 80 -j ACCEPT
```

Step 2.   Save the rule you just created:

```
# service iptables save
Saving firewall rules to /etc/sysconfig/iptables:        [  OK  ]
```

Step 3.   Restart the firewall service for the changes to take effect:

```
# service iptables restart
iptables: Flushing firewall rules:                       [  OK  ]
iptables: Setting chains to policy ACCEPT: filter        [  OK  ]
iptables: Unloading modules:                             [  OK  ]
iptables: Applying firewall rules:                       [  OK  ]
```

Normally, for a service to work, you need to disable SELinux protection as well. In this case, there is no need to make any adjustments to SELinux for the kickstart server to work.

MIGRATION TIP

In RHEL5, SELinux is set up to block services by default. You need to adjust this for the HTTP service to work properly.

Step 1.   Query for the Boolean value you need to change:

```
# getsebool -a | grep httpd_dis
httpd_disable_trans --> off
```

Step 2.   Disable the SELinux protection:

```
# setsebool -P httpd_disable_trans=1
```

Step 3.   Verify that the Boolean has changed:

```
# getsebool -a | grep httpd_dis
```

```
httpd_disable_trans --> on
```

We look at SELinux and Booleans more closely in Chapter 11, "SELinux." For now, if you're using RHEL5, you can just use the commands given here.

Your kickstart server setup is now complete. To get the client to access the kickstart server, you need to boot the client from the Red Hat CD.

When you reach the boot prompt, type the following command:

```
# linux ks=http://172.168.1.1/pub/kickstart/redhat-base.cfg append
ip=172.168.1.105 netmask=255.255.255.0
```

Because you don't have a fully automated kickstart server (yet), you need to point the client to the kickstart file that you want to use as well as define a temporary IP address for it. Make sure that this IP address is in the same subnet as your kickstart server; otherwise, it won't work.

With your kickstart server setup complete, let's create a kickstart file that you can use with it.

Mastering Kickstart Config Files

Building a kickstart file can be fairly easy, until something goes wrong. The one thing I will say is that it requires much trial and error to get everything the way that you want it. Before we go any further, though, bookmark the following page:

> http://docs.redhat.com/docs/en-US/Red_Hat_Enterprise_Linux/6/html/
> Installation_Guide/s1-kickstart2-options.html

This page provides the single best reference on options for kickstart files, along with the syntax and a description of each option. I didn't include it here because the page is huge and it is better to always have an updated version online anyway.

Let's look at a sample kickstart file and break it down:

```
# cat /var/www/pub/kickstart/redhat-base.cfg


# Tells kickstart to start the install
install

# Specifies the language
lang en_US.UTF-8

# Specifies the keyboard layout
keyboard us

# Skip Red Hat key input
```

```
key --skip

# Forces the text install to be used (saves on time because a GUI doesn't need
to be loaded)
text

# Skips the display of any GUI during install
skipx

# Used with an HTTP install to specify where the install files are located
url --url http://172.168.1.1/pub/

# Assign the client a static IP upon first boot & set the hostname
network --device eth0 --hostname Client01 --bootproto dhcp

# Set the root password
rootpw --iscrypted <encrypt_password>

# Enable the firewall and open port 22 for SSH remote administration
firewall --enabled --port=22:tcp

# Setup security and SELinux levels
authconfig --enableshadow --enablemd5
selinux --permissive

# Set the timezone
timezone --utc America/New_York

# Create the bootloader in the MBR with drive sda being the drive to install it on
bootloader --location=mbr --driveorder=hda

# Wipe all partitions and build them with the info below
# ***hda may be different depending on the type of drives you use***
clearpart --drives=hda --all --initlabel

# Create a 100MB /boot partition
part /boot --fstype ext3 --size=100

# Create a 5GB / partition
part / --fstype ext3 --size=5000

# Create a 2GB swap
part swap --size=2000

# Use the rest of the free space on disk to create the /home partition
part /home --fstype ext3 --size=100 --grow
```

```
# Install the Base and Core software packages, plus OpenSSH server & client
# This is the bare minimum for a system to run (with remote access via SSH)
%packages
@Core
@Base
openssh-clients
openssh-server
```

This kickstart file is well documented, so it should be fairly easy to understand what is going on. I also didn't use any kind of complex partitioning here, making the partition layout easier to understand. In the last section, you can also see that you are only going to be installing enough packages to get the system up and running and nothing more. By doing this, you provide a faster install because there aren't as many packages to install first of all, and if you ever decide that you need a package that you left out, you can always install it later. After you generate an encrypted password and replace it in the appropriate line, this kickstart file will provide you with a basic setup for a client using your kickstart server.

Post Install

One great benefit of using the kickstart system is that you can have your kickstart file execute scripts upon completing the installation of your system. At the end of your kickstart file, you would define a %post section. Anything in the %post section is treated as if you were typing it at the console of a system. You can perform customizations or execute other scripts for further configuration of your system. While %post is usually a more useful section because the system is already installed, you should know that there is also a %pre section that is executed before the installation begins.

Advanced Partitioning

Kickstart also enables you to create more advanced partitions. In the kickstart file, you need to use the commands outlined in the web page mentioned earlier to carve out drives and create your advanced partitions. As an example, let's create some LVM partitions for the client.

This is an excerpt from another kickstart file I have:

```
# cat /var/www/pub/kickstart/redhat-base2.cfg
...
# Setup each physical disk to be used for LVM
part pv.01 --size=1 --grow --ondisk=sda

# Create the VolumeGroup to use on the Physical Volume
volgroup VolGroup00 pv.01
```

```
# Carve out the disk with Logical Volumes
logvol / --fstype ext3 --name=LogVol00 --vgname=VolGroup00 --size=5000
logvol /home --fstype ext3 --name=LogVol01 --vgname=VolGroup00 --size=1000
logvol /var/log --fstype ext3 --name=LogVol02 --vgname=VolGroup00 –size=1000

logvol swap --fstype swap --name=LogVol03 --vgname=VolGroup00 --size=1024
```

Although this example might seem similar to the basic partitions, you must define the Physical Volume, Volume Group, and Logical Volumes in this order; otherwise, you get errors (which are not always the best in kickstart). A nice trick for creating a kickstart file without having to manually type one out is to walk through an installation normally. As you may remember from the first chapter in the book, when you finish installing a system, a file called anaconda-ks.cfg is created in the root user's home directory. This file is actually a kickstart file of all the actions you took during the installation of the system. You can copy it over to your kickstart server, and voila, you're done.

Suppose you don't want to go through the process of reinstalling a server every time you need a reference machine. Luckily, there is also a GUI tool that enables you to build kickstart files much more easily. You could use this tool instead of building the kickstart files from the command line. However, you need a desktop manager (because it is a GUI tool), which usually isn't installed on most servers. The GUI tool has different screens that enable you to build a kickstart file from scratch, and it validates the syntax of the file for you as you're building it. This approach may be useful if you're just starting out with kickstart or you're trying to troubleshoot because the syntax is generated by the tool and is in the correct format.

To install the GUI tool, use the following:

```
# yum install -y system-config-kickstart
```

To launch it, use this command:

```
# system-config-kickstart
```

One benefit of installing the GUI tool on a server where you may not have a desktop manager is that it comes with a command-line syntax validator (`ksvalidator`). This command can be used to verify the syntax of your kickstart files, which help in the troubleshooting process. My current production kickstart files are a couple of hundred lines each, so having something to check syntax is always helpful.

Automating Kickstart

So far in this chapter, we've looked at how to set up a kickstart server and make a kickstart file for clients. Now we can take this one step further and automate the process using PXE boots and a TFTP server. The protocol remains the same

(HTTP) for the clients to grab the kickstart files from. You can use the kickstart file created in the previous section for clients.

TFTP Server

To start, let's set up a TFTP server that can hand clients the bootstrap files for a preboot environment. Because you already have a kickstart server in place from the first section of this chapter, much of the work is already done for you.

Step 1.   Check the directory structure, which should look like the following:

```
# tree /var/www/pub
/var/www/pub
|-- EFI
|   |-- BOOT
|   |   |-- BOOTX64.conf
|   |   |-- TRANS.TBL
|   |   `-- splash.xpm.gz
|   `-- TRANS.TBL
|-- EULA
|-- GPL
|-- HighAvailablility
|-- LoadBalancer
|-- Packages
|   README
|-- ResilientStorage
|-- ScalableFileSystem
|-- Server
|-- images
|   |-- README
|   |-- TRANS.TBL
|   |-- efiboot.img
|   |-- efidisk.img
|   |-- install.img
|   |-- product.img
|   `-- pxeboot
|       |-- initrd.img
|       `-- vmlinuz
|-- isolinux
|   |-- boot.cat
|   |-- boot.msg
|   |-- grub.conf
|   |-- initrd.img
|   |-- isolinux.bin
|   |-- isolinux.cfg
|   |-- memtest
|   |-- splash.jpg
|   |-- vesamenu.c32
|   `-- vmlinuz
|-- kickstart
|   `-- redhat-base.cfg
|-- media.repo
`-- repodata
```

If anything is missing, you can create it now to match the directory structure here. You also need to make a directory structure for the TFTP server to serve files from:

```
# cd /
# mkdir -p tftpboot/{images,pxelinux.cfg}
```

Step 2.   You can then verify with the following:

```
# tree /tftpboot/
/tftpboot/
|-- images
`-- pxelinux.cfg
```

You need to copy over the kernel files from the /var/www/pub/images/pxeboot directory to the TFTP directory structure so that these files may be served to the clients.

```
# cp /var/www/pub/images/pxeboot/vmlinuz /tftpboot/images
# cp /var/www/pub/images/pxeboot/initrd.img /tftpboot/images
```

Before going any further with configuration, you need to install some packages.

Step 3.   Install the TFTP server package as well as the syslinux package needed to boot clients:

```
# yum install -y syslinux
# yum install -y tftp-server
```

When these two packages are installed, you can finish configuration of the TFTP server. When the TFTP server package is installed, it is actually a part of the xinetd service (you learn more about this in Chapter 19, "Network Services"). You just need to make a single change to the config file for the TFTP server, specifically telling it in which directory the boot files are located to serve to clients.

Step 4.   Your config file should look like the following:

```
# cat /etc/xinetd.d/tftp
service tftp
{
        disable                 = no
        socket_type             = dgram
        protocol                = udp
        wait                    = yes
        user                    = root
        server                  = /usr/sbin/in.tftpd
        server_arg              = -s /tftpboot
        per_source              = 11
        cps                     = 100 2
        flags                   = IPv4
}
```

Step 5.   After you make the required changes, just restart the `xinetd` service:

```
# service xinetd restart
Stopping xinetd:                                    [  OK  ]
Starting xinetd:                                    [  OK  ]
```

Step 6.   You should also make sure that the server is set to start when the system boots:

```
# chkconfig tftp on
```

Step 7.   Verify with the following:

```
# chkconfig tftp --list
tftp              on
```

Finally, for the TFTP server, you need to move a few additional files from the `syslinux` package just installed. Because these files change location depending on what version and architecture you're using, you can manually search for these files before moving them:

```
# whereis syslinux
syslinux: /usr/bin/syslinux /usr/lib/syslinux
```

The files you need are located in the second directory. Again, this location could be slightly different on your system. Copy the necessary files into the TFTP server directory structure:

```
# cp /usr/share/syslinux/menu.c32 /tftpboot
# cp /usr/share/syslinux/pxelinux.0 /tftpboot
```

Step 8.   You also need to create a blank file called default, which is the place where the PXE menu will exist later:

```
# touch /tftpboot/pxelinux.cfg/default
```

Step 9.   This completes the TFTP server setup. You should now have the following directory structure:

```
# tree /tftpboot/
/tftpboot/
|-- images
|   |-- initrd.img
|   `-- vmlinuz
|-- menu.c32
|-- pxelinux.0
`-- pxelinux.cfg
    `-- default
```

PXE Boot

For clients to be able to PXE boot, you need to ensure two things are set up properly. First, you need a DHCP server to serve IP addresses to the clients. This lets the clients know where the PXE server actually is located.

Step 1.   Set up the DHCP server with the default settings:

```
# yum install -y dhcp
```

Step 2.   Verify the DHCP server was installed properly:

```
# rpm -qa | grep dhcp
dhcp-4.1.1-12.P1.el6.x86_64
```

Step 3.   Use the following sample config file for the DHCP server:

```
# cat /etc/dhcp/dhcpd.conf
ddns-update-style none;
authoritative;

subnet 172.168.1.0 netmask 255.255.255.0 {

        ### Parameters for the local subnet ###

        option routers                          172.168.1.1;
        option subnet-mask                      255.255.255.0;

        option domain-name                      "example.com";
        option domain-name-servers              172.168.1.1;

        default-lease-time                      21600;
        max-lease-time                          43200;

        range dynamic-bootp 172.168.1.100 172.168.1.200;

        ### PXE Server IP ###

        next-server 172.168.1.1;
        filename "pxelinux.0";

}
```

MIGRATION TIP
In RHEL5, the DHCP server config file is /etc/dhcpd.conf. In RHEL6, it has been moved into the /etc/dhcp directory because there is also support for DHCP over IPv6.

Step 4.   Save any changes you made to the file and restart the DHCP service:

```
# service dhcpd restart
Stopping dhcpd:                                          [  OK  ]
Starting dhcpd:                                          [  OK  ]
```

Step 5. Enable the DHCP server to start when the system boots:

```
# chkconfig dhcpd on
```

Step 6. Verify that the DHCP service is set to start on boot as well:

```
# chkconfig dhcpd — list
dhcpd                0:off   1:off   2:on   3:on   4:on   5:on
6:off
```

The final step for PXE boot is creating a PXE menu from which clients can choose the kickstart file to boot from. Earlier, you created the file /tftpboot/pxelinux.cfg/default, which was blank. Here is what the menu file looks like when complete:

```
# cat /tftpboot/pxelinux.cfg/default
default menu.c32
prompt 0
timeout 10

MENU TITLE PXE Menu

LABEL RedHat 6.0 x64
MENU LABEL RedHat 6.0 x64
KERNEL images/vmlinuz
append initrd=images/initrd.img linux
ks=http://172.168.1.1/pub/kickstart/test.cfg
```

The timeout option defines how long the system will wait before choosing the default option for you. Here, you also defined a title for the PXE menu, created two different types of labels representing the operating system that you are going to install, and defined a kernel with options on how to boot the kickstart file. Save and close the file to complete the PXE setup.

Firewall and SELinux Configuration

Because you have added a few additional services, there are, of course, a few additional security settings you need to make. While the original firewall is in place for the HTTP server, you need to add rules for the TFTP service and the DHCP server.

Step 1. Use iptables to create the additional firewall rules:

```
# iptables -I INPUT 5 -p udp -m udp --dport 67 -j ACCEPT
# iptables -I INPUT 5 -p udp -m udp --dport 69 -j ACCEPT
```

Step 2. Save the firewall rules you just created:

```
# service iptables save
Saving firewall rules to /etc/sysconfig/iptables:          [  OK  ]
```

Step 3. Then restart the `iptables` service:

```
# service iptables restart
iptables: Flushing firewall rules:                        [  OK  ]
iptables: Setting chains to policy ACCEPT: filter         [  OK  ]
iptables: Unloading modules:                              [  OK  ]
iptables: Applying firewall rules:                        [  OK  ]
```

MIGRATION TIP

As we discussed earlier, in RHEL5, SELinux is set up to block services by default. With the addition of PXE booting and a DHCP server, you need to adjust a few more values for these services to work properly.

Step 1. Query for the Boolean value you need to change:

```
# getsebool -a | grep tftpd_dis
tftpd_disable_trans --> off
# getsebool -a | grep dhcpd_dis
dhcpd_disable_trans --> off
```

Step 2. Disable SELinux protection:

```
# setsebool -P tftpd_disable_trans=1 dhcpd_disable_trans=1
```

Step 3. Verify that the Boolean has changed:

```
# getsebool -a | grep tftpd_dis
tftpd_disable_trans --> on
# getsebool -a | grep dhcpd_dis
dhcpd_disable_trans --> on
```

We look at SELinux and Booleans more closely in Chapter 11. For now, if you are using RHEL5, you can just use the commands given here.

Now for the ultimate test...to see if it works! Since you set up the kickstart server on RHEL01, you can PXE boot Client02. Because you are using VirtualBox for the lab, you can start Client02 and press F12 to bring up the boot options. Select L to boot from the LAN, and if everything works correctly, you should see the PXE menu you created. Selecting the first (and only) option starts the kickstart installation over the network. Because you tested the original kickstart server, nothing should have changed here, and the installation should go through successfully. You can add different kickstart options to your PXE menu to create different types of servers and clients.

Other Network Installs

Although kickstart installations are not the only network install that you can perform, they are the most convenient and offer the best fully automated approach. You can use NFS, FTP, and HTTP to perform network installs as well. The main setup for these three install types is the same. First, you need to mount the CD-ROM drive:

```
# mount /dev/cdrom /mnt
```

This step provides the files required to install Red Hat. The next step depends on which installation type you would like to perform. For an HTTP network install, you would need to create a separate directory under /var/www as you did with the kickstart install. If you're using NFS or FTP, you need to create a directory that will be served up by those protocols to your clients--for instance, /opt/install_files. After you create the directory you are going to use, copy the contents of the CD to the directory:

```
# cp -R /mnt/* /opt/install_files
```

If the service is running properly, that's really all you need to do from a server standpoint. On the client system, use the Red Hat CD to boot up the system. At the boot prompt, type in `linux askmethod`, which enables you to choose which installation method you'd like to use. We don't cover the setup and security requirements of each service here because we have done that throughout the book. The Red Hat exam also doesn't test on the installation of the operating system anymore, although network installs are listed in the exam prep guide, so it is important to know how each method, including kickstart, works.

Summary

In this chapter, we discussed the different methods you can use to install Red Hat Enterprise Linux over the network. In particular, we covered the kickstart method in depth because it is heavily used in the real world for installations of all different sizes. Knowing how to troubleshoot kickstart installations is also really important as well because the first few times you use this method, you will run into problems and knowing how to resolve them is key.

Review Questions

1. Kickstart can be accomplished only by using a PXE server. True or False?

2. What port on the firewall needs to be open for the TFTP server to work?

3. What three protocols can you use to perform network installations?

4. Can you create a RAID or LVM partition using kickstart?

5. It is possible to run scripts before a kickstart installation. True or False?

6. What is the name of the section used to run scripts after a kickstart installation?

7. What three components are needed to fully automate a kickstart installation?

Answers to Review Questions

1. False. A PXE server eases the automation process but isn't required for kickstart installations to work.

2. The TFTP server uses UDP port 69.

3. Network installations can be performed using the HTTP, FTP, and NFS protocols.

4. Yes. Kickstart supports both basic and advanced partitioning (RAID/LVM).

5. True. This is done by defining a %pre section although it is rarely used.

6. By defining a %post section, you can run scripts after a kickstart installation is complete.

7. By combining a TFTP server, PXE boot, and DHCP server, you can fully automate the kickstart installation process.

Lab 8

Task 1 – Setting Up Kickstart

Step 1.   Create a kickstart server using the following guidelines:
  a. The server must use the FTP protocol.
  b. The server doesn't have to be fully automated (no PXE boot).
  c. The kickstart file should provide only the base packages.
  d. The kickstart file should use only basic partitions (no RAID or LVM).
The task is complete when a client system can be installed using the kickstart server.

Task 2 – Enhancing the Kickstart Server

Step 1.   Convert the kickstart server from Task 1 into a fully automated kickstart server. Use the following guidelines:

   a. The server must use the FTP protocol.

   b. The server must be fully automated.

   c. The kickstart server must provide a PXE boot menu.

   d. The kickstart server must provide IP addresses to any client booting from the network.

   e. The kickstart file should provide only the base packages.

   f. The kickstart file may contain any type of partitioning.

The task is complete when a client system can be installed using the kickstart server.

Task 3 – A Different Kind of Install

Step 1.   Disable the kickstart server.

Step 2.   Perform a network installation of Red Hat using the following guidelines:

   a. The network install must be performed using the HTTP protocol.

   b. No kickstart server may be used.

   c. No automation may be used (PXE boot or DHCP).

   d. Any settings may be used for the client as long as the operating system installs correctly and the system is bootable.

The task is complete when a client system is installed successfully.

This chapter covers the following subjects:

- **Working with Syslog**—This section covers logging, both local and centralized.

- **Monitoring System Performance**—This section looks at how to monitor system performance.

- **Automation with cron and at**—This section covers system automation via scheduled and single-instance jobs.

The following RHCSA exam objectives are covered:

- Identify CPU and memory-intensive processes, adjust process priority with `renice`, and kill processes

- Locate and interpret system log files

- Schedule tasks using `cron`

The following RHCE exam objectives are covered:

- Produce and deliver reports on system utilization (processor, memory, disk, and network)

- Use shell scripting to automate system maintenance tasks

- Configure a system to log to a remote system

- Configure a system to accept logging from a remote system

## CHAPTER 9

System Logging, Monitoring, and Automation

How do you know when something goes wrong on your system? You look at the logs, of course! In all seriousness, understanding system logging is important so that you can troubleshoot when something goes wrong. Logs are kept for almost everything that you can think of, including the kernel, boot process, and different services that are running. Aside from logs, there are also utilities you can use to monitor and check the status of your system. This chapter looks at how you can use these tools and logging to troubleshoot anything that is thrown your way. The chapter also touches on how to automate some of these tasks.

Working with Syslog

Whenever something goes wrong—and sometimes when things go right—on the system, a message is generated by the syslog service. These messages are used to keep track of how the system is performing, what actions are taking place, and if there is a problem with something. Red Hat comes with a syslog service built in and already set to start at boot. In RHEL6, the rsyslog package is installed by default and is the primary logging service used.

MIGRATION TIP

In RHEL5, the default logging service was split between two daemons: syslogd and klogd. Syslogd was used for system messages and klogd for kernel messages. In RHEL6, these have both been replaced with the rsyslogd daemon, which handles both types of messages. If you are still on RHEL5, you can install the syslog service via the sysklogd package.

The rsyslog service has a main config file, /etc/rsyslog.conf, that controls where messages are sent when they are generated. Because logging is a critical piece of the operating system, it is installed by default as part of the core packages.

Step 1.   Just out of good habit, you should verify that the package is installed:

```
# rpm -qa | grep syslog
rsyslog-4.6.2-2.el6.x86_64
```

Because you can see that it is installed, you should also check on two other issues.

Step 2.   First, make sure that the service is set to start when the system boots:

```
# chkconfig rsyslog --list
rsyslog            0:off   1:off   2:on    3:on    4:on    5:on
6:off
```

Step 3.   Second, make sure that the service is currently running:

```
# service rsyslog status
rsyslogd (pid  1279) is running...
```

For RHEL05:

Step 1.   Verify the installation of the package:

```
# rpm -qa | grep klog
sysklogd-1.4.1-44.el5
```

Step 2.   Check that the service will start on boot:

```
# chkconfig syslog --list
syslog             0:off   1:off   2:on    3:on    4:on    5:on
6:off
```

Aside from the name difference, as we have already discussed, there are two daemons that run instead of one. They do, however, both run under a single service name.

Step 3.   Verify that the service is running:

```
# service syslog status
syslogd (pid  2214) is running...
klogd (pid  2217) is running...
```

As you can see here, there are some slight differences between logging on RHEL5 and RHEL6 (such as the naming and single versus double daemons). The rsyslog service provides better logging features, so it is recommended to upgrade if possible.

All the messages sent to the rsyslog service are stored in the /var/log directory, and each message section has its own file or subdirectory. You can also define your own log files or directories. The biggest problem that arises from using any logging service is the files can become uncontrollable if left unchecked. Being able to log different alerts and to obtain information from logs, in my opinion, is an art all unto itself. There are so many ways to customize logs, and each network setup is different. You should know that there are nine different alerts that the syslog service uses. These alerts can be produced by different network devices and Red Hat systems.

The nine severity levels of syslog include the following:

- emerg
- alert
- crit
- err
- warning
- notice
- info
- debug
- none

The Config File

The /etc/rsyslog.conf file is broken down into the following parts:

Modules	Indicate whether they can be loaded or unloaded (rsyslog is modular)
Global directives	Specify config options that apply to the daemon (all start with a $)
Rules	Indicate cooperation of a selector and an action
Selector	Is based on <facility>.<priority>
Action	Defines what to do with messages after they're sorted by the selector

Let's look at the default config file to see some examples:

```
# cat /etc/rsyslog.conf
#rsyslog v3 config file

# if you experience problems, check
```

```
# http://www.rsyslog.com/troubleshoot for assistance

#### MODULES ####

$ModLoad imuxsock.so    # provides support for local system logging (e.g. via
logger command)
$ModLoad imklog.so      # provides kernel logging support (previously done by
rklogd)
#$ModLoad immark.so     # provides --MARK-- message capability

# Provides UDP syslog reception
#$ModLoad imudp.so
#$UDPServerRun 514

# Provides TCP syslog reception
#$ModLoad imtcp.so
#$InputTCPServerRun 514


#### GLOBAL DIRECTIVES ####

# Use default timestamp format
$ActionFileDefaultTemplate RSYSLOG_TraditionalFileFormat

# File syncing capability is disabled by default. This feature is usually not
required,
# not useful and an extreme performance hit
#$ActionFileEnableSync on


#### RULES ####

# Log all kernel messages to the console.
# Logging much else clutters up the screen.
#kern.*                                          /dev/console

# Log anything (except mail) of level info or higher.
# Don't log private authentication messages!
*.info;mail.none;authpriv.none;cron.none         /var/log/messages

# The authpriv file has restricted access.
authpriv.*                                       /var/log/secure

# Log all the mail messages in one place.
mail.*                                          -/var/log/maillog
```

```
# Log cron stuff
cron.*                                                   /var/log/cron

# Everybody gets emergency messages
*.emerg                                                          *

# Save news errors of level crit and higher in a special file.
uucp,news.crit                                           /var/log/spooler

# Save boot messages also to boot.log
local7.*                                                 /var/log/boot.log

# ### begin forwarding rule ###
# The statement between the begin ... end define a SINGLE forwarding
# rule. They belong together, do NOT split them. If you create multiple
# forwarding rules, duplicate the whole block!
# Remote Logging (we use TCP for reliable delivery)
#
# An on-disk queue is created for this action. If the remote host is
# down, messages are spooled to disk and sent when it is up again.
#$WorkDirectory /var/spppl/rsyslog # where to place spool files
#$ActionQueueFileName fwdRule1 # unique name prefix for spool files
#$ActionQueueMaxDiskSpace 1g   # 1gb space limit (use as much as possible)
#$ActionQueueSaveOnShutdown on # save messages to disk on shutdown
#$ActionQueueType LinkedList   # run asynchronously
#$ActionResumeRetryCount -1    # infinite retries if host is down
# remote host is: name/ip:port, e.g. 192.168.0.1:514, port optional
#*.* @@remote-host:514
# ### end of the forwarding rule ###
```

You can see from the output where some of the files are stored. Also shown is a sample rule.

Log Rotation

If left alone, logs can grow to enormous size. Luckily for you, the logrotate command allows you to rotate logs before they become too big. By default, the logrotate command is called daily to cycle the log files into a new file. The parameters of the command are defined in its config file, /etc/logrotate.conf, and the /etc/logrotate.d directory. However, the command itself is called from /etc/cron.daily/logrotate, a cron job that is run daily (as already mentioned). You can always call the logrotate command yourself if you'd like to rotate your logs, but don't do this too frequently because you'll end up with tons of rotated logs and you'll be right back to square one with a mess of unorganized log files.

Syntax: `logrotate [options] configfile`

Options:

-d   Debugs; doesn't do anything but test

-f   Forces file rotation

-v   Provides verbose output

The following example rotates the current logs as defined in the config file:

 # logrotate /etc/logrotate.conf

Centralized Logging

If you'd like to set up a centralized syslog server, you need to choose which server you'd like to store all your logs on. For this example, you can use the RHEL01 system as the centralized server and configure it to receive logs from the other systems on the network.

Step 1.   Look at a section of the /etc/rsyslog.conf file again:

```
#### MODULES ####


$ModLoad imuxsock.so     # provides support for local system log-
ging (e.g. via logger command)
$ModLoad imklog.so       # provides kernel logging support (previ-
ously done by rklogd)
#$ModLoad immark.so      # provides --MARK-- message capability

# Provides UDP syslog reception
#$ModLoad imudp.so
#$UDPServerRun 514

# Provides TCP syslog reception
#$ModLoad imtcp.so
#$InputTCPServerRun 514
```

In the modules section, you can see two areas that will provide the capability to receive logs from other systems. The standard is to use the UDP protocol on port 514. By uncommenting the section related to UDP reception, you essentially can provide a way for the syslog server to become the centralized server for the network.

Step 2.   Uncomment the following two lines:

```
$ModLoad imudp.so
$UDPServerRun 514
```

Step 3.   When you're finished, you need to save the file, exit, and restart the syslog service:

```
# service rsyslog restart
Shutting down system logger:                           [  OK  ]
Starting system logger:                                [  OK  ]
```

As with any service that you'd like to make available to your network, you need to create a firewall allowing UDP 514 to be opened up.

Step 4.   Use iptables to create the required firewall rule:

```
# iptables -I INPUT 5 -p udp -m udp --dport 514 -j ACCEPT
```

Step 5.   Save the firewall rule you just created:

```
# service iptables save
Saving firewall rules to /etc/sysconfig/iptables:      [  OK  ]
```

Step 6.   Then restart the iptables service:

```
# service iptables restart
iptables: Flushing firewall rules:                     [  OK  ]
iptables: Setting chains to policy ACCEPT: filter      [  OK  ]
iptables: Unloading modules:                           [  OK  ]
iptables: Applying firewall rules:                     [  OK  ]
```

The firewall rules might not make sense at the moment because we haven't covered iptables or firewall rules yet. After you read Chapter 12, "System Security," return here to make sure you understand what is happening in the creation of firewall rules.

MIGRATION TIP

Unfortunately, due to the revamp of the syslog service, centralized logging for RHEL5 is quite different. On RHEL5, the syslog config file doesn't contain a modules section to enable remote management. Instead, you need to edit the daemon config file. We cover centralized logging for RHEL5 in the next section.

Now that the security requirements have been addressed and the centralized server is configured, you can shift your attention to the client systems. Let's look at RHEL02 for the client system. You can config RHEL02 to send some or all of its log files to the centralized syslog server (RHEL01).

You can use the following syntax when configuring log files to be sent to the centralized server:

```
<log file>          @<hostname or IP of system (local or remote)>
```

You can edit the RHEL02 system to point all security logs to the central server:

```
# nano /etc/rsyslog.conf
authpriv.*          @172.168.1.1
```

Save the file and restart the `syslog` service on RHEL02:

```
# service rsyslog restart
Shutting down system logger:                          [  OK  ]
Starting system logger:                               [  OK  ]
```

If you log out and log back in on RHEL02, it generates a security event. You can then jump over to the RHEL01 host and check the logs to see the event generated by the client system RHEL02.

REAL-WORLD TIP

When you're pointing logs to a centralized server, either local or remote, there are a few special options you can use:

```
# Send messages using the TCP protocol instead of UDP
Authpriv.*                      @@172.168.1.1
# Displays messages on the console instead of sending them remotely
Authpriv.*                      @system
# Discard all messages generated for this log file
Authpriv.*                      ~
# Send alert to all log files ** use with caution **
Authpriv.*                      *
```

These options can be used in conjunction with forwarding your logs to keep a local copy on your server.

Centralized Logging (The RHEL5 Way)

To set up centralized logging for RHEL5, do the following:

Step 1. Edit the /etc/sysconfig/syslog file to include the `-r` option:

```
# nano /etc/sysconfig/syslog
# Options to syslogd
# -m 0 disables 'MARK' messages.
# -r enables logging from remote machines
# -x disables DNS lookups on messages received with -r
# See syslogd(8) for more details
SYSLOGD_OPTIONS="-m 0 -r"
```

Step 2. Save the file, exit, and restart the `syslog` service:

```
# service syslog restart
Shutting down kernel logger:                          [  OK  ]
Shutting down system logger:                          [  OK  ]
Starting system logger:                               [  OK  ]
Starting kernel logger:                               [  OK  ]
```

With the `syslog` service now accepting remote logs, you need to create a firewall rule. This process is the same as on RHEL6. One last modification that needs to be made on RHEL5 is the adjustment of some SELinux protections.

Step 3.   Query the required Boolean values:

```
# getsebool -a | grep logd
klogd_disable_trans --> off
syslogd_disable_trans --> off
```

Step 4.   Change the values to allow incoming logs:

```
# setsebool -P klogd_disable_trans=1 syslogd_disable_trans=1
```

Step 5.   Verify the preceding Booleans have been changed:

```
# getsebool -a | grep logd
klogd_disable_trans --> on
syslogd_disable_trans --> on
```

Although we haven't covered SELinux yet (it is covered in Chapter 11, "SELinux"), the Boolean values are required here if you are still using RHEL 5. After you read through Chapter 11, you can refer back here to make sure you understand the changes being made.

User Login Events

Aside from the normal logs generated and used by the `syslog` service, there are two special commands that deal with system logins. These two commands have special logs that can be read only through the use of these commands:

`lastlog`	Lists login records
`faillog`	Lists failed login attempts

You can use these two commands for viewing login events. These two commands are useful for hunting down attacks where users are trying to force themselves into other users' accounts (called *a brute-force attack*).

Syntax: `lastlog [options]`

Options:

`-b DAYS`	Displays results older than `DAYS`
`-u LOGIN`	Displays results for the user `LOGIN`

Show the last time the user01 account logged in:

```
# lastlog -u user01
Username        Port    From         Latest
user01          tty                  Fri Sep 10 05:16:42 -0400 2010
```

You can also view more details using the `faillog` command.

Syntax: `faillog [options]`

Options:

`-a`	Displays all events
`-l SEC`	Locks the account for `SEC` seconds after a failed login
`-u LOGIN`	Prints records for user `LOGIN`

Show more information about the user01 account login events:

```
# faillog -u user01
Login        Failures Maximum Latest                On
user01          0        0
```

The ability to work with `syslog` is important to being able to help troubleshoot any issue on Linux, not just Red Hat. When you're trying to find an issue or resolve one, the log files should always be your first stop.

Monitoring System Performance

Every time a program or command is run, a process is created for it. These processes are all unique and identified by the process identification (PID) that becomes allocated to it. System processes are critical to keeping the system up and running or providing services to clients. Management of processes can help keep the system stable or help when the system becomes unstable. Here are some of the process management commands you can use:

`ps`	Displays information about running processes
`kill`	Terminates a process
`pgrop`	Finds a process based on its PID
`pidof`	Displays all processes related to a service or command
`top`	Monitors system resources (similar to Task Manager in Windows)
`renice`	Adjusts the priority of a particular process

First, let's look at the processes the root user currently owns by using the ps command:

```
# ps
  PID TTY            TIME CMD
 4474 pts/3      00:00:00 bash
 4506 pts/3      00:00:00 ps
```

The ps command includes a number of options for producing different types of output, including viewing all processes currently running on the system.

To view processes with more detailed information, you can use the following command:

```
# ps u
USER    PID %CPU %MEM    VSZ    RSS TTY    STAT START    TIME COMMAND
root   2387  0.0  0.1   1660    424 tty1   Ss+  07:30    0:00 /sbin/mingetty tty1
root   2388  0.0  0.1   1660    420 tty2   Ss+  07:30    0:00 /sbin/mingetty tty2
root   2389  0.0  0.1   1660    420 tty3   Ss+  07:30    0:00 /sbin/mingetty tty3
root   2390  0.0  0.1   1660    420 tty4   Ss+  07:30    0:00 /sbin/mingetty tty4
root   2391  0.0  0.1   1660    448 tty5   Ss+  07:30    0:00 /sbin/mingetty tty5
root   2392  0.0  0.1   1660    420 tty6   Ss+  07:30    0:00 /sbin/mingetty tty6
```

Here, you see not only the PID, but also the CPU and memory utilization. A common set of options that I use when working with the ps command is aux combined with the grep command to weed out anything I'm not interested in. This way, I can get detailed information about a particular process. Say you'd like to see what information is available about any process pertaining to the SSH service:

```
# ps aux | grep ssh
root      4286  0.0  0.1  62616  1216 ?     Ss   Sep23  0:00 /usr/sbin/sshd
root     15872  0.0  0.3  90116  3248 ?     Ss   10:06  0:00 sshd: user01 [priv]
user01   15874  0.0  0.1  90116  1740 ?     S    10:06  0:00 sshd: user01@pts/0
user01   15921  0.0  0.0  61176   728 pts/0 R+   10:14  0:00 grep ssh
```

You also could use

```
# ps aux
```

With this command, however, you would receive 59 lines of output that you would have had to go through to view those 4 lines that you actually need. You can see how narrowing down your output can be really helpful.

Let's also look at some of the other options the ps command offers:

```
$ ps —help
********* simple selection *********  ********* selection by list *********
-A all processes                          -C by command name
```

```
-N negate selection                  -G by real group ID (supports names)
-a all w/ tty except session leaders -U by real user ID (supports names)
-d all except session leaders        -g by session OR by effective group name
-e all processes                     -p by process ID
T  all processes on this terminal    -s processes in the sessions given
a  all w/ tty, including other users -t by tty
g  OBSOLETE — DO NOT USE             -u by effective user ID (supports names)
r  only running processes            U  processes for specified users
x  processes w/o controlling ttys    t  by tty
*********** output format **********  *********** long options ***********
-o,o user-defined  -f full           --Group --User --pid --cols --ppid
-j,j job control    s  signal        --group --user --sid --rows --info
-O,O preloaded -o   v  virtual memory --cumulative --format --deselect
-1,l long           u  user-oriented --sort --tty --forest --version
-F    extra full    X  registers     --heading --no-heading --context
                  ********* misc options *********
-V,V  show version      L  list format codes   f  ASCII art forest
-m,m,-L,-T,H  threads   S  children in sum      -y change -l format
-M,Z  security data     c  true command name   -c scheduling class
-w,w  wide output       n  numeric WCHAN,UID    -H process hierarchy
```

You can see here that there are numerous output formats and sort features. Knowing how to manipulate the output of the ps command and find what you're looking for really helps when troubleshooting on the exams, but it also plays a huge role in troubleshooting in the real world.

What happens if one of the processes running on your system becomes out of control? In that case, you can use the kill command to terminate the process, even if it isn't responding (also called a *runaway process*). To use the kill command, however, you need to know the PID of the process that you want to kill (are you starting to see why the ps command is so helpful?).

Syntax: kill PID

If you want to stop the SSH service because it isn't responding, you just have to look for the PID associated with the SSH daemon. If you look back at the output, you can see this is PID 4286. To kill the process forcefully and effectively stop the SSH service, you can do the following:

kill 4286

Sometimes if the kill command doesn't work the way you intended it to, you can also call it with the -9 option to give it priority on the system:

kill -9 4286

What happens if you don't know the PID of the process you want to terminate? How could you look that up if you weren't sure what to query from the output of the `ps` command? There are actually two other commands you can use to determine the PID(s) of a service or command: `pidof` and `pgrep`.

First, let's look at `pidof`, to which you can pass just the name of the service or daemon. To find the PID(s) belonging to the SSH service, use the following:

```
# pidof sshd
15874 15872 4286
```

To achieve the same information in an easier-to-read format, you can use the `pgrep` command:

```
# pgrep sshd
4286
15872
15874
```

It's good to know that you can hunt down and kill processes or even just find out how many are running, but what if you need more information? Suppose you need to know how much of the CPU a particular process is taking up? Let's look at the final command: `top`. This command gives you an overview of processes on the system, including memory usage, CPU utilization, and more.

To check out the system overall, issue the following command and you get results similar to those shown in Figure 9-1:

```
#top
```

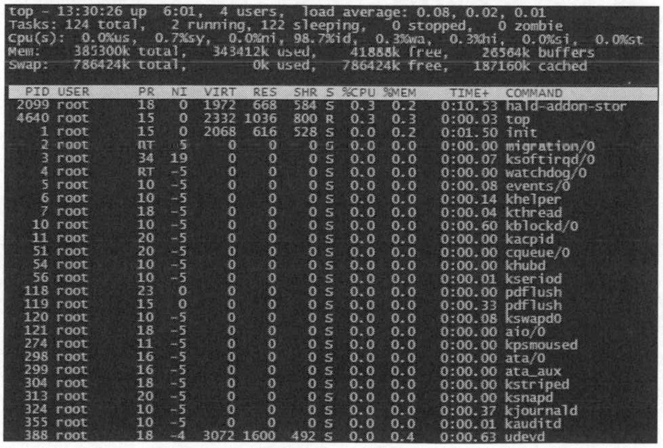

```
top - 13:30:26 up  6:01,  4 users,  load average: 0.08, 0.02, 0.01
Tasks: 124 total,   2 running, 122 sleeping,   0 stopped,   0 zombie
Cpu(s):  0.0%us,  0.7%sy,  0.0%ni, 98.7%id,  0.3%wa,  0.3%hi,  0.0%si,  0.0%st
Mem:    385300k total,   343412k used,    41888k free,    26564k buffers
Swap:   786424k total,        0k used,   786424k free,   187160k cached

  PID USER      PR  NI  VIRT  RES  SHR S %CPU %MEM    TIME+  COMMAND
 2099 root      18   0  1972  668  584 S  0.3  0.2   0:10.53 hald-addon-stor
 4640 root      15   0  2332 1036  800 R  0.3  0.3   0:00.03 top
    1 root      15   0  2068  616  528 S  0.0  0.2   0:01.50 init
    2 root      RT  -5     0    0    0 S  0.0  0.0   0:00.00 migration/0
    3 root      34  19     0    0    0 S  0.0  0.0   0:00.07 ksoftirqd/0
    4 root      RT  -5     0    0    0 S  0.0  0.0   0:00.00 watchdog/0
    5 root      10  -5     0    0    0 S  0.0  0.0   0:00.08 events/0
    6 root      10  -5     0    0    0 S  0.0  0.0   0:00.14 khelper
    7 root      18  -5     0    0    0 S  0.0  0.0   0:00.04 kthread
   10 root      10  -5     0    0    0 S  0.0  0.0   0:00.60 kblockd/0
   11 root      20  -5     0    0    0 S  0.0  0.0   0:00.00 kacpid
   51 root      20  -5     0    0    0 S  0.0  0.0   0:00.00 cqueue/0
   54 root      10  -5     0    0    0 S  0.0  0.0   0:00.00 khubd
   56 root      10  -5     0    0    0 S  0.0  0.0   0:00.01 kseriod
  118 root      23   0     0    0    0 S  0.0  0.0   0:00.00 pdflush
  119 root      15   0     0    0    0 S  0.0  0.0   0:00.33 pdflush
  120 root      10  -5     0    0    0 S  0.0  0.0   0:00.08 kswapd0
  121 root      18  -5     0    0    0 S  0.0  0.0   0:00.00 aio/0
  274 root      11  -5     0    0    0 S  0.0  0.0   0:00.00 kpsmoused
  298 root      16  -5     0    0    0 S  0.0  0.0   0:00.00 ata/0
  299 root      16  -5     0    0    0 S  0.0  0.0   0:00.00 ata_aux
  304 root      18  -5     0    0    0 S  0.0  0.0   0:00.00 kstriped
  313 root      20  -5     0    0    0 S  0.0  0.0   0:00.00 ksnapd
  324 root      10  -5     0    0    0 S  0.0  0.0   0:00.37 kjournald
  355 root      10  -5     0    0    0 S  0.0  0.0   0:00.01 kauditd
  388 root      18  -4  3072 1600  492 S  0.0  0.4   0:00.63 udevd
```

Figure 9-1 Results of running **`top`**.

The output in Figure 9-1 shows real-time information about the system resources. You can use the q to quit from the top command.

When you're comfortable working with processes, you can then make some more advanced adjustments, such as changing the priority of a particular process. Let's say that you have a custom application running on your system. You can use the renice command to give that particular process higher priority on the CPU.

Syntax: renice <priority> [options]

Options:

-p PID	Changes process priority for a particular PID
-u user	Changes process priority for a particular user(s)

The priority values range from –20 (first priority) to 20 (dead last priority). Only the root user may set processes to use a priority under 0. Going back to the example, you can give the application extra priority by using the following:

```
# renice -2 3874
```

This command changes the application process (3874) to have better priority than its default priority of 0. Knowing how to work with system processes and extract information from your system will help you become a better system administrator. It can also help you troubleshoot faster on the Red Hat exams.

In the next section, we look at job scheduling, which can be combined with some of the commands just covered to automate system monitoring.

Automation with cron and at

In any operating system, it is possible to create jobs that you want to reoccur. This process, known as *job scheduling*, is usually done based on user-defined jobs. For Red Hat, this process is handled by the cron service, which can be used to schedule tasks (also called *jobs*). By default, Red Hat comes with a set of predefined jobs that occur on the system (hourly, daily, weekly, monthly, and with arbitrary periodicity). As an administrator, however, you can define your own jobs and allow your users to create them as well.

Step 1. Although the cron package is installed by default, check to make sure it is installed on your system:

```
# rpm -qa | grep cron
cronie-1.4.4-2.el6.x86_64
cronie-anacron-1.4.4-2.el6.x86_64
crontabs-1.10-32.1.el6.noarch
```

Step 2.   If, for some reason, the package isn't installed, install it now:

```
# yum install -y cronie cronie-anacron crontabs
```

MIGRATION TIP
In RHEL5, the cron package was called vixie-cron, which has been replaced in RHEL6 with cronie.

Step 3.   Verify that the cron service is currently running:

```
# service crond status
crond (pid  2239) is running...
```

Step 4.   Also verify that the service is set to start when the system boots:

```
# chkconfig --list crond
crond              0:off   1:off   2:on    3:on    4:on    5:on
6:off
```

To start working with cron, you first need to look at the two config files that control access to the cron service. These two files are:

/etc/cron.allow

/etc/cron.deny

The /etc/cron.allow file:

■   If it exists, only these users are allowed (cron.deny is ignored).

■   If it doesn't exist, all users except cron.deny are permitted.

The /etc/cron.deny file:

■   If it exists and is empty, all users are allowed (Red Hat Default).

For both files:

■   If neither file exists, root only.

EXAM TIP
The rules surrounding these two files can be kind of confusing at first, so you might want to create some sample jobs to gain a better understanding of how changing these two files affects the permissions of the cron service.

Creating cron Jobs

The default setting for Red Hat allows any user to create a cron job. As the root user, you also have the ability to edit and remove any cron job you want. Let's jump into creating a cron job for the system. You can use the crontab command to create, edit, and delete jobs.

Syntax: crontab [-u user] [option]

Options:

-e   Edits the user's crontab

-l   Lists the user's crontab

-r   Deletes the user's crontab

-i   Prompts before deleting the user's crontab

Before you start using the crontab command, however, you should look over the format it uses so you understand how to create and edit cron jobs. Each user has her own crontab file in /var/spool/cron (the file for each user is created only after the user creates her first cron job), based on the username of each user. Any "allow" actions taken by the cron service are logged to /var/log/cron.

View the /etc/crontab file to understand its syntax:

```
# grep ^# /etc/crontab
# For details see man 4 crontabs
# Example of job definition:
# .--------------- minute (0 - 59)
# |  .------------- hour (0 - 23)
# |  |  .---------- day of month (1 - 31)
# |  |  |  .------- month (1 - 12) OR jan,feb,mar,apr ...
# |  |  |  |  .---- day of week (0 - 6) (Sunday=0 or 7) OR sun,mon,tue,etc.
# |  |  |  |  |
# *  *  *  *  *  command to be executed
```

This file clearly spells out the values that can exist in each field. You must make sure that you provide a value for each field; otherwise, the crontab will not be created. You can also define step values by using */<number to step by>. For example, you could put */5 in the minute field to mean every fifth minute.

The best way to understand these fields is to create a crontab file and make some sample jobs. Using a text editor, create the following file in the /tmp directory.

Sample script for cron:

```
# nano /tmp/sample_script
#!/bin/bash
#
# Send a msg to all users on the console
#
wall "Hello World"
```

Save the file and set the following permissions:

```
# chmod 775 /tmp/sample_script
```

Now create a cron job to launch the sample script. Because you are using the root user account, you can create a crontab for the normal user account user01.

Step 1.   Set up user01's crontab:

```
# crontab -u user01 -e
```

Step 2.   Add the following line:

```
* * * * * /tmp/sample_script
```

Step 3.   Save the file and quit the editor.

Because you are using * in every field to test, in about 60 seconds you will see the script execute, and it should display "Hello World" on your screen.

> **EXAM TIP**
>
> The crontab file uses the vi editor to make changes to itself. If you aren't familiar with this editor, be aware that the input commands are slightly different from that of nano or emacs. Make sure you know how to use the vi editor for the Red Hat exams.

Obviously, you don't want messages every 60 seconds on your system, but you get the idea of how cron and crontab should work. Let's list the current jobs that user01 has set up, and you should see the job just created (do this just for verification purposes).

Step 4.   List the current cron jobs of user01:

```
# crontab -u user01 -l
* * * * * /tmp/sample_script
```

You can now edit the crontab again to remove the single line, effectively deleting that individual job, or you can just delete the user's crontab entirely.

Step 5.   To remove a user's crontab jobs, use the following command:

```
# crontab -u user01 -r
```

Step 6.   You can verify the activity on different crontabs by...wait for it...looking at the log files!

```
# tail /var/log/cron
Sep 10 09:08:01 new-host crond[4213]: (user01) CMD
(/tmp/sample_script)
Sep 10 09:08:38 new-host crontab[4220]: (root) LIST (user01)
Sep 10 09:09:01 new-host crond[4224]: (user01) CMD
(/tmp/sample_script)
Sep 10 09:10:01 new-host crond[4230]: (user01) CMD
(/tmp/sample_script)
Sep 10 09:11:01 new-host crond[4236]: (user01) CMD
(/tmp/sample_script)
Sep 10 09:12:01 new-host crond[4242]: (user01) CMD
(/tmp/sample_script)
Sep 10 09:13:01 new-host crond[4248]: (user01) CMD
(/tmp/sample_script)
Sep 10 09:13:06 new-host crontab[4251]: (root) LIST (user01)
Sep 10 09:14:01 new-host crond[4253]: (user01) CMD
(/tmp/sample_script)
Sep 10 09:14:15 new-host crontab[4258]: (root) DELETE (user01)
```

You can see that the cron service is executing the /tmp/sample_script file, and you can see the action after you deleted it. The process of creating crontabs and scheduling jobs is the same for all users on the system, including the root user.

MIGRATION TIP

In RHEL5, the /etc/crontab file was used as the root user's crontab. This crontab followed a different format from that of all other system users. The /etc/crontab file has an extra field between the last time field and command field. In this extra field, you must specify which user you want the job to run as.

Here is what the /etc/crontab file looks like for RHEL5 systems:

```
# cat /etc/crontab
SHELL=/bin/bash
PATH=/sbin:/bin:/usr/sbin:/usr/bin
MAILTO=root
HOME=/

# run-parts
01 * * * * root run-parts /etc/cron.hourly
02 4 * * * root run-parts /etc/cron.daily
22 4 * * 0 root run-parts /etc/cron.weekly
42 4 1 * * root run-parts /etc/cron.monthly
```

Here, the root user is defined to run the specified commands. This user field is now optional in RHEL6.

What do you think happens if you set up cron jobs to run during the night (say, to run some reports) and you shut down the system right before you go home? Well, it turns out that there is another great feature of cron. The /etc/anacrontab file defines jobs that should be run every time the system is started. If your system is turned off during the time that a cron job should have run, when the system boots again, the cron service will call /etc/anacrontab to make sure that all missed cron jobs are run.

Let's look at the /etc/anacrontab file:

```
# cat anacrontab
SHELL=/bin/sh
PATH=/sbin:/bin:/usr/sbin:/usr/bin
MAILTO=root
# the maximal random delay added to the base delay of the jobs
RANDOM_DELAY=45
# the jobs will be started during the following hours only
START_HOURS_RANGE=3-22


#period in days   delay in minutes   job-identifier    command
1        5        cron.daily               nice run-parts /etc/cron.daily
7        25       cron.weekly              nice run-parts /etc/cron.weekly
@monthly 45       cron.monthly             nice run-parts /etc/cron.monthly
```

The comments in this file make it easy to understand how jobs are defined. If your system is constantly on and you don't require anacron to be run, you can uninstall the cronie-anacron package, which controls just the anacron commands for the cron service.

MIGRATION TIP

In RHEL5, anacron was a separate service from cron. The anacron service alone was called when the system booted and similarly ran the /etc/anacrontab file. This file looks similar to the RHEL6 version without any comments:

```
# cat anacrontab
SHELL=/bin/sh
PATH=/sbin:/bin:/usr/sbin:/usr/bin
MAILTO=root


1        65       cron.daily            run-parts /etc/cron.daily
7        70       cron.weekly           run-parts /etc/cron.weekly
30       75       cron.monthly          run-parts /etc/cron.monthly
```

For RHEL5, you need to ensure that this service is set to run when the system boots in order for it to be effective:

```
# chkconfig anacron — list
anacron          0:off    1:off    2:on    3:on    4:on    5:on    6:off
```

MIGRATION TIP

In RHEL5, you also need to disable SELinux protection for the cron service to function properly. Although we haven't covered SELinux yet, you can use the following steps to configure it:

Step 1. Query the required Boolean values:

```
# getsebool -a | grep crond
crond_disable_trans --> off
```

Step 2. Change the values to allow incoming logs:

```
# setsebool -P crond_disable_trans=1
```

Step 3. Verify the preceding Booleans have been changed:

```
# getsebool -a | grep crond
crond_disable_trans --> on
```

Single Jobs with at

Although you can use the cron service to schedule jobs that you want to occur more than once, you can use a service called atd for single-instance jobs.

Step 1.   As with any service thus far, you need to verify that the package is installed:

```
# rpm -qa | grep ^at
at-3.1.10-42.el6.x86_64
```

Step 2.   Check that the service is currently running:

```
# service atd status
atd (pid  2300) is running...
```

Step 3.   Finally, verify that the service is set to start on system boot:

```
# chkconfig --list atd
atd              0:off    1:off    2:off    3:on    4:on    5:on
6:off
```

The atd service uses two files in the same manner that cron does to control access to the service. These files are

/etc/at.allow

/etc/at.deny

The /etc/at.allow file:

- If it exists, only these users are allowed (at.deny is ignored).

- If it doesn't exist, all users except at.deny are permitted.

The /etc/at.deny file:

- If it exists and is empty, all users are allowed (Red Hat default).

For both files:

- If neither file exists, root only.

The atd service also includes a single command, at, that is used to set up the jobs you want to run.

Syntax: at [options]

Options:

-l	Lists all jobs in the queue
-d ID	Removes a job from the queue
-m	Sends mail to the user when the job is complete
-f FILE	Reads input from the file
-v	Shows the time the job will be executed

The at command enables you to specify a time in many different formats, making it really flexible. Let's look at a few examples of the time formats you can use:

```
# at 9am
# at now + 3 days
# at 1:30 3/22/10
```

After you specify a time, your command prompt changes:

```
# at 10:07am
at>
```

Now you just need to enter any commands that you want to execute for your job at the specified time. You can finish by pressing Ctrl+D to end the command input and send the job to the queue:

```
# at 10:07am
at>
at> wall "Hello World"
at> <EOT>
```

Now that a job is queued, let's view what the file that holds this job looks like.

Step 1. Query the /var/spool/at directory for jobs:

```
# ls /var/spool/at
a000010147997f  spool
```

Unlike with the cron service, the names of the at jobs aren't really meaningful. Instead of viewing the directory that holds the at jobs, you might find it easier to list the jobs waiting to be run like you did with the cron service.

Step 2. View the currently queued jobs using the at command:

```
# at -l
1          2010-10-27 10:07 a root
```

Step 3. You can also use the atq command for the exact same results:

```
# atq
1          2010-10-27 10:07 a root
```

You can see one job currently in the queue was sent by the root user and is waiting to run at 10:07 a.m. Instead of typing out all the jobs you might want to run, you could also use the -f option to specify a file containing a list of commands that you want executed instead:

```
# at -f cmds_file 11pm
```

When you put jobs in the queue, notice that they are given ID numbers. This information is important in case there is a job that you want to delete from the queue.

Step 4. Add a temporary job to the queue:

```
# cd ~
# touch test_job && chmod 775 test_job
# at -f test_job 11pm
```

Step 5. Verify that the job made it to the queue:

```
# atq
1          2010-12-04 23:00 a root
```

Step 6.   Delete the job from the queue:

```
# at -d 1
```

Step 7.   You can also use the atrm command to achieve the same results:

```
# atrm 1
```

Step 8.   Verify that the job is truly gone:

```
# atq
```

You should now be able to schedule single jobs and reoccurring jobs. Job management is important in making sure that your system runs smoothly. It also helps when you're automating tasks so you don't have to do them every day.

Summary

Knowing how to work with logs and where to look for information is critical when you're troubleshooting the system. A centralized syslog server helps in many ways with making log collection and management easier. You can also use tools such as ps and top to look into resource issues that the system may be having. In this chapter, we looked at the cron and atd services, each of which can be used for scheduling jobs. Using these tools, you can help track down problems that arise and look for trends of reoccurring issues. In the next chapter, we look at the kernel, the brains behind the Red Hat operating system.

Review Questions

1. What option can you change in the rsyslog config file to accept remote logs (acting as a centralized logging server)?

2. What two commands are special for dealing with user login events?

3. Can you name the two commands that can be used to view the free space on the system?

4. What command can you use to view system processes and their CPU usage?

5. The at command is used to schedule reoccurring system jobs. True or False?

6. What happens to jobs that are scheduled to run while the system is off?

7. What command can be used to view the queue for at service jobs?

8. What is the top command used for?

Answers to Review Questions

1. Uncomment the following line in the /etc/rsyslog.conf file:

   ```
   #$ModLoad imudp.so
   #$UDPServerRun 514
   ```

2. The `lastlog` and `faillog` commands are used to view user login–related events?

3. The `du` and `df` commands are used to view available space on the system.

4. Use the `ps` command to view processes and their CPU usage.

5. False. The `at` command is used to schedule one-time-only jobs. The `cron` service handles reoccurring system jobs.

6. When the system starts up again, the `cron` service will run any jobs that were missed while the system was off. On Red Hat Enterprise Linux 5, the `anacron` service handles this functionality.

7. `atq`

8. Use the `top` command to view CPU and memory usage.

Lab 9

Task 1 – Centralized Logging

Step 1.   Set up a centralized log server on RHEL02 using the following guidelines:
   a. The server must accept logs from all clients on the 172.168.1.0/24 subnet.
   b. All security logs should remain local to the system that they are on.
   c. Only /var/log/messages and /var/log/dmesg should be forwarded to the centralized server.

Step 2.   Set up each server or client system in the lab to forward the appropriate logs to RHEL02.

The task is complete when all logs are set up correctly and the centralized log server (RHEL02) is collecting the correct logs.

Task 2 – System Monitoring

Step 1.   Create a BASH script on RHEL01 using the following guidelines:
   a. The script must output the ps aux command to a file called system_mon located in the /opt directory.
   b. The script must output the amount of free memory to a file called system_mon located in the /opt directory.
   c. The script must append the date to the system_mon file.

The task is complete when the script records the necessary information in the required file and the file is named correctly.

Task 3 – Scheduling Jobs

Perform the following tasks on RHEL01:

Step 1.   Set up a cron job to execute every day at noon. The job should execute the script that you created in Task 2.

Step 2.   Create a single job to occur 10 minutes from now that will output the date and time to all users who are logged in to the system.

The task is complete when all jobs have been scheduled and they execute successfully.

This chapter covers the following subjects:

■ **Kernel Basics**—This section covers the basics of the kernel.

■ **Updating the Kernel**—This section covers different ways to update the kernel.

■ **Tuning the Kernel with /proc/sys**—This section looks at ways you can tune the kernel for performance.

The following RHCSA exam objective is covered:

■ Update the kernel package appropriately to ensure a bootable system

The following RHCE exam objective is covered:

■ Use /proc/sys and sysctl to modify and set kernel runtime parameters

## CHAPTER 10

The Kernel

The heart of Red Hat is the Linux kernel. The kernel is responsible for interacting with the hardware and producing output to the screen. There is also a virtual file system that gets created in the /proc directory to hold information and parameters for the kernel. In this chapter, we look at the basics of the kernel, ways to update it, and ways to tune it using the /proc file system. Although the focus of this book is on Red Hat and the exams, everything in this chapter applies to other versions of the Linux operating system as well.

Kernel Basics

Linux is truly just the kernel. Red Hat and the other distributions in existence today are software and configuration files packaged with the Linux kernel to bring you an entire operating system (although we still refer to any distribution as *Linux*). Because the kernel is really what runs everything, understanding how it works is essential. The kernel can be used to load new drivers, support new hardware, or even offer a custom kernel for individual needs. The Linux kernel is modular, and because of this, you can load and unload kernel modules even after the system has booted. In this chapter, we look at four commands that help when working with the kernel:

uname	Displays information about the kernel
lsmod	Lists currently loaded kernel modules
modinfo	Displays information about a kernel module
sysctl	Enables you to tune kernel parameters

Let's start with the `uname` command to find out some information about the kernel first.

Syntax: `uname [option]`

Options:

`-a`	Prints all information relating to the kernel
`-s`	Shows the kernel name
`-r`	Requests kernel release information
`-v`	Requests the kernel version

Let's check and see which version of the kernel is currently running:

```
# uname -a
Linux RHEL01 2.6.32-71.el6.x86_64 #1 SMP Wed Sep 1 01:33:01 EDT 2010 x86_64 x86_64
x86_64 GNU/Linux
```

The kernel version numbering is important here (`2.6.32-71.el6`). The first number is the major version of the kernel. The second number is the major release of the first number. If the release number is even, which it is (6), it means that this is a stable release of the kernel. Odd numbers are development kernels and should not be used for production systems. The third number is the patch version of the kernel. The last number (71) is added by Red Hat to represent its release version of the kernel. Also note the `el6`, which tells you that you are running Red Hat Enterprise Linux 6. If you couldn't tell, this is an x64-bit version of the operating system (denoted by the `x86_64`).

REAL-WORLD TIP

Although we are talking about even and odd numbers for stability of the kernel, this information is more for historical purposes. Today, everything is referred to as a *2.6 kernel or later*.

You can also get the version of the currently installed kernel through the package manager:

```
# rpm -qa | grep kernel
kernel-2.6.32-71.el6.x86_64
```

You could also use the following:

```
# rpm -q kernel
```

When it comes to working with kernels, you should be familiar with different locations. Let's look at four of these locations:

/boot	Place where the kernel and boot files are kept
/proc	Current hardware configuration and status
/usr/src	Source code of the kernel
/lib/modules	Kernel modules

As you saw in Chapter 2, "System Initialization," the kernel is also used to boot the operating system. Because the kernel is modular, it is important to understand which modules are in use and how to view them. You can use the `lsmod` command to view modules that are currently loaded.

Syntax: `lsmod`

To look at what is currently loaded by the kernel since you booted the system, you use the following command:

```
# lsmod
Module               Size  Used by
autofs4             29253  3
hidp                23105  2
rfcomm              42457  0
l2cap               29505  10 hidp,rfcomm
ext4               353979  2
[output truncated]
```

The preceding output is truncated due to size. With this list of modules in hand, you can further explore what a particular module does by using the `modinfo` command.

Show the details of the ext4 kernel module listed previously:

```
# modinfo ext4
filename:       /lib/modules/2.6.32-71.el6.x86_64/kernel/fs/ext4/ext4.ko
license:        GPL
description:    Fourth Extended Filesystem
author:         Remy Card, Stephen Tweedie, Andrew Morton, Andreas Dilger,
Theodore Ts'o and others
srcversion:     8689F457D14068A36A86631
depends:        mbcache,jbd2
vermagic:       2.6.32-71.el6.x86_64 SMP mod_unload modversions
```

Although you don't need to know the complexities of the kernel or anything hardware related for the Red Hat exams, it is important to know how to find this information. Locating issues and knowing to look for them are half the battle when you're troubleshooting. Now let's move on to ways you can update the kernel.

Updating the Kernel

We all know how important it is to keep up with the patching process on our systems. It prevents people from breaking in and doing malicious things, not to mention it keeps the boss from yelling at us, too! To update the kernel package in Red Hat is fairly straightforward.

Step 1.   View the current version of the kernel:

```
# uname -r
2.6.32-71.el6.x86_64
```

As you learned in Chapter 6, "Package Management," you can use the yum command to query information about packages in the repository. You know from the preceding output that you are using version 71 of the kernel on Red Hat Enterprise Linux 6. You can check to see what information the yum command can provide on the most recent version of the kernel package in the repositories.

Step 2.   To view kernel package information, use the following command:

```
# yum info kernel
Loaded plugins: rhnplugin
This system is not registered with RHN.
RHN support will be disabled.
Installed Packages
Name        : kernel
Arch        : x86_64
Version     : 2.6.32
Release     : 71.el6
Size        : 112 M
Repo        : installed
From repo   : anaconda-RedHatEnterpriseLinux-201009221801.x86_64
Summary     : The Linux kernel
URL         : http://www.kernel.org/
License     : GPLv2
Description : The kernel package contains the Linux kernel (vmlin-
uz), the core of any
            : Linux operating system. The kernel handles the basic
functions
            : of the operating system: memory allocation, process
allocation, device
            : input and output, etc.
```

Because you're using Red Hat Enterprise Linux 6 at the moment, your kernel is up-to-date. What if you were still on Red Hat Enterprise Linux 5, though? On the Client01 system, which uses RHEL5, check what the kernel version is.

Step 1.   On Client01, query the version of the kernel via the package manager:

```
# yum info kernel
Loaded plugins: fastestmirror
Loading mirror speeds from cached hostfile
 * addons: mirrors.xmission.com
 * base: ftp.osuosl.org
 * extras: ftp.usf.edu
```

```
 * updates: mirror.sanctuaryhost.com
Installed Packages
Name        : kernel
Arch        : i686
Version     : 2.6.18
Release     : 164.el5
Size        : 41 M
Repo        : installed
Summary     : The Linux kernel (the core of the Linux operating
system)
URL         : http://www.kernel.org/
License     : GPLv2
Description: The kernel package contains the Linux kernel (vmlin-
uz), the core of any
            : Linux operating system. The kernel handles the basic
functions
            : of the operating system: memory allocation, process
allocation, device
            : input and output, etc.

Available Packages
Name        : kernel
Arch        : i686
Version     : 2.6.18
Release     : 194.11.3.el5
Size        : 17 M
Repo        : updates
Summary     : The Linux kernel (the core of the Linux operating
system)
URL         : http://www.kernel.org/
License     : GPLv2
Description: The kernel package contains the Linux kernel (vmlin-
uz), the core of any
            : Linux operating system. The kernel handles the basic
functions
            : of the operating system: memory allocation, process
allocation, device
            : input and output, etc.
```

The first thing you should notice is the additional section that shows available packages alongside the currently installed package. The first half of the output shows the installed package, and the second half shows the kernel package available for you to upgrade to. Because you are only on version 164.el5 and the latest version is 194.11.3.el5, you should upgrade the kernel.

Step 2.   Using the package manager, you can upgrade the kernel to the latest version:

```
# yum update -y kernel
Loaded plugins: fastestmirror
Loading mirror speeds from cached hostfile
 * addons: mirrors.xmission.com
 * base: ftp.osuosl.org
 * extras: centos-distro.cavecreek.net
 * updates: mirror.sanctuaryhost.com
Setting up Update Process
Resolving Dependencies
```

```
--> Running transaction check
---> Package kernel.i686 0:2.6.18-194.11.3.el5 set to be installed
--> Finished Dependency Resolution

Dependencies Resolved

================================================================
 Package          Arch       Version              Repository        Size
================================================================
Installing:
 kernel           i686       2.6.18-194.11.3.el5   updates           17 M

Transaction Summary
================================================================
Install       1 Package(s)
Update        0 Package(s)
Remove        0 Package(s)

Total download size: 17 M
Downloading Packages:
kernel-2.6.18-194.11.3.el5.i686.rpm                    |  17 MB     00:18
Running rpm_check_debug
Running Transaction Test
Finished Transaction Test
Transaction Test Succeeded
Running Transaction
  Installing     : kernel
1/1

Installed:
  kernel.i686 0:2.6.18-194.11.3.el5

Complete!
```

Now you should have the most updated version of your kernel on Client01. By using the yum command to update the kernel, you are pulling only the most updated version that Red Hat is making available through the repositories. This doesn't mean that this is the most recent version of the Linux kernel available. If you visit http://www.kernel.org, you can find the most up-to-date kernel available. You should download it in a format you are comfortable using (the site has .tar, .gz, .rpm, and more). If you are going to use an .rpm file, remember that you have the rpm command to make installation easier for you. As an example, I pulled the most recent version of the kernel from Red Hat as an .rpm file for the Client01 system. Instead of using the package manager to install the kernel from the repository, as I did, you could also do the following:

```
# rpm -ivh kernel-2.6.18-194.3.1el5
```

WARNING

When updating a kernel with the rpm command, never use the -U option to update. The reason behind this is that the update option erases the prior kernel when updating, whereas the -i option installs the newer kernel alongside the old kernel. If something doesn't work or goes wrong, you have an older kernel to revert to.

You've been warned!

Regardless of what method you use, when the update of the kernel is complete, you should verify that /boot/grub/grub.conf has been updated to contain a stanza with the updated kernel and that it is set to boot from it. This should happen automatically when updating the kernel via the package manager; however, I recommend that you always verify this for yourself (otherwise, your system may boot incorrectly).

Since the kernel hasn't changed on RHEL01 (because it was already up-to-date), look at the grub.conf file on Client01 because you did update the kernel there:

```
# cat /boot/grub/grub.conf
# grub.conf generated by anaconda
#
# Note that you do not have to rerun grub after making changes to this file
# NOTICE: You have a /boot partition. This means that
#         all kernel and initrd paths are relative to /boot/, eg.
#         root (hd0,0)
#         kernel /vmlinuz-version ro root=/dev/VolGroup00/LogVol00
#         initrd /initrd-version.img
#boot=/dev/hda
default=0
timeout=5
splashimage=(hd0,0)/grub/splash.xpm.gz
hiddenmenu
title CentOS (2.6.18-194.11.3.el5)
        root (hd0,0)
        kernel /vmlinuz-2.6.18-194.11.3.el5 ro root=/dev/VolGroup00/LogVol00
        initrd /initrd-2.6.18-194.11.3.el5.img
title CentOS (2.6.18-164.el5)
        root (hd0,0)
        kernel /vmlinuz-2.6.18-164.el5 ro root=/dev/VolGroup00/LogVol00
        initrd /initrd-2.6.18-164.el5.img
```

You can see that the first entry is the newly updated kernel and that the default option is set to 0, making sure you will load your updated kernel the next time you boot the system. Reboot your system to allow the new kernel to be used and check to make sure that there are no errors or issues when booting up with the new kernel. If you encounter any issues, you can reboot again and choose the older kernel at the GRUB boot menu to fix any issues you're having.

Up to this point, you should be comfortable updating and upgrading a kernel on your Red Hat system. Although it is possible to build completely custom kernels, this is a very large undertaking and requires a good deal of knowledge regarding the internals of the Linux kernel. We don't cover this topic here because custom kernel compiling is not part of the Red Hat exams; however, there are many great books on the subject.

The last topic that we address is modifying the kernel through the use of the /proc/sys file system.

Tuning the Kernel with /proc/sys

One of the great things about Linux is that it works on so many different types of hardware out of the box. Although this is a great feature of Linux, it also requires developers of different distributions, such as Red Hat, to generalize settings for their versions of the operating system. This generalization is fine in most cases, but those who want some extra processing power and better performance should tune their kernel.

The kernel has a virtual file system, /proc/sys, that allows you to tune the kernel while the system is running. The kernel creates the /proc/sys virtual file system when the system boots up, which holds all the parameters of the kernel. This virtual file system is then used to manipulate kernel parameters for testing purposes (these changes are valid only until the system reboots). When you have the kernel tuned the way you'd like, you can simply have your settings applied when the system boots (through a special config file), or you can compile your own kernel to have them built in permanently. As you are testing kernel changes, make sure you don't rely on any settings made within the /proc/sys file system because they are erased when the system reboots. During testing, you can use the echo command to change the values of the kernel while the system is running.

Let's look at an example showing how to allow the system to temporarily forward packets.

Step 1.   View the current value in the kernel:

```
# cat /proc/sys/net/ipv4/ip_forward
0
```

Step 2.   Change the kernel option that controls packet forwarding:

```
# echo 1 > /proc/sys/net/ipv4/ip_forward
```

Step 3.   Verify that the value has changed:

```
# cat /proc/sys/net/ipv4/ip_forward
1
```

If you want the changes to be persistent across system reboots, you can put the parameters you'd like to remain during boot in the /etc/sysctl.conf file. This file is manipulated through the sysctl command, which you can also use to tune the kernel.

Syntax: sysctl [options]

Options:

-e	Ignores errors
-w	Enables you to change a setting in the /etc/sysctl.conf file
-p	Loads settings from the /etc/sysctl.conf file
-a	Displays all settings currently available

REAL-WORLD TIP

The /etc/sysctl.conf file and sysctl command are responsible for values only under the /proc/sys directory. There are other areas of the virtual file system that reside in the /proc root directory.

Before you start tuning things, let's look at all the available options:

```
# sysctl -a
```

You may notice that I left out the output of this command. You can run the same command again with a slight modification:

```
# sysctl -a | wc -l
551
```

The output here shows that there are 551 different options available for tuning within the /proc/sys file system (hence, why I left out the output). You could pipe these options to a file for later review and to look up what each one does. For now, let's make the same change to the kernel as before.

Step 1.   Query the parameter responsible for forwarding packets within the kernel:

```
# sysctl -a | grep ip_forward
net.ipv4.ip_forward = 0
```

Step 2.   Using the `sysctl` command, change the option:

```
# sysctl -w net.ipv4.ip_forward=1
net.ipv4.ip_forward = 1
```

Note there is no whitespace between the parameter, equal sign, or value.

Step 3.   Verify that the value has been changed:

```
# sysctl -a | grep ip_forward
net.ipv4.ip_forward = 1
```

You can see that the value has indeed been changed. Because you shouldn't mess with the system settings at the moment, you can change the value back or reboot the system so that the original value is restored.

Step 4.   Return the parameter to its original value:

```
# sysctl -w net.ipv4.ip_forward=0
net.ipv4.ip_forward = 0
```

An alternative to adding different options to the /etc/sysctl.conf file would be to compile a custom kernel. This would include all the custom parameters in the kernel permanently so that they don't need to be set automatically at boot time. You can also remove options that you aren't using and give your system better performance. Compiling a kernel is not an easy task and is also not part of the Red Hat exams. There are some great books and online documentation available, though, if you are interested.

Summary

Although customization and compiling custom kernels are something you are not likely to see on the Red Hat exam, you should be comfortable with updating a kernel and ensuring that the system survives a reboot. You should also be comfortable tuning kernel parameters via the /proc/sys file system. If you find yourself looking for better performance or wanting to learn some more advanced usage of the kernel, I suggest you compile a kernel for yourself on the lab system. Just remember that this is not a simple task and takes time to get right.

Review Questions

1. What is the difference between the update (-U) and install (-i) options when using rpm to update the kernel?

2. What directory is used to represent the virtual file system created by the kernel?

3. What file is used to maintain custom parameters for the kernel during system boot?

4. What critical step must you take after updating the kernel to a newer version?

Answers to Review Questions

1. You should never use the -U option because it erases the prior kernel when updating. This leaves you with no fallback kernel should your system not boot properly.

2. The /proc directory. The /proc/sys directory is the place where you actually tune kernel parameters.

3. The /etc/sysctl.conf file maintains a list of custom kernel parameters that should be applied during system boot.

4. You must ensure that the /boot/grub/grub.conf file has the new entry for your newly updated kernel to be able to boot into it.

Lab 10

Task 1 – Updating the Kernel

Step 1. Using the yum command, update the kernel to the latest version on RHEL02.

Step 2. Using the yum command, update the kernel to the latest version on Client01.

The task is complete when both RHEL02 and Client01 have the most updated kernels and can survive a system reboot.

Task 2 – Kernel Tuning

Step 1. Tune the following parameters in the kernel:
    a. Output the contents of /proc/sys/fs/file-max and increase the size by 100.

The task is complete when all parameter changes can be verified and survive a system reboot.

This chapter covers the following subjects:

- **Understanding SELinux**—This section covers how SELinux works and how to configure it.

- **SELinux Troubleshooting**—This section describes how to troubleshoot SELinux.

The following RHCSA exam objectives are covered:

- Set enforcing and permissive modes for SELinux

- List and identify SELinux and file process context

- Restore default file contexts

- Use Boolean settings to modify system SELinux settings

- Diagnose and address routine SELinux policy violations

## CHAPTER 11

SELinux

Security Enhanced Linux (SELinux) is another layer of security for the Linux operating system. Developed by the National Security Agency (NSA), it adds protection for different files, applications, processes, and so on. Many users who are just starting out tend to turn off SELinux because it is a complex system that can take much time and effort to get used to. Instead of turning it off, however, you could use SELinux in "permissive" mode, which allows everything to function normally but logs warnings when actions or commands would have been blocked. Running in this mode is good for troubleshooting and gaining an understanding of how SELinux works. For the Red Hat Exam, however, you need to know how to work with SELinux enabled and enforcing.

Understanding SELinux

As already stated, SELinux can be quite complex. Let's start with some of the basics to understanding SELinux. It can run in three different modes:

disabled   SELinux is turned off and doesn't restrict anything.

permissive   SELinux is turned on, but it logs warnings only when an action normally would have been blocked.

enforcing   SELinux is turned on and blocks actions related to services.

Aside from these three modes, there are numerous commands that you can use for the management of SELinux:

sestatus   Shows the current status of SELinux

getenforce   Shows the enforcing status of SELinux

setenforce   Changes the enforcing status of SELinux

getsebool   Returns the Boolean value of a service option

setsebool   Sets the Boolean value of a service option

chcon   Changes the context of a file, directory, or service

restorecon   Resets the context of an object

Before you start using commands, you should look at the further breakdown of SELinux. Each file, directory, and service on your system has a context that is used to prevent or allow actions (see Figure 11-1). SELinux uses these contexts along with Boolean values to permit certain actions or services to run.

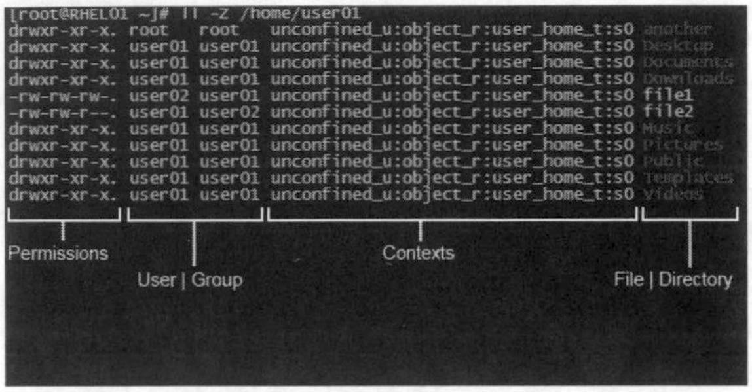

Figure 11-1   Files, directories, and services all have contexts.

Let's start by looking at the current mode that SELinux is running in. For this, you can use the sestatus command.

Syntax: sestatus [options]

Options:

-b   Displays all Booleans and their statuses

-v   Provides verbose output

Determine the current status of SELinux:

```
# sestatus
SELinux status:             enabled
SELinuxfs mount:            /selinux
Current mode:               enforcing
Mode from config file:      enforcing
Policy version:             21
Policy from config file:    targeted
```

You can also use the getenforce command to view the status in a different way:

```
# getenforce
Enforcing
```

When you first installed this system, SELinux was set to be enforcing. In RHEL6, this setting is the default. Because you are working in a lab environment, I suggest that you set SELinux to permissive on Client01 and Client02. For RHEL01 and

RHEL02, you should leave SELinux set to enforcing. If you run into any problems where you suspect SELinux of causing the issue, you can troubleshoot using the two different systems. On the exam, you are required to work with SELinux set to enforcing, so you need to understand how to troubleshoot it and fix any issues that arise.

Configuring SELinux

You can change the mode in which SELinux operates by changing the config file. The main config file is /etc/selinux/config

View the current details of the /etc/selinux/config file:

```
# cat /etc/selinux/config
# This file controls the state of SELinux on the system.
# SELINUX= can take one of these three values:
#       enforcing - SELinux security policy is enforced.
#       permissive - SELinux prints warnings instead of enforcing.
#       disabled - SELinux is fully disabled.
SELINUX=enforcing
# SELINUXTYPE= type of policy in use. Possible values are:
#       targeted - Only targeted network daemons are protected.
#       strict - Full SELinux protection.
SELINUXTYPE=targeted
```

You can see that the three SELinux modes are listed in the comments of the file and that the current mode is enforcing. At any time, you can change the mode that SELinux runs in, but a system reboot is required for it to take effect. After you change the mode in which SELinux is running and reboot the system, SELinux re-labels the file system to change the context of the files. This process can be time consuming depending on the size of your drive and the number of files it contains, so planning ahead with the mode to run SELinux is always advised. Aside from editing the config file, you can also use the setenforce command to change the status.

Syntax: setenforce [Enforcing | Permissive | 1 | 0]

If the current mode is permissive, you can change it to enforcing with the following:

```
# setenforce enforcing
```

Regardless of which method you use when changing the mode in which SELinux runs, you are still required to reboot the system. Now that you know how to find and change the mode in which SELinux operates, let's move on to file contexts.

File Contexts

SELinux uses three different contexts to enforce security: user, role, and domain (also called *type*). New to RHEL6 is the addition of a fourth context known as *level* (this level represents the sensitivity level of a file or directory). These can be further expanded to define values for each context.

User:

unconfined_u	Unprotected user
system_u	System user
user_u	Normal user

Role:

object_r	File
system_r	Users and processes

Domain:

unconfined_r	Unprotected file or process

NOTE: For the domain section listed here, unconfined_r is only one type of context that can be used. More restrictive values can be used, but unconfined_r is the most general, which is why it's listed here.

Each file, folder, and service has an associated label that contains all three contexts. In this section, we look at the SSH service as an example because it is installed with the system by default. You can use the ps command described in Chapter 9, "System Logging, Monitoring, and Automation," to view the labels associated with a service.

Check the SELinux labels associated with SSH service:

```
# ps -ZC sshd
LABEL                                   PID TTY          TIME CMD
system_u:system_r:sshd_t:s0-s0:c0.c1023 1421 ?        00:00:00 sshd
system_u:system_r:sshd_t:s0-s0:c0.c1023 4977 ?        00:00:00 sshd
system_u:system_r:sshd_t:s0-s0:c0.c1023 4982 ?        00:00:00 sshd
```

The first field you see here is system_u, which, you can tell from the expanded context section, is a system user. The second field contains system_r, which again you can reference to see that it is a user or, in this case, a process. The third field shows unconfined_t as the domain. You can ignore the fourth field for the moment.

Let's look a little further at the domain context. The domain is simply a way of categorizing which contexts can talk to one another. Another example should help make this clearer.

Look at the label for the SSH service main config file:

```
# ll -Z /etc/ssh/sshd_config
-rw-------. root root system_u:object_r:etc_t:s0          /etc/ssh/sshd_config
```

Going through the label, you see the user is system_u (a system user), the role is object_r (a file), and the domain is etc_t. Any service that has access to the etc_t domain is able to access this file. System services usually are the only ones aside from the root user that have access to the /etc directory, so a domain of etc_t makes sense.

REAL-WORLD TIP

In RHEL5, the SSH config file had a domain of unconfined_t while the SSH service had a domain of etc_t. You may be wondering why the SSH service has access even though it is in another domain (unconfined_t). The reason is that the unconfined_t domain is unprotected, making it available to anyone. In RHEL6, many of the services and their config files have had their labels changed.

Although you haven't installed a web server yet (that's in Chapter 14, "Web Services"), contexts are important when creating websites because if the site doesn't have the correct context, it is not accessible by the web server. To change the context of a file or directory, you can use the chcon command.

Syntax: chcon [options] CONTEXT FILE

Options:

-f	Suppresses error messages
-u	Sets user context
-r	Sets role context
-t	Sets type context (domain)
-R	Changes recursively
-v	Provides verbose output

Let's look at an example.

Step 1. Change the user context from normal user to system user:

```
# cd ~
# touch myfile
# ls -Z myfile
-rw-r--r--. root root unconfined_u:object_r:admin_home_t:s0 myfile
```

Step 2. Now change the context:

```
# chcon -vu system_u myfile
context of myfile changed to system_u:object_r:user_home_t
```

Step 3.   Verify that it has been changed:

```
# ls -Z myfile
-rw-r--r--. root root system_u:object_r:admin_home_t:s0 myfile
```

> **REAL-WORLD TIP**
>
> A neat trick you can do with the chcon command is to reference the context of another file. This capability is useful when you're using SELinux to enforce security on websites. You could set up a dummy site that acts as a template, say /var/www/html/default_site. When you create a new customer site, you can use the chcon command to reference the template site and apply the correct context:
>
> ```
> # chcon -vR —reference /var/www/html/default_site /var/www/html/customer_site
> ```

If you make a mistake or just want to reset the original contexts of a file or directory, you can use the restorecon command.

Syntax: restorecon [options]

Options:

-i	Ignores files that don't exist
-p	Shows progress
-v	Shows changes as they happen
-F	Resets context

Step 4.   Reset the context of your file back to its original context:
```
# restorecon -F myfile
```

Step 5.   Verify the change was applied correctly:

```
# ls -Z myfile
-rw-r--r--. root root root:object_r:admin_home_t:s0 myfile
```

You may have noticed that instead of going back to user_u, the user context is now set to root. This behavior is normal for the root user, but if you did this for non-root-owned files, it would have been reset to user_u.

This discussion may seem really confusing, but working through the labs will help to clarify any confusion. Creating SELinux policies is an advanced topic that isn't covered here or on the Red Hat exams, but knowing how to work with contexts and troubleshoot issues is definitely a requirement.

Service and Boolean Options

Now that we've looked at the contexts related to files and directories, let's look at the Boolean options associated with services. Each service controls certain actions with a set of options defined as Boolean values (they can be either on or off). This section covers how to work with Boolean options for services and is the most important when it comes to the Red Hat exam because it shows you how to enable access to different services.

To view these Boolean options, you can use the `getsebool` command combined with `grep` to look for specific options.

Syntax: `getsebool [-a | boolean]`

Although you have not installed a web server yet, let's look at the Boolean options from it anyway. The reason behind this is that it has many options, making for a good example.

Query the Boolean options available for the httpd service (Apache):

```
# getsebool -a | grep http
allow_httpd_anon_write --> off
allow_httpd_mod_auth_ntlm_winbind --> off
allow_httpd_mod_auth_pam --> off
allow_httpd_sys_script_anon_write --> off
httpd_builtin_scripting --> on
httpd_can_check_spam --> off
httpd_can_network_connect --> off
httpd_can_network_connect_cobbler --> off
httpd_can_network_connect_db --> off
httpd_can_network_relay --> off
httpd_can_sendmail --> off
httpd_dbus_avahi --> on
httpd_enable_cgi --> on
httpd_enable_ftp_server --> off
httpd_enable_homedirs --> off
httpd_execmem --> off
httpd_read_user_content --> off
httpd_setrlimit --> off
httpd_ssi_exec --> off
httpd_tmp_exec --> off
httpd_tty_comm --> on
httpd_unified --> on
httpd_use_cifs --> off
httpd_use_gpg --> off
httpd_use_nfs --> off
```

You might be thinking that this is a huge list, so how can you tell which options to change so that Apache can provide you with different services? The semanage command can provide you with a description of each Boolean. It is also very useful if you need a specific setting changed.

View the descriptions for the httpd service (Apache):

```
# semanage boolean -l | grep http
httpd_can_network_relay          -> off   Allow httpd to act as a relay
httpd_can_network_connect_db     -> off   Allow HTTPD scripts and modules to
connect to databases over the network.
httpd_use_gpg                    -> off   Allow httpd to run gpg in gpg-web
domain
httpd_enable_cgi                 -> on    Allow httpd cgi support
httpd_use_cifs                   -> off   Allow httpd to access cifs file
systems
allow_httpd_mod_auth_pam         -> off   Allow Apache to use mod_auth_pam
allow_httpd_anon_write           -> off   Allow Apache to modify public files
used for public file transfer services.  Directories/Files must be labeled
public_rw_content_t.
httpd_enable_homedirs            -> off   Allow httpd to read home directories
allow_httpd_sys_script_anon_write -> off   Allow apache scripts to write to
public content. Directories/Files must be labeled public_rw_content_t.
httpd_dbus_avahi                 -> on    Allow Apache to communicate with avahi
service via dbus
httpd_unified                    -> on    Unify HTTPD handling of all content
files.
httpd_can_network_connect        -> off   Allow HTTPD scripts and modules to
connect to the network using TCP.
allow_httpd_mod_auth_ntlm_winbind -> off   Allow Apache to use mod_auth_pam
httpd_tty_comm                   -> on    Unify HTTPD to communicate with the
terminal. Needed for entering the passphrase for certificates at the terminal.
httpd_read_user_content          -> off   Allow httpd to read user content
httpd_use_nfs                    -> off   Allow httpd to access nfs file systems
httpd_tmp_exec                   -> off   Allow Apache to execute tmp content.
httpd_execmem                    -> off   Allow httpd scripts and modules
execmem/execstack
httpd_can_sendmail               -> off   Allow http daemon to send mail
httpd_builtin_scripting          -> on    Allow httpd to use built in scripting
(usually php)
httpd_can_check_spam             -> off   Allow http daemon to check spam
httpd_can_network_connect_cobbler -> off   Allow HTTPD scripts and modules to
connect to cobbler over the network.
httpd_ssi_exec                   -> off   Allow HTTPD to run SSI executables in
the same domain as system CGI scripts.
httpd_enable_ftp_server          -> off   Allow httpd to act as a FTP server by
```

```
listening on the ftp port.
httpd_setrlimit                   -> off   Allow httpd daemon to change system
limits
```

MIGRATION TIP

In RHEL5, there was a Boolean with the value `<service>_disable_trans`. This one Boolean protects each service and prevents it from being accessed unless the value is changed first. In RHEL 6, this Boolean no longer exists for each service, but the number of Booleans for each service has expanded, offering more detailed protection. If you are still using RHEL5, you need to change the `<service>_disable_trans` Boolean to have a value of on for the service to work correctly.

After deciding which Boolean you'd like to change, you need to enable or disable the value appropriately. To enable or disable a Boolean option, you can use the `setsebool` command. When using the command, you also need to use the `-P` option for the change to be persistent.

Syntax: `setsebool [options] [boolean = <on (1) | off (0)>]`

Option:

  `-P`   Makes the changes persistent

From the option listed here, suppose you want to be able to access your home directory through the web server. In that case, you need to adjust the `httpd_enable_homedirs` Boolean for this to happen. Change the value to disable protection of this particular option:

```
# setsebool -P httpd_enable_homedirs=1
```

Notice that this command uses the `-P` option to make sure that the changes are persistent upon reboot. Now verify that it has been enabled:

```
# getsebool httpd_enable_homedirs
httpd_enable_homedirs --> on
```

Now the web server allows you to access your home directory through the Web, making it easy to share files. Although this isn't something I recommend doing, it does serve as a good example of how Booleans work in conjunction with services. As you have already seen in earlier chapters, Booleans are important for different services. The following chapters of this book deal with different services and cover the exact Booleans you need to know for each service to make them work properly.

SELinux Troubleshooting

When you're troubleshooting SELinux issues, there are a few packages that you should install first:

```
# yum install -y policycoreutils-python policycoreutils selinux-policy
setroubleshoot-server
```

You will also find the following two log files handy:

/var/log/audit/audit.log	Logs SELinux denials
/var/log/messages	Logs SELinux denials

Each log file provides specific error messages when denials occur, making them easier to search using grep. Two common commands you can use to hunt for error messages include

```
# grep "SELinux is preventing" /var/log/messages
```

```
# grep "denied" /var/log/audit/audit.log
```

Problems can arise in SELinux for numerous reasons. However, the top three include

- **Labeling problems**—Using a nonstandard directory tends to cause problems if the directory or files aren't labeled correctly.

- **Correct context**—When you're moving files, they can lose or retain incorrect contexts, causing access errors. Use the matchpathcon command to verify the correct context.

- **Confined service**—If certain Booleans are not enabled, a service may have trouble operating or communicating with other services.

Policy Violations

If you are having trouble with Booleans and need to determine what a specific Boolean does, you can use the semanage command as you saw earlier.

To list all the Booleans with their current values and a brief description, use the following:

```
# semanage boolean -l
SELinux boolean                            Description

ftp_home_dir                    -> off     Allow ftp to read and write files in
smartmon_3ware                  -> off     Enable additional permissions needed
xdm_sysadm_login                -> off     Allow xdm logins as sysadm
xen_use_nfs                     -> off     Allow xen to manage nfs files
mozilla_read_content            -> off     Control mozilla content access
[Output Truncated]
```

When a denial occurs on the system, you see an ID associated with it in your log files. This ID can be used to determine a more detailed understanding of what could be causing problems with your files or service.

Use the `sealert` command to obtain more information from an ID:

```
# sealert -l 0621a8c3-b182-49cf-9116-c78a9dd52199
```

You can see that this command should give you enough information to understand what is going on. Although you shouldn't run into too many issues with SELinux on the Red Hat exam, it is important to be able to work with the Boolean values and know how to find what you are looking for among them. Aside from Booleans, most of the SELinux issues should be minor.

Summary

With the release of RHEL6, SELinux has taken on a larger role in securing systems. This chapter covered how to set up and configure SELinux, while still ensuring functionality of your system. For the Red Hat exams, make sure you are comfortable looking up Boolean values and knowing how to adjust them, changing file contexts, and handling SELinux policy violations. Also, this chapter examined contexts and how they play a role in SELinux. If you want to learn more about SELinux, there are entire courses dedicated to SELinux and advanced management.

Review Questions

1. What is the point of using SELinux?

2. What are SELinux Booleans?

3. What command can you use to change the context of files?

4. What command can you use to query Boolean values?

5. What command and option do you use to view the description of Boolean values?

6. How would you view all Boolean options for the HTTP service?

7. Which log file is used to keep track of policy violations?

8. How would you disable SELinux protection for NFS, allowing shares to be read/write?

Answers to the Review Questions

1. SELinux provides enhanced granular security for the Linux operating system.

2. SELinux Booleans provide restrictions to different aspects of a service.

3. `chcon`

4. `getsebool`

5. `semanage boolean -l`

6. `getsebool -a | grep http`

7. The /var/log/audit/audit.log file contains all policy violations.

8. `setsebool -P nfs_export_all_rw=1`

Lab 11

Task 1 – SELinux Setup

Step 1. Ensure that SELinux is set to enforcing on RHEL01.

Step 2. Ensure that SELinux is set to permissive on RHEL02.

Step 3. Ensure that SELinux is set to enforcing on Client01.

Step 4. Ensure that SELinux is set to disabled on Client02.

The task is complete when SELinux is set up properly on all systems in the lab.

Task 2 – Booleans

Step 1. On Client01, change the `httpd_disable_trans` Boolean from off to on.

Step 2. On RHEL01, output all Booleans and their values for the NFS service to a file called nfs_bools in the /opt directory.

Step 3. On RHEL01, output all Booleans and their descriptions for the Samba service to a file called samba_bools in the /opt directory.

The task is complete when all files have been created and Boolean values changed.

This chapter covers the following subjects:

■ **Security Through TCP Wrappers**—This section covers security with the use of the TCP Wrappers utility.

■ **Firewall Rules Using iptables**—This section looks at firewall rules.

■ **Working with NAT**—This section covers more advanced uses of iptables to configure NAT.

■ **Pluggable Authentication Module (PAM)**—This section looks at how security can be enforced with PAM, including password policies.

The following RHCSA exam objective is covered:

■ Configure firewall settings using system-config-firewall or iptables

The following RHCE exam objective is covered:

■ Use iptables to implement packet filtering and configure network address translation (NAT)

## CHAPTER 12

System Security

I'd like to start off this chapter by saying that because I'm a person who is nuts about security, I think this is one of the most important chapters in the book. One of the biggest reasons for system compromise these days isn't that some elite hacker is breaking in and circumventing the multiple layers of security on your network; it's that some system administrators couldn't take five minutes to close the front door! In this chapter, we look at defense in depth, starting with TCP Wrappers, iptables (which are used to set up the firewall), and the Pluggable Authentication Module (PAM). If there is one chapter that you should spend a good deal of time reading, and not just for the exam, this is the one.

Security Through TCP Wrappers

TCP Wrappers is a host service that can be used to limit or control access from remote hosts. Although it is installed by default, verifying things manually is always good. First, check for the TCP Wrappers package to make sure it is installed:

```
# rpm -qa | grep wrappers
tcp_wrappers-7.6-56.3.el6.x86_64
tcp_wrappers-libs-7.6-56.3.el6.x86_64
```

Now that you know the service is installed, you can begin to configure it for access control. You can limit access to either users or hosts via the /etc/hosts.allow and /etc/hosts.deny files (you can mix and match both users and hosts in either file). The order in which items are defined within these two files is important! The TCP Wrappers service scans the two files in the following fashion:

- Search the hosts.allow file.

- Search the hosts.deny file.

- If not found in either, allow.

The TCP Wrapper service itself uses the following syntax in the two already-mentioned files:

```
<daemon_list> : <client_list>
```

Aside from being able to define a hostname or IP address in the client_list field, you can also define any of the following six keywords:

ALL	Specifies all networks
LOCAL	Specifies the local network
EXCEPT	Excludes a particular user/client
KNOWN	Indicates all hosts that can be resolved by the system
UNKNOWN	Indicates all hosts that can't be resolved by the system
PARANOID	Specifies that the forward and reverse lookup IP address don't match

These keywords can be used to help keep your rule count under control. Instead of defining each host within your network, you can just use the keyword LOCAL instead.

Let's look at a few examples to help drive home the point. Suppose that you want to restrict access to the SSH service and allow connections only from the local network. In this case, you would use the following rule in the /etc/hosts.allow:

```
sshd : 172.168.1.
```

First, you are defining the service you want to use, SSH, by listing the name of the daemon (sshd). Next, you are listing the local subnet from which you want to allow access—in this case, the internal lab subnet. Notice that there are only three octets with a trailing "dot" (.) character. This indicates a subnet as opposed to just a single IP address. If you want to allow only a single IP address to be able to access the server, you could do something like this:

```
sshd : 172.168.1.1
```

With the preceding line, connections would be allowed only from the host 172.168.1.1, instead of the entire 172.168.1.0 /24 subnet.

REAL-WORLD TIP

In the real world, it is highly recommended that you use TCP Wrappers to lock down things such as SSH to your local subnets. This even prevents people on the inside from accessing the servers unless they are on the correct subnet. Usually, end users are on their own subnet, denying them access to any management connections.

Going further with this example, what if you want to allow all users from the 172.168.1.0/24 network except the 172.168.1.100 host? Then you could use the following rule in /etc/hosts.allow:

```
sshd : 172.168.1. EXCEPT 172.168.1.100
```

While locking down the number of hosts that can access a particular server, you don't want to go crazy either; otherwise, you'll end up with a management nightmare! A common solution in the real world is to use the domain name in which servers and clients are members to provide you with basic management. You can restrict it to hosts from particular domains with the following:

```
sshd : .example.com
```

With this line in your /etc/hosts.allow file, you allow any system on the example.com domain to access this server. When troubleshooting TCP Wrappers, you can use the /var/log/secure file to view any information that is recorded. This helps you determine if something is wrong or being blocked for a specific reason. You should not use TCP Wrappers as your *only* line of security because there are ways to fool it; however, it is a great *layer* of security. Combined with a firewall and SELinux, TCP Wrappers is a nice addition to hardening your servers.

EXAM TIP

When taking the exam, make sure that you remember the order in which TCP Wrappers applies rules. This information is really helpful when troubleshooting issues with system access.

Firewall Rules Using iptables

Most people think that having a firewall at the edge of their network will protect them from everything. This notion couldn't be more wrong, but having a host-based firewall helps increase your system's and network's security. By default, Red Hat comes with a built-in firewall called iptables, which is enabled by default as well. Managing the firewall is essential because many services depend on being able to interact with the outside world or the rest of your network. Because the firewall is set up by default, you don't need to install it, but you should verify that the package is installed anyway.

Step 1. Verify the installation:

```
# rpm -qa | grep iptables
iptables-ipv6-1.4.7-3.el6.x86_64
iptables-1.4.7-3.el6.x86_64
```

Step 2. You should also take a moment to verify that iptables is set to start when the system boots up:

```
# chkconfig iptables --list
iptables        0:off   1:off   2:on    3:on    4:on    5:on
6:off
```

During boot, the /etc/rc.d/init.d/iptables script executes and starts the `iptables` service with the rules found in /etc/sysconfig/iptables. There are a few issues that you should understand before we jump into any examples. The `iptables` command is actually the tool used to manage a networking subsystem within the Linux kernel called *netfilter*. This subsystem is used to filter packets at different levels and is what actually implements the firewall portion.

Configuring iptables

To start, let's look at the syntax for `iptables`.

Syntax: `iptables [options] [chain] -j [target]`

Options:

`-A chain`	Appends to the chain
`-D chain`	Deletes from the chain
`-I chain`	Inserts into the chain
`-L chain`	Lists all rules
`-p proto`	Uses the protocol specified
`-m match`	Matches the extended expression
`-s address`	Defines a source address
`-d address`	Defines a destination address

Chains:

`INPUT`	Packets coming into the system
`OUTPUT`	Packets leaving the system
`FORWARD`	Incoming packets that should be forwarded

Targets:

`ACCEPT`	Allows the packets
`DROP`	Drops the packets and gives no response
`REJECT`	Rejects the packets and sends a rejection response

First, note that these are not all the options; however, they are the most commonly used and are absolutely necessary to work with services on the system.

When you're defining an `iptables` rule, there are a few factors to take into consideration: which direction the packet is heading, the action that should be taken, the protocol in use, and the port being used. You can also create your own chains aside from the ones listed here, which is what Red Hat has done for its version of Linux. The default INPUT chain for Red Hat is INPUT.

EXAM TIP

Before you start configuring rules, you can view any existing firewall rules with

```
# iptables --list
```

The reason it is not used here is that RHEL6 has no firewall rules except for incoming SSH connections by default.

MIGRATION TIP

For RHEL5, the default INPUT chain is actually RH-Firewall-1-INPUT.

Let's look at a basic `iptables` example to see how a rule is created.

Allow SSH connections over TCP port 22:

```
# iptables -I INPUT -p tcp -m tcp --dport 22 -j ACCEPT
```

Breaking down this rule, you can see that it is inserting this rule (I); using the default Red Hat input chain (INPUT); matching only TCP connections (-m tcp); using the TCP protocol (-p tcp); looking for incoming connections on port 22 (--dport 22); and, if a packet is found, jumping (-j) to the acceptance chain (ACCEPT) to allow the packet. In plain terms, this rule allows incoming TCP connections on port 22 of this system. After you work with a few rules, creating firewall rules will become easier. I chose this rule for a particular reason: because it is a rule that you will use all the time.

The SSH service, which is discussed in Chapter 13, "Remote Access," is used heavily in the Linux world to remotely administer servers. You need a firewall rule to allow incoming connections to your system to be able to connect remotely, and the preceding rule does just that.

REAL-WORLD TIP

Here is a great tip to use when working with `iptables` and firewall rules. Suppose you are testing rules for a remote location and you accidentally lock yourself out. Do you really want to explain to your boss why you need to take tomorrow off to fly across the country to reset the server? Before you create any new rules, make a copy of your current working `iptables` rules and name it iptables.bak:

```
# cp /etc/sysconfig/iptables /etc/sysconfig/iptables.bak
```

Because you learned about scheduled jobs in Chapter 9, you can put that information to good use here. Use the following command to schedule a job to replace any changes to the `iptables` file with the backup copy you made in a specified amount of time:

```
# echo "mv /etc/sysconfig/iptables.bak /etc/sysconfig/iptables && service
iptables restart" | at now+20min
```

This way, if you get locked out, the rules reset themselves after the time threshold has been reached. If your rules work correctly, you can just delete the job. Trust me: This one is a lifesaver.

Let's look at the default firewall rules that come with Red Hat:

```
# cat /etc/sysconfig/iptables
# Generated by iptables-save v1.4.7 on Thu Dec  2 15:39:03 2010
*filter
:INPUT ACCEPT [0:0]
:FORWARD ACCEPT [0:0]
:OUTPUT ACCEPT [22:3572]
-A INPUT -m state --state RELATED,ESTABLISHED -j ACCEPT
-A INPUT -p icmp -j ACCEPT
-A INPUT -i lo -j ACCEPT
-A INPUT -p tcp -m state --state NEW -m tcp --dport 22 -j ACCEPT
-A INPUT -j REJECT --reject-with icmp-host-prohibited
-A FORWARD -m physdev --physdev-is-bridged -j ACCEPT
-A FORWARD -j REJECT --reject-with icmp-host-prohibited
COMMIT
# Completed on Thu Dec  2 15:39:03 2010
```

MIGRATION TIP

In RHEL5, the default set of firewall rules is completely different! The rules have been cut down in RHEL6 to include only an SSH incoming rule. The default rules for RHEL5 are as follows:

```
# cat /etc/sysconfig/iptables
# Manual customization of this file is not recommended.
*filter
:INPUT ACCEPT [0:0]
```

```
:FORWARD ACCEPT [0:0]
:OUTPUT ACCEPT [0:0]
:RH-Firewall-1-INPUT - [0:0]
-A INPUT -j RH-Firewall-1-INPUT
-A FORWARD -j RH-Firewall-1-INPUT
-A RH-Firewall-1-INPUT -i lo -j ACCEPT
-A RH-Firewall-1-INPUT -p icmp --icmp-type any -j ACCEPT
-A RH-Firewall-1-INPUT -p 50 -j ACCEPT
-A RH-Firewall-1-INPUT -p 51 -j ACCEPT
-A RH-Firewall-1-INPUT -p udp --dport 5353 -d 224.0.0.251 -j ACCEPT
-A RH-Firewall-1-INPUT -p udp -m udp --dport 631 -j ACCEPT
-A RH-Firewall-1-INPUT -p tcp -m tcp --dport 631 -j ACCEPT
-A RH-Firewall-1-INPUT -m state --state ESTABLISHED,RELATED -j ACCEPT
-A RH-Firewall-1-INPUT -m state --state NEW -m tcp -p tcp --dport 22 -j ACCEPT
-A RH-Firewall-1-INPUT -j REJECT --reject-with icmp-host-prohibited
COMMIT
```

By looking through the firewall rules, you might notice a few things. First, you should notice the default reject-all rules at the end of this file. These can be found on any set of firewall rules and are usually referred to as "cleanup" rules. Second, make sure you always check this file to ensure your rule is included. As already mentioned, there is only a single rule for SSH by default. Like TCP Wrappers, the firewall rules are parsed in order, so it does matter where you append and insert rules.

EXAM TIP

A mistake that many people (including myself) make is using the `-A` option to append a new rule to the firewall rules and then not understanding why the new rule isn't working. My suggestion is to check the `iptables` file and find out where in the file your rule is located because many times it ends up on the bottom, below the REJECT rule. If this is the case, your rule will never be hit because no packet will ever get past the catchall REJECT rule.

The last line of this file is COMMIT, which writes the rules into memory for use on the system.

Dealing with `iptables` is probably one of the hardest topics until you have worked with them for a while. There are many different ways to configure rules, and understanding how they work from start to finish can be overwhelming. In fact, many companies make firewall appliances based on Linux and custom versions of `iptables`, which goes to show you how powerful yet complex Linux can be. The most important point to understand, especially for the exam, is how to add and troubleshoot firewall rules so that your services can function properly on the system. If you're having difficulty figuring out why something is being blocked, you can quickly disable the firewall to verify that it is indeed the firewall causing the trouble.

To look at another real-world example, suppose you need to allow SSH access to your server but you'd like to restrict the subnet that can connect.

Step 1.   You could do something like this:

```
# iptables -I INPUT 5 -s 172.168.1.1/24 -p tcp --dport 22 -j ACCEPT
```

This rule is a little more complex than the previous one. Here, you are appending to the input chain a rule that says anything from the source (-s) network 172.168.1.1/24, using the TCP protocol (-p tcp), allow on port 22 incoming (--dport 22). The lab at the end of this chapter covers multiple iptables rules to help you gain a better understanding. As you get further into this book, you need to start configuring iptables rules for different services, so learning how to work with the rules now will only help you in the long run. When creating rules with iptables, make sure that you save and restart the iptables service after you finish editing your rules because the new rules do not take effect until the service is restarted.

Step 2.   Save the rule just created:

```
# service iptables save
Saving firewall rules to /etc/sysconfig/iptables:          [  OK  ]
```

Step 3.   Restart the firewall service for the changes to take effect:

```
# service iptables restart
iptables: Flushing firewall rules:                         [  OK  ]
iptables: Setting chains to policy ACCEPT: filter          [  OK  ]
iptables: Unloading modules:                               [  OK  ]
iptables: Applying firewall rules:                         [  OK  ]
```

WARNING: The iptables command does have a GUI version, which makes generating rules and putting them in place a snap. I want to warn you, however, that using the GUI version overwrites any custom rules that you have in the iptables file. For example, if you write out a few rules using a shell and then make one addition via the GUI, only the GUI rule shows up when you open the iptables file. Again, I caution you away from using the GUI tool unless you are going to make all rules in one shot using this tool.

REAL-WORLD TIP

In the real world, you will work with firewall rules constantly. One important point to remember is that when testing firewall rules, you will not always be in front of the system you're working on. When tuning or creating your rules, you need to be careful that you don't create a rule that will lock you out of your system! Nothing is worse than tuning a rule and saving it, only to realize later you have now locked yourself out of the system and need to drive three hours to your disaster recovery site because you can't get access to your server!

Troubleshooting Firewall Rules

When troubleshooting firewall rules and connections, you can temporarily disable the firewall to make sure that the firewall is really what is causing your problem in the first place. You can also use the status option of the service command to view the current status of iptables.

```
# service iptables status
Table: filter
Chain INPUT (policy ACCEPT)
num   target     prot opt source          destination
1     ACCEPT     all  --  0.0.0.0/0       0.0.0.0/0           state
RELATED,ESTABLISHED
2     ACCEPT     icmp --  0.0.0.0/0       0.0.0.0/0
3     ACCEPT     all  --  0.0.0.0/0       0.0.0.0/0
4     ACCEPT     tcp  --  0.0.0.0/0       0.0.0.0/0           state NEW tcp dpt:22
5     REJECT     all  --  0.0.0.0/0       0.0.0.0/0           reject-with icmp-
host-prohibited

Chain FORWARD (policy ACCEPT)
num   target     prot opt source          destination
1     ACCEPT     all  --  0.0.0.0/0       0.0.0.0/0           PHYSDEV match --
physdev-is-bridged
2     REJECT     all  --  0.0.0.0/0       0.0.0.0/0           reject-with icmp-
host-prohibited

Chain OUTPUT (policy ACCEPT)
num   target     prot opt source          destination
```

You can also check in the /var/log/messages file to look for any messages that iptables produces because this is the default log file. If there is a lot going on with the system, it may be difficult to pick out messages because this file houses logs for many different services. While this topic isn't on the exam, it is really useful in the real world to get solid feedback from only the firewall service.

Working with NAT

One final use for `iptables` is network address translation (NAT). This allows you to use a server as a gateway to a subnet, essentially controlling what goes in and out of your network. You actually use this in the lab so that all systems can use RHEL01 as a gateway to get in and out of the private network.

Earlier, we described the syntax of `iptables`:

Syntax: `iptables [options] [chain] -j [target]`

However, there is actually one extra piece to this, the table type:

Syntax: `iptables -t [table-type] [options] [chain] -j [target]`

The reason I left off the table-type field originally is that there are two types of tables: filter and nat. By default, a filter table type is used, which is why you don't have to specify it. Because you're working with NAT, however, you need to specify the table type along with your `iptables` rule. NAT rules are created based on what type of rule you need. Destination NAT (DNAT) uses the PREROUTING chain to manipulate the destination IP address. Source NAT (SNAT) uses the POSTROUTING chain to manipulate the source IP address. With SNAT, packets are adjusted right before they are about to be routed. You need to create a firewall rule that makes use of this to allow all your clients on the internal network to be able to communicate with the outside world.

Step 1.   Use the following rule to implement NAT for the internal network:

```
# iptables -t nat -I POSTROUTING -o eth0 -s 172.168.1.0/24 -j
MASQUERADE
```

The interface `eth0` contains the outside network IP address (192.168.1.5 for me). The internal network is 172.168.1.0/24 (which is configured on `eth1`). This rule allows clients on the internal network to point to this system (RHEL01) as the default gateway and have their requests for outside traffic, such as a web page or package download, forwarded to the correct external network. You also need to make an adjustment to the kernel for this NAT rule to function properly.

Step 2.   Make the following change to the kernel:

```
# echo 1 > /proc/sys/net/ipv4/ip_forward
```

The preceding change is valid only until the system is rebooted, however. If you want the kernel parameter change to become permanent, you need to modify the kernel parameter on boot. Make sure that you save and restart the firewall service for the changes to take effect.

> **TIP:**   For the IP forward change to be persistent across reboots, add the following line to /etc/sysctl.conf:
>
> ```
> net.ipv4.ip_forward = 0
> ```
>
> Whenever the system boots, the parameter is automatically changed in the kernel for you.

Although you won't see too much NAT configuration unless you are on a small home or office network, you should still know how it works and be able to troubleshoot it should there be a problem.

Pluggable Authentication Module

Pluggable Authentication Module (PAM) includes a set of dynamically loadable library modules that can be used to enforce security on the system. It does this by using a set of configuration files that check for different criteria (depending on the application or service being called). These config files are located in /lib/security for 32-bit systems and /lib64/security for 64-bit systems. Here are some of the available library modules:

```
# ls /lib/security
pam_access.so          pam_oddjob_mkhomedir.so
pam_ccreds.so          pam_passwdqc.so
pam_chroot.so          pam_permit.so
pam_console.so         pam_pkcs11.so
pam_cracklib.so        pam_postgresok.so
pam_debug.so           pam_pwhistory.so
pam_deny.so            pam_rhosts_auth.so
pam_echo.so            pam_rhosts.so
```

Although this is not the full list, you can tell what some of these modules do by just looking at their names. If a service can make use of PAM, you can find a config file available in the /etc/pam.d directory. Again, there are many files located here that you can work with. To work with and make use of PAM, you need to understand how the config files work.

Securing Access

Each config file contains four columns using the following syntax:

```
module_type            control_flag      module_name      [arguments]
```

Further breaking down different options, there are four different module types used as a security mechanism:

`auth`	Establishes identity
`account`	Allows or denies access
`password`	Manages password policies
`session`	Applies settings to an application

There are also five different control flags that determine the action to take based on success or failure:

`required`	Proceeds if passed; continues even on fail
`requisite`	Stops on failure
`sufficient`	Requires no other verification if true
`optional`	Ignores success or failure
`include`	Includes all module-type directives from another file

The third column is the name of a file that should be called (usually the dynamic library file), including any optional arguments as well. Let's look at one of the config files as an example:

```
# cat /etc/pam.d/reboot
#%PAM-1.0
auth        sufficient    pam_rootok.so
auth        required      pam_console.so
#auth        include      system-auth
account     required      pam_permit.so
```

This PAM config file handles who can reboot the system. The first line uses the pam_rootok.so module, which returns true if the user who calls the command is the root user. If you are the root user because of the "sufficient" control flag, no other requirements are necessary and the system reboots. If you are not the root user, the next line is called; it checks to see that you are logged in to the console. The logic here is that you wouldn't want to reboot the system and have it come up in an unstable state without having physical console access. If this is the case, the final line is called (pam_permit.so), which always returns true so the system will reboot.

PAM modules and their config files aren't hard to use, but knowing how to read them and what they mean can take some practice. Make sure you understand the module types and control flags.

Here's another example of a commonly called module:

```
# cat /etc/pam.d/system-auth
#%PAM-1.0
# This file is auto-generated.
# User changes will be destroyed the next time authconfig is run.
auth            required        pam_env.so
auth            sufficient      pam_unix.so nullok try_first_pass
auth            requisite       pam_succeed_if.so uid >= 500 quiet
auth            required        pam_deny.so

account         required        pam_unix.so
account         sufficient      pam_succeed_if.so uid < 500 quiet
account         required        pam_permit.so

password        requisite       pam_cracklib.so try_first_pass retry=3
password        sufficient      pam_unix.so md5 shadow nullok try_first_pass
use_authtok
password        required        pam_deny.so

session         optional        pam_keyinit.so revoke
session         required        pam_limits.so
session         [success=1 default=ignore] pam_succeed_if.so service in crond
quiet use_uid
session         required        pam_unix.so
```

Without going through the whole file, I want to point out the third line. Here, you see the use of arguments as well as a module name. This line requires the user to have a UID with a value that is greater than or equal to 500 (a nonsystem user). You can make changes to the config files with /etc/pam.d, but make sure you know that some of these are regenerated by other system commands like this one (noted in the third comment line).

PAM Troubleshooting

No one is expected to remember what all the modules for PAM do or what their options are. Knowing where to look when you need to troubleshoot PAM will help you quickly resolve or customize anything you need when working with PAM. First, you should know that the /usr/share/doc/pam-<version>/txts directory contains text readme files that provide details and arguments for each of the PAM modules you can use. This information helps you when trying to figure out exactly what a particular module does. Second, you should know that PAM logs to a separate log file, making it easier to find issues. The /var/log/secure log file provides information relating to PAM events. If you're troubleshooting or trying to customize something, you can use this log file as a reference to make sure that everything is working properly. One last issue to check with PAM is to see whether there is limited access to a system. Check to see whether the /etc/nologin file exists. If it does, no regular users are allowed to log in to the system console; instead, the /etc/nologin file text is displayed to the user. This is common for system hardening at the console but might be something you need to know how to detect and troubleshoot as well.

Managing Password Policies

Ensuring that a good password policy is in place helps ease administration of your system. It also prevents break-ins and brute-force attacks on account passwords. There are a few different ways you can manage the password policies on your system.

Step 1.   Look at the /etc/login.defs file, which controls password length, age, and expiration:

```
# cat /etc/login.defs
...
# Password aging controls:
#
#       PASS_MAX_DAYS   Maximum number of days a password may be
used.
#       PASS_MIN_DAYS   Minimum number of days allowed between
password changes.
#       PASS_MIN_LEN    Minimum acceptable password length.
#       PASS_WARN_AGE   Number of days warning given before a
password expires.
#
PASS_MAX_DAYS   99999
PASS_MIN_DAYS   0
PASS_MIN_LEN    5
PASS_WARN_AGE   7
```

Next, turn your attention back to PAM for a moment. Both the pam_cracklib and pam_passwdqc modules are used in enforcing password length and complexity. Already defined by default as part of the password requirements, the pam_cracklib module can be changed to incorporate stricter requirements.

Step 2.   View the current pam_cracklib policy:

```
password      requisite     pam_cracklib.so try_first_pass retry=3
type=
```

You can add some additional parameters to increase (or decrease) the complexity and length of the password. You can't, however, take all the options available at face value. You can gain "credit points" by using complexity within your password. For example, if the minlen option is set to 6, you can have a four-character password with one uppercase character and one number, giving you two additional strength "credits." By default, you get only one credit for each category, but you can also adjust that. Here are the available configurable options:

minlen   Controls the minimum password length (default is 6)

retry   Specifies the number of times to retry before an error is issued

difok   Specifies the number of characters that need to be different between password changes (default is 5)

dcredit   Credit for digits in password (default is 1)

ucredit   Credit for uppercase letters in password (default is 1)

lcredit   Credit for lowercase letters in password (default is 1)

ocredit   Credit for special characters in password (default is 1)

You can edit each option to give credit (or not) when creating a user password. You need to consult your company's password policy to determine which options should be set. You can practice editing each option to see how they will affect the complexity of your system passwords.

Summary

Dealing with security either for the Red Hat exam or in the real world is no small task. In the first section, we described TCP Wrappers, which helps with securing services that support it. Next, we looked at firewall rules with `iptables` and NAT, which help to enforce security on the system. Finally, we discussed PAM, which provides modules for security of different services and actions on the system. Each part of this chapter plays a different role in providing security to different parts of the system. It takes practice and experience to learn the proper way to configure, monitor, and troubleshoot security effectively for a Red Hat system. Security is also important throughout the rest of the book because you need to use what you learned here to work with the other services.

Review Questions

1. All services in Red Hat can use TCP Wrappers. True or False?

2. The firewall service is disabled by default. True or False?

3. When Red Hat Enterprise Linux 6 is installed, SELinux is set to enforcing by default. True or False?

4. What does the following firewall rule accomplish: `iptables -I INPUT 5 -p tcp -m tcp --dport 80 -j ACCEPT`?

5. What is the last rule in the `iptables` file?

6. What is PAM used for?

7. What is NAT? How is it used?

8. The following firewall rule works under Red Hat Enterprise Linux 6: `iptables –I RH-Firewall-1-INPUT –p tcp –m tcp --dport 22 –j ACCEPT`. True or False?

Answers to the Review Questions

1. False. A service needs to have support for TCP Wrappers to be able to use it.

2. False. The firewall service is enabled by default.

3. True. For Red Hat Enterprise Linux 6, SELinux comes set up in enforcing mode. When installing Red Hat Enterprise Linux 5, you have the option to choose which mode you'd like it to operate in.

4. The firewall rule is inserted into the fifth line of the `iptables` rules and opens up TCP port 80 (for the HTTP service) on the firewall to allow incoming connections.

5. The last rule is always an implicit deny statement rejecting anything that wasn't matched by previous rules.

6. PAM is used as a modular way to leverage security. In this chapter, the main function we discussed was for managing password policies and complexity.

7. Network address translation (NAT) maintains a table that allows the use of multiple internal IP addresses to a multiple public IP address (called address translation). It can also be used for one-to-one or one-to-many relationships as well.

8. False. The `INPUT` chain being used is the default under Red Hat Enterprise Linux 5. This rule generates errors under Red Hat Enterprise Linux 6.

Lab 12

Task 1 – TCP Wrappers

Step 1.   Set up TCP Wrappers using the following guidelines:

    a. RHEL01 should allow SSH access from the 192.168.1.0 /24 and 172.168.1.0 /24 networks.

    b. Client02 should allow SSH access from the 172.168.1.0 /24 network only.

    c. All other access from any network on the two systems listed here should be denied.

The task is complete when TCP Wrappers is set up properly.

Task 2 – Firewall Rules

Step 1.   Create the following firewall rules:

    a. Allow access to TCP port 3306 on RHEL02.

    b. Allow access to TCP port 22 on all servers in the lab.

    c. Deny access to port 80 and port 3306 on Client02.

    d. Deny access to port 80 from Client02 on Client01.

The task is complete when all firewall rules are in place successfully.

This chapter covers the following subjects:

- **SSH**—This section covers remote management of systems using the SSH protocol.

- **SSH Security Revisited**—This section looks at the SSH protocol again and some more advanced ways to secure it.

- **VNC Servers**—This section looks at remote management using GUI connections.

The following RHCSA exam objectives are covered:

- Access remote systems using SSH and VNC

- Deploy a VNC server that allows multiple desktops to be shared

The following RHCE exam objectives are covered:

- Install the packages needed to provide the service

- Configure SELinux to support the service

- Configure the service to start when the system is booted

- Configure the service for basic operation

- Configure host-based and user-based security for the service

- Configure key-based authentication

- Configure additional options described in the documentation

## CHAPTER 13

Remote Access

You walk into the server room and install Red Hat on your new server. After the installation is complete, you need to configure numerous packages and then begin setting up users. All these tasks take time, and if you work in a data center, chances are your office is located somewhere else. Remote access to any system that you work on makes managing and troubleshooting much easier because you don't physically need to be in the same location as your systems. In this chapter, we discuss using SSH for command-line remote access and VNC for graphical remote access.

Secure SHell (SSH)

You know that at some point or another you will need to be able to administer servers remotely, and you wouldn't want to do this without some sort of security in place, right? SSH can protect the traffic that passes from your computer to a remote computer, making the tunnel secure for administration. The tunnel that SSH uses for communication is encrypted, unlike protocols such as Telnet that don't employ any encryption. SSH is a fairly easy service to set up and is useful in many different ways. Although it is usually installed by default, you also should verify.

Step 1. Verify that the SSH server package is installed:

```
# rpm -qa | grep ssh
libssh2-1.2.2-7.el6.x86_64
openssh-5.3p1-20.el6.x86_64
openssh-server-5.3p1-20.el6.x86_64
openssh-clients-5.3p1-20.el6.x86_64
```

Step 2. If the SSH server package isn't installed, do the following:

```
# yum install -y openssh-server
```

Step 3. Make sure to verify again:

```
# rpm -qa | grep ssh
openssh-server-5.3p1-20.el6.x86_64
```

Step 4.   Ensure that the service is currently running (or start it if it isn't):

```
# service sshd status
sshd (pid  678) is running...
```

Now that the service is running, you should also make sure that the service is set to start when the system boots.

Step 1.   Enable the service Ïduring boot:

```
# chkconfig sshd on
```

Step 2.   Verify that the service is enabled during boot:

```
# chkconfig --list sshd
sshd              0:off   1:off   2:on   3:on   4:on   5:on
6:off
```

Now let's move on to configuring the SSH service for use.

Configuring SSH

After the SSH package is installed, you can start the configuration by looking at the main config file. The config file, which is located at /etc/ssh/ssh_config, comes with a set of "safe" default settings. Before making any changes, however, you should make a backup copy of the original file in case something happens that you need to revert to a clean config file later and you want to restore the original.

Make a backup of the main config file:

```
# cp /etc/ssh/sshd_config /etc/ssh/sshd_config.orig
```

By default, Red Hat has the SSH service installed, running, and a firewall rule allowing incoming connections for the service. Because the config file also has a decent set of default options, you could log in at this point and begin doing work on your server. As discussed in the preceding chapter, you should never run a service with a default config file because such files tend to lack security for the service as a whole. Let's look through the config file at some options:

```
# cat /etc/ssh/sshd_config
...
Port 22
Protocol 2

ListenAddress 0.0.0.0

SyslogFacility AUTHPRIV

PermitRootLogin yes

PasswordAuthentication yes
```

```
ChallengeResponseAuthentication no
UsePAM yes

X11Forwarding yes

Subsystem        sftp      /usr/libexec/openssh/sftp-server
```

Let's discuss some of the options laid out here:

`Port`	Defines the port used for SSH
`Protocol`	Specifies the protocol being used (1 or 2)
`ListenAddress`	Defines the IP address to listen on
`PermitRootLogin`	Determines whether the root user can log in
`X11Forwarding`	Allows the forwarding of GUI programs

All these options should be self-explanatory, but there are two options that I recommend changing before you use the SSH service:

```
PermitRootLogin = No
X11Forwarding = No
```

Changing these two options provides a little extra security on your system. As you learned in Chapter 7, "User Administration," you should never use the root account locally, so allowing that account to log in remotely is just not a good idea. After you finish making any changes to the SSH service, you need to restart the service for the changes to take effect.

Restart the SSH service:

```
# service sshd restart
Stopping sshd:                                          [  OK  ]
Starting sshd:                                          [  OK  ]
```

Now that the SSH server is set up, you should test it from one of the client systems.

Step 1.   Log in to Client02 and verify that the SSH packages are installed:

```
# rpm -qa | grep ssh
libssh2-1.2.2-7.el6.x86_64
openssh-5.3p1-20.el6.x86_64
openssh-server-5.3p1-20.el6.x86_64
openssh-clients-5.3p1-20.el6.x86_64
```

Here, you are specifically looking for the client package to be installed so that you can connect to the SSH server. Using the `ssh` command, you can remotely connect to the RHEL01 system.

Syntax: `ssh [options]`

Options:

`-f`	Moves the command to the background
`-g`	Enables remote hosts to connect to local forwarded ports
`-i <id file>`	Uses the specified key file
`-L`	Enables port forwarding
`-p <port>`	Uses the specified port for the SSH connection
`-R`	Enables port forwarding
`-v`	Provides verbose output

The first time you connect to a host, you are required to accept that you trust the host. After you accept the connection, the host is stored permanently in the ~/.ssh/known_hosts file. Because you are in a lab environment, there should be no question as to the authenticity of the hosts you are connecting to, but in the real world, make sure that you trust the host you are connecting to.

Step 2.   Connect to RHEL01 using the ssh command:

```
# ssh user01@172.168.1.1
The authenticity of host '172.168.1.1 (172.168.1.1)' can't be
established.
RSA key fingerprint is
5a:29:fd:c7:e1:5a:3d:4f:b1:99:05:f1:5f:ac:46:cb.
Are you sure you want to continue connecting (yes/no)? yes
Warning: Permanently added '172.168.1.1' (RSA) to the list of known
hosts.
user01@172.168.1.1's password:
Last login: Thu Jun  3 06:22:12 2010 from 172.168.1.20
[user01@RHEL01 ~]$
```

Based on the login prompt, you can tell that you are signed in to a different host and what user you are signed in as. In this case, you can see that you are signed in to RHEL01 as user01. When you're finished working on the remote host, you can return to your local system or just close the connection by using the exit command.

Because SSH is such a common tool for a system administrator to use, I recommend two different products. If you use Windows clients (laptop/desktop) and want to connect via SSH to a Linux server, you can download and use PuTTY (free) or SecureCRT (not free, but better). If you are on Linux already, you can just use the shell built into the system although there are many free utilities to help manage your SSH connections more easily.

Firewall and SELinux Configuration

When it comes to remote management in Linux, SSH is the standard. Because SSH is installed by default in Red Hat and there is a firewall rule already in place for you to begin remote management, you do not need to create any additional rules. As is good practice, though, you should verify that the rule is, in fact, in place.

Because SSH uses TCP port 22 for remote access, you should query any rule from the /etc/sysconfig/iptables file:

```
# cat /etc/sysconfig/iptables | grep 22
-A INPUT -m state --state NEW -m tcp -p tcp --dport 22 -j ACCEPT
```

With the firewall rule already in place, you also need to look at SELinux restrictions on the SSH service.

Step 1.   Query the Boolean values associated with SSH:

```
# getsebool -a | grep ssh
allow_ssh_keysign --> off
sftpd_write_ssh_home --> off
ssh_sysadm_login --> off
```

EXAM TIP

The `sftpd_write_ssh_home` Boolean is new to RHEL6, and the `run_ssh_inetd` has been removed.

You need to change only one of the options here. Later in this chapter, we discuss host-based security through the use of public and private keys, which requires the first Boolean to be turned on.

Step 2.   Enable the required Boolean value:

```
# setsebool -P allow_ssh_keysign=1
```

Step 3.   Verify that the value has changed:

```
# getsebool -a | grep ssh
allow_ssh_keysign --> on
sftpd_write_ssh_home --> off
ssh_sysadm_login --> off
```

At this point, the firewall and SELinux requirements are taken care of for SSH. SSH doesn't require too many changes to work out of the box, but as you work your way through the book, you will encounter services that require multiple changes to firewall rules and SELinux.

SSH Security

SSH has many different options when it comes to security. First, let's look at some host security. The SSH service can make use of the TCP Wrappers service for additional protection when you are setting it up. Suppose you want to allow connections only from the 172.168.1.0 /24 network to the RHEL01 host.

Step 1.   Use TCP Wrappers to limit the hosts that can connect to the server:

```
# echo "sshd: 172.168.1." >> /etc/hosts.allow
# echo "ALL: ALL" >> /etc/hosts.deny
```

This allows all clients within the 172.168.1.0 /24 subnet to connect into the SSH server (provided they have a valid user account), and it disallows any other host outside this subnet. Although TCP Wrappers is a good starting point for host-based security, you should also change a few of the options in the config file to really improve the security of your SSH server. You should take into account the default port that the SSH service will use, the IP address that the server listens on, and the protocol version.

Step 2.   Change the options just discussed to improve security:

```
Protocol 2
Port 2222
ListenAddress 172.168.1.1
```

When you change these options, the default port isn't known to everyone, and only the internal network adapter listens for connections. Be careful not to lock yourself out from the external network, though.

Let's switch focus for a second and look at user-based security. Although this type of security is not in the config file by default, you can also limit the users or groups that you'd like to connect to your SSH server. The SSH service processes these options in the following order:

```
DenyUsers □  AllowUsers □  DenyGroups □  AllowGroups
```

Step 3.   Add the following to your config file to allow only specific users to connect:

```
AllowUsers user01,user02
```

Now only the two users who have been listed are allowed to connect to the SSH server. Although security for SSH is great, make sure that you have documented your security somewhere because hardened systems tend to lead to connection issues if not planned out properly. You need to be able to review what security mechanisms you have in place when troubleshooting.

Troubleshooting SSH

When it comes to troubleshooting SSH, the service tends to either work or not work. A key part of working with SSH is also being able to troubleshoot it. The first place to always look with SSH is in the log file located at /var/log/secure. This file should provide you with any information as to why you can't connect to a remote machine. If you run into errors about the remote host refusing the connection, the problem is most likely something blocking your connection. This could be due to the service not running, firewall rules being incorrect, or extra security measures such as TCP Wrappers. Another common error that occurs often when testing is the remote key of the server changing. If the key changes on the remote host, you get a big warning message:

```
@@@@@@@@@@@@@@@@@@@@@@@@@@@@@@@@@@@@@@@@@@@@@@@@@@@@@@@@@@@
@    WARNING: REMOTE HOST IDENTIFICATION HAS CHANGED!    @
@@@@@@@@@@@@@@@@@@@@@@@@@@@@@@@@@@@@@@@@@@@@@@@@@@@@@@@@@@@
IT IS POSSIBLE THAT SOMEONE IS DOING SOMETHING NASTY!
Someone could be eavesdropping on you right now (man-in-the-middle attack)!
It is also possible that the RSA host key has just been changed.
```

If this is the case, you can open the ~/.ssh/known_hosts file to edit or delete the line containing the key that has changed.

> **WARNING:**   The known_hosts file contains ONE key PER line!

The reason I'm warning you here is that not all displays are long enough to display the full length of the key, so they wrap it, giving the illusion of a multiline key. It would not be a good thing to try to delete the four- or five-line key from this file in the nano text editor because you would actually just end up erasing everything below it.

SSH Security Revisited

The previous section described ways to set up an SSH server, configuration, and some ways to make SSH more secure. Here, we look at two additional steps that can be added to the SSH server to increase security further. These two features are key authentication and port forwarding. With key authentication, users have a private key (on their local client machines) and a public key (on the server that they want to connect to). When a user tries to log in to the server, the two keys are used (with an optional passphrase) to allow the user to log in. This provides additional security because it requires you to not only know a user's password, but also have a copy of that user's private key. With port forwarding, you can set up a management gateway requiring you to connect to the gateway first before connecting to any additional servers within the network. This provides for centralized administration of logins and good auditing.

Public/Private Keys

To start the key authentication section, I'd like to point out a few files:

~/.ssh/id_rsa	Your private key
~/.ssh/id_rsa.pub	Your public key
~/.ssh/authorized_keys	Place on the server where the public key is located

When creating your keys, you can specify either DSA or RSA encryption. For this example, use RSA. The ssh-keygen command enables you to create a set of keys to use with the SSH service.

Step 1. Generate the keys on Client02 as user01:

```
# ssh-keygen -t rsa
Generating public/private rsa key pair.
Enter file in which to save the key (/home/user01/.ssh/id_rsa):
[Press Enter]
Created directory '/home/user01/.ssh'.
Enter passphrase (empty for no passphrase): [Enter a STRONG
password]
Enter same passphrase again:
Your identification has been saved in /home/user01/.ssh/id_rsa.
Your public key has been saved in /home/user01/.ssh/id_rsa.pub.
The key fingerprint is:
8f:a2:03:e9:5b:df:52:a4:8d:80:ad:3b:50:01:7e:23 user01@Client02
```

Here, you can see both the private and public keys being generated. You should now have an .ssh directory in user01's home directory. Now you need to copy the public key (id_rsa.pub) over to the server so you can use it to log in. There is actually a nice little command that can do this for you.

Step 2. Copy the public key over to RHEL01 as user01:

```
# ssh-copy-id -i ~/.ssh/id_rsa.pub RHEL01
29
The authenticity of host 'rhel01 (172.168.1.1)' can't be estab-
lished.
RSA key fingerprint is
5a:29:fd:c7:e1:5a:3d:4f:b1:99:05:f1:5f:ac:46:cb.
Are you sure you want to continue connecting (yes/no)? yes
Warning: Permanently added 'rhel01' (RSA) to the list of known
hosts.
```

Now try logging into the machine, with "ssh 'RHEL01'", and check in:

```
.ssh/authorized_keys
```

to make sure we haven't added extra keys that you weren't expecting.

When the public key is in place, you also need to adjust your main config file on the SSH server (RHEL01) to allow authentication via public/private keys.

Step 3.   In the sshd_config file, change the following two options:

```
PasswordAuthentication no
PubKeyAuthentication yes
```

This change prevents users from logging on with anything but their public/private key combination.

Step 4.   Restart the SSH service for the settings to take effect:

```
# service sshd restart
Stopping sshd:                                          [  OK  ]
Starting sshd:                                          [  OK  ]
```

Step 5.   Try to connect to RHEL01 as user01 from the Client02 host to ensure that the key authentication is working properly:

```
# ssh user01@172.168.1.1
user01@172.168.1.1's password:
Last login: Thu Jun  3 06:22:12 2010 from 172.168.1.20
[user01@RHEL01 ~]$
```

Port Forwarding

As already mentioned, port forwarding allows you to connect to a centralized gateway before forming additional connections within your network. This capability increases security by forcing all connections to flow through a centralized gateway where auditing usually takes place to keep track of who is logged in. This centralized management is accomplished through the use of port forwarding, where each connection is made to the gateway and then forwarded to another server.

Syntax: `ssh username@hostname -L local-port:remote-hostname:remote-port`

Let's look at an example. Suppose on RHEL01 you want to create a port forward to RHEL01 and allow SSH connections to come only from RHEL01. You can use the following command to set up the initial tunnel on RHEL01:

```
# ssh user01@172.168.1.2 -L 1234:172.168.1.2:22
```

After executing this command on RHEL01, you should now have a tunnel formed to RHEL02. Other users can now use SSH locally on RHEL01 to be forwarded to RHEL02.

Another example would be sending all traffic to a specific site:

```
# ssh -N -L 8080:localhost:80 <site>
```

The -N keeps the SSH connection from being interactive. Now if you were to set up your browser to use a proxy connecting to a localhost on port 8080, you would be able to securely visit the site specified in the command. Although port forwarding is useful for quick testing or connections, there are actually great programs out there that allow for easier management and tunnel creation than just using the command line.

VNC Servers

Having remote access into a server is great, but what happens if an end user calls in and says she's having problems with her system? Chances are she isn't using just a shell and her desktop has somehow become messed up. You don't have to use SSH to fix the problem remotely because there is always an alternative: VNC. The VNC server allows you to remote into the user's system and view her desktop. With the end user's desktop in view, you can more easily troubleshoot any issues she is having. Setting up a VNC server isn't hard, and in fact, it sometimes comes pre-installed as part of a desktop package.

Step 1.   Install the vnc-server package on RHEL02:

```
# yum install -y tigervnc-server
```

Step 2.   Query to make sure the package is installed correctly:

```
# rpm -qa | grep tiger
tigervnc-server-1.0.90-0.10.20100115svn3945.el6.x86_64
```

MIGRATION TIP

On RHEL6, the available VNC package is called tigervnc and tigervnc-server. On RHEL5 and earlier, a different package called vnc and vnc-server was available.

EXAM TIP

The vino package, which is similar to vnc-server, provides the same functions through the Gnome Desktop Manager.

With the packages installed, you need to adjust the two lines in the main config file telling the VNC server how to run.

Step 3.   View the default line items:

```
# cat /etc/sysconfig/vncservers
# VNCSERVERS="2:myusername"
# VNCSERVERARGS[2]="-geometry 800x600 -nolisten tcp -nohttpd -
localhost"
```

The first line defines the user who is allowed to log in to the system. The second line lists the arguments passed to the VNC server when the service starts.

-geometry	Defines the size of the viewer when the client connects
-nolisten tcp	Denies TCP connections to the VNC server
-nohttpd	Denies web VNC clients from connecting
-localhost	Forces the use of a secure gateway (port forwarding)

The number that appears (2 in this case) is the number of the session for the defined user. The VNC server runs on port 5900, but the actual port that will be used is 5900 + the number defined = 5902 in this case.

Step 4.   Change your config file to the following:

```
# nano /etc/syconfig/vncservers
VNCSERVERS="2:helpdesk"
VNCSERVERARGS[2]="-geometry 1024x768 -nolisten tcp -nohttpd"
```

Step 5.   Save the file and exit.

Because you are on a local network, you don't need to worry about secure connections. You will be using the helpdesk user to connect as well.

Step 6.   Set the password for the helpdesk user to be able to connect with him:

```
# vncpasswd
Password:
Verify:
```

Step 7.   Start the VNC server to be able to connect to it:

```
# vncserver :1
xauth: creating new authority file /root/.Xauthority

New RHEL02:1 (root)' desktop is RHEL02:1

Creating default startup script /root/.vnc/xstartup
Starting applications specified in /root/.vnc/xstartup
Log file is /root/.vnc/RHEL02:1.log
```

This creates the files required for the VNC server because it has now been started for the first time.

MIGRATION TIP

On RHEL5, the VNC has a configuration issue: It will not start the desktop manager without an edit to the ~/.vnc/xstartup file. To prevent the issue of not seeing the desktop manager correctly, you need to edit this file.

Step 1. Edit the ~/.vnc/xstartup file to uncomment the first two lines:

```
# nano ~/.vnc/xstartup
# Uncomment the following two lines for normal desktop:
unset SESSION_MANAGER
exec /etc/X11/xinit/xinitrc
```

At this point, you need to restart the VNC server session for the changes to take effect.

Step 2. Kill the current VNC session:

```
# vncserver -kill :1
Killing Xvnc process ID 12865
```

Step 3. Start a new session:

```
# vncserver :1
xauth: creating new authority file /root/.Xauthority

New RHEL02:1 (root)' desktop is RHEL02:1

Creating default startup script /root/.vnc/xstartup
Starting applications specified in /root/.vnc/xstartup
Log file is /root/.vnc/RHEL02:1.log
```

At this point, your VNC server should be running properly, but you also need to make sure that you create a firewall rule for the port that the VNC server is using. I don't show how to create one here because you will use a different port when setting up your VNC server.

Connecting Clients

So far, you have set up a VNC server on RHEL02 and also created a firewall rule allowing you to gain access to the system. All that is left to do at this point is connect from a client system. You can install the client package on Client02 and give the connection a try.

Step 1. Install the VNC package that contains the client software to connect:
```
# yum install -y tigervnc
```

Step 2. Verify that the package was installed successfully:
```
# rpm -qa | grep tiger
tigervnc-1.0.90-0.10.20100115svn3945.el6.x86_64
```

Step 3. At this point you can use the `vncviewer` command to connect to the VNC server:

```
# vncviewer 172.168.1.2:5902
```

The system now prompts you for the password that you set up for the helpdesk user on Client01. After you enter the password, a display of the remote desktop appears as if you were sitting at the system.

VNC can be useful when you're trying to help end users troubleshoot or show them how to do something. Many times in the real world, however, the desktop managers are not used (only the shell is), so there isn't really a need for VNC on servers.

Summary

In this chapter, we looked at two different types of remote access. We discussed SSH and how it creates secure tunnels to provide system administrators with secure remote access to their systems. We also looked at VNC and how it can be used to remotely connect to desktops. Remote access is critical in the real world because no one manages systems from the console (unless there is an issue with the system). Knowing how to set up remote access and configure it to be secure is a vital real-world skill. For the Red Hat exams, make sure that you are comfortable working on systems remotely.

Review Questions

1. What is SSH used for?

2. Should you allow remote root access? Why or why not?

3. What happens if a host changes its IP address and the keys don't match?

4. Which version of SSH should you use?

5. SSH can run only on TCP port 22. True or False?

6. TCP Wrappers can be used with SSH. True or False?

7. What is the benefit of using public/private key authentication?

8. What is VNC?

9. What is the name of the package that allows you to install VNC?

Answers to the Review Questions

1. SSH is used for secure remote management of Linux systems.

2. You should never allow remote root access. Should your root account become compromised and you use the same password, someone could gain access to all your systems. You also don't want the most powerful user of your system (with no accountability) logging in and making changes.

3. A large warning message appears indicating that the key doesn't match the host you are connecting to. You have to remove the key/host pair from the known_hosts file to proceed.

4. Version 2 is the latest and most secure version of SSH.

5. False. Through its main config file, SSH can be configured to run on any port you'd like (provided that port is available).

6. True. SSH does support TCP Wrappers.

7. Public/private key authentication provides an additional layer of security because you need the correct key instead of just knowing someone's password. Passwords combined with public/private keys take the security one additional step.

8. VNC is used to control a remote desktop session.

9. The VNC package for Red Hat Enterprise Linux 6 is `tiger-vnc`.

Lab 13

Task 1 – SSH Servers

Step 1. Set up an SSH server on all systems with the lab using the following settings:
   a. Each server must have a user account called tech_support with the password tech1234.
   b. Each SSH server must use password-based authentication.
   c. Each SSH server must use the version 2 protocol.
   d. The root user should not be allowed to log in via SSH on any server.

The task is complete when a user can log in to each server via SSH.

Task 2 – SSH Revisited

Step 1.   Change the SSH servers on RHEL01 and RHEL02 to meet the new guidelines:

   a. Each SSH server must use public key authentication instead of passwords.

   b. Each tech_support user must be able to log in with a password.

   c. The root user should be allowed to log in via SSH on RHEL02 only.

The task is complete when a user can log in to each server via SSH.

Task 3 – VNC

Step 1.   Set up a VNC server on Client01.

Step 2.   Set up a VNC server on Client02.

Step 3.   Ensure that you can connect to each VNC server from each Client*XX* system.

The task is complete when all VNC servers are accessible.

This chapter covers the following subjects:

- **Apache Web Server**—This section covers the basics of Apache.
- **Apache Security**—This section covers security and how to protect your web server.
- **CGI Applications**—This section covers how to set up and run a CGI application on Apache.
- **Virtual Hosts**—This section looks at how to host multiple websites.
- **Squid Web Proxy**—This section covers how to set up and configure a proxy server.

The following RHCSA exam objective is covered:

- Configure a system to run a default configuration HTTP server

The following RHCE exam objectives are covered:

- Install the packages needed to provide the service
- Configure SELinux to support the service
- Configure the service to start when the system is booted
- Configure the service for basic operation
- Configure host-based and user-based security for the service
- Configure a virtual host
- Configure private directories
- Deploy a basic CGI application
- Configure group-managed content

## CHAPTER 14

Web Services

The most commonly used web server in the world today is Apache—and with good reason. Built with security in mind, Apache is a solid and stable web server that has been around for years. The module design allows for scalability and ease of use. Apache can also be used to host multiple websites at a single time through the use of its virtual hosts feature. There is also an option to use the SSL protocol, making websites safe and secure. This secure base provides a platform for developers to use when writing secure code for banks, retail sites, and so on. Because Apache has all these great options, it means there is a lot to cover, which is why this whole chapter focuses on the Apache web server and Squid, a web proxy.

The Apache Web Server

Today, with Web 2.0 on the rise and Software as a Service (SaaS) becoming more prevalent, Apache has begun to play a larger role. It is important to know how to install and secure Apache correctly. To start, let's look at some of the new features in Red Hat 6:

- Apache has been upgraded to version 2.2 (from 2.0).

- It has improved caching modules: `mod_cache` and `mod_disk_cache`.

- It provides support for proxy load balancing through `mod_proxy_balancer`.

- It provides support for large files, allowing web servers to handle files larger than 2GB.

- It has improved authentication and authorization support.

These features help increase the scalability and security that Apache is known for.

Installing Apache

When you're working with Apache, you need two packages. The first is `httpd`, which actually installs the Apache web server. The second is the `mod_ssl` package, which provides the ability to create secure websites later in this chapter.

Step 1.   Install the two required packages:

```
# yum install -y httpd mod_ssl
```

Step 2.   Verify that the packages were installed correctly:

```
# rpm -qa | grep http
httpd-2.2.15-5.el6.x86_64
httpd-tools-2.2.15-5.el6.x86_64

# rpm -qa | grep ssl
mod_ssl-2.2.15-5.el6.x86_64
openssl-1.0.0-4.el6.x86_64
```

Step 3.   With the packages installed, make sure that the service is set to start when the system boots:

```
# chkconfig httpd on
```

Step 4.   Verify your changes:

```
# chkconfig httpd --list
httpd           0:off   1:off   2:on    3:on    4:on    5:on
6:off
```

Configuring the Web Server

Now that the web server is installed, we can shift our attention to the config files and directories. During the installation, a directory (/var/www) is created with a set of subdirectories. This directory tree is the place where you store your websites. There are also a few config files to look at:

/etc/httpd/conf/httpd.conf	Main config file
/var/log/httpd	Log file directory for the web server
/usr/lib64/httpd/modules	Modules for Apache

The main config file for Apache is completely usable right out of the box, which is great if you'd like to just get up and running. You should spend some time looking through the main config file because it provides many options and good documentation in the comments. The top of the config file is grouped into three sections.

From the /etc/httpd/conf/httpd.conf file:

```
# The configuration directives are grouped into three basic sections:
#  1. Directives that control the operation of the Apache server process as a
#     whole (the 'global environment').
#  2. Directives that define the parameters of the 'main' or 'default' server,
#     which responds to requests that aren't handled by a virtual host.
#     These directives also provide default values for the settings
#     of all virtual hosts.
```

```
#   3. Settings for virtual hosts, which allow Web requests to be sent to
#      different IP addresses or hostnames and have them handled by the
#      same Apache server process.
```

In this section, we discuss specifically the global environment and main server options. Here are some common options for the global section:

ServerRoot	Defines where the config files are held
Timeout	Specifies the time before a request times out (120 seconds is the default)
Listen	Indicates the port number to listen on (default is 80)
User	Identifies the user to run the web server as
Group	Identifies the group to run the web server as
LoadModule	Defines a module to load when the web server starts

These options apply to the server as a whole, usually changing from server to server instead of section to section. Let's also look at a few basic options for the main server section:

DocumentRoot	Defines where the website files are located
ServerName	Defines a server name or IP address and port number

These main server options are the default for the server. As you see later in this chapter, when you host multiple sites on a single server, any option that isn't defined uses the global section options as the default. If you have worked with Apache before or know something about Apache, you already should have an understanding of how large of a topic Apache can be. There are numerous texts dedicated to just configuring and maintaining Apache web servers because of the complexity behind it. For the Red Hat exams and basic real-world setups, you need to know only the basics of Apache.

Let's start by defining the location of a website on the file system. By default, it is located in the /var/www/html directory, although this can be changed if you'd like. In the main config file, you see a section denoted by the Directory option.

Section of /etc/httpd/conf/httpd.conf:

```
<Directory "/var/www/html">
    Options Indexes FollowSymLinks
    AllowOverride None
    Order allow,deny
    Allow from all
</Directory>
```

The options defined within this section apply specifically to the website and directory structure, as defined by the `Directory` option. For the preceding example, this means the site located in the /var/www/html directory. If you want to change the directory where your site is located, you need to change the `DocumentRoot` option as well as the `Directory` option. The default option is

```
DocumentRoot "/var/www/html"
```

There is also a way to have multiple sites using *virtual hosts*, as you see later. When your config file is completely set up the way you want it, you can use the `httpd` service options to test your config file. Using the `configtest` argument, the service parses the main config file for any errors and reports back if something is found. It is always a good idea to check your config file before trying to use it because it will prevent the server from starting if it contains any errors.

Test the config file:

```
# service httpd configtest
Syntax OK
```

There is also another cool option that the `httpd` service has (many services have it, but it is more useful here). Normally, for a service to use a new config file, it requires that the service is restarted. This restart process actually stops the service from running before starting it over again. Normally, this isn't a big deal, but when hundreds of people are hitting your site, can you afford to have even a two-second outage? To circumvent this issue, you can use the `reload` argument, which allows the main config file to be reread without the actual service being brought down. This is why it is important to test your config files first.

To restart the httpd service, use the following command:

```
# service httpd restart
Stopping httpd:                                     [  OK  ]
Starting httpd:                                     [  OK  ]
```

To only reload the service and reread the config file, use this command instead:

```
# service httpd reload
Reloading httpd:                                    [  OK  ]
```

One other option to keep in mind is the `graceful` parameter. It restarts the web server, allowing it to read the new config file changes without disconnecting any currently connected clients. The only downfall here is that the currently active connections use the old config file until they terminate their connection and reconnect. You can use it as follows:

```
# service httpd graceful
```

Firewall and SELinux Configuration

For your web server to become fully functional, you need to make some security changes. First and foremost, the firewall needs to be opened on port 80.

Step 1.   Use `iptables` to create the additional firewall rules:

```
# iptables -I INPUT 5 -p tcp -m tcp --dport 80 -j ACCEPT
```

Step 2.   Save the firewall rules you have just created:

```
# service iptables save
Saving firewall rules to /etc/sysconfig/iptables:        [  OK  ]
```

Step 3.   Then restart the `iptables` service:

```
# service iptables restart
iptables: Flushing firewall rules:                       [  OK  ]
iptables: Setting chains to policy ACCEPT: filter        [  OK  ]
iptables: Unloading modules:                             [  OK  ]
iptables: Applying firewall rules:                       [  OK  ]
```

Additionally, you need to look at SELinux protection for the web server. Table 14-1 presents the available options.

Table 14-1   SELinux Options

Option	Description
httpd_can_network_relay	Allow httpd to act as a relay.
httpd_can_network_connect_db	Allow httpd scripts and modules to connect to databases over the network.
httpd_use_gpg	Allow httpd to run gpg in the gpg-web domain.
httpd_enable_cgi	Allow httpd CGI support.
httpd_use_cifs	Allow httpd to access CIFS file systems.
allow_httpd_mod_auth_pam	Allow Apache to use mod_auth_pam.
allow_httpd_anon_write	Allow Apache to modify public files used for public file transfer services. Directories/Files must be labeled public_rw_content_t.
httpd_enable_homedirs	Allow httpd to read home directories.
allow_httpd_sys_script_anon_write	Allow Apache scripts to write to public content. Directories/Files must be labeled public_rw_content_t.
httpd_dbus_avahi	Allow Apache to communicate with the avahi service via dbus.
httpd_unified	Unify httpd handling of all content files.

Table 14-1   SELinux Options

Option	Description
httpd_can_network_connect	Allow httpd scripts and modules to connect to the network using TCP.
allow_httpd_mod_auth_ntlm_winbind	Allow Apache to use mod_auth_pam.
httpd_tty_comm	Unify httpd to communicate with the terminal. Needed for entering the passphrase for certificates at the terminal.
httpd_read_user_content	Allow httpd to read user content.
httpd_use_nfs	Allow httpd to access NFS file systems.
httpd_tmp_exec	Allow Apache to execute tmp content.
httpd_execmem	Allow httpd scripts and modules execmem/execstack.
httpd_can_sendmail	Allow http daemon to send mail.
httpd_builtin_scripting	Allow httpd to use built in scripting (usually PHP).
httpd_can_check_spam	Allow the http daemon to check spam.
httpd_can_network_connect_cobbler	Allow httpd scripts and modules to connect to cobbler over the network.
httpd_ssi_exec	Allow httpd to run SSI executables in the same domain as system CGI scripts.
httpd_enable_ftp_server	Allow httpd to act as an FTP server by listening on the FTP port.
httpd_setrlimit	Allow the httpd daemon to change system limits.

To provide basic web services to your network, you don't need to make any changes. Almost any extension or nonbasic functionality requires modification of SELinux protection.

MIGRATION TIP

In RHEL6, the available Boolean options for web services have changed completely. Make sure that you are familiar with the new options available.

MIGRATION TIP

For RHEL5, you need to disable the SELinux service protection to be able to utilize basic web services.

Step 1. Query for the Boolean value you need to change:

```
# getsebool -a | grep httpd_dis
httpd_disable_trans --> off
```

Step 2. Disable the SELinux protection:

```
# setsebool -P httpd_disable_trans=1
```

Step 3. Verify that the Boolean has changed:

```
# getsebool -a | grep httpd_dis
httpd_disable_trans --> on
```

When you're working with web services, there is an additional requirement when it comes to SELinux. Apache makes use of file contexts because of the different web content available on disk. The context of any newly created directory needs to be set for the web server user to be able to access it properly. For example, suppose you create the following two directories to hold two customer websites.

Step 1. Create the customer web directories:

```
# mkdir /var/www/site1
# mkdir /var/www/site2
```

Step 2. Check the current context of the files:

```
# ls -Z /var/www
drwxr-xr-x. root root system_u:object_r:httpd_sys_script_exec_t:s0
cgi-bin
drwxr-xr-x. root root system_u:object_r:httpd_sys_content_t:s0 error
drwxr-xr-x. root root system_u:object_r:httpd_sys_content_t:s0 html
drwxr-xr-x. root root system_u:object_r:httpd_sys_content_t:s0 icons
drwxr-xr-x. root root unconfined_u:object_r:httpd_sys_content_t:s0
site1
drwxr-xr-x. root root unconfined_u:object_r:httpd_sys_content_t:s0
site2
```

You can change the context of the customer sites to match the default site (the html directory).

Step 3. Use the chcon command to change the context of the user and domain:

```
# chcon -Rvu system_u site1
changing security context of 'site1'

# chcon -Rvu system_u site1
changing security context of 'site1'
```

Step 4.   You also could reference the default directory for a single command:

```
# chcon --reference=html site2
```

This changes the site2 directory to match the html directory's SELinux context.

Step 5.   You can now check again and verify that all the context fields for the two customer site directories have been changed correctly:

```
# ll -Z
drwxr-xr-x. root root system_u:object_r:httpd_sys_script_exec_t:s0
cgi-bin
drwxr-xr-x. root root system_u:object_r:httpd_sys_content_t:s0 error
drwxr-xr-x. root root system_u:object_r:httpd_sys_content_t:s0 html
drwxr-xr-x. root root system_u:object_r:httpd_sys_content_t:s0 icons
drwxr-xr-x. root root system_u:object_r:httpd_sys_content_t:s0 site1
drwxr-xr-x. root root system_u:object_r:httpd_sys_content_t:s0 site2
```

Troubleshooting Apache

One of the best tools available for troubleshooting Apache is its log files. Each log file has a separate directory from the other log files on the system, which makes them easy to pick out. There are two basic files you can use to troubleshoot with:

/var/log/httpd/access_log	Logs all access to the server
/var/log/httpd/error_log	Logs error messages from the server

Usually, browsing these two logs provides you with enough information when troubleshooting to resolve your issues. In the main config file, there is also a section for logging that enables you to change the information recorded by the httpd service. If you'd like different output (or more output), you can adjust the logging section accordingly.

If you're using a secure site, there are three additional files for SSL.

/var/log/httpd/ssl_access_log	Logs access to the secure site
/var/log/httpd/ssl_error_log	Logs error messages from the secure site
/var/log/httpd/ssl_request_log	Logs requests made to the server from clients

As you have already seen, you can use the config-test parameter when looking for errors in the main config file. One common error that everyone seems to get when starting the service is about the ServerName option not being set, so the web server assumes 127.0.0.1 by default. To correct this issue, you should set the ServerName option within the main config file to the name of your server. You can also change the amount of output generated in the log files by changing the LogLevel option within the main config file.

REAL-WORLD TIP

The default LogLevel is set to warn, but you can change it to info or debug to see detailed information about what is going on. Be very careful when changing this, though, because it can produce a huge amount of data and negatively impact your system or lock it up entirely.

Another useful tool to troubleshoot web server issues with is the elinks browser. This text-based browser lets you easily check websites. To make use of this utility, you need to install an additional package.

Step 1.   Install the required package:

```
# yum install -y elinks
```

Step 2.   When it's installed, you can test your site with the following:

```
# elinks 172.168.1.1
```

After running the command, you should see the screen shown in Figure 14-1.

```
                  Test Page for the Apache HTTP Server on Red Hat Enterprise Linux (1/2)
                                Red Hat Enterprise Linux Test Page

    This page is used to test the proper operation of the Apache HTTP server after it has been
    installed. If you can read this page, it means that the Apache HTTP server installed at
    this site is working properly.


If you are a member of the general public:

    The fact that you are seeing this page indicates that the website you just visited is
    either experiencing problems, or is undergoing routine maintenance.

    If you would like to let the administrators of this website know that you've seen this page
    instead of the page you expected, you should send them e-mail. In general, mail sent to the
    name "webmaster" and directed to the website's domain should reach the appropriate person.

    For example, if you experienced problems while visiting www.example.com, you should send
    e-mail to "webmaster@example.com".

    For information on Red Hat Enterprise Linux, please visit the Red Hat, Inc. website. The
    documentation for Red Hat Enterprise Linux is available on the Red Hat, Inc. website.



If you are the website administrator:

http://www.redhat.com/                                                              [------]
```

Figure 14-1   Test page for the Apache HTTP server.

Step 3.   If you don't specify between HTTP and HTTPS, normal HTTP is assumed. If you want to test for a secure site, you can use the following:

```
# elinks https://172.168.1.1
```

Step 4.   To quit the elinks browser, just press q.

Apache Security

In the previous section, we addressed the firewall rules and SELinux policy changes required to get the `httpd` service working. This section goes more in depth with Apache security because it is such a large topic. For the exam and particularly in the real world, you need to be able to configure host-based and user-based security for Apache. You also are required to set up a secure website using the HTTPS protocol.

Host-Based Security

To start, you can limit the IP address on which the server can listen for incoming connections. You use the `Listen` option to define an IP address and a port, usually 80. This capability is helpful if you have multiple IP addresses because it allows access only to the IP address, and therefore that network, you specify.

On the RHEL01 system, there are two IP addresses: 172.168.1.1 and 192.168.1.5. Let's configure this Apache server to allow clients to access it only from the 172.168.1.0/24 network:

```
Listen 172.168.1.1:80
```

Now RHEL01 will listen only on the 172.168.1.1 IP address on port 80 for incoming requests.

Next, let's look at the `<Directory>` section, which holds options pertaining to the main server config. Within this section, the first thing you do is restrict the networks, IP addresses, or domains that have access to the web server. In the `<Directory>` section, let's set up `Allow from` and `Deny from` options.

Step 1.   Allow all hosts to connect:
```
Allow from all
```

Step 2.   To allow only a specific IP or host, use the following:
```
Allow from 172.168.1.2
```

Step 3.   You could also use the hostname:
```
Allow from RHEL02
```

Step 4.   You can also specify a domain:
```
Allow from .example.com
```

Step 5.   The deny options work in the same manner. To deny from a whole subnet, use the following:
```
Deny from 192.168.1
```

WARNING: There are two things to watch out for here. First, when you're specifying a domain to allow or deny from, make sure you include the leading dot (.); otherwise, the restriction won't work properly. Second, when you specify a subnet, there is no ending dot (.) or last octet.

After you determine the hosts that you want to allow or deny access to your web server, you next need to define which order they are applied in:

`Order allow,deny`	Allows first and then denies everything else
`Order deny, allow`	Denies first and then allows everything else

Because the goal is to make the web server more secure, let's use the first option, which denies everything by default. To finish the `<Directory>` section, let's look at general options and the `AllowOverride` option. The default setup in the config file is pretty secure:

`Options Indexes FollowSymLinks`	Allows indexing of directories and allows symlinks outside this `<Directory>` section
`AllowOrverride None`	Does not allow any normal user to make changes in DocumentRoot

There are quite a few different option settings you can define here. I suggest spending some time in the man pages and the default config file, which contains detailed documentation to the different options for Apache.

The complete `<Directory>` section now looks like this:

```
<Directory "/var/www/html">
    Options Indexes FollowSymLinks
    AllowOverride None
    Order allow,deny
    Allow from 172.168.1
</Directory>
```

The options we just covered allow you to have a more secure server through host-based security. Don't forget that these options are specific to this one `<Directory>` section and they can be different in each section. If you want to define the defaults for any further subsections you want to have, you can define all your options in the `<Directory />` section, which is the default option.

NOTE: By default, the `httpd` service runs with the following credentials:

- User apache
- Group apache

This is a great default setting because it allows the httpd service to run only as the Apache user. Should something on the server get compromised, the hacker would be able to access only resources that the Apache user has access to, which usually isn't anything outside the web directories.

User-Based Security

Now that we have configured some host-based authentication, we can move on to user-based authentication. This provides a way to allow only certain users or groups to access the web server or portions of the web server. Here are the options that can be used for used based security:

AuthType	Defines the authentication type
AuthName	Adds a comment for the user to see on login
AuthUserFile	Specifies the file used to define username and password
AuthGroupFile	Is similar to the user file but for groups
Require	Specifies the users or groups that can log in

Let's look at an example to make the usage of these options more clear. Suppose you want to password protect the main site because it contains information for human resources (HR) that shouldn't get out.

Step 1. Define the following under the main server section in the config file:

```
<Directory "/var/www/html">


    AuthType Basic
    AuthName "Password Restricted Area"
    AuthUserFile /etc/httpd/userfile
    Require user user01

</Directory>
```

Now you can go over to the /etc/httpd directory and create a userfile to hold the user accounts. You can use the htpasswd command to create the user and group accounts.

Step 2. Create the sole user who will need access to this site:

```
# htpasswd -cm /etc/httpd/userfile user01
New password:
Re-type new password:
Adding password for user user01
```

There are two very important issues to note here. First, notice the -c option when calling this command, which creates the file and populates it with the first user and password. DO NOT use this option again when creating subsequent users; otherwise, it will completely override the file and you will lose all users in the file. The second is the -m option, which uses MD5 encryption when writing the passwords to the file. You should always use this; otherwise, anyone will be able to see the username and password combo in clear-text!

Step 3.   Restart the web server:

```
# service httpd reload
Reloading httpd:                                        [  OK  ]
```

Access the main page by pointing your browser from any system on the 172.168.1.0 /24 network to http://172.168.1.1/index.html. You should be prompted for a username and password. This is great! You now have a secure main site, and HR can begin posting documents here. There is a problem, however. Suppose HR would like the main site to be fully accessible to the company, for public news. But they also want to have a section where only HR employees can go to view things (like everyone's salary). Not a problem. You can just make a few changes to make all this happen.

Step 4.   First, open your main config file and change your <Directory> section:

```
<Directory "/var/www/html">


      AllowOverride authconfig

</Directory>
```

Step 5.   Save your config file and navigate to your web directory structure.

Step 6.   Here, create a new directory to hold the documents for the HR group:

```
# cd /var/www/html
# mkdir hr
```

Now, you need to create a file called .htaccess that defines who has access to this directory. This is allowed on a per-directory basis because you are allowing this file to "override" the default access of anyone (this is why you change the AllowOverride option in the main config file).

Step 7.   Enter the following into the file:

```
# nano .htaccess
AuthType Basic
AuthName "Password Restricted Area"
AuthGroupFile /etc/httpd/groupfile
Require group hr_users
```

Like the user-defined access, this allows only users from the hr_users group, defined in the /etc/httpd/groupfile. Save this file and close it. The last step you need to do is add a few user accounts for the HR users to the already-existing userfile and then allow the hr_users in the group file.

Step 8.   Create a few user accounts:

```
# htpasswd -m /etc/httpd/userfile hr01
New password:
Re-type new password:
Adding password for user hr01

# htpasswd -m /etc/httpd/userfile hr02
New password:
Re-type new password:
Adding password for user hr02
```

Step 9.   In /etc/httpd/groupfile, add the following:

```
hr_users: hr01 hr02
```

Step 10.   With everything in place, you can restart the web server:

```
# service httpd reload
Reloading httpd:                                          [  OK  ]
```

Now if you try to access http://172.168.1.1/index.html, you will have no problem. This area is no longer password-protected. However, if you were to go over to http://172.168.1.1/hr/test.html, you would be prompted for a username and password. You will also notice, however, that if you enter user01 as the username, you are not able to access this area. The reason is that you used the Require group option, which requires a member of the hr_users group you defined.

There is one other option that falls under user security that you should be aware of in case it comes up on the exam. The option is called UserDir, and when it's enabled, it allows users to browse and access the public_html directory within their home folder. This option can be useful if you want each user to share some files over the Web, but I shouldn't even need to tell you what a security issue this is if left unchecked. By default, this option is disabled, and with good reason.

If you need to be able to share content out of a user's home directory for the exam, set the following option in the main config file:

```
Userdir public_html
```

Then navigate to any user account on the system, create a public_html directory if it doesn't exist, and set the appropriate permissions:

```
# cd /home/user01
# mkdir public_html
# chmod 701 /home/user01
# chmod 705 -R /home/user01/public_html
```

CAUTION: I can't begin to stress the importance of not using this `UserDir` option. You would be allowing your user's home directory to be world executable and his public_html would be readable and executable. This just screams security problem! The only reason I cover it in this book is so that you are aware of the option for the exam. In the real world, use caution when setting up this option!

Setting Up HTTPS

Aside from normal websites, you can also have secure websites using the HTTPS protocol. Configuring secure websites in Apache is simple. If you haven't already installed the mod_ssl package, you need to do so before anything else. When this package is installed, the /etc/httpd/conf.d/ssl.conf file is added to your system. This file contains the configuration settings for your secure web server.

Here is what the default file looks like:

```
# grep -v ^# /etc/httpd/conf.d/ssl.conf

LoadModule ssl_module modules/mod_ssl.so

Listen 443

SSLPassPhraseDialog   builtin

SSLSessionCache               shmcb:/var/cache/mod_ssl/scache(512000)
SSLSessionCacheTimeout   300

SSLMutex default

SSLRandomSeed startup file:/dev/urandom   256
SSLRandomSeed connect builtin

SSLCryptoDevice builtin

<VirtualHost _default_:443>

ErrorLog logs/ssl_error_log
TransferLog logs/ssl_access_log
```

```
LogLevel warn

SSLEngine on

SSLProtocol all -SSLv2

SSLCipherSuite ALL:!ADH:!EXPORT:!SSLv2:RC4+RSA:+HIGH:+MEDIUM:+LOW

SSLCertificateFile /etc/pki/tls/certs/localhost.crt

SSLCertificateKeyFile /etc/pki/tls/private/localhost.key

<Files ~ "\.(cgi|shtml|phtml|php3?)$">
    SSLOptions +StdEnvVars
</Files>
<Directory "/var/www/cgi-bin">
    SSLOptions +StdEnvVars
</Directory>

SetEnvIf User-Agent ".*MSIE.*" \
         nokeepalive ssl-unclean-shutdown \
         downgrade-1.0 force-response-1.0

CustomLog logs/ssl_request_log \
          "%t %h %{SSL_PROTOCOL}x %{SSL_CIPHER}x \"%r\" %b"

</VirtualHost>
```

The most important elements here are the Listen option and the options defined within the <VirtualHost _default_:443> </VirtualHost> tags. By default, the secure site is hosted as a virtual host (which is nice because this allows you to run it alongside other nonsecure sites). We cover virtual hosts later in this chapter.

You should also take note of the following two options:

```
SSLCertificateFile /etc/pki/tls/certs/localhost.crt
SSLCertificateKeyFile /etc/pki/tls/private/localhost.key
```

They define the options and locations of your certificate file and key, which are used when hosting a secure website. Although the default options will work, if you ever change the IP address or domain name pair, you will need to generate a new certificate and key. Installing the crypto-utils package provides you with the openssl and genkey commands required to accomplish this. Because this topic isn't part of the exam, however, I don't go through the full steps here.

One additional step that you need to take for your secure website is opening an additional port on the firewall.

Step 1. Use the `iptables` command to create your firewall rules:

```
# iptables -I INPUT 5 -p tcp -m tcp – dport 80 -j ACCEPT
# iptables -I INPUT 5 -p tcp -m tcp – dport 443 -j ACCEPT
```

Step 2. Save the rule you just created:

```
# service iptables save
Saving firewall rules to /etc/sysconfig/iptables:          [  OK  ]
```

Step 3. Restart the firewall service for the changes to take effect:

```
# service iptables restart
iptables: Flushing firewall rules:                         [  OK  ]
iptables: Setting chains to policy ACCEPT: filter          [  OK  ]

iptables: Unloading modules:                               [  OK  ]
iptables: Applying firewall rules:                         [  OK  ]
```

CGI Applications

Now that you know how to configure and secure a web server, let's look at some more advanced deployments and how to share data. For this first example, let's deploy a CGI application on the web server.

Step 1. Create a directory to hold your web application:

```
# mkdir /var/www/web-app-01
```

Step 2. Copy any required files into the newly created directory:

```
# cp /home/user01/app.py /var/www/web-app-01
```

NOTE: You can get the app.py from http://sourceforge.net/projects/rhcelabscripts/.

Step 3. Add the following section to your /etc/httpd/conf/httpd.conf file:

```
ScriptAlias /webapp "/var/www/web-app-01"
<Directory "/var/www/web-app-01/">
    Options ExecCGI FollowSymLinks
    Order allow,deny
    Allow from all
</Directory>
```

Step 4. Check the config file for syntax errors:

```
# service httpd configtest
Syntax OK
```

Step 5. Set the correct permissions for the directory:

```
# chmod 755 -R /var/www/web-app-01
```

Step 6.   Restart the web service:

```
# service httpd restart
Stopping httpd:                                          [  OK  ]
Starting httpd:                                          [  OK  ]
```

Now if you navigate to http://172.168.1.1/webapp/app.py, you should see the CGI application be executed in the browser! If you have worked with Apache before, you know that there is already a directory set up by default for CGI applications. When Apache is installed, the /var/www/cgi-bin directory is created to hold CGI applications. You also see the following section in the main config file:

```
ScriptAlias /cgi-bin/ "/var/www/cgi-bin/"


#
# "/var/www/cgi-bin" should be changed to whatever your ScriptAliased
# CGI directory exists, if you have that configured.
#
<Directory "/var/www/cgi-bin">
    AllowOverride None
    Options None
    Order allow,deny
    Allow from all
</Directory>
```

Instead of creating your own directory, you could have also just used this one (although doing your own thing is good, too). There are many other types of applications that you can run, such as PHP, RUBY, and JAVA. Although the Red Hat exams only require you to be able to work with CGI applications, it is very common to see different application types in the real world.

Virtual Hosts

One of the big benefits of Apache is that you can run multiple websites on a single host. This is done through a virtual host configuration, where you can define different sites in your main Apache config file. We have already discussed the global options and main server options in the main config file. The third section deals with virtual host options:

NameVirtualHost	Specifies the hostname or IP address for the virtual host
ServerAdmin	Indicates the email address for the webmaster
DocumentRoot	Defines the directory for the virtual host files
ServerName	Defines the URL for the virtual host

| ErrorLog | Specifies the location for the error log |
| CustomLog | Specifies the location for a custom log |

Many of these options are similar to options provided in the main server section of the config file. If an option is not defined in the virtual host section, it defaults to whatever is set in the main server section.

Setting up virtual hosts is easy; just do the following:

Step 1.   Copy the main server section default site as an example:

```
<VirtualHost *:80>


        ServerAdmin webmaster@example.com
        DocumentRoot /var/www/site1
        ServerName www.site1.com
        ErrorLog logs/site1_error_log
        CustomLog logs/site1_access_log common


</VirtualHost>
```

Step 2.   Don't forget to verify the syntax before running with the config:

```
# httpd -S
VirtualHost configuration:
wildcard NameVirtualHosts and _default_ servers:
*:80                     www.site1.com
(/etc/httpd/conf/httpd.conf:985)
Syntax OK
```

Step 3.   If you have multiple virtual host sites, you can check them with the following:

```
# httpd -D DUMP_VHOSTS
VirtualHost configuration:
wildcard NameVirtualHosts and _default_ servers:
*:80                     www.site1.com
(/etc/httpd/conf/httpd.conf:985)
Syntax OK
```

Squid Web Proxy

A proxy server is a device that usually sits between a client and the destination the user is trying to reach. It can provide security, anonymity, and even protection for the client behind the proxy. To help in this process is Squid, which is a web proxy server for Red Hat. It sits between the client and web server that the user is trying to connect to. Many times these devices are used when you want to control access to the Internet (think web filtering). As a web proxy, it can also cache data that users request from the Web and make it locally available, reducing the load on your external devices such as gateways and firewalls. Here, we look at how to set up a web proxy, define access control lists, and troubleshoot it.

Installing Squid

Much as you did with the web server, you need to start by installing the package(s) needed for Squid. There is only one package required to install the Squid proxy server.

Step 1.   Install the package with the following command:

```
# yum install -y squid
```

Step 2.   After it's installed, verify:

```
# rpm -qa | grep squid
squid-3.1.4-1.el6.x86_64
```

Next, you should turn on Squid at boot time. You use the chkconfig command to do this.

Step 3.   Enable Squid to start at boot:

```
# chkconfig squid on
```

Step 4.   Verify the service will start at boot:

```
# chkconfig squid —list
squid               0:off   1:off   2:on    3:on    4:on    5:on
6:off
```

Now that you know the package is installed and will start at boot, you can turn your attention to configuration.

Configuring the Proxy

When setting up your proxy server, you need to know the following items:

/etc/sysconfig/squid	Startup options for the config file
/etc/squid/squid.conf	Main config file for the service
/var/spool/squid	Cache location on the proxy server
/var/log/squid	Log files for the proxy server

As with most services you configure, the first item on the agenda is the main config file. I want to warn you first that although this config file has huge amounts of documentation and numerous examples, it contains over 4,000+ lines, so make sure you put aside some time if you plan to take on reading and going through this whole config file! As with Apache, configuring a web proxy server can be a daunting and sometimes lengthy process until you have it set up correctly. This lab, however, requires just the basic functionality from the proxy server, so it shouldn't be too difficult to get running. Let's look at some of the main configuration options:

`http_port`	Specifies the port to listen on
`visible_hostname`	Identifies the name of the Squid server
`hierarchy_stoplist`	Provides a list of words that tell the Squid server to handle the request
`access_log`	Keeps track of the web pages that are downloaded
`acl`	Defines an access control list
`http_access`	Defines which system or networks have access

You can use the default port to run the Squid proxy, which will make testing a little easier. However, you can set the `visible_hostname` option to the name of your server:

```
# nano /etc/squid/squid.conf
visible_hostname = RHEL01
```

EXAM TIP

Be aware that many proxies like to use port 8080. Why Squid chose to use 3128 as a default, I have no idea, but be prepared to know how to change the default port that Squid listens on if required for the exam. You should also change the default port if running Squid in a production environment because it is never a good idea to leaving anything with its default option for security reasons.

You should also define the URL syntax for which the Squid server should not handle. An example would be form data that you want the server to submit directly and not cache your private data:

```
hierarchy_stoplist cgi-bin ?
Acl QUERY urlpath_regex cgi-bin \?
cache deny QUERY
```

Firewall and SELinux Configuration

The firewall and SELinux requirements for Squid are actually quite simple. Squid uses port 3128 by default for its communication, so you should open this port on the firewall. Both the TCP and UDP protocols are used.

Step 1. Use the `iptables` command to create your firewall rules:

```
# iptables -I INPUT 5 -p tcp -m tcp — dport 3128 -j ACCEPT
# iptables -I INPUT 5 -p udp -m udp — dport 3128 -j ACCEPT
```

Step 2.   Save the rules you just created:

```
# service iptables save
Saving firewall rules to /etc/sysconfig/iptables:          [  OK  ]
```

Step 3.   Restart the firewall service for the changes to take effect:

```
# service iptables restart
iptables: Flushing firewall rules:                        [  OK  ]
iptables: Setting chains to policy ACCEPT: filter         [  OK  ]
iptables: Unloading modules:                              [  OK  ]
iptables: Applying firewall rules:                        [  OK  ]
```

By default, you do not have to change SELinux for your Squid setup. You should know what the available options are, though:

squid_use_tproxy   Allows Squid to run as a transparent proxy (TPROXY)

squid_connect_any   Allows Squid to connect to all ports, not just HTTP, FTP, and Gopher ports

If you want to enable either of these features, just make sure to adjust the SELinux Boolean value appropriately.

TIP: In RHEL5, you need to disable SELinux protection for the Squid service for it to work.

Step 1.   Query for the Boolean value you need to change:

```
# getsebool -a | grep squid_dis
squid_disable_trans --> off
```

Step 2.   Disable the SELinux protection:

```
# setsebool -P squid_disable_trans=1
```

Step 3.   Verify that the Boolean has changed:

```
# getsebool -a | grep squid_dis
squid_disable_trans --> on
```

As you can see, the firewall rules and SELinux requirements are really light for Squid. Before starting the service, though, we need to cover Squid security a little more in depth.

Web Proxy Security

Squid uses host-based security through the use of access control lists. These ACLs are configured in the main config file, /etc/squid/squid.conf. In the config file, you can define an ACL for your network and give all other networks access to the proxy server.

In the /etc/squid/squid.conf file:

```
acl my_local_net src 172.168.1.0/24
acl allow_dom dstdomain example.com
```

You also need to enable HTTP access for those networks:

```
http_access allow my_local_net
http_access allow allow_dom
```

Save the config file before exiting. Now you can start the squid service to test the proxy:

```
# service squid start
init_cache_dir /var/spool/squid... Starting squid: .      [  OK  ]
```

Verify:

```
# service squid status
squid (pid  4577) is running...
```

When Squid begins, it creates its cache in /var/spool/squid, as defined by the init_cache_dir option in the startup script. You can also check in the log file /var/log/squid/access.log to see whether any error messages are being generated. On the Client01 system, you can connect to the proxy and test the connection.

From Client01, use the elinks command to connect to the proxy from the command line:

```
# HTTP_PROXY=172.168.1.1:3128 elinks
```

If you can't connect, make sure the firewall rules are set properly and check the logs for any error messages.

Summary

Web services are important because they play a critical role on the Internet. Learning how to set up and manage an Apache web server's inner workings efficiently takes a good deal of time. For the exam, make sure you know the basics of configuration and virtual hosts. Proxies also help in offloading the pounding that web servers would take without them. Both of these services, combined with DNS, make up the web infrastructure for websites.

Review Questions

1. What port does the Apache web server run on? What about HTTPS?

2. Are additional packages besides httpd required for a secure website? If so, what are they?

3. What command can you use to create a password-protected page?

4. What happens if you call the command from question 3 with the -c option after it has already been run?

5. What command can you use to validate the syntax of the Apache config file?

6. What is a virtual host?

7. How can virtual hosts be used?

8. How can you change the security context of a directory to work with Apache?

9. What benefit does a web proxy provide to your network?

10. What is the default port that Squid runs on?

Answers to Review Questions

1. Apache uses port 80 for HTTP and port 443 for HTTPS.

2. Yes. For Apache to run a secure site, the mod_ssl package is required to be installed.

3. The htpasswd command can be used to password-protect a web page.

4. The file that stores usernames and their encrypted passwords is erased and replaced with a new file.

5. `service httpd configtest`

6. A virtual host is a way of hosting multiple sites using a single IP address.

7. If you are a hosting company or want to run multiple websites/applications from a single IP address, you can use virtual hosts to accomplish this.

8. Using the chcon command, you can change the context of a file to work with Apache.

9. A web proxy can provide multiple benefits, including security, web page caching for faster load times, and load balancing.

10. By default, Squid runs on port 3128.

Lab 14

Task 1 – Web Server Setup

Step 1. Set up an Apache web server with the following guidelines:
The web server should be accessible only on port 80.

The default website should be located in the /var/www/first_site directory.

The site should be accessible only from the local network (172.168.1.0 /24).

Step 2. Create an index.html file in the first_site directory. Use the following text for the file:

```
<html>
<body>
<h2>This is my first web site!</h2>
</body>
</html>
```

The task is complete when any client on the local network can access the first_site website.

Task 2 – Secure Websites

Step 1. Set up another website using the following guidelines:
The website should be accessible only on port 443 (HTTPS).
The secure website should be located in the /var/www/secure_site directory.
The site should be accessible only from the local network (172.168.1.0 / 24).

Step 2. Create an index.html file in the first_site directory. Use the following text for the file:

```
<html>
<body>
<h2>This is the secure version of my site!</h2>
</body>
</html>
```

The task is complete when any client on the local network can access the secure_site website.

Task 3 – A Web Proxy

Step 1. Set up a web proxy using Squid with the following guidelines:

The proxy should be able to handle all web traffic for the 172.168.1.0 / 24 subnet.
Configure Client02 to use the proxy for its web traffic.
The proxy should listen on port 3128.

The task is complete when Client02 can access the Internet through the proxy.

This chapter covers the following subjects:

- **Network File Systems**—This section covers network file systems and how clients can use them.

- **NFS Security**—This section covers NFS security.

- **Troubleshooting NFS**—This section looks at troubleshooting NFS.

- **Connecting Clients**—This section looks at how to connect clients to the NFS server.

The following RHCE exam objectives are covered:

- Install the packages needed to provide the service

- Configure SELinux to support the service

- Configure the service to start when the system is booted

- Configure the service for basic operation

- Configure host-based and user-based security for the service

- Provide network shares to specific clients

- Provide shares suitable for group collaboration

## CHAPTER 15

NFS

There are many different ways you can share files with users on your network. This chapter is the first of three chapters dealing with sharing files over the network. Specifically, in this chapter we will look at NFS, Samba in the next chapter, and FTP in Chapter 17. NFS provides a way for other systems on the network to store files in a centralized place. This ensures that backups are easier and security remains intact on a single point (instead of spread over multiple servers throughout your network). Keeping your data in a centralized place will make your life much easier as a system administrator. Let's just jump into NFS and centralized storage.

Network File Systems

The Network File Systems (NFS) protocol works great when it comes to Linux systems because it allows for client flexibility, centralized management of files, and some other great features. To get NFS working properly, you need to set up the NFS server first and then set up the client to test access to the server. As with any other service, you need to install a few packages before doing anything else. The actual NFS service is the same for both servers and clients, with the difference being found in the services running and the config files.

There are four different versions of NFS; version 4 is the most current. Although you can disable what versions the server listens for, the client actually determines which version it will use when connecting to the server (unless, of course, the server is offering the version the client is asking for). This description will make more sense as you move along in the chapter.

> **MIGRATION TIP**
>
> When RHEL5 was introduced, it came with both NFS versions 3 and 4 available for use, but version 3 was used by default. In RHEL6, again both versions are available, but version 4 is now the default. It is recommended that even if you are still on RHEL5, you use version 4 because of the numerous improvements.

Installing an NFS Server

Follow these steps to install an NFS server.

Step 1.   To begin the NFS server setup, install the required packages:

```
# yum install -y nfs-utils nfs4-acl-tools
```

Step 2.   Verify the package installation:

```
# rpm -qa | grep nfs
nfs4-acl-tools-0.3.3-5.el6.x86_64
nfs-utils-1.2.2-7.el6.x86_64
nfs-utils-lib-1.1.5-1.el6.x86_64
```

> **MIGRATION TIP**
>
> RHEL6 no longer includes any of the system-config GUI packages. This includes the removal of the system-config-nfs package.

Step 3.   The NFS server uses three different services to function properly. You need to enable them all at boot for the NFS server to function the way it should:

```
# chkconfig nfs on
# chkconfig nfslock on
# chkconfig rpcbind on
```

> **MIGRATION TIP**
>
> RHEL6 now uses the rpcbind service, which replaces the portmapper service from RHEL5. If you are still using RHEL5, you need to replace the rpcbind commands in these examples with portmap instead.

Step 4.   Verify that all three services are set to start on system boot:

```
# chkconfig --list nfs
nfs             0:off   1:off   2:on    3:on    4:on    5:on    6:off

# chkconfig --list nfslock
nfslock         0:off   1:off   2:on    3:on    4:on    5:on    6:off
```

```
# chkconfig --list rpcbind
netfs            0:off   1:off   2:on   3:on   4:on   5:on   6:off
```

You should also verify that the NFS service is currently stopped because you need to make some configuration changes before you can start it.

Step 5.   Verify that the service is off:

```
# service nfs status
rpc.mountd is stopped
nfsd is stopped
rpc.rquotad is stopped
```

Configuring NFS

The nfs and rpcbind services both control a number of daemons on the system when they are started. Let's look at the different daemons these two services are composed of:

rpcbind	Forwards incoming requests to the appropriate subservice
rpc.idmapd	Maps the UID and GID to users and groups
rpc.lockd	Manages file locks and releases in case of client disconnect
rpc.nfsd	Responds to client requests for file access
rpc.rquotad	Provides statistics on disk quotas to clients
rpc.statd	Works with rpc.lockd to provide recovery services

Let's also look at the config files that you will be dealing with:

/etc/sysconfig/nfs	Contains the main config files for the NFS service
/etc/exports	Contains a list of resources that will be exported (made available) to clients

Here are some additional files that you will use when working with NFS:

/var/lib/nfs/etab	Contains a list of currently exported resources
/var/lib/nfs/rmtab	Contains a list of remotely mounted resources

For the first configuration step, you need to make a few changes to the main config file.

Step 1.   Open the main config file for editing:

```
# nano /etc/sysconfig/nfs
```

Step 2. Uncomment the following lines:

```
MOUNTD_NFS_V1="no"
MOUNTD_NFS_V2="no"
MOUNTD_NFS_V3="no"

RPCNFSDARGS="-N 2 -N 3"
```

The first three lines disable the `mountd` daemon from accepting anything below version 4. The last line disables the NFS service from even advertising anything but version 4 as well.

> **MIGRATION TIP**
> If you are still on RHEL5, there is an unresolved bug that causes strange errors if you disable all versions of the `mountd` daemon from being advertised. For RHEL5, I recommend uncommenting only the following lines:
> ```
> MOUNTD_NFS_V1="no"
> MOUNTD_NFS_V2="no"
> ```

Step 3. Save the file and exit.

Next, let's work with the /etc/exports file because this defines what resources will be available to your clients. If the file doesn't exist already, you can create it. The syntax of the /etc/exports file is

```
<mountpoint>          <host><permissions/options>
```

> **WARNING:** Notice there is no space between the `<host>` field and the `<permissions/options>` field. If you include a space, you receive a syntax error and the resource will not export properly.

Mount Options:

`rw`	Sets read/write permissions
`ro`	Sets read-only permissions
`insecure`	Allows the use of ports over 1024
`sync`	Specifies that all changes must be written to disk before a command completes
`no_wdelay`	Forces the writing of changes immediately (useful for logs if something crashes)
`root_squash`	Prevents root users

As an example, you can use the following two locations to export to the clients:

/home   The home directory containing your users' data

/opt/company_data   The directory created earlier in the book that holds company data

Step 4.   Set up your exports in the /etc/exports files to be available to any client on the network:

```
# nano /etc/exports
/home                    *(ro,sync)
/opt/company_data        *(rw,sync)
```

Here, you define two resources that you will make available. The first line defines the /home directory to be exported and allows read-only access to all clients. The second line provides the /opt/company_data directory to all of your clients with read and write permissions. After you finish defining all the resources you want to export, save and close the file.

Step 5.   Start the two NFS services (rpcbind should be running already by default):

```
# service nfslock start
Starting NFS statd:                                    [  OK  ]

# service nfs start
Starting NFS services:                                 [  OK  ]
Starting NFS quotas:                                   [  OK  ]
Starting NFS daemon:                                   [  OK  ]
Starting NFS mountd:                                   [  OK  ]
```

Step 6.   Verify that the services have started successfully:

```
# service rpcbind status
rpcbind (pid  25068) is running...

# service nfslock status
rpc.statd (pid  17726) is running...

# service nfs status
rpc.svcgssd is stopped
rpc.mountd (pid 17780) is running...
nfsd (pid 17777 17776 17775 17774 17773 17772 17771 17770) is
running...
rpc.rquotad (pid 17764) is running...
```

NOTE: For some reason, the first time you start the NFS services, they don't always produce an output showing that they started successfully. If you want to verify that they have started successfully, you can restart the service to view the correct output on the console screen.

If you already started the services before creating an /etc/exports file, you can also use the `exportfs` command to manually export any new resources added to the /etc/exports file.

Syntax: `exportfs [options]`

Options:

`-a`   Exports or unexports all directories

`-r`   Reexports all directories

`-u`   Unexports one or more directories

`-v`   Provides verbose output

Step 1.   Here is what a manual export of resources would look like:

```
# exportfs -avr
exporting *:/opt/company_data
exporting *:/home
```

Step 2.   Alternatively, you can also get the same effect by restarting only the NFS service, which in turn restarts all daemons:

```
# service nfs restart
Shutting down NFS mountd:                                    [  OK  ]
Shutting down NFS daemon:                                    [  OK  ]
Shutting down NFS quotas:                                    [  OK  ]
Shutting down NFS services:                                  [  OK  ]
Starting NFS services:                                       [  OK  ]
Starting NFS quotas:                                         [  OK  ]
Starting NFS daemon:                                         [  OK  ]
Starting NFS mountd:                                         [  OK  ]
```

REAL-WORLD TIP

It is better to manually export the directories than to restart the service because you don't disconnect your clients when exporting new directories, but you do disconnect them when the service is restarted.

Now that all the resources have been exported properly and the NFS service has been started, you can use the `rpcinfo` command to verify that all the parts of the NFS service are running properly.

Syntax: `rpcinfo -p [host]`

You can view both local and remote connection information with the `rpcinfo` command. Because you are looking for information about the local server, you don't have to specify a host when calling the command. View the current running `nfs` daemons:

```
# rpcinfo -p
   program vers proto   port  service
    100000    4   tcp    111  portmapper
    100000    3   tcp    111  portmapper
    100000    2   tcp    111  portmapper
    100000    4   udp    111  portmapper
    100000    3   udp    111  portmapper
    100000    2   udp    111  portmapper
    100024    1   udp  41853  status
    100024    1   tcp  40535  status
    100011    1   udp    875  rquotad
    100011    2   udp    875  rquotad
    100011    1   tcp    875  rquotad
    100011    2   tcp    875  rquotad
    100003    4   tcp   2049  nfs
    100003    4   udp   2049  nfs
    100021    1   udp  32769  nlockmgr
    100021    3   udp  32769  nlockmgr
    100021    4   udp  32769  nlockmgr
    100021    1   tcp  32803  nlockmgr
    100021    3   tcp  32803  nlockmgr
    100021    4   tcp  32803  nlockmgr
```

Where you see the `nfs` daemon running, notice that only version 4 is listed. The reason is that you disabled all other versions in the config file. Although some of the other daemons listed use other versions as well, you should verify that at least the `nfs` daemon shows version 4.

Firewall and SELinux Configuration

NFS is one of the many Red Hat services that can take advantage of TCP Wrappers as well as firewall rules for security. We don't use TCP Wrappers here, but should you run into trouble on the exam with the NFS service not working, don't forget to check to see whether anything is being filtered by TCP Wrappers. Because you are using NFS version 4 here, you need to create only a single firewall rule.

Step 1.   Use `iptables` to create the additional firewall rules:

```
# iptables -I INPUT 5 -p tcp -m tcp --dport 2049 -j ACCEPT
```

Step 2.   Save the firewall rules you just created:

```
# service iptables save
Saving firewall rules to /etc/sysconfig/iptables:          [  OK  ]
```

Step 3.   Restart the `iptables` service:

```
# service iptables restart
iptables: Flushing firewall rules:                         [  OK  ]
iptables: Setting chains to policy ACCEPT: filter          [  OK  ]
iptables: Unloading modules:                               [  OK  ]
iptables: Applying firewall rules:                         [  OK  ]
```

> **WARNING:**   According to Red Hat's documentation, NFS version 3 is the default on RHEL5 (this isn't the case with later versions of RHEL5). If you choose to stay with NFS version 4, you need to statically define ports in the /etc/sysconfig/nfs file for each of the four daemons required for the NFS service to run. You also need to add these ports to the /etc/services file and create a firewall rule for each one. For all this trouble, you are better off using NFS version 4 instead.
>
> Each setup of NFS can vary slightly based on other firewall rules and security restrictions that you might have in place, so testing with these options will help.

> **Exam Tip**
>
> If you are using NFS version 4 and having issues with firewall rules, you can take the following steps:
>
> **Step 1.** Define static ports in /etc/sysconfig/nfs for each of the four required daemons NFS uses.
>
> **Step 2.** Create a firewall rule for the `rpcbind` server (TCP and UDP port 111).
>
> **Step 3.** Create a firewall rule for the `MOUNTD_PORT` you specified (TCP and UDP).
>
> **Step 4.** Create a firewall rule for the `STATD_PORT` you specified (TCP and UDP).
>
> **Step 5.** Create a firewall rule for the `LOCKD_TCPPORT` you specified (TCP).
>
> **Step 6.** Create a firewall rule for the `LOCKD_UDPPORT` you specified (UDP).

To complete this section, let's make some adjustments to SELinux for the NFS service to function properly. Table 15-1 shows some of the Boolean options available for the NFS server.

Table 15-1 SELinux Booleans

Booleans	Description
nfs_export_all_ro	Allows NFS to share files and directories as read-only
nfs_export_all_rw	Allows NFS to share files and directories as read/write
httpd_use_nfs	Allows httpd to access NFS file systems
use_nfs_home_dirs	Supports NFS home directories
samba_share_nfs	Allows Samba to export NFS volumes
allow_nfsd_anon_write	Allows NFS servers to modify public files
allow_ftpd_usr_nfs	Allows FTP servers to use NFS for public file transfer services

Step 1. Query for the Boolean value you need to change:

```
# getsebool -a | grep nfs
allow_ftpd_use_nfs --> off
allow_nfsd_anon_write --> off
git_system_use_nfs --> off
httpd_use_nfs --> off
nfs_export_all_ro --> off
nfs_export_all_rw --> off
qemu_use_nfs --> on
samba_share_nfs --> off
use_nfs_home_dirs --> off
virt_use_nfs --> off
xen_use_nfs --> off
```

Step 2. Disable SELinux protection for only the options that you need:

```
# setsebool -P nfs_export_all_ro=1 nfs_export_all_rw=1
```

Step 3. Verify that the Boolean has changed:

```
# getsebool -a | grep nfs
allow_ftpd_use_nfs --> off
allow_nfsd_anon_write --> off
git_system_use_nfs --> off
httpd_use_nfs --> off
nfs_export_all_ro --> on
nfs_export_all_rw --> on
qemu_use_nfs --> on
samba_share_nfs --> off
use_nfs_home_dirs --> off
virt_use_nfs --> off
xen_use_nfs --> off
```

MIGRATION TIP

In RHEL5, the NFS service is blocked by default because of SELinux protection. You need to make a change to a single Boolean to disable SELinux protection to the service.

Step 1. Query for the Boolean value you need to change:

```
# getsebool -a | grep nfsd_dis
nfsd_disable_trans --> off
```

Step 2. Disable SELinux protection:

```
# setsebool -P nfspd_disable_trans=1
```

Step 3. Verify that the Boolean has changed:

```
# getsebool -a | grep nfsd_dis
nfsd_disable_trans --> on
```

Now your basic security requirements should be taken care of. The SELinux Booleans have been set and firewall rules added. Let's look now at additional security you can provide for the NFS server.

NFS Security

In NFS, much of the security is built in through other means. When you're dealing with security, there are always two main areas to focus on: host-based security and user-based security. Let's look at user-based security first.

Because the resources that are exported from the server are just standard directories and files, they use the common file permissions or ACLs that the system administrator provides. This means that it is important to set up permissions and test them when setting up directory structures to export. Aside from these standard permissions, there isn't really anything else that needs to be covered from a user-based security perspective.

For host-based security, there are some features you can use for NFS. Table 15-2 shows some of the options that can be used on NFS shares.

Table 15-2 Options for NFS Shares

Mount Options	Description
ro	Sets the exported file system as read-only
rw	Sets the exported file system as read/write
sync	Prevents the NFS server from replying unless the changes are written to disk
wdelay	Delays the NFS server from writing to the disk if it suspects another write request is imminent
root_squash	Prevents root users connected remotely from having root privileges
noexec	Prevents execution of binaries on mounted file systems
nosuid	Disables set-user-identifier or set-group-identifier bits

You can also use access control lists (ACLs) in conjunction with NFS to restrict access to certain hosts. This can also be accomplished with firewall rules depending on which method you're more comfortable with. Make sure that you restrict access to only clients that need access to NFS shares. Also, make sure that you use the root_squash command if you can because it prevents other users with root permissions from causing trouble on your NFS shares.

Troubleshooting NFS

There are three management commands that help with troubleshooting NFS from both the server and client sides:

mountstats	Shows information about mounted NFS shares
nfsstat	Shows statistics of exported resources
nfsiostat	Shows statistics of NFS mounted shares

MIGRATION TIP

The mountstats and nfsiostat commands are available only under RHEL6.

First, let's look at which resources are exported. For this, you can check the /var/lib/nfs/etab file.

Step 1.   View exported resources (whether or not they are mounted):

```
# cat /var/lib/nfs/etab
/home
*(ro,sync,wdelay,hide,nocrossmnt,secure,root_squash,no_all_squash,n
o_subtree_check,secure_locks,acl,anonuid=65534,anongid=65534)
/opt/data
*(rw,sync,wdelay,hide,nocrossmnt,secure,root_squash,no_all_squash,n
o_subtree_check,secure_locks,acl,anonuid=65534,anongid=65534)
```

Step 2.   From the client side, you can use the nfsstat command for similar results.

Syntax: nfsstat [options]

Options:

-m   Shows statistics on mounted NFS file systems

-n   Shows NFS statistics

-v   Provides verbose output

Step 3.   To display the exported resources from the client (mounted only), use the following:

```
# nfsstat -m
/mnt/home from 172.168.1.1:/home
 Flags:
rw,relatime,vers=4,rsize=262144,wsize=262144,namlen=255,hard,proto=
tcp,timeo=6
00,retrans=2,sec=sys,clientaddr=172.168.1.10,minorversion=0,addr=17
2.168.1.1

/mnt/data from 172.168.1.1:/opt/data
 Flags:
rw,relatime,vers=4,rsize=262144,wsize=262144,namlen=255,hard,proto=
tcp,port=0
,timeo=600,retrans=2,sec=sys,clientaddr=172.168.1.10,minorversion=0,a
ddr=172.16
8.1.1
```

After clients are connected to the server, you can again use the nfsstat command to get some statistical information.

Step 4. View NFS version 4 stats from connected clients:

```
# nfsstat
Server rpc stats:
calls           badcalls        badauth         badclnt         xdrcall
465             3               3               0               0

Server nfs v4:
null            compound
19          4%  446         95%

Server nfs v4 operations:
op0-unused      op1-unused      op2-future      access          close           commit
0          0%   0          0%   0          0%   39         3%   5          0%   0          0%
create          delegpurge      delegreturn     getattr         getfh           link
0          0%   0          0%   0          0%   253       24%   55         5%   0          0%
lock            lockt           locku           lookup          lookup_root     nverify
0          0%   0          0%   0          0%   64         6%   0          0%   0          0%
open            openattr        open_conf       open_dgrd       putfh           putpubfh
45         4%   0          0%   5          0%   0          0%   403       38%   0          0%
putrootfh       read            readdir         readlink        remove          rename
30         2%   0          0%   73         6%   0          0%   0          0%   0          0%
renew           restorefh       savefh          secinfo         setattr         setcltid
0          0%   5          0%   45         4%   0          0%   6          0%   13         1%
setcltidconf    verify          write           rellockowner    bc_ctl          bind_conn
13         1%   0          0%   0          0%   0          0%   0          0%   0          0%
exchange_id     create_ses      destroy_ses     free_stateid    getdirdeleg     getdevinfo
0          0%   0          0%   0          0%   0          0%   0          0%   0          0%
getdevlist      layoutcommit    layoutget       layoutreturn    secinfononam    sequence
0          0%   0          0%   0          0%   0          0%   0          0%   0          0%
set_ssv         test_stateid    want_deleg      destroy_clid    reclaim_comp
0          0%   0          0%   0          0%   0          0%   0          0%

Client rpc stats:
calls       retrans     authrefrsh
131         0           0
```

You can also use the `nfsiostat` command for similar statistics. In addition, if you want some detailed debug information about mounted NFS shares, you can use the `mountstats` command. This information would be useful only if you are looking to fine-tune NFS or track down a serious problem, though.

Connecting Clients

Setting up a client to use NFS is relatively simple when you have the NFS server in place. Let's set up the Client01 system to use a share on the RHEL01 NFS server.

Step 1.   To start, you need to install the required packages:

```
# yum install -y nfs-utils nfs4-acl-tools
```

These two packages include the necessary files for you to connect to the NFS server and use the exported resources. On the client side, you need only the `rpcbind` service running to mount NFS resources on the server.

Step 2.   Ensure that the required service is set to start on boot:

```
# chkconfig rpcbind on
```

You can now create some directories to hold the NFS shares on the local system.

Step 3.   Create two local directories:

```
# mkdir /mnt/{company_data,temp}
```

Step 4.   Mount the `company_data` NFS share:

```
# mount -t nfs 172.168.1.1:/opt/company_data /mnt/company_data
```

MIGRATION TIP

In RHEL5, the `mount` command uses NFS version 3, so you need to specify the version. You would use the following command instead:

```
# mount -t nfs nfsvers=4 172.168.1.1:/opt/company_data /mnt/company_data
```

In RHEL6, version 4 is used by default, so there is no need to specify.

Assuming your permissions and security restrictions are correctly in place, you should now be able to move into the /mnt/company_data directory and actually access the NFS share on the server. If you don't want to always mount NFS shares after your system has booted, you can, of course, add an entry to the /etc/fstab file to have them mounted automatically at system boot.

Step 1.   In the /etc/fstab, add the following line:

```
# nano /etc/fstab
rhel01:/opt/company_data          /opt/company_data     nfs
rw,sync   0 0
```

You should recall the syntax of this file from Chapter 4, "File Systems and Such." It mounts the remote /opt/company_data to the local /mnt/company_data directory.

MIGRATION TIP

Again, if you are on RHEL5, make sure you specify the version of NFS that you want to use (nfs for version 2 and 3; nfs4 for version 4).

```
rhel01:/opt/company_data        /opt/company_data       nfs4    rw,sync   0 0
```

Step 2.   Save your file and exit.

Step 3.   Using the mount command, you can verify that the resource was mounted properly:

```
# mount | grep nfs
sunrpc on /var/lib/nfs/rpc_pipefs type rpc_pipefs (rw)
nfsd on /proc/fs/nfsd type nfsd (rw)
172.168.1.1:/home on /mnt/temp type nfs
(rw,vers=4,addr=172.168.1.1,clientaddr=172.168.1.10)
172.168.1.1:/opt/company_data on /mnt/company_data type nfs
(rw,vers=4,addr=172.168.1.1,clientaddr=172.168.1.10)
```

The remote resource should now be available just as if it were a local resource.

Summary

File sharing makes life a lot easier when you don't have files all over the place. Centralized file storage also helps when it comes to security and auditing. Knowing how to work with file sharing services is a big part of collaboration in the workplace. Users always need a place to put their files, and security is always a growing concern. Make sure that you try to plan ahead for growth of file servers, and from time to time, test their security. At this point, you should know how to set up a file sharing server using NFS. This chapter provided a lot of information due to the requirements of setting up such services, so make sure you practice doing labs and different configuration styles until you are comfortable setting up and troubleshooting all the different file sharing services.

Review Questions

1. Red Hat Enterprise Linux 6 uses the portmap service alongside the NFS service. True or False?

2. What is the /var/lib/nfs/etab file used for?

3. To export directories as resources, what file needs to be edited?

4. The exportfs command is used to view currently exported resources. True or False?

5. What port does NFS use by default?

6. What command can you use to view NFS statistics?

7. What option needs to be used with the mount command to mount an NFS resource?

Answers to Review Questions

1. False. The portmap service was replaced by the rpcbind service in Red Hat Enterprise Linux 6.

2. The /var/lib/nfs/etab file is used to keep track of currently exported resources.

3. The /etc/exports file needs to contain any directory that you want to export, including which options you'd like to use as well.

4. False. The exportfs command is used to export one or all resources.

5. The NFS service uses TCP port 2049 by default.

6. The nfsstat command can be used to view NFS statistics.

7. The -t nfs option is used with the mount command to mount NFS resources.

Lab 15

Task 1 – NFS Server Setup

Step 1.   Set up an NFS server on RHE01 using the following guidelines:

a. Create two directories: /opt/lab1 and /opt/lab2.

b. Both the lab1 and lab2 directories should be exported on the NFS server.

c. The server should support only NFS version 4.

d. The lab1 directory should have read/write access for everyone in the lab.

e. The lab2 directory should have read-only access for everyone in the lab.

f. All access from Client01 should be blocked.

Step 2.   When the server is set up, perform the following action:

a. Create a script that collects the output of the nfsstat command and outputs it to /opt/nfs_stats.

b. Set up a oron job to run the script previously created once a week (Friday at 4 p.m.).

The task is complete when the NFS server is set up and accessible from other systems in the lab.

This chapter covers the following subjects:

- **Samba**—This section covers file sharing using Samba.
- **Samba Security**—This section looks at Samba security.
- **Samba Clients**—This section looks at how to connect clients to the Samba server.

The following RHCE exam objectives are covered:

- Install the packages needed to provide the service
- Configure SELinux to support the service
- Configure the service to start when the system is booted
- Configure the service for basic operation
- Configure host-based and user-based security for the service
- Provide network shares to specific clients
- Provide shares suitable for group collaboration

## CHAPTER 16

Samba

As a Linux administrator, when you think Windows, you should also think Samba. Samba is a great technology that you can run on Linux allowing you to communicate and interact with Windows servers and clients. A Samba server can host Windows shares, act as a print server, and in some more advanced cases act as a backup domain controller for Windows domains. This chapter examines how to set up Samba for basic use providing your clients with network shares similar to NFS. The biggest difference here, though, is the ability for Windows systems to also have access to your shares. We will also look at how to secure these shares just like we did in the previous chapter with NFS.

Samba

Samba, which uses the CIFS/SMB protocol, is commonly brought up when you want Linux and Windows machines to be able to share files together. Aside from the file sharing uses, Samba also has some built-in functionality to run as a member server on a Windows domain, print server, or file server. Let's get started with the setup.

Step 1. Install the required packages for Samba:

```
# yum install -y samba samba-common samba-client
```

Step 2. Verify the package installation:

```
# rpm -qa | grep samba
samba-client-3.5.4-68.el6.x86_64
samba-3.5.4-68.el6.x86_64
samba-winbind-clients-3.5.4-68.el6.x86_64
samba-common-3.5.4-68.el6.x86_64
```

Step 3. Enable the service to start during boot:

```
# chkconfig smb on
```

Step 4. Verify that the service is set to start on boot:

```
# chkconfig smb --list
smb             0:off   1:off   2:on    3:on    4:on    5:on
6:off
```

Configuring Samba

If you have never worked with Samba before, the number of options can seem overwhelming. First, let's look at the two services responsible for running Samba:

smbd	Samba server daemon
nmbd	NetBIOS service daemon

There are also a handful of config files:

/etc/samba/smb.conf	Contains the main config file
/etc/samba/smbusers	Maps Samba and Red Hat users
/etc/samba/smbpasswd	Contains Samba user passwords

I'm sure you could have guessed by now that no service this complex comes without a group of management commands as well:

mount.cifs	Mounts a Samba resource without root privileges
smbclient	Connects to a Samba resource
smbpasswd	Configures Samba users and passwords
smbstatus	Displays the status of Samba connections
testparm	Tests the syntax of the main config file for issues
umount.cifs	Unmounts a Samba resource without root privileges

Now that you are completely overwhelmed with config files and commands, let's take a step back and see what these things are actually used for. You need to edit the main config file to set up the Samba server and directories that you'd like to make into Samba shares. Here is a sample /etc/samba/smb.conf config file you can use (just read through it for now):

```
# cat /etc/samba/smb.conf


### Global Data Section ###

[global]

    ### Define our workgroup and hostname information ###

    workgroup               = INET
    server string           = My Samba Server
    netbios name            = RHEL01
```

```
        ### Define the log file and its size ###

        log file          = /var/log/samba/%m.log
        max log size      = 50

        ### Use a local password file (/etc/samba/smbpasswd) ###

        security          = user
        passdb backend    = tdbsam

        ### Define printer settings ###

        load printers             = yes
        printcap name             = /etc/printcap
        cups options              = raw

### Samba Share for Company Data ###

[company_data]

    ### Define a comment for the share ###

    comment = Directory for all employees within the company

    ### Allow users to access the share and define its location ###

    browseable      = yes
    path            = /opt/company_data

    ### Make the share writable and define access for valid users ###

    valid users     = user01
    writable        = yes

### Share for Samba printers ###

[printers]

    ### Define a comment for the share ###

    comment = All Printers

    ### Allow users to access the share and define its location ###
```

```
browseable      = no
path            = /var/spool/samba

### Set permissions and user access ###

guest ok        = no
writable        = no
printable       = yes
```

To set up the file, do the following:

Step 1.   Make a backup of the main config file so you can review the comments in it later:

```
# cp /etc/samba/smb.conf /etc/samba/smb.bk
```

Step 2.   Copy the sample file provided here into a new main config file:

```
# nano /etc/samba/smb.conf
```

Step 3.   Save the file and exit. Now you need to check that the config file has no syntax errors by using the testparm command:

Syntax: testparm [options] <config file> [hostname] [host IP]

Options:

-s   Suppresses the prompt

-v   Provides verbose output (shows the default options)

Check the syntax of the config file:

```
# testparm
Load smb config files from /etc/samba/smb.conf
Processing section "[company_data]"
Processing section "[printers]"
Loaded services file OK.
Server role: ROLE_STANDALONE
Press enter to see a dump of your service definitions

[global]
        workgroup = INET
        netbios name = RHEL01
        server string = My Samba Server
        log file = /var/log/samba/%m.log
        max log size = 50
        printcap name = /etc/printcap
        cups options = raw

[company_data]
        comment = Directory for all employees within the company
        path = /opt/company_data
        valid users = user01
        read only = No
```

```
[printers]
        comment = All Printers
        path = /var/spool/samba
        printable = Yes
        browseable = No
```

There are no errors in the output shown here, but you can see the global options displayed, including the different shares that are accessible to users. Before you can start connecting clients, however, you also need to create Samba users because they are separate from system users. You can use the smbpasswd command to create a new Samba user.

Syntax: smbpasswd [options] [user]

Options:

-a	Adds a user
-d	Disables a user
-e	Enables a user
-x	Deletes a user

WARNING: Because you have specified to use the tdbsm back end, any user that you want to create for Samba must have an account locally on the Samba server.

MIGRATION TIP

For legacy purposes, you can specify smbpasswd as a back-end storage choice. If you do this, all username/password combinations are stored in the /etc/samba/smbpasswd file.

Step 1.   Create your first Samba user:

```
# smbpasswd -a user01
New SMB password:
Retype new SMB password:
Added user user01.
```

Step 2.   Verify that the user was created successfully by using the pdbedit command:

```
# pdbedit -w -L
user01:501:XXXXXXXXXXXXXXXXXXXXXXXXXXXXXXXXX:17601CAE62CBC5D649CF7D1
951C42806:[
U          ]:LCT-4D498DE8:
```

EXAM TIP

Whenever you make changes to the Samba users, you need to restart the service before you are able to use them.

At this point, everything should be in place for your Samba server. You just need to make sure that the directories you specified to be a Samba share exist (yours does because you created /opt/company_data back in Chapter 4, "File Systems and Such").

Step 1.   If you haven't done so already, start the Samba service:

```
# service smb start
Starting SMB services:                                      [  OK  ]
```

Step 2.   Verify that the service is running:

```
# service smb status
smbd (pid  3145) is running...
SELinux and Firewall Configuration
```

If you are accustomed to Windows systems, you should already know what ports you need to open on the firewall.

Step 1.   Use the iptables command to create your firewall rules:

```
# iptables -I INPUT 5 -p tcp -m tcp --dport 137 -j ACCEPT
# iptables -I INPUT 5 -p udp -m udp --dport 138 -j ACCEPT
# iptables -I INPUT 5 -p udp -m udp --dport 139 -j ACCEPT
# iptables -I INPUT 5 -p tcp -m tcp --dport 445 -j ACCEPT
```

Step 2.   Save the rules you just created:

```
# service iptables save
Saving firewall rules to /etc/sysconfig/iptables:           [  OK  ]
```

Step 3.   Restart the firewall service for the changes to take effect:

```
# service iptables restart
iptables: Flushing firewall rules:                          [  OK  ]
iptables: Setting chains to policy ACCEPT: filter           [  OK  ]
iptables: Unloading modules:                                [  OK  ]
iptables: Applying firewall rules:                          [  OK  ]
```

These four ports are very common to Windows administrators, as they are heavily used in Windows environments. Next, you need to deal with the SELinux protection for the Samba service. Due to the complexities of Samba and its integration with Windows, there are quite a few different Boolean values that you need to change. Table 16-1 shows the Booleans available for Samba.

Table 16-1   SELinux Booleans

Booleans	Description
samba_domain_controller	Allows Samba to act as the domain controller, add users and groups, and change passwords.
samba_enable_home_dirs	Allows Samba to share users' home directories.
samba_export_all_ro	Allows Samba to share any file/directory as read-only.
samba_export_all_rw	Allows Samba to share any file/directory as read/write.
use_samba_home_dirs	Supports Samba home directories.
samba_create_home_dirs	Allows Samba to create new home directories (via PAM, for example).
allow_smbd_anon_write	Allows Samba to modify public files used for public file transfer services. Files/directories must be labeled public_content_rw_t.
samba_share_fusefs	Allows Samba to export ntfs/fusefs volumes.
samba_share_nfs	Allows Samba to export NFS volumes.
samba_run_unconfined	Allows Samba to run unconfined scripts.
virt_use_samba	Allows virt to manage CIFS files.

Step 1.   Query for available Boolean options:

```
# getsebool -a | egrep '(samba)|(smb)|(nmb)|(win)'
allow_httpd_mod_auth_ntlm_winbind --> off
allow_smbd_anon_write --> off
samba_create_home_dirs --> off
samba_domain_controller --> off
samba_enable_home_dirs --> off
samba_export_all_ro --> off
samba_export_all_rw --> off
samba_run_unconfined --> off
samba_share_fusefs --> off
samba_share_nfs --> off
use_samba_home_dirs --> off
virt_use_samba --> off
wine_mmap_zero_ignore --> off
```

Step 2.   You need to change only a few settings for the shares to work properly:

```
# setsebool -P samba_export_all_ro=1 samba_export_all_rw=1
```

Step 3.   Verify that the changes have been made:

```
# getsebool -a | egrep '(samba)|(smb)|(nmb)|(win)'
allow_httpd_mod_auth_ntlm_winbind --> off
```

```
allow_smbd_anon_write --> off
samba_create_home_dirs --> off
samba_domain_controller --> off
samba_enable_home_dirs --> off
samba_export_all_ro --> on
samba_export_all_rw --> on
samba_run_unconfined --> off
samba_share_fusefs --> off
samba_share_nfs --> off
use_samba_home_dirs --> off
virt_use_samba --> off
wine_mmap_zero_ignore --> off
```

MIGRATION TIP

In RHEL5, you need to disable SELinux protection for Samba for it to work. Three daemons are protected, so three values need to be changed.

Step 1. Query for the Boolean values you need to change:

```
# getsebool -a | egrep '(smbd_dis)|(nmbd_dis)|(winbind_dis)'
nmbd_disable_trans --> off
smbd_disable_trans --> off
winbind_disable_trans --> off
```

Step 2. Disable the SELinux protection:

```
# setsebool -P nmbd_disable_trans=1 smbd_disable_trans=1
winbind_disable_trans=1
```

Step 3. Verify that the Boolean has changed:

```
# getsebool -a | egrep '(smbd_dis)|(nmbd_dis)|(winbind_dis)'
nmbd_disable_trans --> on
smbd_disable_trans --> on
winbind_disable_trans --> on
```

Don't forget that you can always look up the available Boolean options in the /selinux/booleans directory if you forget which options you need.

Another huge benefit with Samba is that if you read the comments in the main config file, it tells you which Boolean values need to be enabled for the different services that Samba can provide. When creating directories that you'd like to make into a Samba share, you can mark them as a Samba share with the correct SELinux context:

```
# chcon -Rt samba_share_t /opt/company_data
```

Now the directory is accessible to the Samba service.

Samba Security

This section on Samba security is probably one of the hardest and shortest sections in the book to write. Samba has so many different options and different configuration choices that it is hard to focus on just a subset of them. The /etc/samba/smb.conf file is heavily documented for different configuration choices. It is important that you read the requirements on the Red Hat exams to know what is required for the Samba configuration (share access restriction, viewable shares, etc). Make sure you spend time reading through the config file to familiarize yourself with the different options. We have already covered how to set up Samba shares and some of the options to restrict usage. You can also use firewall rules to allow or restrict access to other systems on the network.

Samba Clients

Now that all your Samba shares are set up, you can access them from one of the client systems (Client02). Be aware that you need to install the client Samba packages before you can connect to any Samba shares.

Step 1. Install the client packages:

```
# yum install -y samba-client samba-common
```

Step 2. Verify that the install was successful:

```
# rpm -qa | grep samba
samba-client-3.5.4-68.el6.x86_64
samba-winbind-clients-3.5.4-68.el6.x86_64
samba-common-3.5.4-68.el6.x86_64
```

Step 3. Create a local directory where you will mount your Samba share. For this example, make it the same as the Samba share directory to keep things simple:

```
# mkdir /opt/company_data
```

Using the smbclient command, you can now mount the Samba share.

Syntax: smbclient [options]

Options:

-L	Lists Samba shares
-U	Defines the user to connect with
-P	Defines the password to connect with
-A	Gets credentials from a file

Step 4.   List the Samba shares on the RHEL01 Samba server:

```
# smbclient -L 172.168.1.1 -U user01%<you password here>
Domain=[RHEL01] OS=[Unix] Server=[Samba 3.0.33-3.29.el5_5.1]

        Sharename       Type        Comment
        ---------       ----        -------
        company_data    Disk        Directory for all employees
within the
company
        IPC$            IPC         IPC Service (My Samba Server)
Domain=[INET] OS=[Unix] Server=[Samba 3.5.4-68.el6]

        Server                  Comment
        ---------               -------

        Workgroup               Master
        ---------               -------
        INET                    RHEL01
```

You can see here that the share named company_data is available for access. Recall from Chapter 4 that the mount command allows you to connect additional resources to the file system hierarchy. You can use the mount command here with the cifs option to mount the Samba share.

Step 5.   Mount the remote Samba share:

```
# mount.cifs //172.168.1.1/company_data /opt/test -o
username=user01,password=<password>
```

You can verify that the mount worked successfully by using the smbstatus command.

Syntax: smbstatus [options]

Options:

-p   Shows processes only

-v   Provides verbose output

-S   Shows shares only

-L   Shows locks only

Step 6.   Verify the mount was successful:

```
# smbstatus

Samba version 3.5.4-68.el6
PID     Username        Group           Machine
----------------------------------------------------------------
 3378   user01          user01          172.168.1.20 (172.168.1.20)

Service         pid     machine         Connected at
----------------------------------------------------------------
company_data    3378    172.168.1.20    Tue Oct 12 16:06:47 2010
```

```
No locked files
```

So far, you are doing well with the client being able to connect to the Samba server. You need to know that any share that is mounted without being added to the /etc/fstab file will be unmounted after the system is rebooted. To remedy this situation, you can create an entry in the /etc/fstab file.

Step 1.   Create an entry in the /etc/fstab file:

```
//172.168.1.1/company_data /opt/test cifs  user=user01,pass=
<password>      0 0
```

Can anyone find a problem with this entry? The problem here is that the username and password are exposed in clear-text for anyone to see. Another way that you can create an entry in the /etc/fstab file without exposing credentials is to put the credentials inside a file to be referenced from the /etc/fstab file.

Step 2.   Add the credentials that you'd like to use to a file:

```
# echo "username=user01" > /etc/samba/smbcred
# echo "password=password" >> /etc/samba/smbcred
```

EXAM TIP
Make sure to set the permissions of the /etc/samba/smbcred file properly.

Step 3.   Update the entry in the /etc/fstab file to reflect the changes to how the credentials are read:

```
//172.168.1.1/company_data /opt/test cifs
credentials=/etc/samba/smbcred 0 0
```

You can use the umount.cifs command to unmount the Samba share and reboot the system to make sure that the share mounts correctly when the system reboots.

Summary

Samba is great for being able to share files with Windows systems. It also can provide a good backup strategy for Windows domain controllers. This chapter showed some great benefits, such as being able to provide print services and Windows logon services. There is a lot of information to take in when learning to configure Samba. Luckily, the config file is heavily documented to help you along. In the next chapter, we look at FTP servers and clients.

Review Questions

1. What are the two types of back-end authentication mechanisms discussed in this chapter?

2. When you're creating a share, there is no option to make it browseable. True or False?

3. What does the `testparm` command do?

4. What command is used to create a user for Samba?

5. What command can you use to view mounted Samba shares?

6. Samba servers can serve files only to users. True or False?

Answers to the Review Questions

1. This chapter described `tdbsm` and `smbpasswd` back-end authentication.

2. False. The browseable option is available for each share.

3. The `testparm` command allows you to check for syntax errors in the /etc/samba/smb.conf file.

4. The `smbpasswd` command is used to create Samba users.

5. The `smbstatus` command shows you currently mounted Samba resources.

6. False. Samba servers can serve both files and printers to users.

Lab 16

Task 1 – Samba Shares

Step 1.   Set up a Samba server on RHEL02.

Step 2.   Create a share called /opt/temp_backup with the following settings:
   a. The share should be browseable.
   b. The share should not be writeable.
   c. Create a sample file called instructions inside the share.
The task is complete when the share is accessible from other systems on the network.

Task 2 – Boot Issues

Step 1.   On RHEL01, change the back-end authentication from tdbsm to
   smbpasswd.

Stop 2.   Ensure that all users are created in the new back-end authentication
   mechanism (passwords may be different if you don't remember them).

The task is complete when the authentication mechanisms have been changed successfully and users can access shares.

This chapter covers the following subjects:

- **File Transfer Protocol**—This section looks at how to share files using an FTP server.

- **FTP Security**—This section covers the security of FTP.

- **Troubleshooting FTP**—This section covers troubleshooting FTP services.

The following RHCSA exam objective is covered:

- Configure a system to run a default configuration FTP server

The following RHCE exam objectives are covered:

- Install the packages needed to provide the service

- Configure SELinux to support the service

- Configure the service to start when the system is booted

- Configure the service for basic operation

- Configure host-based and user-based security for the service

- Configure anonymous-only downloads

## CHAPTER 17

FTP

There are many different ways you can share files with users on your network. This capability is important because you don't always want your users storing things locally on their desktop or laptop. Should something happen to your end users' systems, they would lose all their work...not to mention that it would cause a backup strategy nightmare. An easier solution for management and security would be to store all your files in a centralized location. In this chapter, we look at File Transfer Protocol (FTP) and how it can be used to share files or provide them in an easy manner.

File Transfer Protocol

While we're on the topic of sharing files (we covered file sharing in Chapters 15, "NFS," and 16, "Samba"), let's finish out file sharing in this chapter by diving right into FTP. In my opinion, this is one of the easiest to use, most convenient, and yet completely insecure protocols (because it tends to be set up insecurely). With that being said, let's look at how these things hold true.

To transfer a file using the FTP protocol, a user must log in to an FTP server, which can be done with credentials or anonymously. When the user is connected, she can traverse the directory structure for any directory or file for which she has permissions. If the protocol is not configured properly, this can leave your entire system open to attack and make it hard to track if the attack is done through an anonymous connection!

The second big issue with the FTP protocol is that when the user logs in with a username and password, they are passed over the network in clear-text, meaning that anyone listening can see them.

So, why use the FTP protocol at all? It's easy to set up, and when used correctly, it's highly effective for delivering files to end users. Almost all major computer makers (HP, Dell, Apple) offer drivers for their systems over FTP, which allows for simple download by end users and organized structure on the back end for the drivers themselves.

Installing an FTP Server

In this chapter, we use the `vsftpd` package, which stands for Very Secure FTP Daemon. This particular FTP server offers additional features that make it a more secure choice if you have to use FTP. As with all services that you'd like to offer to your network users, you need to make sure that the appropriate packages are installed. Here's how.

Step 1.   Grab the required package:
```
# yum install -y vsftpd
```

Step 2.   When the installation is complete, verify it was installed successfully:
```
# rpm -qa | grep vsftpd
vsftpd-2.2.2-6.el6.x86_64
```

Step 3.   Ensure that the service will start on system boot:
```
# chkconfig vsftpd on
```

Step 4.   Verify the service starts on boot:
```
# chkconfig vsftpd --list
vsftpd          0:off   1:off   2:on    3:on    4:on    5:on    6:off
```

Configuring vsftp

To start the configuration of the FTP server, you need to look at the config file. For `vsftpd`, there is only one main config file; it's located at /etc/vsftpd/vsftpd.conf, which is where you configure the settings of the FTP server.

Step 1.   Look at which options are available in the config file:
```
# grep -v ^# vsftpd.conf
anonymous_enable=YES
local_enable=YES
write_enable=YES
local_umask=022
dirmessage_enable=YES
xferlog_enable=YES
connect_from_port_20=YES
xferlog_std_format=YES
listen=YES
pam_service_name=vsftpd
userlist_enable=YES
tcp_wrappers=YES
```

Step 2.   Now let's go over what each of these options can be used for:

`anonymous_enable=YES`   The default; sets security, although it should be changed to NO for better host-based security

`local_enable=YES`   Allows local users to log in

`write_enable=YES`	Enables users to write to directories
`local_umask=022`	Sets the umask for all uploaded files
`dirmessage_enable=YES`	Displays directory messages
`xferlog_enable=YES`	Logs all transfer activity to /var/log/xferlog
`connect_from_port_20=YES`	Forces port transfers to originate from port 20
`xferlog_std_format=YES`	Logs everything in standard transfer format
`listen=YES`	Allows the server to listen for connections
`pam_service_name-vsftpd`	Specifies the name used for the PAM service
`userlist_enable=YES`	Enables the service to consult user_list
`tcp_wrappers=YES`	Allows incoming requests based on the TCP Wrappers configuration
`userlist_deny=YES`	Enables users listed in user_list to log in via FTP

These default settings for the `vsftpd` service allow you to get off the ground running with the FTP service. At this point, any one of your system's users is able to log in to the `vsftpd` service, but because the firewall is enabled by default, the connection will be denied. Before you open the connection to your users, take some time to become familiar with the different options you can configure on your FTP server. The config file is heavily documented as to what each option does.

EXAM TIP
If you can't find or remember what a particular option does within the config file, you can also reference the man page for it during the exam. To access the config file man page, use this command:

```
# man vsftpd.conf
```
If you look through the man pages, you will notice that there are tons of options you can use to configure and lock down the `vsftpd` service, although the options you have set up already are good for basic usage. While only basic configuration is required for the exam, you can make this service a viable option to offer files or host projects for your users in a secure, centralized fashion.

EXAM TIP
When editing the config file, make sure you don't include any spaces between the option you're using and the value you're assigning it. This could cause an error during startup of the service.

Firewall and SELinux Configuration

Before you can begin using the FTP service, you need to make some firewall adjustments and SELinux changes. Let's start with the firewall rules. FTP uses both TCP ports 20 and 21, which you can open on the firewall.

Step 1.   Use the `iptables` command to create your firewall rules:

```
# iptables -I INPUT 5 -p tcp -m tcp —dport 20 -j ACCEPT

# iptables -I INPUT 5 -p tcp -m tcp —dport 21 -j ACCEPT
```

Step 2.   Save the rules you just created:

```
# service iptables save
Saving firewall rules to /etc/sysconfig/iptables:          [  OK  ]
```

Step 3.   Restart the firewall service for the changes to take effect:

```
# service iptables restart
iptables: Flushing firewall rules:                         [  OK  ]
iptables: Setting chains to policy ACCEPT: filter          [  OK  ]
iptables: Unloading modules:                               [  OK  ]
iptables: Applying firewall rules:                         [  OK  ]
```

Now that the firewall rules are taken care of, let's move on to SELinux.

REAL-WORLD TIP

It is possible to get your FTP server to interact over a single firewall port. This is possible because of the different ways that FTP functions (active versus passive), but because this isn't a requirement for the exams, we don't discuss it here.

Depending on what features you are trying to configure, you need to adjust SELinux accordingly. Table 17-1 presents the available options.

Table 17-1   SELinux Booleans

Booleans	Description
ftp_home_dir	Allows FTP to read and write files in the users' home directories.
allow_ftpd_full_access	Allows FTP servers to log in to local users and read/write all files on the system, governed by DAC.
allow_ftpd_use_nfs	Allows FTP servers to use NFS for public file transfer services.
allow_ftpd_anon_write	Allows FTP servers to upload files used for public file transfer services. Directories must be labeled public_content_rw_t.
ftpd_connect_db	Allows FTP servers to connect to the MySQL database.

Table 17-1   SELinux Booleans

Booleans	Description
allow_ftpd_use_cifs	Allows FTP servers to use CIFS for public file transfer services.
httpd_enable_ftp_server	Allows httpd to act as an FTP server by listening on the FTP port.

For now, let's enable the system users to have read/write access to the system.

Step 1.   Query for the Boolean value you need to change:

```
# getsebool -a | grep ftpd_full
allow_ftpd_full_access --> off
```

Step 2.   Disable the SELinux protection:

```
# setsebool -P allow_ftpd_full_access=1
```

Step 3.   Verify that the Boolean has changed:

```
# getsebool -a | grep ftpd_full
allow_ftpd_full_access --> off
```

If you need to enable additional features for your FTP server, make sure to disable SELinux protection for that feature.

MIGRATION TIP

In RHEL5, the FTP service needs to have SELinux protection disabled for it to run properly.

Step 1. Query for the Boolean value you need to change:

```
# getsebool -a | grep ftpd_dis
ftpd_disable_trans --> off
```

Step 2. Disable the SELinux protection:

```
# setsebool -P ftpd_disable_trans=1
```

Step 3. Verify that the Boolean has changed:

```
# getsebool -a | grep ftpd_dis
ftpd_disable_trans --> on
```

One of the features you need to be able to set up is anonymous access to your FTP server. For this feature to function properly, you need to make sure that you adjust the allow_ftpd_anon_write Boolean. This allows you to have anonymous users upload files. This capability can be dangerous because there is no way to track which user is uploading or writing files. It is recommended to leave this option disabled unless you know what you're doing.

Let's now shift focus to FTP host-based and user-based security.

FTP Security

After you configure SELinux properly for the vsftpd service, you also should configure some basic security. When dealing with security for FTP, you can run into a little trouble if you don't plan things out ahead of time.

The FTP protocol supports two different types of file transfers. The first is known as active mode, which uses port 20 to connect back to the client. The second is known as passive mode, which uses a custom-defined range of ports above 1024. Because there are two different modes for FTP, you need to decide which mode you want to use so that you can configure the correct security settings and open the correct ports on the firewall. Back in the configuration section, the option connect_from_port_20 is set to YES by default. This means that, by default, active mode is used for the vsftpd service.

Let's look at some other options that can be used for basic security. You can disable the anonymous_enable option to prevent nonauthorized users from accessing the FTP server. The local_enable option, which is enabled by default, allows local system users to log in to the FTP server. Keeping this option is usually safe option so that you don't need to maintain a second list of users that you want to be able to log in to the FTP server.

There is one other security step you should take for the FTP server. The userlist_enable option, which is set to YES by default, allows the vsftpd service to consult the /etc/vsftpd/user_list file. When this option is used in conjunction with the userlist_deny option, all users in this file are denied access to the server and not even prompted for a password. This prevents them from submitting clear-text passwords over the network. If you want to change this setting, however, you could set the userlist_deny option to NO. Then all users except for those listed in /etc/vsftpd/user_list are denied access. This setting is useful if you want only select individuals to be able to log in and not all your system users.

Here is what the file contains by default:

```
# cat user_list
# vsftpd userlist
# If userlist_deny=NO, only allow users in this file
# If userlist_deny=YES (default), never allow users in this file, and
# do not even prompt for a password.
# Note that the default vsftpd pam config also checks /etc/vsftpd/ftpusers
# for users that are denied.
```

```
root
bin
daemon
adm
lp
sync
shutdown
halt
mail
news
uucp
operator
games
nobody
```

As you can see, this file can get very confusing with options quickly, which is why you should plan out ahead of time what you want your FTP server policy to be.

REAL-WORLD TIP

The file called /etc/vsftpd/ftpusers denies access to log in to the FTP server no matter what. A few system users are populated in this file when the vsftpd service is installed. If you want to ban a user, you can use this file. The difference is that users in this file are not allowed to log in but still receive a login and password prompt allowing them to submit their credentials over the network in clear-text.

REAL-WORLD TIP

If you'd like to control user security through the use of PAM modules, vsftpd comes with /etc/pam.d/vsftpd. This file defines the requirements that a user must meet to log in to the FTP server.

For additional security, the vsftpd service supports the use of TCP Wrappers, which can be used for access control. Although you don't need to configure TCP Wrappers for the server in this lab, it is good to know that the service supports it.

Troubleshooting FTP

Now that the setup is complete, you need to test the FTP server from one of the clients, Client01. To save time during the exam and when testing in the real world, you can use the command-line FTP client lftp. This command includes many features for quick testing and verification that the FTP server is functioning properly.

Step 1.   Install the lftp package on the Client01 system:

```
# yum install -y lftp
```

Step 2.   Verify the installation of the lftp package:

```
# rpm -qa | grep lftp
lftp-4.0.9-1.el6.x86_64
```

Step 3.   On the Client01 system, you can connect to RHEL01:

```
# lftp 172.168.1.1 -u user01
```

You are prompted for your password, and then you have FTP access to the server. From here, you can upload and download files using standard FTP commands.

If you're having trouble getting the FTP server to function properly, there is a process you can follow to help narrow down where the trouble is. First, disable the firewall and SELinux. Next, you can check the config files to make sure that everything is set properly (don't forget that there should be no spaces between options and values). Next, restart the service and check to see whether you can connect. Verify that you are allowed to log in and not blocking the user you are testing with in the user_list or ftpusers files. When the server is functioning properly, add back the firewall (with the correct rules, of course). If the service suddenly stops working, you have a firewall issue, which usually translates to a port not being opened. When the service is functioning again with the firewall, add back SELinux for a final verification.

Summary

File sharing makes life a lot easier when you don't have files all over the place. Centralized file storage also helps when it comes to security and auditing. Knowing how to work with file sharing services is a big part of collaboration in the workplace. Users always need a place to put their files, and security is always a growing concern. Make sure that you try to plan ahead for growth of file servers, and from time to time, test their security. Make sure you are comfortable troubleshooting and configuring FTP servers and verifying that your clients can connect.

Review Questions

1. What is the name of the package used to install an FTP?

2. What command can be used to easily list all the options in the FTP main config file?

3. What option is used to allow anonymous uploads to the FTP server?

4. What two ports should be opened on the firewall for the FTP server to function properly?

5. What is the /etc/vsftpd/user_list file used for?

6. What client-side command can you use to test your FTP server connection?

7. FTP is one of three protocols that can be used for kickstart and/or network installs. True or False?

Answers to Review Questions

1. The vsftpd package is used to install an FTP server.

2. The grep -v ^# /etc/vsftpd/vsftpd.conf command shows you all the options currently being used with the FTP server.

3. The anonymous_enable=YES option in the main config file allows anonymous uploads.

4. You must open TCP ports 20 and 21 for the FTP server to function properly.

5. The user_list file can be used to limit which users have access to the FTP server.

6. The lftp command can be used on a client to test FTP server connections.

7. True. FTP is one of three protocols used for kickstart and/or network installs. The other two protocols are NFS and HTTP.

Lab 17

Task 1 – Anonymous FTP

Step 1.   On RHEL02, set up an anonymous FTP server.

Step 2.   Copy all files from the /opt directory on RHEL01 to the FTP server on RHEL02.

The task is complete when the FTP server on RHEL02 contains all the files from the /opt directory on RHEL01.

Task 2 – Secure FTP

Step 1.   Set up an FTP server on RHEL01.

Step 2.   Allow FTP access to the /home directory for all users on RHEL01.

Step 3.   Ensure access from all other users on other systems in the lab is denied.

The task is complete when the FTP server is set up correctly.

This chapter covers the following subjects:

- **Setting Up BIND**—This section covers how to set up a DNS server.

- **Configuring a DNS Server**—This section walks through the configuration of different types of DNS servers.

- **DNS Utilities and Troubleshooting**—This section covers the different utilities used to configure and troubleshoot a DNS server.

- **BIND Security**—Nothing is more important than securing a service, so this section covers all the details of DNS security.

The following RHCE exam objectives are covered:

- Install the packages needed to provide the service

- Configure SELinux to support the service

- Configure the service to start when the system is booted

- Configure the service for basic operation

- Configure host-based and user-based security for the service

- Configure a caching-only nameserver

- Configure a caching-only nameserver to forward DNS queries (forwarding server)

## CHAPTER 18

DNS

When you're trying to access a website, you type in the name you are looking for and it comes up. In the background, though, Domain Name Service (DNS) is what translates that website name into an IP address so that the site may be accessed. This translation also occurs when you are connecting to other systems on your network through their hostnames instead of their IP addresses. DNS plays a critical role not only in your networks, but also on the Internet as a whole. Knowing how to set up, maintain, and troubleshoot such a server is vital to any network. The root DNS servers for the world run BIND as their DNS software choice, so naturally Red Hat also includes it on the exams. This chapter covers BIND in great detail because it is such a critical network component.

Setting Up BIND

Just as with any other service, you need to install the packages for BIND first.

Step 1. Install the required packages:
```
# yum install -y bind bind-utils bind-libs
```

Step 2. Verify that the packages have been installed:
```
# rpm -qa | grep ^bind
bind-utils-9.7.0-5.P2.el6.x86_64
bind-9.7.0-5.P2.el6.x86_64
bind-libs-9.7.0-5.P2.el6.x86_64
```

Step 3. Ensure that the service is set to start on system boot:
```
# chkconfig named on
```

Step 4. Verify that the service is set to start on boot:
```
# chkconfig --list named
named        0:off   1:off   2:on   3:on   4:on   5:on   6:off
```

At this point, you need to decide what type of DNS server you would like to set up. According to Red Hat, there are two types of nameservers:

- **Authoritative**—These nameservers answer to resource records that are part of their zones only. This includes both primary (master) and secondary (slave) nameservers.

- **Recursive**—These nameservers offer resolution services but are not authoritative for any zone. All query answers are cached in memory for a fixed period of time.

There is another way you can classify nameservers:

- **Master**—This nameserver stores original and authoritative zone records for a particular namespace. It also answers queries about the namespace from other nameservers. Each domain must have at least one master.

- **Slave**—Although this nameserver receives its namespace information from a master nameserver, this nameserver type can answer queries for which it has authority. Used for load balancing and redundancy.

- **Caching**—This nameserver has no authority and is primarily used for name-to-IP resolution. All resolutions are cached for a fixed period of time. Heavily used by Internet service providers (ISPs).

- **Forwarding**—This nameserver has no authority and is used only to forward requests to specific nameservers for resolution.

Each domain for which your server has authority is called a *zone* and the information for that zone in kept in....wait for it...*zone files*. The caching DNS server requires an additional package to be installed, so let's start by setting up a master DNS server and its zone first. Each zone file also requires that you use the fully qualified domain name (FQDN) when defining hostnames. Although we usually address the configuration first, let's look at the SELinux and firewall requirements instead because the configuration of BIND can become complex.

Firewall and SELinux Configuration

For your clients to be able to query the DNS server, you need to open a single port on the firewall, but for both protocols. The DNS clients can use both TCP and UDP port 53.

Step 1. Use the `iptables` command to create your firewall rules:

```
# iptables -I INPUT 5 -p udp -m udp --dport 53 -j ACCEPT
# iptables -I INPUT 5 -p tcp -m tcp --dport 53 -j ACCEPT
```

Step 2. Save the rules you just created:

```
# service iptables save
Saving firewall rules to /etc/sysconfig/iptables:          [  OK  ]
```

Step 3.   Restart the firewall service for the changes to take effect:

```
# service iptables restart
iptables: Flushing firewall rules:                        [  OK  ]
iptables: Setting chains to policy ACCEPT: filter         [  OK  ]
iptables: Unloading modules:                              [  OK  ]
iptables: Applying firewall rules:                        [  OK  ]
```

For the DNS server, there is only a single SELinux Boolean value that you can change:

`named_write_master_zones`   Allows master zone files to be written

If you would like to have a dynamic DNS server or allow zone file transfers, you need to disable this value; otherwise, you can leave the default protection as is.

MIGRATION TIP

In RHEL5, an additional SELinux Boolean provides protection to the DNS service. You need to adjust it for the DNS service to work properly.

Step 1.   Query for the Boolean value you need to change:

```
# getsebool -a | grep named_dis
named_disable_trans --> off
```

Step 2.   Disable the SELinux protection:

```
# setsebool -P named_disable_trans=1
```

Step 3.   Verify that the Boolean has changed:

```
# getsebool -a | grep named_dis
named_disable_trans --> on
```

TIP: For additional security, you can set SELinux to allow only the named system user to be able to read the /etc/named.conf file. This ensures additional security should you need it. To allow only the named user to be able to read the /etc/named.conf file, use the following command:

```
# chcon -t named_conf_t /etc/named.conf
```

Verify with this command:

```
# ls -Z /etc | grep named.conf
```

Configuring a DNS Server

To begin configuring the DNS server, check out these key config files for a BIND server:

/etc/named.conf	Main config file
/etc/rndc.key	Key file
/etc/rndc.conf	Key config file
/usr/share/doc/bind-9*/sample	Directory that holds sample files

Before you do anything, you should make a backup of the /etc/named.conf file:

```
# cp /etc/named.conf /etc/named.conf.orig
```

You should also remove this file for now because you will be making a new one in the coming sections:

```
# rm /etc/named.conf
```

MIGRATION TIP

For RHEL5 users, the /etc/named.conf file *does not* exist by default, so you don't need to worry about backing it up or removing it.

The first step for configuration is to make sure that your system has a static IP address and that the /etc/resolv.conf file is pointing to localhost as the nameserver:

Step 1. Verify that the localhost is used for DNS queries on RHEL01:

```
# cat /etc/resolv.conf
search example.com
nameserver 127.0.0.1
nameserver 192.168.1.1
```

The secondary server listed here is actually my personal router, which can provide DNS as well. Before going any further, you should also understand the different types of resource records used with DNS and why each one is important.

A	Maps the hostname to an IP address
NS	Contains the IP address or CNAME of the nameserver
MX	Defines where mail for a particular domain goes
PTR	Maps the IP address to a hostname
SOA	Contains general administrative control for the domain
CNAME	Used as an alias

There are four different DNS server types, so let's start with the configuration of each one.

Master Server

A master server is the basis for the DNS infrastructure. It provides a place to define all DNS records and extend them to secondary servers that can help with load balancing and redundancy. For this master server configuration, you need to create a new /etc/named.conf file. You can use the sample /etc/named.conf file to get started. Here is what the named.conf looks like:

```
/* Global options for the BIND Server */
options
{

        directory "/var/named"; // the default
        dump-file              "data/cache_dump.db";
        statistics-file        "data/named_stats.txt";
        memstatistics-file     "data/named_mem_stats.txt";

};

/* Logging options so you know where your logs are going */
logging
{
        channel default_debug {
                file "data/named.run";
                severity dynamic;
        };
};

/* Our sample domain is example.com defined here */
zone "example.com" {
        type master;
        file "example.com.zone";
        allow-update { none; };
};

/* This is a reverse lookup for our subnet 172.168.1.0/24 */
zone "1.168.172.in-addr.arpa" {
        type master;
        file "example.com.revzone";
        allow-update { none; };
};

/* File containing root hints (points directly to root DNS servers) */
```

```
zone "." IN {
        type hint;
        file "named.ca";
};

/* The zone file for our localhost (good for troubleshooting) */
zone "localhost." IN {
        type master;
        file "named.localhost";
        allow-update { none; };
};

/* The reverse lookup zone for our localhost (good for troubleshooting) */
zone "0.0.127.in-addr.arpa." IN {
        type master;
        file "named.loopback";
        allow-update { none; };
};
```

MIGRATION TIP

The /var/named directory in RHEL6 is no longer writable (it was writable in RHEL5). If you have a zone file or reverse zone file that needs to be written to, you should store it in /var/named/dynamic.

WARNING: In the sample template here, the zone files are kept in /var/named, but in the real world, these files should actually exist in /var/named/dynamic. If you run into write errors on RHEL6, you should move your zone and reverse zone files into the /var/named/dynamic directory and update your /etc/named.conf file to reflect the changes.

The comments included here should make this config file self-explanatory. Take particular notice of the `logging` section. The locations defined here specify where your log files go for BIND (however, some information is also logged to /var/log/messages). This information is extremely helpful for troubleshooting should the DNS server not work properly. You can change the logging options for more or less information, but it is set up here to initially include enough information for someone to be able to know exactly what is going on. Now that you have an /etc/named.conf file, you need to create the zone and reverse zone files.

In the /var/named directory, you can set up the following example.com.zone file:

```
# nano example.com.zone
;
; Zone file for example.com
```

```
;
$TTL    86400

@       IN  SOA   rhel01.example.com. root.example.com. (
                  2010120710        ; Serial
                  1d                ; refresh
                  2h                ; retry
                  4w                ; expire
                  1h )              ; min cache


@               IN   NS   rhel01.example.com.
@               IN   A    172.168.1.1


;
; Network Hosts
;

rhel01      IN  A    172.168.1.1
rhel02      IN  A    172.168.1.2
client01    IN  A    172.168.1.10
client02    IN  A    172.168.1.20
```

There are a few issues to make note of here. First, notice that when defining the domain, you put a dot (.) at the end of each FQDN. The root.example.com is the email address of the administrator for the DNS server, which is defined here without an at sign (@). In the middle of the file, you create two entries for this server, making it the primary nameserver for this domain. Now if a client were to ping the domain name or the server's hostname (RHEL01), it would respond because it is the primary nameserver. The last few lines define the clients and their IP addresses (notice that these hostnames are not FQDNs).

Let's now look at the reverse zone file that will allow the DNS server to map IP addresses to hostnames. Again, you can work with the sample provided here:

```
# nano /var/named/example.com.revzone
;
; Reverse Zone file for example.com
;
$TTL    86400

@       IN  SOA   rhel01.example.com. root.example.com. (
                  2010120710        ; Serial
                  1d                ; refresh
                  2h                ; retry
                  4w                ; expire
                  1h )              ; min cache
```

```
@                IN  NS  rhel01.example.com.

;
; Network Hosts
;

1   IN  PTR    rhel01.example.com.
2   IN  PTR    rhel02.example.com.
10  IN  PTR    client01.example.com.
20  IN  PTR    client02.example.com.
```

This file looks almost the same as the forward zone except that instead of A records there are PTR records. The number you see for each client is actually the number in the fourth octet of the IP address (2 correlates to 172.168.1.2). After each PTR definition, you specify the FQDN.

At this point, you still need three files. Two are for the localhost zone and one is the root hints file. On RHEL6, these files are all provided for you in the /var/named directory by default, making the configuration process much easier.

MIGRATION TIP

If you are still on RHEL5, the last three files you need are also provided as samples, but they are each named differently. Here is a breakdown of how you can add the required files.

First, you add the named.localhost file to the /var/named directory. You grab this from one of the provided samples:

```
# cp /usr/share/doc/bind-9.7.0/sample/var/named/localhost.zone
/var/named/named.localhost
```

Next, you need to provide the reverse zone file for the localhost. For this file, you just copy it over from the samples provided:

```
# cp /usr/share/doc/bind-9.3.6/sample/var/named/named.local
/var/named/named.loopback
```

Finally, you need to create the root hints file. You also copy this over from the samples provided:

```
# cp /usr/share/doc/bind-9.3.6/sample/var/named/named.root /var/named/named.ca
```

Everything is now in place for you to begin using your DNS server. Before starting the service, however, make sure that the config files don't have any syntax errors.

Step 1.   You can use the configtest option of the named command to accomplish this:

```
# service named configtest
```

```
zone localhost/IN: loaded serial 42
zone 0.0.127.in-addr.arpa/IN: loaded serial 2010120710
zone example.com/IN: loaded serial 2010120711
zone 1.168.172.in-addr.arpa/IN: loaded serial 2010120710
```

Step 2.   Because no errors are displayed, you can start the service:

```
# service named start
Starting named:                                          [  OK  ]
```

REAL-WORLD TIP

Don't forget that to allow zone transfers or zone files to be written, you need to change the value of the named_write_master_zones Boolean.

At this point, you should have a fully functional master DNS server. Although you aren't required to know how to set up a master DNS server for the Red Hat exams, this task is commonly performed in the real world. The master DNS server is only the first of four, so let's move on to the second type: a slave DNS server.

Slave Server

A slave DNS server is similar to a master DNS server. It can help with load balancing and provide redundancy should the master DNS server fail. Because it serves as a "secondary" DNS server, it actually pulls the necessary files from its master counterpart, making configuration of a slave DNS server quite easy. Because the slave server pulls all the DNS records from the master, you need to set up the slave DNS server on RHEL02.

NOTE: On RHEL02, you need to install the BIND packages, make a backup of the /etc/named.conf file, and copy the following template.

When you have RHEL02 set up, you can use the following template for your /etc/named.conf file:

```
/* Global options for the BIND Server */
options
{

        directory "/var/named"; // the default
        dump-file               "data/cache_dump.db";
        statistics-file         "data/named_stats.txt";
        memstatistics-file      "data/named_mem_stats.txt";


};
```

```
/* Logging options so you know where your logs are going */
logging
{
        channel default_debug {
                file "data/named.run";
                severity dynamic;
        };
};

/* Our sample domain is example.com defined here */
zone "example.com" {
        type slave;
        file "slaves/example.com.zone";
        masters { 172.168.1.1; };
};

/* This is a reverse lookup for our subnet 172.168.1.0/24 */
zone "1.168.172.in-addr.arpa" {
        type slave;
        file "slaves/example.com.revzone";
        masters { 172.168.1.1; };
};

/* File containing root hints (points directly to root DNS servers) */
zone "." IN {
        type hint;
        file "named.root";
};

/* The zone file for our localhost (good for troubleshooting) */
zone "localhost." IN {
        type master;
        file "localhost.zone";
        allow-update { none; };
};

/* The reverse lookup zone for our localhost (again good for troubleshooting) */
zone "0.0.127.in-addr.arpa." IN {
        type master;
        file "named.local";
        allow-update { none; };
};
```

Because the slave server can provide redundancy or load balancing, its /etc/named.conf is similar to that of the master DNS server. The difference here, though, is that the slave server doesn't actually need the zone files to exist. You can see here that you define a masters option, which is actually the master DNS server. The slave DNS server will periodically check with the master DNS server, pull down the data for a zone, and create the zone file if it doesn't exist. The slave zone files exist in the /var/named/slaves directory.

> **NOTE:**   Make sure that your named.ca, named.localhost, and named.loopback files are in place on RHEL02.

Step 1.   With the files in place, you can check for syntax errors:

```
# service named configtest
zone localhost/IN: loaded serial 42
zone 0.0.127.in-addr.arpa/IN: loaded serial 1997022700
```

Step 2.   Start the named service:

```
# service named start
Starting named:                                         [  OK  ]
```

Step 3.   Check the /var/named/slaves directory to see if the zone files copied over from the master DNS server correctly:

```
# ls /var/named/slaves
example.com.revzone   example.com.zone
```

You can manually pull the zone files from the master DNS server by using the dig command to perform a zone transfer. We look at the full syntax of the dig command later, but here you can see how to manually transfer a zone file:

```
# dig -t axfr example.com @rhel01

; <<>> DiG 9.3.6-P1-RedHat-9.3.6-4.P1.el5 <<>> @rhel01 example.com axfr
; (1 server found)
;; global options: printcmd
example.com.            86400   IN      SOA     rhel01.example.com.
root.example.com. 2010120711 86400 7200 2419200 3600
example.com.            86400   IN      NS      rhel01.example.com.
example.com.            86400   IN      A       172.168.1.1
client02.example.com.   86400   IN      A       172.168.1.20
client01.example.com.   86400   IN      A       172.168.1.10
rhel02.example.com.     86400   IN      A       172.168.1.2
rhel01.example.com.     86400   IN      A       172.168.1.1
example.com.            86400   IN      SOA     rhel01.example.com.
root.example.com. 2010120711 86400 7200 2419200 3600
;; Query time: 50 msec
;; SERVER: 172.168.1.1#53(172.168.1.1)
```

```
;; WHEN: Tue Feb  1 10:21:25 2011
;; XFR size: 8 records (messages 1)
```

If you get any errors, the slave DNS server is not able to pull the zone files from the master DNS server until the errors are resolved. In the "DNS Utilities and Troubleshooting" section later, you see how to resolve any errors that are thrown here.

Caching-Only Server

The setup of a name caching-only server is a little different from what you have done already. The first thing we mentioned before starting any configuration is that you back up the original /etc/named.conf file (RHEL6 only). This original /etc/named.conf file is actually a sample named.conf file for name caching-only DNS servers! On RHEL01 again, make a backup of any current named.conf file:

```
# cp /etc/named.conf /etc/named.conf.bk
```

Restore the original named.conf file:

```
# mv /etc/named.conf.orig /etc/named.conf
```

TIP: If you are on RHEL5, you need to install an additional package to get the caching-only nameserver config files.

Step 1. Install the required package:

```
# yum install -y caching-nameserver
```

Step 2. As with all installs, verify:

```
# rpm -qa | grep caching
caching-nameserver-9.3.6-4.P1.el5_4.2
```

Step 3. Copy the sample file:

```
# cp /etc/named.caching-nameserver.conf /etc/named.conf
```

Use the following as your caching-only nameserver /etc/named.conf config file:

```
/* General options for our caching-only name server */
options {
        listen-on port 53 { 127.0.0.1; };
        listen-on-v6 port 53 { ::1; };
        directory       "/var/named";
        dump-file       "/var/named/data/cache_dump.db";
        statistics-file "/var/named/data/named_stats.txt";
        memstatistics-file "/var/named/data/named_mem_stats.txt";
        allow-query     { localhost; };
        recursion yes;
};
```

```
/* Logging options so you know where your logs are going */
logging
{
        channel default_debug {
                file "data/named.run";
                severity dynamic;
        };
};


/* This view statement forces cached lookups only */
zone "." IN {
        type hint;
        file "named.ca";
};


include "/etc/named.rfc1912.zones";
```

Make sure to save this file as named.conf and ensure it is in the /etc/directory.
For a caching-only nameserver, there is only one other file you need:
/etc/named.rfc.1912.zones (as defined in the sample file). This file should
already exist by default in the /etc directory.

MIGRATION TIP

The /etc/named.rfc.1912.zones file is put in the /etc directory when you install the
caching-nameserver package.

The named.rfc.1912.zones file looks for the named.localhost and named.loopback
files created earlier. It also looks for a named.empty file, which should already exist
in your /var/named directory.

MIGRATION TIP

The /etc/named.1912.zones file that is provided looks for different filenames as
pointed out in the "Master Server" section. Ensure that each file referenced by the
named.1912.zones file exists in /var/named; otherwise, you get errors when you try
to start the service.

Step 1.   When you have everything set up, make sure that you test the config file
for any errors:

```
# service named configtest
zone localhost/IN: loaded serial 42
zone 0.0.127.in-addr.arpa/IN: loaded serial 1997022700
```

Step 2.   Now you can start the service:

```
# service named start
Starting named:                                    [  OK  ]
```

> **WARNING:**   If you set up a caching-only nameserver, you should now switch your /etc/named.conf file back to the master DNS server configuration. The rest of this chapter deals with DNS security and troubleshooting assuming that you still have the master DNS server in place.

Forwarding-Only Server

A forwarding-only server does not actually handle any queries, but instead just forwards them to the correct location. This might be something you see if you work for an ISP that handles thousands of requests at a time. Forwarding-only servers are actually the easiest to set up because they require almost no configuration. In the named.conf file, let's set up the following section:

```
options {
    directory "/var/named";
    fowarders { 172.168.1.0/24; forward first; };
};
```

This section sends all queries to the first DNS server in the match-list and to the root DNS servers if no match is made. You also can specify `forward only` to check only the match-list servers and no root DNS server. If you don't include the directive, it defaults to `forward first`. If you are going to allow the query of root DNS servers, you must have the /var/named/named.ca file, which contains a list of root DNS servers. This is the entire setup required for a forwarding-only DNS server.

DNS Utilities and Troubleshooting

For the server and client, there are a handful of utilities you can use to verify the functionality of DNS. These utilities include

`dig`	DNS lookup utility
`host`	DNS lookup utility
`ping`	Network or hostname verification utility
`nslookup`	Utility to lookup a hostname from an IP addresses
`hostname`	Utility to sets or show the system hostname (FQDN)

Although four different types of DNS servers have been described up to this point, I'm going to assume you still have a master DNS server configured. For this reason, you can use your utilities to check the setup and configuration of the master DNS server to verify that everything is working properly. The most basic test after the DNS server has been set up properly is to ping the hostname of the nameserver and the domain itself. If both return a reply, your nameserver is querying properly.

Step 1.   Ping the hostname of the nameserver for your network—in this case, RHEL01:

```
# ping rhel01
PING rhel01.example.com (172.168.1.1) 56(84) bytes of data.
64 bytes from rhel01.example.com (172.168.1.1): icmp_seq=1 ttl=64
time=0.036
ms
64 bytes from rhel01.example.com (172.168.1.1): icmp_seq=2 ttl=64
time=0.020
ms

--- rhel01.example.com ping statistics ---
2 packets transmitted, 2 received, 0% packet loss, time 1001ms
rtt min/avg/max/mdev = 0.020/0.028/0.036/0.008 ms
```

Step 2.   Next, you can ping the domain name to ensure that the primary nameserver is again functioning properly:

```
# ping example.com
PING example.com (172.168.1.1) 56(84) bytes of data.
64 bytes from rhel01.example.com (172.168.1.1): icmp_seq=1 ttl=64
time=0.030
ms
64 bytes from rhel01.example.com (172.168.1.1): icmp_seq=2 ttl=64
time=0.020
ms

--- example.com ping statistics ---
2 packets transmitted, 2 received, 0% packet loss, time 1001ms
rtt min/avg/max/mdev = 0.020/0.028/0.036/0.008 ms
```

Another useful tool that can help test whether your DNS server is functioning properly is the host command.

Syntax: host [option] HOSTNAME

Options:

-l	Allows you to perform zone transfers
-r	Disables recursive processing
-t	Specifies the query type
-v	Provides verbose output

You can use this command for two simple purposes to ensure functionality.

Step 3.   First, perform a forward lookup to test the main zone file:

```
# host rhel01
rhel01.example.com has address 172.168.1.1
```

Step 4.   Second, perform a reverse lookup to test the reverse lookup zone file:

```
# host 172.168.1.1
1.1.168.172.in-addr.arpa domain name pointer rhel01.example.com.
```

If the results that you are expecting don't match what is displayed, or if the hostname or IP address can't be found, it is a good indication there is a problem with that particular zone file. This is a good way to test a few of the entries in each zone file to verify functionality of the DNS server. Aside from the host command, you can also use the nslookup command that offers slightly different information about lookups.

Step 5.   Query the domain name again:

```
# nslookup example.com
Server:        172.168.1.1
Address:       172.168.1.1#53

Name:  example.com
Address: 172.168.1.1
```

This time you see the nameserver for the example.com domain respond. This is a good way to find out which DNS server is responsible for a particular domain.

Step 6.   You can also use nslookup like the host command to perform forward lookups:

```
# nslookup rhel01
Server:        172.168.1.1
Address:       172.168.1.1#53

Name:  rhel01.example.com
Address: 172.168.1.1
```

Step 7.   Plus, you can use it to perform reverse lookups:

```
# nslookup 172.168.1.1
Server:        172.168.1.1
Address:       172.168.1.1#53

1.1.168.172.in-addr.arpa      name = rhel01.example.com.
```

Next, we look at a more in-depth utility: the dig command. The dig command offers you the most information when querying a domain or a particular host within the domain.

Syntax: dig [@global-server] [domain][q-type]

The q-type can be any type of resource record that you'd like to query. If you don't specify one, the dig command just queries information from the primary nameserver, showing the root hints. Let's look at how to use this utility for more information to troubleshoot the network.

Step 1. Do a forward lookup of your DNS server directly:

```
# dig @RHEL01

; <<>> DiG 9.3.6-P1-RedHat-9.3.6-4.P1.el5 <<>> @rhel01
; (1 server found)
;; global options: printcmd
;; Got answer:
;; ->>HEADER<<- opcode: QUERY, status: NOERROR, id: 10633
;; flags: qr rd ra; QUERY: 1, ANSWER: 13, AUTHORITY: 0, ADDITION-
AL: 14

;; QUESTION SECTION:
;.                               IN      NS

;; ANSWER SECTION:
.                       517028  IN      NS      g.root-servers.net.
.                       517028  IN      NS      h.root-servers.net.
.                       517028  IN      NS      i.root-servers.net.
.                       517028  IN      NS      j.root-servers.net.
.                       517028  IN      NS      k.root-servers.net.
.                       517028  IN      NS      l.root-servers.net.
.                       517028  IN      NS      m.root-servers.net.
.                       517028  IN      NS      a.root-servers.net.
.                       517028  IN      NS      b.root-servers.net.
.                       517028  IN      NS      c.root-servers.net.
.                       517028  IN      NS      d.root-servers.net.
.                       517028  IN      NS      e.root-servers.net.
.                       517028  IN      NS      f.root-servers.net.

;; ADDITIONAL SECTION:
a.root-servers.net.     517028  IN      A       198.41.0.4
a.root-servers.net.     517028  IN      AAAA    2001:503:ba3e::2:30
b.root-servers.net.     517028  IN      A       192.228.79.201
c.root-servers.net.     517028  IN      A       192.33.4.12
d.root-servers.net.     517028  IN      A       128.8.10.90
e.root-servers.net.     517028  IN      A       192.203.230.10
f.root-servers.net.     517028  IN      A       192.5.5.241
f.root-servers.net.     517028  IN      AAAA    2001:500:2f::f
g.root-servers.net.     517028  IN      A       192.112.36.4
h.root-servers.net.     517028  IN      A       128.63.2.53
h.root-servers.net.     517028  IN      AAAA
2001:500:1::803f:235
i.root-servers.net.     517028  IN      A       192.36.148.17
i.root-servers.net.     517028  IN      AAAA    2001:7fe::53
j.root-servers.net.     517028  IN      A       192.58.128.30

;; Query time: 12 msec
;; SERVER: 172.168.1.1#53(172.168.1.1)
;; WHEN: Tue Feb  1 10:13:23 2011
;; MSG SIZE  rcvd: 500
```

Step 2.   Do a forward lookup of your domain name:

```
# dig @RHEL01 example.com

; <<>> DiG 9.3.6-P1-RedHat-9.3.6-4.P1.el5 <<>> @rhel01 example.com
; (1 server found)
;; global options: printcmd
;; Got answer:
;; ->>HEADER<<- opcode: QUERY, status: NOERROR, id: 2847
;; flags: qr aa rd ra; QUERY: 1, ANSWER: 1, AUTHORITY: 1, ADDI-
TIONAL: 1

;; QUESTION SECTION:
;example.com.                    IN      A

;; ANSWER SECTION:
example.com.            86400    IN      A       172.168.1.1

;; AUTHORITY SECTION:
example.com.            86400    IN      NS
rhel01.example.com.

;; ADDITIONAL SECTION:
kickstart-01.example.com. 86400 IN      A       172.168.1.1

;; Query time: 11 msec
;; SERVER: 172.168.1.1#53(172.168.1.1)
;; WHEN: Tue Feb  1 10:13:36 2011
;; MSG SIZE  rcvd: 88
```

Step 3.   Also check the reverse lookup of your domain name:

```
# dig -x 1.168.172.in-addr.arpa

; <<>> DiG 9.3.6-P1-RedHat-9.3.6-4.P1.el5 <<>> -x 1.168.172.in-
addr.arpa
;; global options: printcmd
;; Got answer:
;; ->>HEADER<<- opcode: QUERY, status: NXDOMAIN, id: 51122
;; flags: qr rd ra; QUERY: 1, ANSWER: 0, AUTHORITY: 0, ADDITIONAL: 0

;; QUESTION SECTION:
;arpa.in-addr.172.168.1.in-addr.arpa. IN         PTR

;; Query time: 1584 msec
;; SERVER: 172.168.1.1#53(172.168.1.1)
;; WHEN: Tue Feb  1 10:19:46 2011
;; MSG SIZE  rcvd: 53
```

You might want to check whether your DNS server allows you to perform a zone transfer as well. If it does, make sure you restrict it to certain servers or clients only because the information it provides can allow someone to map out your entire network.

Step 4.   Test for zone transfer functionality:

```
# dig @RHEL01 example.com axfr


; <<>> DiG 9.3.6-P1-RedHat-9.3.6-4.P1.el5 <<>> @rhel01
example.com axfr
; (1 server found)
;; global options: printcmd
example.com.            86400    IN      SOA
rhel01.example.com.
root.example.com. 2010120711 86400 7200 2419200 3600
example.com.            86400    IN      NS
rhel01.example.com.
example.com.            86400    IN      A        172.168.1.1
client02.example.com.   86400    IN      A        172.168.1.20
client01.example.com.   86400    IN      A        172.168.1.10
rhel02.example.com.     86400    IN      A        172.168.1.2
rhel01.example.com.     86400    IN      A        172.168.1.1
example.com.            86400    IN      SOA
rhel01.example.com.
root.example.com. 2010120711 86400 7200 2419200 3600
;; Query time: 50 msec
;; SERVER: 172.168.1.1#53(172.168.1.1)
;; WHEN: Tue Feb  1 10:21:25 2011
;; XFR size: 8 records (messages 1)
```

Up to this point, you have been querying different hostnames and IP addresses, but what happens if different DNS servers return different information? You may have a problem with propagation between your servers. To fix this problem and make sure that all DNS servers are using the most updated information, increment the serial number on your master DNS server. Incrementing the serial number forces a replication of the DNS records and propagation to occur.

If you still haven't set up the FQDN for your system, you can use the hostname command to set it up.

Syntax: hostname [FQDN]

Step 1.   Query the current FQDN of your system:

```
# hostname
rhel01
```

Step 2.   If you want to change it, you can again use the hostname command, but specify the FQDN after the command:

```
# hostname rhel01.example.com
```

This changes your system's hostname to include the domain in the hostname. If you make any changes to the hostname, you should reboot your system before continuing. As a final troubleshooting step, make sure that your clients have the correct information located in the /etc/resolv.conf file. As discussed in Chapter 5, "Networking," this file is used by clients to query other systems on the network as well as which DNS servers to use as primary and secondary servers.

Step 3.   Change these DNS settings for Client01:

```
# cat /etc/resolv.conf
search example.com
nameserver 172.168.1.1
```

BIND Security

The BIND DNS server offers plenty of ways in which to make your DNS server more secure. When you are creating your /etc/named.conf file, there is a section where you can define options that you'd like to use with the server. I purposely left out some options at the beginning of this chapter so as to show the security they provide by adding them in. You can create a more refined list of hosts and subnets that you'd like to allow access to perform particular actions or tasks against your DNS server.

The first option you can use is listen-on, which defines the port and IP address(es) that your server will listen on. This limits the subnets on which the DNS server can be reached from. You can also use the allow-query option to limit which subnets even have access to the DNS server to begin with. A third option, allow-transfer, defines the slave servers that are allowed to query data from the master and transfer its zone file. This should not be allowed from any other host on your network.

Here is part of the /etc/named.conf file:

```
/* Global options for the BIND Server */
options
{

        listen-on port 53 { 127.0.0.1; 172.168.1.1; };
        allow-query { 127.0.0.1; 172.168.1.0/24; };

        allow-transfer { 172.168.1.2; };

        directory "/var/named"; // the default
        dump-file               "data/cache_dump.db";
        statistics-file         "data/named_stats.txt";
        memstatistics-file      "data/named_mem_stats.txt";

};
```

Although being able to query from any system on the network might seem convenient, it can become a huge pain to remember IP addresses and subnets that are all over your network. To help with this situation, BIND allows you to create an ACL that controls access and allows the use of a "name" instead of just IP addresses and subnets.

Step 1. Define an ACL directive:

```
acl "home-lab" { 127.0.0.1; 172.168.1.0/24; };
acl "local-srv" { 127.0.0.1; 172.168.1.1; };
acl "slave-srv" { 172.168.1.1; };
```

Now you can replace these directives within the /etc/named.conf file for easier use.

Now here is part of the /etc/named.conf file reworked:

```
/* Global options for the BIND Server */
options
{
        listen-on port 53 { local-srv; };
        allow-query { home-lab; };

        allow-transfer { slave-srv; };

        directory "/var/named"; // the default
        dump-file               "data/cache dump.db";
        statistics-file         "data/named_stats.txt";
        memstatistics-file      "data/named_mem_stats.txt";

};
```

Now that you have configured some additional options, you can move on to file ownership to help secure the BIND server. All the files should be owned by the named user, which runs as a system user.

Step 2. After you finish configuring all the files and zones you need, you can simply use the following two commands:

```
# chown root:named /etc/named/*
# chown root:named /var/named/*
```

All the files that relate to the BIND setup should now be owned correctly. To take it one step further, you could use an additional SELinux step to lock down the main config file. If you change the SELinux context of the main config file, only the named user is able to have access to it.

Step 3. To change the context, do the following:

```
# chcon -t named_conf_t named.conf
```

Another piece of BIND security that we discuss is using rndc for secure local management of your DNS server. Although it is included with the installation of the BIND package, you have to do a few things to set it up correctly. First, you need to include a line in your /etc/named.conf file. I again purposely left out this feature during the original configuration to highlight the additional security you get from it. In your /etc/named.conf file at the bottom, add the following two lines:

```
/* Authentication key file */
include "/etc/rndc.key";
```

Step 4.   Now you need to generate a secure key for the key file:

```
# dns-keygen
J991RthErgClGAjsGlQ52FSxXsNsdX98HWBxgq7q1Gr8wv2mrwmfWHGJW9tY
```

Step 5.   Insert the generated key into the /etc/rndc.key file:

```
# nano /etc/rndc.key
key "rndckey" {
        algorithm        hmac-md5;
        secret
"J991RthErgClGAjsGlQ52FSxXsNsdX98HWBxgq7q1Gr8wv2mrwmfWHGJW9tY";
};
```

Step 6.   You should also generate a config file for rndc as well:

```
# rndc-confgen > /etc/rndc.conf
```

This file contains some default settings for rndc, such as which IP address and port the rndc service should listen on.

Step 7.   Open the /etc/rndc.conf file and paste the key generated in step 4:

```
# nano /etc/rndc.conf
# Start of rndc.conf
key "rndckey" {
        algorithm hmac-md5;

        # This should be the key we generated in step 4
        secret
"J991RthErgClGAjsGlQ52FSxXsNsdX98HWBxgq7q1Gr8wv2mrwmfWHGJW9tY";
};

options {
        default-key "rndckey";
        default-server 127.0.0.1;
        default-port 953;
};

# End of rndc.conf

# Use with the following in named.conf, adjusting the allow list
as needed:
# key "rndckey" {
#       algorithm hmac-md5;
#       secret "QmnAAgdU3sUMGb3DXQ1gAw==";
# };
#
# controls {
#       inet 127.0.0.1 port 953
#                   allow { 127.0.0.1; } keys { "rndckey"; };
```

```
# };
# End of named.conf
```

Now your key in the /etc/rndc.conf file and the /etc/rndc.key file should match. To complete the setup of rndc, you also need to edit the /etc/named.conf file.

Step 8. Insert the following at the bottom of your /etc/named.conf file:

```
controls {
        inet 127.0.0.1 port 953
                allow { 127.0.0.1; } keys { "rndckey"; };
};

include "/etc/rndc.key";
```

The controls statement specifies which hosts or subnets are allowed to manage the DNS server through the rndc utility. The final line references the key file so that anyone trying to read the /etc/named.conf file won't see the secret key.

Step 9. Like the /etc/named.conf file, these two files that you have just created for rndc should be owned only by the named user:

```
# chown root:named /etc/rndc.*
```

Step 10. You should also limit the rndc files to be readable only by the root user:

```
# chmod 400 /etc/rndc.*
```

Step 11. While you're at it, also change the SELinux context for enhanced security:

```
# chcon -t named_conf_t rndc.key rndc.conf
```

Although rndc should now be set up, you need to create a firewall rule on port 953 for it to function properly (and for your clients to be able to connect and manage the DNS server).

Step 1. Use iptables to create the additional firewall rules:

```
# iptables -I INPUT 5 -p udp -m udp --dport 953 -j ACCEPT
```

Step 2. Save the firewall rules you just created:

```
# service iptables save
Saving firewall rules to /etc/sysconfig/iptables:          [  OK  ]
```

Step 3. Then restart the iptables service:

```
# service iptables restart
iptables: Flushing firewall rules:                         [  OK  ]
iptables: Setting chains to policy ACCEPT: filter          [  OK  ]
iptables: Unloading modules:                               [  OK  ]
iptables: Applying firewall rules:                         [  OK  ]
```

A few more bits of housekeeping finish this off.

Step 1.   Check the syntax of your config files:

```
# service named configtest
zone localhost/IN: loaded serial 42
zone 0.0.127.in-addr.arpa/IN: loaded serial 2010120710
zone example.com/IN: loaded serial 2010120711
zone 1.168.172.in-addr.arpa/IN: loaded serial 2010120710
```

Step 2.   Restart the named service:

```
# service named restart
Stopping named:                                      [  OK  ]
Starting named:                                      [  OK  ]
```

Step 3.   Verify the status of the rndc service:

```
# rndc status
number of zones: 4
debug level: 0
xfers running: 0
xfers deferred: 0
soa queries in progress: 0
query logging is OFF
recursive clients: 0/1000
tcp clients: 0/100
server is up and running
```

The last topic we discuss deals with BIND security in the chroot environment. This is quite possibly one of the best features that Linux has to offer. When you are installing select services that support chroot environments, you can actually install the software package within its own "container." The security benefit to this is that if the system ever becomes hacked, the attacker has access to only that one service within the container and not the rest of your system! BIND is one of the many great services that you can implement within a chroot environment. To accomplish this, you need to do two things. First, you need to install a special package for BIND to run within the chroot environment:

```
# yum install -y bind-chroot
```

Second, you need to edit the /etc/sysconfig/named directory and change it to a specific directory out of which you want to host BIND (such as /var/named/chroot). When this task is complete, you copy all your files and directories into the /var/named/chroot directory as if it were the root (/) directory. Your directory structure might look something like the following:

```
# tree /var/named/chroot/
/var/named/chroot/
|-- dev
|   |-- null
|   |-- random
|   `-- zero
```

```
|-- etc
|   `-- localtime
`-- var
    |-- named
    |   |-- data
    |   `-- slaves
    `-- run
        `-- named
```

As a special note, the only thing you don't put inside this directory structure is the rndc config file and key. You can actually just create a link to them from your true /etc/directory:

```
# ln -s /var/named/chroot/etc/rndc.conf /etc/rndc.conf
# ln -s /var/named/chroot/etc/rndc.key /etc/rndc.key
```

Summary

Working with DNS servers is never an easy topic. If you have never worked with them before, understanding the process of DNS queries and the setup to make them work correctly is even more difficult. BIND is quietly flexible, however, and is the most widely used implementation in the world.

This chapter covered four different types of DNS servers in detail and how to set them up. We also looked at security pertaining to DNS servers and troubleshooting any issues that come up. DNS servers play a big role in the network and are considered one of the critical parts of a network infrastructure in the real world. Make sure you understand the concepts as well as implementation because you will have to handle this, not just on the Red Hat exam, but also in the real world.

Review Questions

1. There are four types of DNS servers. Name them.

2. What is the difference between an A record and a PTR record?

3. A slave DNS server offers no additional benefits. True or False?

4. What is the rndc utility used for?

5. What command can you use to test the config files before starting the DNS service?

6. What three commands can you use to help verify that the DNS server is functioning properly?

7. What port must be opened on the firewall for DNS?

8. What does the `rdnc-confgen` command do?

9. What port does the `rndc` utility listen on by default?

Answers to the Review Questions

1. The four types of DNS servers are master, slave, caching-only, and forwarding.

2. An `A` record translates translated hostnames to IP addresses, and a `PTR` record works the other way around.

3. False. A slave DNS server provides load balancing and redundancy benefits.

4. The `rndc` utility provides a method for managing the DNS server remotely and securely.

5. `service named configtest`

6. The `dig`, `host`, and `ping` commands can be used to test DNS server functionality.

7. DNS uses port 53.

8. The `rdnc-confgen` command generates an rndc.conf file for the `rndc` utility.

9. By default, the `rndc` utility listens on port 953.

Lab 18

Task 1 – DNS

Step 1.   Open the GRUB config file in any text editor.

Step 2.   Add a new entry to the config file:
   a. The new entry should have the title Red Hat Recovery.
   b. The new entry should not be the default.
   c. The recovery entry should allow you to boot into recovery mode.

Step 3.   Change the timeout of the boot selection to 10 seconds.

The task is complete when the system boots with both entries in the GRUB menu and they both work correctly.

Task 2 – Boot Issues

Step 1.   Make sure you have your Red Hat installation CD available. Delete the /etc/inittab file and reboot the system.
   You will receive an error message that the system can't find the file.

Step 2.   Boot from the Red Hat installation CD into recovery mode.

Step 3.   Replace the file from the CD into the correct location on the system.

Step 4.   You may need to use the command `mount /dev/cd-rom /mnt` to access the CD drive.

The task is complete when the system boots up again.

This chapter covers the following subjects:

- **Xinetd: The Master Service**—This section covers the xinetd service and how it interacts with network services.

- **Dynamic Host Configuration Protocol (DHCP)**—This section covers the DHCP service and how to give out IP addresses.

- **Network Time Protocol (NTP)**—This section looks at the NTP protocol and how to keep the time on your network synced.

The following RHCE exam objectives are covered:

- Install the packages needed to provide the service

- Configure SELinux to support the service

- Configure the service to start when the system is booted

- Configure the service for basic operation

- Configure host-based and user-based security for the service

- Synchronize time using other NTP peers

## CHAPTER 19

Network Services

Need the time? How about an IP address for your client system? TFTP server? These are all network services that can be provided to different systems on your network. This chapter looks at the different network services that can be offered in Red Hat, including DHCP for IP addressing; NTP for time; and xinetd, which provides multiple services. These types of services are commonly found on many networks of different sizes. Each service plays a particular role in keeping the network functioning and servicing clients with different needs. Although xinetd, DHCP, and TFTP servers aren't explicitly defined on any of the Red Hat Exam Prep Guides, they are important pieces to a real-world network, which is why they are covered in this chapter.

Xinetd: The Master Service

As a system administrator, you will most likely need to provide your users with network and Internet services. These services may include FTP, HTTP, or Telnet. Although some software packages like Apache provide a single service (HTTP), there is also a master service called xinetd that can run multiple services at the same time. Although the Red Hat Exam Prep Guide doesn't specify any particular xinetd service, you may need it to configure basic services on the exam. It is also a widely used service in the real world, particularly when it comes to automating the installation of Red Hat. There are really only a few things that you need to know to be able to use the xinetd service. This package doesn't always come installed by default, so first let's install it.

Step 1. Install the xinetd package:

```
# yum install -y xinetd
```

Step 2. Verify that the package is installed correctly:

```
# rpm -qa | grep xinetd
xinetd-2.3.14-29.el6.x86_64
```

With the service installed, you can shift your focus to the config files. The xinetd service has a master config file (/etc/xinetd.conf), which inherits all the settings of the services that it controls. Aside from this master config file, a single directory (/etc/xinetd.d) contains individual config files for each service you would like xinetd to run. As an example, let's set up a TFTP server, which can be used to back up config files for Cisco switches or to deliver data to clients during a PXE boot process (also known as a network installation). We looked at PXE boot earlier in Chapter8, "Network Installs." To get started, you just need to install the TFTP server package.

Step 3.   Install the required package:

```
# yum install -y tftp-server
```

Step 4.   Verify that the package is installed correctly:

```
# rpm -qa | grep tftp
tftp-server-0.49-5.1.el6.x86_64
```

Now that the package is installed, you can go into the /etc/xinetd.d directory and see the config file for the new service. By default, the TFTP service is disabled. Let's look at the config file, which is small and simple to understand.

```
# cat /etc/xinetd.d/tftp
service tftp
{
        socket_type             = dgram
        protocol                = udp
        wait                    = yes
        user                    = root
        server                  = /usr/sbin/in.tftpd
        server_args             = -s /tftpboot
        disable                 = yes
        per_source              = 11
        cps                     = 100 2
        flags                   = IPv4
}
```

Here, you can see the basics, such as which protocol it uses, whether the service is disabled, and what arguments are passed to the service during startup. For this example, all the defaults work fine. You may be wondering why I suggest leaving the service disabled if you want to use it. Services that are controlled by xinetd can be enabled in the config file when you enable them during the boot process.

Step 5.   Enable the TFTP server to start when the system boots:

```
# chkconfig tftp on
```

Step 6.   Verify that the service will start during boot:

```
# chkconfig tftp --list
tftp              on
```

Looking back in the config file now, notice that the service has been automatically enabled to start. You can verify this by checking the file:

```
# cat /etc/xinetd.d/tftp | grep disable
        disable = no
```

Step 7. At this point, you should also enable the xinetd service itself to start on system boot:

```
# chkconfig xinetd on
```

Step 8. Verify that the service will start during boot:

```
# chkconfig xinetd --list
xinetd          0:off   1:off   2:off   3:on    4:on    5:on
6:off
```

There is also one other thing you can verify. You can get a list of all services enabled during boot by using the chkconfig command. The difference here, though, is that the xinetd service lists not only its boot levels, but also those of all the services that it controls.

Step 9. Use chkconfig to view all the xinetd services:

```
# chkconfig --list
xinetd          0:off   1:off   2:on    3:on    4:on    5:on
6:off
xinetd based services:
        chargen-dgram: off
        chargen-stream: off
        daytime-dgram: off
        daytime-stream: off
        discard-dgram: off
        discard-stream: off
        echo-dgram:    off
        echo-stream:   off
        tcpmux-server: off
        tftp:          on
        time-dgram:    off
        time-stream:   off
```

You can see here that the xinetd service is set to start on boot and that the TFTP service is the only service it will start.

Step 10. To get the service up and running without a system reboot, just adjust any config file options you'd like and restart the xinetd service:

```
# service xinetd restart
Stopping xinetd:                                          [  OK  ]
Starting xinetd:                                          [  OK  ]
```

Step 11. Verify that the xinetd service is now running on the system and listening on UDP port 69 for connections:

```
# netstat -a | grep tftp
udp        0        0 *:tftp                              *:*
```

EXAM TIP

Remember that even though the TFTP server is mentioned here, it is actually the xinetd service that is running and providing all functionality over UDP port 69 on behalf of any TFTP requests.

EXAM TIP

Remember also that for any service you set up to run under xinetd, you need to make a firewall rule to allow incoming connections.

The xinetd service understands services from /etc/services and ports from /etc/rpc. These two files define all services and ports that the system can use to offer different network services to clients using the xinetd master service. The xinetd service is fairly simple to configure, but you should make sure that you define the config file for the services that you want to use within the /etc/xinetd.d directory and restart the service before use. For simple troubleshooting of any xinetd service, you can check the /var/log/messages file, which is the place where the /etc/xinetd.conf config file defines all logs to be sent. Although the default configuration options are usually fine, you can also edit the information sent to the log file by editing the main config file. The following options are available for logging:

- Attempt

- Duration

- Exit

- Pid

- Host

- Userid

You also have the following host access options:

- `only_from`

- `no_access`

- `access_times`

They can be defined within the main config file for security restrictions. Usually, it is better to let the firewall and TCP Wrappers take care of restricting certain clients, but you should know that the options are available. Although the xinetd service can actually handle multiple services, you need to ensure that you have created the appropriate firewall rule for each server you intend to use. Because you have configured a TFTP server for this example, you need to ensure that you create a rule to allow the TFTP server to be used.

NOTE: You may already have this firewall rule in place from Chapter 8, when you set up the automated kickstart server.

Step 1.   Use `iptables` to create the required firewall rule:

```
# iptables -I INPUT 5 -p udp -m udp – dport 69 -j ACCEPT
```

Step 2.   Save the firewall rule you just created:

```
# service iptables save
Saving firewall rules to /etc/sysconfig/iptables:          [  OK  ]
```

Step 3.   Then restart the `iptables` service:

```
# service iptables restart
iptables: Flushing firewall rules:                         [  OK  ]
iptables: Setting chains to policy ACCEPT: filter          [  OK  ]
iptables: Unloading modules:                               [  OK  ]
iptables: Applying firewall rules:                         [  OK  ]
```

MIGRATION TIP

Aside from firewall rules, if you are still on RHEL5, you need an SELinux change as well.

Step 1. Query for the Boolean value you need to change:

```
# getsebool -a | grep dhcpd_dis
tftpd_disable_trans --> off
```

Step 2. Disable SELinux protection:

```
# setsebool -P tftpd_disable_trans=1
```

Step 3. Verify that the Boolean has changed:

```
# getsebool -a | grep dhcpd_dis
tftpd_disable_trans --> on
```

Dynamic Host Configuration Protocol

One of the basics elements found on all networks is a Dynamic Host Configuration Protocol (DHCP) server, making it an important part of any network. DHCP makes network administration easy because you can make changes to a single point (the DHCP server) on your network and let those changes filter down to the rest of the network. Although DHCP is not explicitly covered in the Red Hat Exam Prep Guide, it is an integral part of any network and a core functionality that every network contains.

Before you can begin the installation or setup of a DHCP server, you need to verify that the server is configured with a static IP address. To verify this, you can look at the interface config file:

```
# cat /etc/sysconfig/network-scripts/ifcfg-eth1
DEVICE="eth1"
NM_CONTROLLED="yes"
ONBOOT=yes
HWADDR=00:0C:29:8E:F1:FD
TYPE=Ethernet
BOOTPROTO=static
DEFROUTE=yes
PEERDNS=yes
PEERROUTES=yes
IPV4_FAILURE_FATAL=yes
IPV6INIT=no
NAME="System eth1"
UUID=5fb06bd0-0bb0-7ffb-45f1-d6edd65f3e03
```

If your network adapter is not set up with a static IP address, check Chapter 5, "Networking," to see how to configure it. Your server should have a static IP address, however, if you have been following along in all the labs. With your static IP in hand, you can begin the installation of the DHCP server.

Installing a DHCP Server

Strangely, the DHCP server package is called dhcp, while the service is called dhcpd.

Step 1.   Start by installing the dhcp package:
```
# yum install -y dhcp
```

Step 2.   Verify that the package is installed correctly:
```
# rpm -qa | grep dhcp
dhcp-4.1.1-12.P1.el6.x86_64
```

Step 3.   With the package installed, make sure that the dhcpd service starts when the system boots as well:

```
# chkconfig dhcpd on
```

Step 4.   Verify that the DHCP service starts on boot:

```
# chkconfig dhcpd --list
dhcpd              0:off   1:off   2:on    3:on    4:on    5:on
6:off
```

Configuring the DHCP Server

To start the configuration, let's look at the important files that handle the options for the DHCP service:

/etc/dhcp/dhcpd.conf   Main config file for the DHCP service using IPv4 addresses

/etc/dhcp/dhcpd6.conf   Main config file for the DHCP service using IPv6 addresses

/var/lib/dhcpd/dhcpd.leases   IPv4 client lease file

/var/lib/dhcpd/dhcpd6.leases IPv6 client lease file

MIGRATION TIP

In RHEL5, the location of the main config file was /etc/dhcpd.conf. Now in RHEL6, the config file has been moved into a directory (/etc/dhcp) because there are additional config files for IPv6 addresses.

The main config file is usually empty aside from a comment or two. The good news is that the package does provide a sample config file for you to use. This sample file provides examples and comments on how you can configure options for your DHCP server.

To copy the sample file, use the following command:

```
# cp /usr/share/doc/dhcp-4.1.1/dhcpd.conf.sample /etc/dhcp/dhcpd.conf
```

If you are new to working with DHCP servers, this sample file will prove helpful in that the comments included in the file explain the different options. The following sample config file gives you the basics to get started. It is less cluttered than the sample, so it is easier to explain.

Here is the sample DHCP server config file:

```
# Global Options
ddns-update-style none;
authoritative;

# Subnet definition
```

```
subnet 172.168.1.0 netmask 255.255.255.0 {

    # Parameters for the local subnet
    option routers                          172.168.1.1;
    option subnet-mask                      255.255.255.0;

    option domain-name                      "example.com";
    option domain-name-servers              172.168.1.1;

    default-lease-time                      21600;
    max-lease-time                          43200;

    # Client IP range
    range dynamic-bootp 172.168.1.100 172.168.1.200;

}
```

Let's break down this file into sections. The first section contains two options for
the DHCP server itself, also called global options:

`ddns-update-style: none`	This means that the DHCP server won't update client DNS records.
`authoritative`	This informs the client that the DHCP server contains legitimate information.

REAL-WORLD TIP

If the server doesn't contain an `authoritative` option and the client switches subnets, it is not able to obtain a new IP address until its old lease has fully expired.
There are also security benefits of sending a DHCPNAK to incorrectly configured
clients.

The next section defines a subnet. Any options that you list in a subnet section are
specific to the subnet for which you define them. If you want to set global options
(such as `authoritative`), you need to define them outside the subnet section. In
this section, the following options are used:

`option routers`	Defines the default gateway to the subnet
`option subnet-mask`	Defines the subnet mask for the subnet
`option domain-name`	Defines the name of the domain
`option domain-name-servers`	Defines the DNS server for the subnet

default-lease-time	Specifies how long each client keeps its lease until a renewal is requested (in seconds)
max-lease-time	Specifies the maximum amount of time a client can keep a lease (in seconds)
range dynamic-bootp	Specifies the range of IP addresses that can be given out to clients

With a config file in place, you have everything you need for the DHCP server to function properly. Although this section does not describe anywhere near all the options available for the DHCP service, this is a good start to getting a DHCP server up and running. For the exams, you can always reference the documentation if you forget the name of an option. Although I hate pointing you to man pages, it is impossible to remember everything for every service. Knowing where to find information when you need it is critical on the exams and in the real world. Here are the three man pages you should know:

```
# man dhcpd.conf
# man dhcpd.leases
# man dhop optiono
```

If you want to have multiple subnets, you can just define a new subnet section with its own set of options. There is no limit to the number of sections you can have.

REAL-WORLD TIP

If you want to set up multiple subnets, you usually have multiple interfaces on the server. If this is the case and you would like to service multiple subnets of clients, you need to adjust the /etc/sysconfig/dhcpd file. In this case, you need to edit the following daemon option:

```
DHCPDARGS="eth0"
```

Change this option to include all the interfaces for which you want to offer clients leases in different subnets. If you have two interfaces in two different subnets, for example, your option might look like this:

```
DHCPDARGS="eth0 eth1"
```

The options we've covered so far are really all you need to set up your DHCP server to work. Even though the DHCP server is set to run, there is another example to consider. It is common in the real world to have to reserve an IP address for a particular client. If you don't want to make the IP address of the client static, you can reserve it instead on the DHCP server. Reservations are common when dealing with printers on networks, but they can be used for clients, too. Here is how you define a reservation for a client. In your /etc/dhcpd.conf file, do the following:

```
host client01 {


    option host-name "client01.example.com";
    hardware ethernet 02:B4:7C:43:DD:FF;
    fixed-address 172.168.1.50;


}
```

Again, let's look at each of these options and what they do.

`option host-name`	Defines the fully qualified domain name of the client
`hardware ethernet`	Defines the MAC address of the client
`fixed-address`	Specifies the IP address that you want the client to receive

These three options are defined in a `host` subsection, just like you defined a subnet section earlier. With the config files in place, you are now ready to start the service. The DHCP server offers a particularly nice feature built into the startup scripts; it can check the syntax of your config file for errors. This capability is nice because prior to actually starting the service, you can check to make sure nothing is set incorrectly.

Check the config file for any errors:

```
# service dhcpd configtest
Syntax: OK
```

If the DHCP service does find errors, it attempts to tell you where in the config file the error exists. Open your config file and remove the brace (}) that ends the subnet section. Save your config file and run the syntax check on your config file again:

```
# service dhcpd configtest
Internet Systems Consortium DHCP Server V3.0.5-RedHat
Copyright 2004-2006 Internet Systems Consortium.
All rights reserved.
For info, please visit http://www.isc.org/sw/dhcp/
/etc/dhcpd.conf line 18: unexpected end of file

^
Configuration file errors encountered -- exiting
```

Here, the service points out that the } is missing from the config file by giving you the line where the issue occurs as well as a general description of what the problem is. Now replace the } again and restart the DHCP service:

```
# service dhcpd start
Starting dhcpd:                                          [  OK  ]
```

Verify that the service is running:

```
# service dhcpd status
dhcpd (pid  3366) is running...
```

Security Configuration

Before any of the clients can start obtaining an IP address from the DHCP server, you need to deal with the security requirements for the DHCP server. They include adding a firewall rule with iptables and disabling any SELinux options that prevent the DHCP service from running. For the firewall rule, you need to know that the DHCP server listens on UDP port 67 for incoming DHCP requests.

Step 1.   Use iptables to create the required firewall rule:

```
# iptables -I INPUT 5 -p udp -m udp --dport 67 -j ACCEPT
```

Step 2.   Save the firewall rule you just created:

```
# service iptables save
Saving firewall rules to /etc/sysconfig/iptables:       [  OK  ]
```

Step 3.   Then restart the iptables service:

```
# service iptables restart
iptables: Flushing firewall rules:                      [  OK  ]
iptables: Setting chains to policy ACCEPT: filter       [  OK  ]
iptables: Unloading modules:                            [  OK  ]
iptables: Applying firewall rules:                      [  OK  ]
```

With the firewall rules in place, you can shift your focus to SELinux. Well, wouldn't you know...there are no SELinux requirements for a DHCP server.

TIP: As you have seen in numerous chapters already, RHEL5 requires some SELinux configuration. For the DHCP server to function, you need to disable SELinux protection of the DHCP service itself.

Step 1. Query for the Boolean value you need to change:

```
# getsebool -a | grep dhcpd_dis
dhcpd_disable_trans --> off
```

Step 2. Disable SELinux protection:

```
# setsebool -P dhcpd_disable_trans=1
```

Step 3. Verify that the Boolean has changed:

```
# getsebool -a | grep dhcpd_dis
dhcpd_disable_trans --> on
```

You should now have a fully functional DHCP server! You can boot up your clients and see if they pick up an IP address, or if the client is already powered on, you can use the `dhclient` command to request an IP address from the server.

Step 4.   Request a dynamic IP from the server:

```
# dhclient
Internet Systems Consortium DHCP Client V3.0.5-RedHat
Copyright 2004-2006 Internet Systems Consortium.
All rights reserved.
For info, please visit http://www.isc.org/sw/dhcp/

Listening on LPF/eth0/08:00:27:74:5b:11
Sending on   LPF/eth0/08:00:27:74:5b:11
Sending on   Socket/fallback
DHCPDISCOVER on eth0 to 255.255.255.255 port 67 interval 7
DHCPOFFER from 192.168.1.1
DHCPREQUEST on eth0 to 255.255.255.255 port 67
DHCPACK from 192.168.1.1
bound to 192.168.1.7 — renewal in 40126 seconds.
```

Troubleshooting DHCP

Not all configurations go as smoothly as you might like. When you're troubleshooting the DHCP server, there are a few things to watch out for. For example, in the main config file, /etc/dhcp/dhcpd.conf, make sure that you end all your options with a semicolon (;). If you don't, the service throws an error when you check the config file. Also, make sure that you also test the DHCP server after the firewall rules are in place. For client troubleshooting, the DHCP server provides a client leases file. This file contains all the lease information about each client that has obtained an IP address from the server. When you have a client that has a DHCP address, you can view the leases file by using the following:

```
# cat /var/lib/dhcpd/dhcpd.leases
lease 172.168.1.200 {
  starts 2 2010/05/11 12:24:10;
  ends 2 2010/05/11 18:24:10;
  tstp 2 2010/05/11 18:24:10;
  binding state free;
  hardware ethernet 08:00:27:74:5b:11;
}
lease 172.168.1.199 {
  starts 4 2010/05/20 11:24:03;
  ends 4 2010/05/20 17:24:03;
  tstp 4 2010/05/20 17:24:03;
  binding state free;
  hardware ethernet 08:00:27:2f:80:8c;
}
```

As you can see from the file output, two clients have active leases. When viewing the leases file, you should be careful that all times in the dhcpd.leases file are in UTC (GMT). The reason for this is that there is no daylight savings in that time zone, making it internationally usable. Make sure you pay attention to this issue if you're trying to troubleshoot with this file. As a final tip, make sure you use the `configtest` option to test the syntax of your config files before starting or restarting the service. This prevents any errors from occurring when you try to start the service.

REAL-WORLD TIP

You may want to consider setting up a secondary DHCP server as a failover. It provides you with a backup should your primary server fail (don't just rely on this secondary server, though; make sure you test it). If you create a failover server, you should follow the 80/20 rule: 80% of your IP addresses should be used on your primary DHCP server, and 20% should be used on your secondary server.

Network Time Protocol

Do you know what time it is? If you don't, that's okay because we're going to discuss the network time protocol (NTP) service. This service is responsible for maintaining the system time, which is highly important in any environment because so many things rely on time (logs, error messages, applications, and so on). There are a few different roles that your system can have when using NTP. They include

Primary NTP Server	Provides time to secondary NTP servers or clients
Secondary NTP Server	Provides time to clients; helps load balance primary NTP servers
NTP Peer	Provides and receives time
NTP Client	Receives time from primary or secondary NTP servers

According to the Red Hat Exam Prep Guide, you need to be able to synchronize clients with a higher-stratum server. The term *stratum* is used to define different levels, from 1 to 15, of time servers that are available to sync with. A stratum 1 time server is the most accurate. For load balancing and redundancy, you would probably want to configure a primary NTP server and a secondary NTP server to sync with a stratum 1 time server (which is located off your network). Now let's look more closely at both the server and client side of NTP.

Installing a Time Server

Usually, the NTP package comes installed as part of your Red Hat system, but it is always good to know how to install it should you ever need to.

Step 1.   If you need to, install the package:

```
# yum install -y ntp
```

Step 2.   Verify that the package has been installed:

```
# rpm -qa | grep ntp
ntp-4.2.4p8-2.el6.x86_64
ntpdate-4.2.4p8-2.el6.x86_64
```

Step 3.   Make sure that the service will start when the system boots up:

```
# chkconfig ntpd on
```

Step 4.   Verify the service starts on boot:

```
# chkconfig ntpd --list
ntpd            0:off   1:off   2:on    3:on    4:on    5:on    6:off
```

Before starting the service, let's configure the system first.

Configuring NTP

To configure the primary NTP server, let's look at part of the config file that comes with the system:

```
# cat /etc/ntp.conf
...
server 0.rhel.pool.ntp.org
server 1.rhel.pool.ntp.org
server 2.rhel.pool.ntp.org
...
#server   127.127.1.0
#fudge    127.127.1.0 stratum 10
```

The first three lines shown here are the Internet (public) NTP servers that you sync with for the correct time. The fourth server option, which is commented out, defines a local clock driver that you can use to update the time. This is usually based on the BIOS click if used. The final option, fudge, defines the stratum level to which your server is set. The server here is set at a stratum level of 10; a local system clock is also defined, and there are three public Internet servers you can sync with for accurate time.

MIGRATION TIP
In RHEL6, the local server and fudge options are both commented out by default.

For now, just let the system sync with the public Internet time servers.

Step 1. Start the NTP service:

```
# service ntpd start
Starting ntpd:                                          [  OK  ]
```

With the server configured, you can turn your attention over to one of the client systems. For this example, use the Client01 system to sync with the RHEL01 primary NTP server. On Client01, you need to verify that the NTP package is already installed:

```
# rpm -qa | grep ntp
ntp-4.2.4p8-2.el6.x86_64
```

With the client installed, again look at the config file. Instead of public servers, you can set the RHEL01 system as the primary server to sync with.

Step 2. Define RHEL01 as the primary time server and make sure the driftfile line is uncommented:

```
# cat /etc/ntp.conf
...
Server       172.168.1.1
driftfile    /var/lib/ntp/drift
```

Now the client is looking at RHEL01 to sync its time. The additional option, driftfile, is a scratch place for the NTP service to calculate time checks and errors for accuracy. It is recommended for better results but not required.

MIGRATION TIP
In RHEL6, there is no longer a driftfile defined by default in the config file.

EXAM TIP

Configuration of the /etc/ntp.conf file works the same for NTP servers or clients. Regardless of which you are configuring, the steps are still the same; the difference comes when choosing which upstream server to sync with.

Step 3.   Now that the client is configured, you just need to start the service:

```
# service ntpd start
Starting ntpd:                                              [  OK  ]
```

EXAM TIP

Like many services that you will work with in Red Hat, any change to the config files requires that the NTP service be restarted.

Firewall and SELinux Configuration

Like the DHCP server, NTP requires only firewall rules to operate (no SELinux configuration is necessary). The NTP service uses TCP and UDP port 123, so you need to open both on the firewall.

Step 1.   Use `iptables` to create the required firewall rules:

```
# iptables -I INPUT 5 -p udp -m udp --dport 123 -j ACCEPT
# iptables -I INPUT 5 -p tcp -m tcp --dport 123 -j ACCEPT
```

Step 2.   Save the firewall rules you just created:

```
# service iptables save
Saving firewall rules to /etc/sysconfig/iptables:          [  OK  ]
```

Step 3.   Then restart the `iptables` service:

```
# service iptables restart
iptables: Flushing firewall rules:                         [  OK  ]
iptables: Setting chains to policy ACCEPT: filter          [  OK  ]
iptables: Unloading modules:                               [  OK  ]
iptables: Applying firewall rules:                         [  OK  ]
```

MIGRATION TIP

Also like the DHCP service, NTP for RHEL5 requires some SELinux configuration. For the NTP server to function, you need to disable SELinux protection of the NTP service itself.

Step 1. Query for the Boolean value you need to change:

```
# getsebool -a | grep ntp
ntpd_disable_trans_fi off
```

Step 2. Disable SELinux protection:

```
# setsebool -P ntpd_disable_trans=1
```

Step 3. Verify that the Boolean has changed:

```
# getsebool -a | grep ntp
ntpd_disable_trans_fi on
```

NTP Security

Security with NTP is predefined for you in the config file when you're setting up an NTP server. Again, let's look through part of the /etc/ntp.conf file. Notice the following two lines:

```
restrict default kod nomodify notrap nopeer noquery
restrict 127.0.0.1
```

These security settings prevent access from any other time server making changes. They also restrict the interface to performing administrative duties on the local loopback. The options listed do the following:

kod	Prevents "kiss of death" packets
nomodify	Prevents other time servers from making changes
notrap	Disables messages from being trapped
nopeer	Prevents other systems from becoming an NTP peer with this server
noquery	Disallows queries from other NTP servers

All these options provide better security but sometimes may restrict certain functionality. You can remove any options you don't want to have an effect on this NTP server. This file is also a great place to look when you're troubleshooting to see if one of these options is preventing a sync of information to your NTP server. If you want to add in another administrative interface, you can simply add a `restrict` option to the /etc/ntp.conf file:

```
restrict 172.168.1.0 mask 255.255.255.0
```

Now you can make changes and manage this NTP server from any system on the local subnet. Don't forget to restart the NTP service if you make any changes.

Troubleshooting NTP

When you want to troubleshoot the NTP service, there are a few commands that can help you out. First, if you want to update the time manually, you can use the `ntpdate` command.

Syntax: `ntpdate <server>`

MIGRATION TIP

RHEL6 comes with the `ntpdate` package installed by default, but RHEL5 does not.

WARNING: Before you run the `ntpdate` command, you must stop the NTP service!

Step 1. Stop the NTP service:

```
# service ntpd stop
Shutting down ntpd:                                    [  OK  ]
```

Step 2. Specify the upstream server that you want to sync against:

```
# ntpdate 0.rhel.pool.ntp.org
23 Aug 16:29:15 ntpdate[7047]: adjust time server 209.234.249.11
offset 0.031852 sec
```

Step 3. Start the service again:

```
# service ntpd start
Starting ntpd:                                         [  OK  ]
```

Step 4. Verify that the time is accurate with the `date` command:

```
# date
Mon Aug 23 16:29:34 GMT 2010
```

The next troubleshooting command is `ntpq`, which enables you to query for other NTP servers. Here, the only concern is the `-p` option, which polls for other NTP servers:

```
# ntpq -p
     remote          refid      st t when poll reach   delay   offset  jitter
==============================================================================
 pool-test.ntp.o .INIT.          16 u    -   64    0   0.000   0.000   0.061
 knowledge.globa .INIT.          16 u    -   64    0   0.000   0.000   0.061
 bindcat.fhsu.ed .INIT.          16 u    -   64    0   0.000   0.000   0.061
 LOCAL(0)        .LOCL.          10 l    -   64    0   0.000   0.000   0.061
```

Finally, you can also go really in depth by tracing where the NTP server is getting its time sync from. To do this, you can use the `ntptrace` command.

Syntax: `ntptrace <server>`

You can specify the public Internet server from before to determine how high in the stratum the server is on other various sync statistics:

```
# ntptrace 0.rhel.pool.ntp.org
0.rhel.pool.ntp.org: stratum 2, offset -0.000210, synch distance 0.
```

Summary

Providing network services to your network is important for other systems to be able to interact. In this chapter, we described providing IP addresses, time, and multiservice management through `xinetd`. Each of these components plays a part in making up the services that you will be able to provide for your network. Although many of these services aren't specifically covered in the exam prep guide, they are crucial components in any network and help integrate other services on your network. The next chapter covers email services.

Review Questions

1. What is the `xinetd` service used for?

2. Editing the /etc/xinetd.d/tftp file and enabling the service are the same as running the `chkconfig tftp on` command. True or False?

3. What command is used to show all services being controlled by the `xinetd` daemon?

4. What is the main config file for the DHCP service?

5. Does a DHCP server allow reserved IP addresses? If so, how?

6. What command can you use to check the config file of the DHCP server?

7. What port does the DHCP server listen on by default?

8. Which file shows you all the client IP addresses?

9. What command and options can you use to update the time?

Answers to the Review Questions

1. The `xinetd` daemon is used to control and/or run multiple system services. One example is a TFTP server.

2. True. Both of these actions have the same effect.

3. `chkconfig xinetd --list`

4. The /etc/dhcp/dhcpd.conf file is the main config file for the DHCP service.

5. Yes. Using the host option in the dhcpd.conf file allows you to reserve a client IP address based on its MAC address.

6. service dhcpd configtest

7. The DHCP server listens on port 67 by default.

8. The /var/liv/dhcpd/dhcpd.leases file contains all clients IP address currently in use.

9. After the ntpd service is stopped, you can use the ntpdate <server> command to update/sync the time.

Lab 19

Task 1 – DHCP Server

Step 1. Set up a DHCP server on RHEL01 with the following settings:
   a. Use the 172.168.1.1 /24 subnet.
   b. The client IP range should be 172.168.1.100 – 172.168.1.110.
   c. Reserve the IP 172.168.1.31 (use any MAC address).

The task is complete when users can receive an IP address on their systems with the allowable IP range.

Task 2 – NTP

Step 1. Set up an NTP server on RHEL01.

Step 2. Sync RHEL01 with any public time server.

Step 3. Sync all other systems in the lab with RHEL01.

The task is complete when all systems on the lab have their time synced correctly.

This chapter covers the following subjects:

- **Email Service Overview**—This section provides a general overview of email services.

- **SMTP with Postfix**—This section covers the setup of outgoing mail with SMTP.

- **Receiving Mail with Dovecot**—This section covers the setup of incoming mail with POP3 and IMAP.

- **Testing the Mail Server**—This section looks at how to test the mail server you have just set up.

The following RHCE exam objectives are covered:

- Install the packages needed to provide the service

- Configure SELinux to support the service

- Configure the service to start when the system is booted

- Configure the service for basic operation

- Configure host-based and user-based security for the service

- Configure a mail transfer agent (MTA) to accept inbound email from other systems

- Configure an MTA to forward (relay) email through a smart host

## CHAPTER 20

Email Services

The world today runs on email, and without it, we would have a hard time functioning. Because of this, we need solid and reliable email servers to ensure that our email is processed correctly and either delivered or received on time. This chapter covers the different email services that can be used on Red Hat and how the email process works as a whole. For Red Hat, Sendmail is the default for sending mail and Dovecot is the default for receiving. Here, we focus more on Postfix for sending and Dovecot for receiving. Let's start with an overview of how email services work.

Email Service Overview

The email system is divided into three different parts: MUA, MDA, and MTA. The mail user agent (MUA) deals specifically with end users. It is what they use to type and read emails they receive. The MUA is a mail client of some sort, such as Thunderbird or Evolution. The mail delivery agent (MDA) handles the delivery of mail from the receiving mail server to the spool where the mail sits until an MUA picks it up for the user. Finally, the mail transfer agent (MTA) is responsible for moving mail from one server to another until it arrives at its destination. In the next few sections, we cover the setup of Postfix and Dovecot to provide mail functionality needed for the network.

SMTP with Postfix

Red Hat provides both Sendmail and Postfix as viable mail programs. We focus only on Postfix in this book for multiple reasons. Postfix provides for easier administration, allows increased security, and supports virtual domains. It is also the default mail program on RHEL6.

MIGRATION TIP

Up until RHEL5, Sendmail was the default mail program for the Red Hat operating system, but this has changed to Postfix with the release of RHEL6.

EXAM TIP

For the exam, you can use either Postfix or Sendmail as long as the system functions properly and the required task is met. As pointed out in the preceding tip, Sendmail is no longer the default, so it may be easier to learn Postfix even if you aren't really familiar with it.

Step 1.   To get started, you just need to verify that Postfix is installed correctly:

```
# rpm -qa | grep postfix
postfix-2.6.6-2.el6.x86_64
```

If the package isn't installed for some reason, you should install it now with the following:

```
# yum install -y postfix
```

Step 2.   The service should be already set to start during system boot, so you should just verify that:

```
# chkconfig postfix --list
postfix           0:off   1:off   2:on    3:on    4:on    5:on
6:off
```

If the service isn't set to start on boot, you can enable it with the following:

```
# chkconfig postfix on
```

Because the Postfix service comes installed by default, you really don't need to do much to get started.

MIGRATION TIP

Because RHEL5 has Sendmail set up as the default mail program, you need to take some additional steps before moving on to configuring Postfix.

Step 1. Install the Postfix package because it isn't there by default:

```
# yum install -y postfix
```

Step 2. Verify that the package installed correctly:

```
# rpm -qa | grep postfix
postfix-2.3.3-2.1.el5_2
```

Step 3. Because you are going to use Postfix in place of the default Sendmail, you also need to stop the Sendmail service:

```
# service sendmail stop
Shutting down sm-client:                                    [  OK  ]
Shutting down sendmail:                                     [FAILED]
```

Step 4. You also need to prevent it from starting during system boot:

```
# chkconfig sendmail off
```

Step 5. Verify:

```
# chkconfig sendmail --list
sendmail        0:off   1:off   2:off   3:off   4:off   5:off   6:off
```

Step 6. Change the default mail program to Postfix:

```
# alternatives --config mta


There are 2 programs which provide 'mta'.

  Selection    Command
-------------------------------------------------
*+ 1            /usr/sbin/sendmail.sendmail
   2            /usr/sbin/sendmail.postfix

Enter to keep the current selection[+], or type selection number: 2
```

Step 7. Verify that the current default for mail is Postfix:

```
# alternatives --display mta | grep current
 link currently points to /usr/sbin/sendmail.postfix
```

Configuring Postfix

Postfix actually starts a service called master, which is its main service. This master service starts three other services besides itself: nqmgr, pickup, and smtpd. The nqmgr service is responsible for mail transmission, relay, and delivery. The pickup service transfers messages, and the smtpd service directs incoming mail. There are numerous things to know when working with Postfix, so let's take a look.

Here are the management commands for Postfix:

mailq   Allows you to view the mail queue (* means active, ! means on hold)

postmap   Postfix lookup table management

postsuper   Allows you to perform maintenance jobs on the Postfix queue

postconf   Postfix configuration utility

The main config files for Postfix are located in the /etc/postfix directory:

master.cf	Contains settings to control the master service
main.cf	Opens the primary config file for Postfix
access	Provides access control
transport	Maps email addresses to relay hosts

The master.cf file is broken down into eight columns:

service	Identifies the name of the service
type	Names the transport mechanism used
private	Names the service used by Postfix only
unpriv	Names the service to be run by nonroot users
chroot	Indicates whether the mail queue should be run in a chrooted environment
wakeup	Specifies the wakeup interval for the service
maxproc	Indicates the maximum number of processes the service can execute
command	Names the command to be executed plus arguments

In the master.cf file, the columns are arranged in the following order:

```
<service> <type> <private> <unpriv> <chroot> <wakeup> <maxproc> <cmd>
```

EXAM TIP

The default /etc/postfix/main.cf file doesn't allow Postfix to accept network connections from any host other than the local system.

Before you can change any of the options in the config file, make sure that the Postfix service is not running. Now let's look at the default options for Postfix:

```
# head -n 35 /etc/postfix/master.cf
#
# Postfix master process configuration file. For details on the format
# of the file, see the master(5) manual page (command: "man 5 master").
#
# =============================================================
# service type  private unpriv  chroot  wakeup  maxproc command + args
#               (yes)   (yes)   (yes)   (never) (100)
# =============================================================
smtp      inet  n       -       n       -       -       smtpd
```

```
pickup     fifo  n       -      n      60      1      pickup
cleanup    unix  n       -      n      -       0      cleanup
qmgr       fifo  n       -      n      300     1      qmgr
...
```

You can make adjustments here for any of the subservices that you'd like to edit, but for purposes of this example, keep the default values for now.

Next, let's look at the main config file, which requires some editing before you can use Postfix. Because the config file is 667 lines long, the whole file is not shown here. Instead, we look at key sections. The following variables need to be set for the Postfix server to work properly:

myhostname	Defines the full hostname of the Postfix server
mydomain	Defines the domain name
myorigin	Defines the name that outgoing mail originates from
inet_interfaces	Identifies the interface on which to receive mail
mydestination	Defines the domains for which Postfix accepts mail
mynetworks	Lists trusted networks
virtual_alias_maps	Defines virtual aliases for incoming mail

You can proceed as follows:

Step 1.   Open the master.cf file with any text editor and set the preceding variables:
```
# nano /etc/postfix/main.cf
```

Step 2.   Change the following options to reflect the lab environment:
```
myhostname = rhel01.example.com
mydomain = example.com
myorigin = $mydomain
inet_interfaces = all
mydestination = $myhostname, localhost.$mydomain, localhost
mynetworks = 172.168.1.0/24, 127.0.0.0/8
```

When you have these settings in place, save the file and exit. Mail servers rely heavily on DNS to function properly. If you don't have a DNS server already configured or you use an external DNS server, make sure it is set up with the correct MX records before you start the Postfix service.

Step 3.   Check that the directory structure and config file are correct:
```
# postfix check
```

Step 4. When you are confident that the DNS records are in place, the Postfix options are set correctly, and the config checks out, you can start the Postfix service:

```
# service postfix start
Starting postfix:                                    [  OK  ]
```

EXAM TIP

The first time you start Postfix, it may not display a notification that it started properly. In this case, you can restart the service as follows:

```
# service postfix restart
Shutting down postfix:                               [  OK  ]
Starting postfix:                                    [  OK  ]
```

Alternatively, you can query to ensure the three daemons are running properly:

```
# ps aux | grep post
root        1479  0.0  0.1  61972  2700 ?   Ss    Jan31    0:00
/usr/libexec/postfix/master
postfix     1488  0.0  0.1  62120  2728 ? S    Jan31    0:00 qmgr -l -t fifo -u
postfix    13900  0.0  0.1  62052  2680 ? S    04:21    0:00 pickup -l -t fifo
-u
root       14194  0.0  0.0 103156   820 pts/1 S+   05:51    0:00 grep post
```

Step 5. Verify:

```
# service postfix status
master (pid 3156) is running...
```

Because Postfix is the default outgoing mail server, you don't need to change the default MTA. It doesn't hurt, though, to check that it is set correctly.

Step 6. Verify that the current default for the outgoing mail is Postfix:

```
# alternatives — display mta | grep current
 link currently points to /usr/sbin/sendmail.postfix
```

An alternative to adjusting the main.cf config file by hand is to use the `postconf` utility.

Syntax: `postconf [options] [parameter=value]`

Options:

-a   Lists the available SASL server plug-in types

-d   Prints the default parameter settings instead of the actual settings

-e   Edits the main.cf config file

-n   Prints all parameter settings that are not at their default values

-v   Enables verbose logging for debugging

For example, if you want to set the mynetworks option, you could do the following:

```
# postconf -e mynetworks="127.0.0.1 /8 172.168.1.0 /24"
```

Verify the change with the following command:

```
# postconf -n | grep mynet
mynetworks = 127.0.0.0/8 172.168.1.0/24
```

Firewall and SELinux Configuration

For Postfix, only a single firewall rule is required. You need to open TCP port 25 for the SMTP service.

Step 1. Use the iptables command to create your firewall rule:

```
# iptabloc  I INPUT 5 -p tcp -m tcp --dport 25 -j ACCEPT
```

Step 2. Save the rule you just created:

```
# service iptables save
Saving firewall rules to /etc/sysconfig/iptables:          [  OK  ]
```

Step 3. Restart the firewall service for the changes to take effect:

```
# service iptables restart
iptables: Flushing firewall rules:                         [  OK  ]
iptables: Setting chains to policy ACCEPT: filter          [  OK  ]
iptables: Unloading modules:                               [  OK  ]
iptables: Applying firewall rules:                         [  OK  ]
```

Postfix is one of those rare Linux services that doesn't really have much in terms of SELinux configuration. There is a single Boolean option that is already enabled by default.

Verify that protection to mailboxes is disabled:

```
# getsebool -a | grep postfix
allow_postfix_local_write_mail_spool --> on
```

MIGRATION TIP

In RHEL5, SELinux protection for Postfix is enabled by default. You need to adjust this for the Postfix service to work properly.

Step 1. Query for the Boolean value you need to change:

```
# getsebool -a | grep postfix_dis
postifx_disable_trans --> off
```

Step 2. Disable the SELinux protection:

```
# setsebool -P postfix_disable_trans=1
```

Step 3. Verify that the Boolean has changed:

```
# getsebool -a | grep postfix_dis
postfix_disable_trans --> on
```

Postfix Security

Because mail servers are omnipresent, it is vital that you understand how to lock down particular features of them. For outgoing mail servers that deal with the SMTP protocol like Postfix, you should make sure that it is not left open to be used as a mail relay. This would allow outsiders to use your server for spam. To do this, you can open the /etc/postfix/access file and add the hostname or IP address of any server(s) that you'd like to be allowed to relay mail through your outgoing mail server.

If you want to allow RHEL02 to relay mail, but not either of the client systems, you could do the following:

```
# nano /etc/postfix/access
172.168.1.2              RELAY
172.168.1.10             REJECT
Client02                 REJECT
```

For additional security, you can also use the following four options in the /etc/postfix/main.cf file:

```
smtpd_helo_required = yes
smtpd_recipient_limit = 500
smptd_recipient_restrictions = mynetworks
smtpd_sender_restrictions = reject_unknown_sender_domain
```

These settings limit access to your mail server to only those within your network. They also limit the number of recipients that can be addressed in a single message.

Aside from locking down your mail server, you can also relay your mail through another smarthost SMTP server. In the /etc/postfix/main.cf config file, define a `relayhost` option with the name of the smarthost you'd like to relay through:

```
# nano /etc/postfix/main.cf
relayhost = mail.example-a.com
```

This now relays your mail through the specified host server. If you'd like to add a little security here, you can also configure the relay to work with SASL for a secure connection. Again, edit the /etc/postfix/main.cf config file:

```
# nano /etc/postfix/main.cf
relayhost = mail.example-a.com
smtp_use_tls = yes
smtp_sasl_auth_enable = yes
smtp_sasl_password_maps = hash:/etc/postfix/smtp_auth
smtp_sasl_security_options = noanonymous
```

You can see that these changes force the use of SASL so that the connection will be secure. They also define a file (/etc/postfix/smtp_auth) to keep the credentials for authentication purposes.

Create the credentials file and populate it:

```
# nano /etc/postfix/smtp_auth
mail.example-a.com              <account_number | account_info>:<password>
```

Notify the Postfix service that you want to add the newly created credentials with the postmap command:

```
# postmap /etc/postfix/smtp_auth
```

Finally, restart the Postfix service for the changes to take effect:

```
# service postfix restart
Shutting down postfix:                                  [  OK  ]
Starting postfix:                                       [  OK  ]
```

Although this section doesn't describe all the security features Postfix provides, it's a good start and will give you the basics for protecting your mail server.

Alias Mapping

Postfix is able to use aliases for managing domains and users. The /etc/aliases file contains the current mappings and should be edited to reflect any changes required for your network. Using the newaliases command, you can view the statistics of the file or update the aliases database. You can use the aliases file to create distribution groups or redirect mail to users who no longer exist in your domain. For example, add the following line to the /etc/aliases file:

```
helpdesk:  user01, user02
```

Then run the newaliases command to update the database:

```
# newaliases
```

Now when you email helpdesk@example.com, the message goes to both users.

Receiving Mail with Dovecot

Now that you can send mail, you also need to be able to receive it. Dovecot enables you to set up an incoming mail server that allows for multiple protocols to be used when accessing mail.

Step 1.   Unlike you did with Postfix, you first need to set up Dovecot by installing the correct package:

```
# yum install -y dovecot
```

Step 2.   Verify the installation:

```
# rpm -qa | grep dovecot
dovecot-2.0-0.10.beta6.20100630.el6.x86_64
```

Step 3.   Enable the service to start on system boot:

```
# chkconfig dovecot on
```

Step 4.   Verify the service will start at boot:

```
# chkconfig dovecot --list
dovecot          0:off   1:off   2:on    3:on    4:on    5:on    6:off
```

Configuring Dovecot

Dovecot, unlike Postfix, has only a single config file that you need to configure. Like its partner Postfix, the Dovecot config file is long—more than 1,000+ lines. Although the entire file is not shown here, you need to configure a few key options.

MIGRATION TIP

In RHEL6, the config file for Dovecot has been moved. It is now located at /etc/dovecot/dovecot.conf. Previously in RHEL5, it was located at /etc/dovecot.conf.

Step 1.   Start by opening the file for editing:

```
# nano /etc/dovecot/dovecot.conf
```

Step 2.   Define the protocols that you'd like to have the Dovecot server use:

```
protocols = imap pop3
```

Step 3.   You should also define the IP address for the server to listen on, disable SSL, and define where user mailboxes should be stored:

```
listen = 172.168.1.1
ssl_disable = yes
mail_location = maildir:~/Maildir
```

Step 4.   Save the file and exit.

Normally, Dovecot attempts to find a mailbox for a user, but if one is not found, it runs into trouble, which is why you explicitly define the `mail_location` option. From these changes, you can also see that you will listen using the IMAP and POP3 protocols. If necessary, you can use the secure versions of both protocols (including SSL).

The following protocols can be used with Dovecot:

IMAP	TCP port 143
POP3	TCP port 110
IMAPS	TCP port 995
POP3S	TCP port 993
LMTP	TCP port 24

MIGRATION TIP

In RHEL5, you can choose from IMAP, POP3, IMAPS, and POP3S. RHEL6 now uses the updated version (2.x) of Dovecot, which also allows you to use the LMTP protocol. This is similar to the SMTP protocol for sending mail.

As already mentioned, use only the first two protocols for this setup. This is all you really need to configure to get the Dovecot server working.

Step 5.   Now start the Dovecot service:

```
# service dovecot start
Starting Dovecot Imap:                                    [  OK  ]
```

Step 6.   Verify that it is running properly:

```
# service dovecot status
dovecot (pid  2909) is running...
```

EXAM TIP

For whatever reason, when you start the Dovecot service, it reports that the IMAP protocol has started, but it is actually starting POP3 as well.

Firewall and SELinux Configuration

Dovecot requires a little more on the security end than Postfix did, mainly because there are more protocols involved. First, you need to make sure to open only the firewall ports for the protocols you are actually using—in this case, 143 and 110.

Step 1. Use the `iptables` command to create your firewall rules:

```
# iptables -I INPUT 5 -p tcp -m tcp --dport 110 -j ACCEPT
# iptables -I INPUT 5 -p tcp -m tcp --dport 143 -j ACCEPT
```

Step 2. Save the rules you just created:

```
# service iptables save
Saving firewall rules to /etc/sysconfig/iptables:          [  OK  ]
```

Step 3. Restart the firewall service for the changes to take effect:

```
# service iptables restart
iptables: Flushing firewall rules:                         [  OK  ]
iptables: Setting chains to policy ACCEPT: filter          [  OK  ]
iptables: Unloading modules:                               [  OK  ]
iptables: Applying firewall rules:                         [  OK  ]
```

When it comes to SELinux, the Dovecot service doesn't have any SELinux protections; therefore, there is nothing required for you to configure.

MIGRATION TIP

In RHEL5, a single SELinux Boolean protects the Dovecot service. You need to disable it for the Dovecot service to work properly.

Step 1. Query for the Boolean value you need to change:

```
# getsebool -a | grep dovecot
dovecot_disable_trans --> off
```

Step 2. Disable the SELinux protection:

```
# setsebool -P dovecot_disable_trans=1
```

Step 3. Verify that the Boolean has changed:

```
# getsebool -a | grep dovecot
dovecot_disable_trans --> on
```

Dovecot Security

Dovecot's security is actually handled through the use of its protocols. You have already set up the mail server to use the IMAP and POP3 protocols. If you want to provide additional security, you can also use their secure counterparts, IMAPS and POP3S, along with SSL. Setting up these protocols takes some additional work because you need to create a certificate for your SSL encryption.

Step 1. You need to edit the information in the certificate file:

```
# nano /etc/pki/dovecot/dovecot-openssl.cnf
[ req ]
default_bits = 1024
encrypt_key = yes
distinguished_name = req_dn
x509_extensions = cert_type
```

```
prompt = no

[ req_dn ]
# country (2 letter code)
C=US

# State or Province Name (full name)
ST=New York

# Locality Name (eg. city)
L=New York

# Organization (eg. company)
O=Example

# Organizational Unit Name (eg. section)
OU=Mail server

# Common Name (*.example.com is also possible)
CN=rhel01.example.com

# E-mail contact
emailAddress=user01@example.com

[ cert_type ]
nsCertType = server
```

After you fill in your details correctly, save the file and exit. Now you need to generate a new certificate for the mail server.

Step 2.   Back up the original certificate files:

```
# mv /etc/pki/dovecot/certs/dovecot.pem
/etc/pki/dovecot/certs/dovecot.pem.bk
# mv /etc/pki/dovecot/private/dovecot.pem
/etc/pki/dovecot/private/dovecot.pem.bk
```

Step 3.   Now you can generate a new certificate:

```
# /usr/share/doc/dovecot-1.0.7/examples/mkcert.sh
Generating a 1024 bit RSA private key
............++++++
.................................................................
..........
.....................................................++++++
writing new private key to '/etc/pki/dovecot/private/dovecot.pem'
-----

subject= /C=US/ST=New York/L=New York/O=Example/OU=Mail
server/CN=rhel01.example.com/emailAddress=user01@example.com
SHA1
Fingerprint=4B:F3:70:0A:1E:B8:86:36:7A:AF:51:5E:3A:24:DC:EC:1E:AF:9
6:B9
```

With the new certificate in place, you also need to make a few adjustments to the original setup. You need to change the protocols that you were using and enable SSL.

Step 4. Change your Dovecot settings in /etc/dovecot/dovecot.conf:

```
# nano /etc/dovecot/dovecot.conf
protocols = imaps pop3s
listen = 172.168.1.1
ssl_disable = no
mail_location = maildir:~/Maildir
```

Step 5. Use the iptables command to create or adjust your firewall rules:

```
# iptables -I INPUT 5 -p tcp -m tcp --dport 993 -j ACCEPT
# iptables -I INPUT 5 -p tcp -m tcp --dport 995 -j ACCEPT
```

Step 6. Save the rules you just created:

```
# service iptables save
Saving firewall rules to /etc/sysconfig/iptables:          [  OK  ]
```

Step 7. Restart the firewall service for the changes to take effect:

```
# service iptables restart
iptables: Flushing firewall rules:                         [  OK  ]
iptables: Setting chains to policy ACCEPT: filter          [  OK  ]
iptables: Unloading modules:                               [  OK  ]
iptables: Applying firewall rules:                         [  OK  ]
```

You are all set. Restart the Dovecot service, and you should now have a secure incoming mail server.

Testing the Mail Server

If you've been following along, you've likely been so busy setting up the mail servers that you still haven't had the chance to test them. Verifying the functionality of your mail servers is always a good idea to make sure they are working properly. Even though you configured a secure Dovecot server in the preceding section, I changed it back to the unsecure version for testing purposes. First, you need to check the Postfix server both locally and remotely to make sure outgoing mail is working. You can use the mail command to make some quick tests to the SMTP protocol.

Step 1. For the local mail test, use the following:

```
# echo "Hello User01" | mail -s "Local Test" user01
```

If you don't see any error messages, your message went through.

Step 2. For the remote mail test, use the following:

```
# echo "Hello again User01" | mail -s "Remote Test"
user01@example.com
```

After your messages are sent, you can use the mailq command with the -v option to view the queue of messages that have been sent or are waiting to be sent. This command produces a lot of output, so you may need to scroll around to find what you're looking for.

Step 3. A third way to test that the mail server is accepting connections properly is to telnet into the Postfix server on port 25:

```
# telnet 172.168.1.1 25
Trying 172.168.1.1...
Connected to localhost.localdomain (127.0.0.1).
Escape character is '^]'.
220 rhel01.example.com ESMTP Postfix
quit
221 2.0.0 Bye
Connection closed by foreign host.
```

NOTE: On RHEL6, the Telnet package is not installed by default. If you plan to use the Telnet client to verify functionality, you need to install it before use.

You can see that everything for the Postfix server seems to be operating normally. Now let's move on to the Dovecot server. You can use the `mutt` command to read mail from the Dovecot server that you just sent to user01.

Syntax: `mutt -f <imap | imaps | pop | pops>://<user><port>`
Check your mail:

```
# mutt -f imap://user01143
```

As with Postfix, you can also use Telnet to verify the connection is working properly:

```
# telnet 172.168.1.1 110
Trying 172.168.1.1...
Connected to rhel01.example.com (172.168.1.1).
Escape character is '^]'.
+OK Dovecot ready.
user user01
+OK
pass password
+OK Logged in.
list
+OK 0 messages:
.
quit
+OK Logging out.
Connection closed by foreign host.
```

Again, you can see that everything connected fine. Both the mail services are running properly. If you run into a situation in which the mail server isn't working properly, you can also check the queue to make sure mail is being sent out properly.

Display current mail in the queue:

```
# mailq
-Queue ID- --Size-- ----Arrival Time---- -Sender/Recipient-------
099FCA110E       441 Thu Feb  3 06:40:21  root@example.com
                     (connect to example.com[192.0.32.10]:25: Connection timed out)
                                          user01@example.com
```

For some reason, this message seems to be stuck in the queue (I disabled the network interface to generate an error). You can just delete it from the queue and send it again later.

Syntax: `postsuper [options]`

Options:

`-d queue_id`	Deletes one message with the named queue ID (you can also specify `ALL` as the `queue_id` to erase all messages in the queue)
`-h queue_id`	Puts the specific message defined by `queue_id` "on hold"
`-H queue_id`	Releases the message that was put "on hold"
`-r queue_id`	Requeues a message
`-s`	Performs a structure check of directories
`-v`	Provides verbose logging

Delete the stuck message on the queue:

```
# postsuper -d 099FCA110E
postsuper: 099FCA110E: removed
postsuper: Deleted: 1 message
```

Verify that the queue is now clean:

```
# mailq
Mail queue is empty
```

Summary

In this chapter, we covered the different types of mail servers that Red Hat has to offer. We also looked at how critical email is in the real world. The basic configuration of email service for the Red Hat exam isn't too difficult, but when it comes to having secure mail servers in the real world, this is a larger undertaking. There are full books dedicated to the subject of configuring and securing email servers, so make sure to do your due diligence before deploying an email server in the real world. You should also have a good understanding of how the different parts of email services work together to provide the flow of email.

Review Questions

1. What port does the SMTP service run on?

2. What command is used to change the mail server from Sendmail to Postfix (useful only if you have both installed)?

3. What are the two config files for Postfix called?

4. Sendmail is the default SMTP service for Red Hat Enterprise Linux 6. True or False?

5. What protocols are used with Dovecot?

6. What command-line program can you use to check your mail?

7. What command can you use to create a new SSL certificate?

Answers to the Review Questions

1. The SMTP service runs on TCP port 110.

2. `alternatives --config mta`

3. The two main config files are master.cf and main.cf.

4. False. The default SMTP service has been changed to Postfix in Red Hat Enterprise Linux 6.

5. Dovecot supports the POP3, POP3S, IMAP, and IMAPS protocols.

6. Typing the `mail` or `mutt` command allows you to read mail from the command line.

7. Use the /usr/share/doc/dovecot-1.0.7/examples/mkcert.sh command after editing the /etc/pki/dovecot/dovecot-openssl.cnf file.

Lab 20

Task 1 – Outgoing Mail

Step 1.   Set up a Postfix mail server on RHEL01 with the following settings:
a. The SMTP service must run on port 25.
b. Only the local subnet may send outgoing mail.
c. Create a user called mail_test with the password mail123.

The task is complete when you can send out mail with the mail_test user over port 25.

Task 2 – Incoming Mail

Step 1.   Set up a Dovecot mail server on RHEL01 with the following settings:
a. The POP3 protocol must be used.
b. Only the example.com domain may receive mail.
c. SSL must be disabled.

The task is complete when you can read the mail for the mail_test user.

This chapter covers the following subjects:

- **Boot Issues**—This section covers issues that arise during system boot.

- **Troubleshooting File Systems**—This section looks at how to troubleshoot file systems.

- **Miscellaneous**—This section looks at various troubleshooting topics.

## CHAPTER 21

Troubleshooting

This chapter is all about troubleshooting the system. Although there is no wrong or right way to go about accomplishing this, there are some common issues to look at here. This chapter covers a variety of issues that could arise while you're working or configuring services. This chapter is also written in a slightly different format, using a problem-and-answer style. Let's get started.

Boot Issues

Many issues can arise when you are working with the boot process of the system. Here are some of the common issues you might run into on the exam or in the real world.

I Lost My Root User Password

If you forget your root user password or you are taking over a system where the root password isn't documented, you can still get into the system. You need to perform the following actions at the physical console of the system.

Step 1. Boot into single-user mode by appending the command line during boot with the following:

```
single
```

Step 2. When you are presented with a command prompt, change the root user password:

```
# passwd root
Changing password for user root.
New password:
Retype new password:
Passwd: all authentication tokens updated successfully.
```

Step 3. Reboot the system and validate that the new root password works correctly:

```
# reboot
```

Password Change Not Available in Single-User Mode

When you enter single-user mode, you may encounter an issue where the root user's password can't be changed. You can use the following steps to resolve this issue.

Step 1.   Verify the existence of the /etc/shadow file:

```
# ls /etc | grep shadow
```

Step 2.   If the /etc/shadow file doesn't exist (which would be the cause of the error in this case), use the pwconv command to re-create the /etc/shadow file:

```
# pwconv
```

Step 3.   Now execute the passwd command to reset or change the root user's password:

```
# passwd root
Changing password for user root.
New password:
Retype new password:
Passwd: all authentication tokens updated successfully.
```

Step 4.   Reboot the system and validate that the new root password works correctly:

```
# reboot
```

The MBR Is Corrupt

If you are having trouble booting the system and you have determined that the master boot record (MBR) is corrupt, you need to boot into rescue mode. Use the Red Hat DVD, boot from it, and choose the option to enter rescue mode.

Step 1.   After you boot, enter the GRUB shell:

```
# grub
Probing devices to guess BIOS drives. This may take a long time.


    GNU GRUB  version 0.97  (640K lower / 3072K upper memory)

 [ Minimal BASH-like line editing is supported. For the first word,
TAB
   lists possible command completions. Anywhere else TAB lists the
possible
   completions of a device/filename.]
grub>
```

Step 2.   Locate the root drive:

```
grub> root
 (hd0,0): Filesystem type is unknown, partition type 0x8e
```

Step 3.   Reinstall the MBR from the GRUB shell:

```
grub> setup (hd0)
 Checking if "/boot/grub/stage1" exists... no
 Checking if "/grub/stage1" exists... yes
 Checking if "/grub/stage2" exists... yes
 Checking if "/grub/e2fs_stage1_5" exists... yes
 Running "embed /grub/e2fs_stage1_5 (hd0)"... 26 sectors are embed-
ded.
 Running "install /grub/stage1 (hd0) (hd0)1+26 p (hd0,0)/grub/stage2
/grub/grub.conf"... succeeded
Done.
```

Step 4.   Reboot the system to validate that the system boots properly:

```
# reboot
```

The Partition or Root File System Can't Be Found

Many times when you're having boot issues with the system, the problem is something in the /boot/grub/grub.conf file. In this case, you need to reboot the system and enter the GRUB menu to edit the grub.conf file. It should resemble the following:

```
# grub.conf generated by anaconda
#
# Note that you do not have to rerun grub after making changes to this file
# NOTICE:  You have a /boot partition. This means that
#          all kernel and initrd paths are relative to /boot/, eg.
#          root (hd0,0)
#          kernel /vmlinuz-version ro root=/dev/mapper/vg_rhel01-lv_root
#          initrd /initrd-[generic-]version.img
#boot=/dev/sda
default=0
timeout=5
splashimage=(hd0,0)/grub/splash.xpm.gz
hiddenmenu
title Red Hat Enterprise Linux (2.6.32-71.el6.x86_64)
        root (hd0,0)
        kernel /vmlinuz-2.6.32-71.el6.x86_64 ro root=/dev/mapper/vg_rhel01-
lv_root rd_LVM_LV=vg_rhel01/lv_root rd_LVM_LV=vg_rhel01/lv_swap rd_NO_LUKS
rd_NO_MD rd_NO_DM LANG=en_US.UTF-8 SYSFONT=latarcyrheb-sun16 KEYBOARDTYPE=pc
KEYTABLE=us crashkernel=auto rhgb quiet
        initrd /initramfs-2.6.32-71.el6.x86_64.img
```

Take note of the different sections of this file (as described in Chapter 2, "System Initialization," as well). Many times a portion or this entire file is missing and you need to use the GRUB shell to re-create this file to get the system to boot properly.

Troubleshooting File Systems

This section covers details about file system and partition issues.

The System Complains About a File System Label

When creating entries in the /etc/fstab file (which are read at boot time), you can use a label instead of the actual partition path to make things easier for you to read and find. If, for some reason, the label changes and you haven't updated the /etc/fstab file, you receive an error. If this error is on the root file system, you need to enter single-user mode and adjust the /etc/fstab file there before the system will boot properly.

The Superblock Has Become Corrupt

If the superblock on your system has become corrupt, you can re-create it with one of the backup superblocks. If the primary file system has the corruption, you may need to use single-user mode or the rescue environment to perform the recovery.

Step 1.   Check the state of the file system:

```
# dumpe2fs -h /dev/hda1
dumpe2fs 1.41.12 (17-May-2010)
Filesystem volume name:    <none>
Last mounted on:           /boot
Filesystem UUID:           0f5576a9-3f08-4fd9-9c73-a02e59a2e8f3
Filesystem magic number:   0xEF53
Filesystem revision #:     1 (dynamic)
Filesystem features:       has_journal ext_attr resize_inode
dir_index filetype
needs_recovery extent flex_bg sparse_super huge_file uninit_bg
dir_nlink
extra_isize
Filesystem flags:          signed_directory_hash
Default mount options:     user_xattr acl
Filesystem state:          clean
Errors behavior:           Continue
Filesystem OS type:        Linux
Inode count:               128016
Block count:               512000
Reserved block count:      25600
Free blocks:               465251
Free inodes:               127978
First block:               1
Block size:                1024
Fragment size:             1024
Reserved GDT blocks:       256
Blocks per group:          8192
Fragments per group:       8192
Inodes per group:          2032
Inode blocks per group:    254
Flex block group size:     16
Filesystem created:        Mon Nov 29 06:00:26 2010
Last mount time:           Wed Dec 15 10:04:07 2010
Last write time:           Wed Dec 15 10:04:07 2010
Mount count:               4
```

```
Maximum mount count:       -1
Last checked:              Mon Nov 29 06:00:26 2010
Check interval:            0 (<none>)
Lifetime writes:           44 MB
Reserved blocks uid:       0 (user root)
Reserved blocks gid:       0 (group root)
First inode:               11
Inode size:                128
Journal inode:             8
Default directory hash:    half_md4
Directory Hash Seed:       7f916fc7-0592-4623-bc42-dc997907268c
Journal backup:            inode blocks
Journal features:          (none)
Journal size:              8M
Journal length:            8192
Journal sequence:          0x00000023
Journal start:             0
```

Step 2.   Find a valid backup superblock:

```
# dumpe2fs /dev/hda1 | grep -i superblock
dumpe2fs 1.41.12 (17-May-2010)
  Primary superblock at 1, Group descriptors at 2-3
  Backup superblock at 8193, Group descriptors at 8194-8195
  Backup superblock at 24577, Group descriptors at 24578-24579
  Backup superblock at 40961, Group descriptors at 40962-40963
  Backup superblock at 57345, Group descriptors at 57346-57347
  Backup superblock at 73729, Group descriptors at 73730-73731
  Backup superblock at 204801, Group descriptors at 204802-204803
  Backup superblock at 221185, Group descriptors at 221186-221187
  Backup superblock at 401409, Group descriptors at 401410-401411
```

Step 3.   Repair the file system with a backup superblock:

```
# e2fsck -f -b 8193 /dev/hda1
```

Users Can't Create Files in Their Home Directories

If users can't create files in their home directories, your first thought should be that the partition is out of space. When it comes to users hoarding files in their home directories, they tend to keep everything, which just eats away at file space.

Step 1.   Verify that the partition isn't full:
```
# df -h
```

Step 2.   If the partition isn't full, check to see whether the user has reached his quota:

```
# quota
```

If neither of these situations is the issue (which is highly unlikely), the next step is to verify whether the issue pertains to only a single user or all users.

Miscellaneous

This section covers numerous different issues you might run into while running Linux.

I Can't Remote into My System

When you run into issues with SSH, you need to follow a process to determine the problem. When you're trying to track down an issue, think of the path that a packet would take from your remote system to enter your server via SSH. Ask yourself the following questions:

- Are TCP Wrappers being used?

- Are the firewall rules set up correctly?

- Is the service running?

- Am I connecting over the correct port?

- Am I using the correct authentication mechanism (public/private key versus password)?

- Is there an issue with the config file?

By working your way methodically through this list, you can narrow down where the issue lies and train your mind to look for certain circumstances when troubleshooting services. If you make any changes to config files, don't forget to restart the service.

I Can't Access Service X

One of the most frustrating issues with Linux is that you might not always remember the different security mechanisms that can be used. Many times you will configure a service, set up security for that service, configure firewall rules, and the service still won't work. You may then realize only after hours of troubleshooting that you never disabled the SELinux protection for the service to function in the way you intended it to. When setting up the security for any service, use the following list of questions to troubleshoot:

- Are firewall rules required? Are they correct?

- Is TCP Wrappers in play?

- Is SELinux protecting a function or the whole service?

- Have you verified whether the Boolean values for SELinux are set correctly?

- What host-based security is in place?

- What user-based security is in place?

- Is the service running, and who is it running as?

Many times you will find that you missed answering one of these questions when configuring or troubleshooting, which is the cause of your issue. Don't forget that all troubleshooting is a methodical process.

When I Start a Service, It Tells Me "Cannot Bind to Address"

All services in Linux have a config file somewhere on the system. Those that allow access to them over the network also need to use an IP address and a port to service clients properly. When a service tells you that it can't bind to an address, it usually indicates that the IP or port is already in use.

Step 1.   Verify your current IP address:

```
# ifconfig
```

Step 2.   Look at the current list of ports being used by the system:

```
# netstat -tuape
```

Step 3.   View the log file, the service, or the general log file to find out which port is in conflict:

```
# tail /var/log/messages
```

I Get the Error Message "No Route to Host"

Although you may think right away that there is a routing issue if you receive the "No route to host" message, many times there isn't. To make sure, however, verify your current IP address.

Step 1.   View the current IP address:

```
# ifconfig
```

Step 2.   View the current routes:

```
# route
```

If your IP, subnet, and gateway are, in fact, set up correctly, this error indicates there is a firewall rule blocking you. When a service is blocked by the firewall, not allowing clients to connect, this is a common error message. You can create a rule on the firewall using the iptables command if you know which service is causing the issue, or you can simply stop the firewall temporarily to verify that it is indeed causing the problem.

Step 3.   Stop the firewall services:

```
# service iptables stop
iptables: Flushing firewall rules:                       [  OK  ]
iptables: Setting chains to policy ACCEPT: filter        [  OK  ]
iptables: Unloading modules:                             [  OK  ]
```

Step 4. Test the service or connection, and then restart the firewall:

```
# service iptables start
iptables: Applying firewall rules:                      [  OK  ]
```

My Ping to Another Host Has Failed

When you are unable to ping a particular host in the network, the problem usually boils down to a few items. Use the following questions to find the answer:

- Is the network interface I am using up and running?

- Does my network interface have a valid IP and netmask?

- Is my gateway set correctly?

- If pinging by hostname, is the /etc/hosts or DNS server entry correct?

- Is there a firewall rule blocking ICMP requests?

Summary

This chapter touched on a few different areas that commonly need troubleshooting. Although it doesn't cover everything, each individual chapter has a troubleshooting section that you can refer to. The topics covered here commonly cause issues, and the advice here can be viewed as quick steps to fix each one. The next, and final, chapter in this book deals with virtualization and KVM.

This chapter covers the following subjects:

■ **Setting Up the Physical Host**—This section covers the setup of the physical host that will be used to host all your virtual systems.

■ **Installing a Virtual Client**—This section covers installation and setup of virtual systems on your physical host.

■ **Monitoring Virtual Resources**—This section looks at how to monitor the resources of your physical and virtual systems.

The following RHCSA exam objectives are covered:

■ Access a virtual machine's console

■ Start and stop virtual machines

■ Configure a physical machine to host virtual guests

■ Install Red Hat Enterprise Linux systems as virtual guests

■ Configure systems to launch virtual machines on boot

## CHAPTER 22

Virtualization with KVM

Kernal-based Virtualization Module (KVM) is a kernel module built for RHEL6. Because support for KVM is officially built in to the RHEL6 kernel only, if you're still on RHEL5, you need to upgrade before proceeding in this chapter. KVM can be used to create and manage virtual systems built on the physical host with the KVM package. This capability is useful for consolidating servers and keeping costs down. There is also a security and ease of management benefit as well. Although the Red Hat exams don't require you to know virtualization in depth, there are some basic requirements. This chapter covers the basics of setting up a physical host and creating virtual machines. We also look at how to manage virtual resources.

Working with Virtual Machines

When choosing a system to serve as your physical host for any number of virtual clients, you need to do some planning. Your host system requires enough resources to support itself and the virtual machines. Ensure that you have sufficient CPU processing power, memory, and storage space. You need to plan how many virtual machines you'd like to build on top of your host and scale your physical host system accordingly.

Setting Up the Physical Host

The creation of virtual machines is done through the use of a hypervisor. This hypervisor allows the sharing of resources between the physical and virtual systems. In RHEL6, the KVM hypervisor requires a 64-bit host system with the correct extensions (Intel 64 or AMD64).

When you're getting started with virtualization, there are a few packages that need to be installed (and many different ways to do it). If you install Red Hat from the DVD, you can select the Virtual Host option to install the required packages automatically. If you're installing from a kickstart file, you can use the @kvm directive to accomplish the same thing. Another option is to install the files from the repositories as normal if your installation is already in place.

> **WARNING:**   You won't receive any updates from Red Hat unless you have a virtualization entitlement license.

> **NOTE:**   Because you are using virtual machines already to emulate the lab, you won't be able to follow along with the commands in this chapter unless you have a separate side machine lying around.

To start, install the required packages for KVM:

```
# yum install -y python-virtinst libvirt virt-manager libvirt-client
```

Verify that the packages were installed correctly:

```
# rpm -qa | grep virt
libvirt-client-0.8.1-27.el6.x86_64
libvirt-0.8.1-27.el6.x86_64
python-virtinst-0.500.3-7.el6.noarch
libvirt-python-0.8.1-27.el6.x86_64
virt-manager-0.8.4-8.el6.noarch
```

Installing a Virtual Client

If you've worked in VMware or VirtualBox before, at this point you're probably thinking of looking for the GUI to set up your clients. For purposes of this chapter, first install the client from the command line and then do it again using the GUI front end. Using KVM from the command line makes for easier administration (mostly because you can automate processes through scripts). Using the `virt-install` command, you can create, manage, and automate the virtual machines.

Syntax: `virt-install —name NAME —ram RAM STORAGE INSTALL [options]`

One problem is that there are tons of options for this command, so there is not enough room here to list them all. For a complete list of options, use the following:

```
# virt-install -help
```

This command can be used interactively or through scripts, making it easier to create virtual guests. Aside from the `virt-install` command, you also can use `virt-manager`, which can accomplish many of the same tasks. This GUI `virt-manager` utility (front end) is used to create virtual guests. If you have an aversion to the command line, you can use the `virt-manager` utility to achieve the same results. Regardless of which method you use, there are few a things that remain constant. You can install virtual guests just as you would any normal physical host: through local installation media, network installation, or PXE.

REAL-WORLD TIP

Red Hat recommends that you use the /var/lib/libvirt/images directory to hold the virtual guest image files. These image files are the virtual disks used to run each virtual guest. You can also store ISO files here for local installation. This location is preconfigured for use with SELinux, so any other location requires a custom written policy within SELinux to work (which is beyond the scope of this book).

Let's create a single virtual guest using `virt-install`:

```
# virt-install --name Client03 --ram 512 --disk
path=/var/lib/libvirt/images/clicnt03.img,size=8 --network network=default --
cdrom /dev/cdrom
```

This looks like a lot to take in for one command; however, it is quite simple when you break down the parts. This command creates a virtual guest named Client03 with 512GB of memory and 8GB of storage. The network interface is set to the default (which is the first virtual network adapter), and the installation occurs from the DVD mounted on /dev/cdrom. Remember that you can also use the `virt-manager` utility if you are more comfortable with a graphical interface.

Give your virtual guest a name and choose the install media, as shown in Figure 22-1.

Figure 22-1   Choosing a name.

Provide a storage path to the virtual disk (see Figure 22-2).

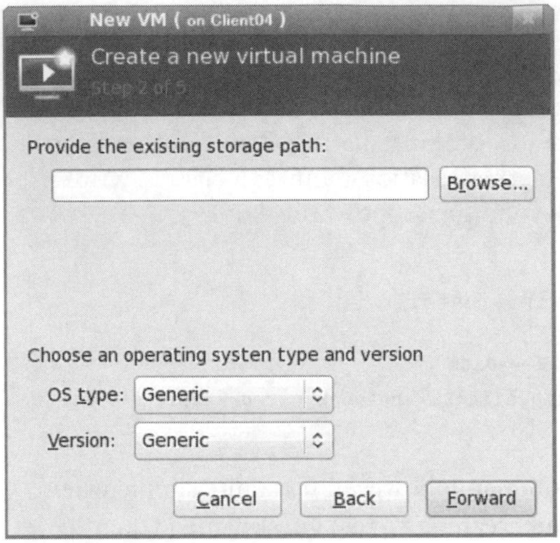

Figure 22-2   Choose the storage path.

Set the memory amount and number of virtual CPUs to use (see Figure 22-3).

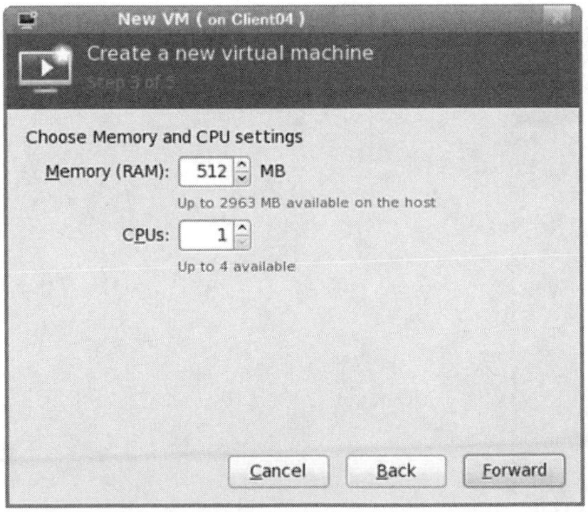

Figure 22-3   Setting memory and number of CPUs.

Choose the storage size (see Figure 22-4).

Choose the network adapter to use (see Figure 22-5).

At this point, your virtual guest is created back on the main window. If you view the settings, you see additional options that you can edit for your virtual machine.

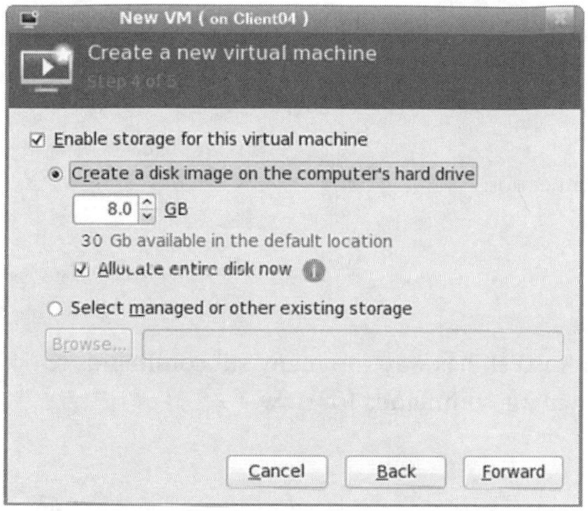

Figure 22-4   Choosing the storage size.

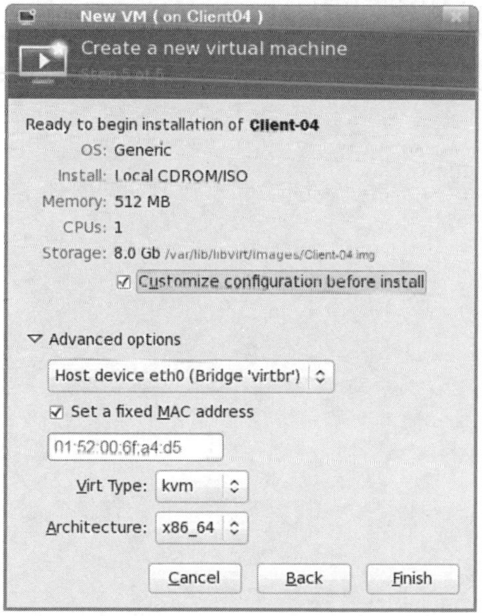

Figure 22-5   Choosing a network adapter.

Managing a Virtual Client

Much as you can create virtual guests, you also need to manage them after they have been created. Management includes tasks such as starting/stopping, rebooting, taking a snap-shot (also called saving), and migrating. These tasks can all be accomplished through the virt-manager utility, but on the command line, you can use the virsh command.

Syntax: `virsh [options] [commands]`

Options:

`-c`	Connects to a hypervisor
`-r`	Connects with a read-only connection
`-q`	Opens in quiet mode
`-l`	Outputs logging to a file

Similar to the `virt-install` command, `virsh` has way too many subcommands to list here. Let's look at only the management commands for now:

`help`	Prints basic help information
`list`	Lists all the virtual guests
`dumpxml`	Outputs the XML config file for a guest
`create`	Creates a virtual guest based on an XML file
`start`	Starts an inactive guest
`destroy`	Forces a guest to stop
`define`	Outputs the XML config file for a guest
`domid`	Displays the guest ID
`domuuid`	Displays the guest UUID
`dominfo`	Displays the guest information
`domname`	Displays the guest's name
`domstate`	Displays the state of the guest
`quit`	Quits the interactive terminal
`reboot`	Reboots a guest
`restore`	Restores a previously saved guest from a file
`resume`	Resumes a paused guest
`save`	Saves the present state of a guest
`shutdown`	Shuts down a guest gracefully
`suspend`	Pauses a guest
`undefine`	Deletes all files relating to a guest
`migrate`	Migrates the guest to another host (live migration possible)

You can see that this is a hefty list, but you should know most of these commands if you've worked with virtualization previously. Before you can use the `virsh` command to manage your virtual guests, you need to connect to the correct hypervisor (on the physical host) to gain access to the virtual guests.

Connect to the hypervisor on RHEL03, the physical host:

```
# virsh connect RHEL03
```

Now that you have connected, you can manage any of the virtual hosts attached to this hypervisor.

REAL-WORLD TIP

After you attach to a hypervisor, use the `list` command to display all available virtual guests:

```
# virsh list --all
```

Monitoring Virtual Resources

If you recall all the way back in Chapter 9, "System Logging, Monitoring, and Automation," we discussed tools and commands that could be used to monitor system resources. When you're dealing with virtualization, there is also a need to monitor system resources; however, this time you want to see what's going on with all your virtual guests, not just the physical host. To accomplish this, let's look at the `virsh` command again with a different set of options.

setmem	Sets the allocated memory for a guest
setmaxmem	Sets the maximum memory limit for the hypervisor
setvcpus	Changes the number of virtual CPUs assigned to a guest
vcpuinfo	Displays virtual CPU information about a guest
vcpupin	Controls the virtual CPU affinity of a guest
domblkstat	Displays block device statistics for a guest
domifstat	Displays network interface statistics for a guest
attach-device	Attaches a device to a guest
attach-disk	Attaches a new disk to a guest
attach-interface	Attaches a new network interface to a guest

`detach-device`	Detaches a device from a guest
`detach-disk`	Detaches a disk from a guest
`detach-interface`	Detaches a network interface from a guest

Just as when you're managing virtual guests, you need to connect to a hypervisor before you can begin using these commands. Within each virtual guest, you have available the same utilities discussed in Chapter 9; however, these additional options for `virsh` give you an external view of what is going on between the physical host and virtual guest system. When monitoring system resources, you also have the option of using the `virt-manager` utility. This utility has all the same options, but it allows you to see them in a graphical form. It is important to create a baseline with your virtual guests when you create them for the first time. This allows you to monitor resources and determine if there is a problem by comparing the current utilization to the baseline of the system. This is an important skill to have, especially when you're trying to determine whether your current hardware is enough to support your virtual guest systems.

Summary

In this chapter, we discussed using KVM on RHEL6 to create and manage virtual guests. We also discussed how to monitor these virtual guests after they have been created. Although there is a separate Red Hat certification based solely on virtualization, system administrators need to understand the basics of creating and managing virtual machines, particularly in today's world where virtualization is everywhere. If you have an interest in virtualization using Red Hat technologies, I suggest you look at the RHCVA certification and training courses.

Review Questions

1. The `virt-install` package allows you to manage virtual machines via a GUI interface. True or False?

2. By default, all virtual machines are created with the same amount of RAM. True or False?

3. What is the `virsh` command used for?

4. What does `virsh reboot Client04` do?

5. How can you display all virtual guests after they're connected to a hypervisor?

Answers to the Review Questions

1. False. The `virt-install` package allows you to manage virtual machines via the command line. The `virt-manager` package allows you to manage virtual machines via a GUI interface.

2. False. You must dictate the amount of RAM you want allocated to your virtual machine when you create it.

3. The `virsh` command is used to manage virtual guests.

4. This command reboots virtual guest Client04.

5. After you connect to a hypervisor, you can use `virsh list —all` to list all virtual guests.

Lab 22

Task 1 – KVM

Step 1.   Open the GRUB config file in any text editor.

Step 2.   Add a new entry to the config file:
   a. The new entry should have the title Red Hat Recovery.
   b. The new entry should not be the default.
   c. The recovery entry should allow you to boot into recovery mode.

Step 3.   Change the timeout of the boot selection to 10 seconds.

The task is complete when the system boots with both entries in the GRUB menu and they both work correctly.

Task 2 – Boot Issues

Step 1.   Make sure you have your Red Hat installation CD available. Delete the /etc/inittab file, and reboot the system.
   You will receive an error message that the system can't find the file.

Step 2.   Boot from the Red Hat installation CD into recovery mode.

Step 3.   Replace the file from the CD into the correct location on the system.

Step 4.   You may need to use the command `mount /dev/cd-rom /mnt` to access the CD drive.

The task is complete when the system boots up again.

Instructions: This lab is based on the lab setup outlined in the introduction to this book. It requires that you have a basic Red Hat installation on host RHEL01 and RHEL02. You have 2.5 hours to complete this lab.

Task 1: Using RHEL02 as your server, perform a network install of host Client01 using the FTP protocol. No desktop manager (Gnome or KDE) is required on Client01 during the installation.

Task 2: Run the t_root_password script on RHEL02. The root password should be changed to something random. Recover the root password and change it to `SecurePassWord`.

Task 3: On Client01, change the default system runlevel to 3.

Task 4: Create a new user called User03. Give the user any password, but force it to expire and be changed on the first login of User03.

Task 5: On RHEL02, output the status of each network service at each runlevel to a file called runlevel_stats.

Task 6: On RHEL01, implement the following:

- On /dev/hdb, configure this disk to use LVM and create three logical volumes of equal size.

- Give the second logical volume the name backups.

- On /dev/hdc, create the following basic partitions: one partition 3GB in size, a swap 2GB in size, and one partition 1GB in size.

- Create ext4 file systems on all created partitions except the swap partition.

- Enable the swap partition.

Task 7: Modify the default timeout for kernel selection during boot to be 20 seconds. Also, create a second entry in the GRUB config file that allows you to boot into single-user mode.

Lab Exam 1

Task 8: Create a user called jsmith on Client01. Create the directory /opt/jsmith. When the user logs in to the system, his home directory should be /opt/jsmith.

Task 9: Create the following files: /opt/secret_data and /opt/salaries. Create an ACL on both files so that users user01 and jsmith can both read them, neither can write to them, and the files must be owned by root.

Task 10: Set up SELinux to be enforcing on RHEL01 and RHEL02. All other systems on the network should have SELinux disabled.

Task 11: Create a user called user02 on RHEL02. Create a script that will output the amount of free disk space and write the results to the file /opt/free_space. Have user02 create a cron job running the newly created script once every three hours.

Task 12: Set up an FTP server on RHEL01. Create the directory /opt/ftp_data and make it the only accessible directory to the FTP server. Anonymous access should be allowed to the FTP server.

Task 13: Create the following firewall rule:

- All systems on the 172.168.1.0/24 subnet should have access to the FTP server on RHEL01. All other systems should be denied access.

- Users from Client01 should be able to remote into RHEL01 via SSH. No other systems should have SSH access to RHEL01.

- On RHEL02, open TCP port 69 for the IP 172.168.1.50 only.

Instructions: This lab is based on the lab setup outlined in the introduction to this book. It requires that you have a basic Red Hat installation on host RHEL01 and RHEL02. You have 2.5 hours to complete this lab.

Task 1: On RHEL01, create a kickstart server and a DHCP server. Using this kickstart server, perform a basic installation (no desktop managers) on Client02.

Task 2: On RHEL02, implement the following:

- Create the directory /opt/server_data.
- Create a cron job that outputs the amount of free disk space in a file called data in the /opt/server_data directory.
- This script should run every day at 3 p.m.

Task 3: On RHEL01, configure an NTP server using GMT as the time zone.

Task 4: Sync Client01 to the time server RHEL01.

Task 5: On RHEL02, implement the following:

- Set up an Apache web server.
- Create two customer websites: csite_1 and csite_2 (these sites must be located in the /var/www/html directory).
- Customer site 2 (csite_2) should be accessible only through the HTTPS protocol.

Lab Exam 2

Task 6: Set up a Samba server on RHEL02. It should have two shares: /opt/company_data and /opt/paychecks. The first share should be accessible by any user and have read/write permissions for the share. The second share should have read-only permissions. The two shares should be accessible only by hosts on the local subnet.

Task 7: Set up RHEL01 as a caching-only DNS server for the local 172.168.1.0/24 subnet. The domain should be example.org.

Task 8: On RHEL02, set up user quotas on the /home directory. Create two users called user01 and user04. These users should not be able to create more than 20MB worth of data in their home directories (hard limit).

Task 9: On RHEL01, create virtual hosts called example.com and example.net. Each site should have its own home directory and be accessible over the HTTP protocol only. Block Client01 from accessing either website.

Task 10: On RHEL01, set up a Squid proxy server on port 2228. Client01 and Client02 should be able to access the Web through this proxy.

Task 11: On RHEL01, set up an SMTP server. Users from Client01 and Client02 should be able to send out mail using this SMTP server (no TLS required).

Task 12: On RHEL02, create a user called bjones. Generate a public/private key for bjones (no password required for key), and set up RHEL02 to allow only public key authentication from RHEL02. The user bjones should be able to connect into RHEL01 via SSH public key authentication.

Task 13: On RHEL02, set up an NFS version 4 server. Create shares called /opt/students and opt/teachers. All users from Client01 and Client02 should have read/write access to the /opt/students share. The /opt/teachers share should be read-only. RHEL01 users should have no access to this NFS server. In addition, no root user from any remote system should have access to this server.

Index

W

X-Y-Z

DAMIAN TOMMASINO

Cert Guide
Learn, prepare, and practice for exam success

Hands-on Guide to
the Red Hat® Exams:
**RHCSA™ and RHCE
Cert Guide and
Lab Manual**

PEARSON

FREE Online Edition

Your purchase of **Hands-on Guide to the Red Hat Exams** includes access to a free online edition for 45 days through the Safari Books Online subscription service. Nearly every Pearson IT Certification book is available online through Safari Books Online, along with more than 5,000 other technical books and videos from publishers such as Addison-Wesley Professional, Cisco Press, Exam Cram, IBM Press, O'Reilly, Prentice Hall, Que, and Sams.

SAFARI BOOKS ONLINE allows you to search for a specific answer, cut and paste code, download chapters, and stay current with emerging technologies.

Activate your FREE Online Edition at
www.informit.com/safarifree

> **STEP 1:** Enter the coupon code: DURXAZG.

> **STEP 2:** New Safari users, complete the brief registration form.
> Safari subscribers, just log in.

If you have difficulty registering on Safari or accessing the online edition,
please e-mail customer-service@safaribooksonline.com